Law for Business Students

We work with leading authors to develop the strongest educational materials in business and law, bringing cutting-edge thinking and best learning practice to a global market.

Under a range of well-known imprints, including Longman, we craft high quality print and electronic publications which help readers to understand and apply their content, whether studying or at work.

To find out more about the complete range of our publishing please visit us on the World Wide Web at: www.pearsoneduc.com

Law for Business Students

Third Edition

Alix Adams

LLB (Bristol), LLM (Cardiff), Cert. Ed., Barrister.
Senior Lecturer in Law, Croydon College

Harlow, England • London • New York • Boston • San Francisco • Toronto • Sydney • Singapore • Hong Kong
Tokyo • Seoul • Taipei • New Delhi • Cape Town • Madrid • Mexico City • Amsterdam • Munich • Paris • Milan

For Cherry, who makes all the difference

Pearson Education Limited

Edinburgh Gate
Harlow
Essex CM20 2JE
England
and Associated Companies throughout the world

Visit us on the World Wide Web at:
http://www.pearsoneduc.com

First published under the Pitman Publishing imprint in Great Britain in 1996
Second edition published 2000
Third edition published 2003

ISBN 0 582 47318 7

British Library Cataloguing-in-Publication Data
A catalogue record for this book is available from the British Library.

10 9 8 7 6 5 4 3 2 1
08 07 06 05 04 03

Typeset by 30
Printed by Ashford Colour Press Ltd, Gosport

The publisher's policy is to use paper manufactured from sustainable forests.

Contents

Preface

Thirty years of teaching law on a variety of further and higher education courses from GCSE to degree level has taught me much about the difficulties experienced by students in grasping legal concepts. It can be particularly hard for students following an intensive course of which law forms only one part. Hopefully this text will meet their needs. I have tried to make it accessible, without over-simplification of the subject matter. Working on the basis that 'a light touch sometimes illuminates', I believe that it may entertain as well as instruct its readers, and hope that it will encourage an interest in further study.

A downloadable Lecturer's Guide, containing suggested solutions to some of the assignments, is available at http://www.booksites.net/adams

The content is intended to meet the demands of students requiring an introduction to business law at degree and diploma level and also reflects the syllabi of a variety of vocational courses, including those of the ACCA, CIMA, ICSA, CIPS and IPD.

Many thanks to the following bodies for allowing publication of examination questions:

The Institute of Chartered Secretaries and Administrators;
The Chartered Institute of Purchasing & Supply.

Thanks are also due to my publishers: Patrick Bond, who gave me the opportunity to write this book in the first place, and Michelle Gallagher, who took over from him recently and has been a great support. Thanks also to my editor Karen Mclaren for her invaluable and friendly professional assistance in producing this third edition.

Thanks again to my friends and colleagues at Croydon College for their continuing interest in my writing. I am grateful to Pam Rogers, who has kept me apprised of company law developments. Special thanks are due to Stella Diamantidi who checked the EU and Human Rights sections and made invaluable suggestions for improvement.

Last but definitely not least, especially warm thanks to my partner Cherry Potts. She yet again has shared with me all the excitement of the editing process, and has still managed to retain a sense of humour and be a constant source of emotional and practical support.

Alix Adams
February 2003

Source: Cherry Potts

Table of cases

Table of legislation

Regulations

CHAPTER I

Getting started: an introduction to studying law

INTRODUCTION

This chapter provides an overview of some of the concepts and principles which form the background to the topics covered in the rest of the book. It also contains some hints on studying law.

WHAT IS LAW?

English law may be defined as a body of rules, created by the state, binding within its jurisdiction and enforced with the authority of the state through the use of sanctions. Here is an analysis of this definition.

Rules

Rules are commands aimed at regulating behaviour. Rules tell us what we can and cannot do; sometimes they may permit behaviour subject to fulfilling a condition. For example, an extension of business premises is illegal unless planning permission is obtained; a shop may not sell alcohol without a licence.

Created by the state

Parliament is responsible for creating most of the law applicable in the UK. Such law is contained in *Acts of Parliament* or *statutes*. Increasingly the content of much of this law is determined by the European Union, and in this respect Parliament does not have complete independence. Since the Human Rights Act 1998 the European Convention on Human Rights is directly enforceable in the English courts.

The jurisdiction of the state

The law of any country is binding only within its territory. The UK Parliament may introduce laws applicable to the UK as a whole, but this book is concerned with the law as it applies in England and Wales.

Enforcement

A legal dispute may require formal resolution by the court or tribunal. The state or a party to the dispute may initiate the enforcement proceedings.

A sanction or penalty may be imposed in order to compensate the injured party or punish the wrongdoer.

THE CHARACTERISTICS OF ENGLISH LAW

English law has characteristics which make it very different from the law of other countries in the European Union.

It has evolved slowly and without interruption over many centuries

The origins of the English legal system can be traced to the Norman Conquest in 1066. Although huge changes have taken place since then, development has been gradual and piecemeal. As a result a rather untidy and conservative evolution has taken place, with historical relics rubbing shoulders with more modern developments. For example, two divisions of the High Court today still carry traces of the names of their forebears in medieval times: the Court of King's Bench (now the Queen's Bench Division) and the Court of Chancery (the Chancery Division).

Lack of Roman law influence

English law has been little influenced by the Roman law principles which dominate the legal systems of other European countries and which also have some influence on Scots law.

Judges have creative powers

Judges were the principal lawmakers until their powers were superseded by Parliament in the eighteenth century; senior judges today still have some limited powers to develop principles of case law. The powers of other European judges are restricted to interpretation of the legal codes created by the relevant state legislatures.

The doctrine of binding precedent

When deciding a case English judges must apply any relevant decisions of a senior court, unlike their other European counterparts who are guided, rather than bound, by previous cases.

Adversarial nature

Case names look rather like football fixture lists: *Bloggs* v *Snodgrass*. A case in the courts is essentially a contest before an umpire (the judge) whose principal tasks are to see that the rules of evidence are obeyed and to decide who is the winner. The main burden of proof is on the accuser, and the case is won by the party who can produce the most convincing evidence. The judge plays very little part in drawing out that evidence; too much judicial intervention may lead to the decision being reversed at an appeal. It has been said that the adversarial system is about proving facts rather than discovering truth.

The function of judges on mainland Europe is an inquisitorial one; this gives the judge power to call witnesses and question them during the hearing of the case. English judges are currently being encouraged to take a more interventionist role as case managers before the hearing of complex cases, but this extension of their function is still a long way from a truly inquisitorial approach.

WHY DO WE NEED LAW?

Any society, or group within it, however small, will make rules for the purposes of organisation, to promote the safety and convenience of members and to regulate their relationships with each other. An affluent industrialised state requires a complex system of law which aims to fulfil a number of purposes. Figure 1.1 shows how the law may be classified.

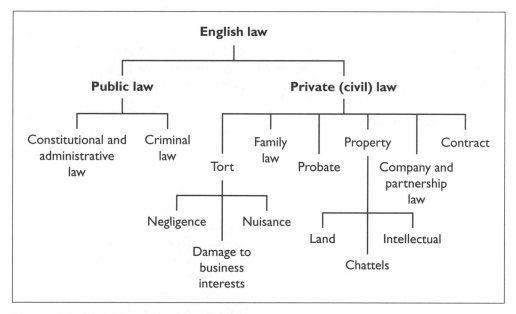

Figure 1.1 Classification of English law

A system of law may be needed for the following reasons:

1 to provide a governmental structure and legislative procedures: constitutional law;

2 to provide public services and to raise taxes to pay for them: administrative and revenue law;

3 to regulate and promote the economy: administrative, civil and criminal law are all involved;

4 to promote public order and preserve national security: criminal law;

5 to give individual members personal rights and duties in relation to others and to enable personal enforcement of these rights: the civil law. Civil law duties may arise through agreement between the parties (the law of contract), or be imposed directly (the law of tort);

6 to give legal validity to approved relationships and transactions between members of the society: this involves the law of contract, the law of property and succession, company and partnership law, and family law.

THE DIFFERENCES BETWEEN CRIMINAL AND CIVIL LAW

It is important from the outset to understand the differences between civil and criminal law. Dual liability for a breach of both civil and criminal law may arise from the same set of facts; but since these two branches of the law have very different purposes, their procedures and penalties differ radically. The following example illustrates these crucial differences.

Alice is treated to a hot lobster lunch at 'The Fat Cat Wine Bar' by Cyril. Subsequently both Alice and Cyril become ill with food poisoning, which they claim was caused by the insanitary condition of Fat Cat's kitchen.

The criminal proceedings

R[egina] v Fat Cat

Selling impure food is a criminal offence under the Food Safety Act 1990: it is in the interests of public safety to control and punish such behaviour.

In this sort of case, Fat Cat may be prosecuted in the magistrates' court by the local authority's trading standards department, rather than by the police. The burden of proving Fat Cat's guilt lies on the prosecutor, who has to prove *beyond all reasonable doubt* that the food poisoning was caused by the condition of the lobster.

If Fat Cat is found guilty he may be fined: a fine is a sum of money payable to the court, it does not go to the victims of the crime.

The civil proceedings

Cyril v Fat Cat

Alice v Fat Cat

Cyril and Alice want compensation for having been made ill. Both are self-employed and, in addition to the pain and inconvenience of their illness, they have also lost earnings while they were laid low.

Two separate claims are involved: Cyril, who bought the food, will sue for breach of contract, as the lobster was clearly not of satisfactory quality; Alice, who was harmed by the food but had no contract with Fat Cat, will sue in tort claiming negligence or breach of the Consumer Protection Act 1987.

Cyril and Alice will take action in the county court and will have to prove that *on the balance of probabilities* Fat Cat caused their problems. This is a lower standard of proof than that required in criminal proceedings, as the court requires it to be proved only that it is more likely than not that Fat Cat was responsible.

If Cyril and Alice win, damages will be payable to them by Fat Cat to compensate them for their pain and suffering and all economic loss resulting from it, including medical costs and loss of earnings. Cyril will also be able to reclaim the cost of the meal.

A summary of the differences between civil and criminal law

Criminal law	Civil law
Purpose	
Regulates behaviour perceived as being anti-social and dangerous to the public.	Gives legal rights to individuals to govern their formal and informal relationships with each other.
Provides machinery by which the state may take action against offenders.	Provides the means by which they may enforce the rights arising from these relationships.
Procedure	
Generally started by the police, but some legislation is enforced by other agencies like local authorities or Customs and Excise.	Civil proceedings are taken against the alleged lawbreaker by the party who claims that they have been wronged.
Exceptionally, a private prosecution may be brought by an individual.	The case may not go to trial even if proceedings are started. Most civil law claims are settled out of court without any threat of legal action. In many others the proceedings are abandoned before trial.
The victim usually plays no part in the decision to prosecute.	

Once started a case will proceed to trial in the magistrates' court or the Crown Court.

Most civil cases are heard in the county court and the High Court and in certain specialised tribunals.

The prosecution must prove that the accused is guilty beyond all reasonable doubt.

The claimant must prove that the defendant is liable on the balance of probability.

Penalties

Focus on the accused and the need to protect society against criminal conduct.

Focus on the needs of the victim and generally require the wrongdoer to pay damages which are often covered by insurance.

The ultimate aim is to punish the criminal, while protecting society from future anti-social conduct.

A penalty may be used to contain criminals by depriving them of their freedom, or to rehabilitate them; it may be intended to deter them or others from committing future crimes.

Exceptionally the court, by injunction or other equitable remedy, may require some practical correction of the wrong. This is usual in domestic violence cases.

CHANGING THE LAW

It is important to realise that the law is subject to frequent change. Very few principles actually remain constant. These changes reflect social, political, economic and technological developments taking place within society.

Social change

Changes in moral values have influenced a number of legal developments in the last 30 years, including reform of the divorce law, limited decriminalisation of homosexuality and abortion, as well as the introduction of legislation to prevent sex, race and disability discrimination.

Political change

No government can initiate new policies unless it has legal authority to do so. This means that the law may require constant, and often radical, change. The privatisation of the water, gas, and electricity industries was achieved by repeal of previous legislation which had introduced a policy of nationalisation.

Economic and technological change

Much of the law governing commerce and industry, including the regulation of health and safety at work, is subject to such influence. As industrial practice changes, old hazards disappear and new ones develop. For example, the commercial exploitation of the internal combustion engine has led to the development of a huge body of road traffic law.

In practice, these influences and political change may be interlinked: an economic or social issue is often the focus of a political policy.

ESSENTIAL LEGAL TERMS

This book has been kept as free as possible from lawyers' jargon. However, there are a few common words and phrases, which you may meet here and elsewhere, which are useful shorthand.

The claimant and defendant

These are the parties in a civil case (*action*). The claimant *sues* (brings the case against) the defendant.

The prosecution and the defence

These are the parties to a criminal case. The 'defence' is sometimes called the *defendant* or the *accused*. The prosecution is sometimes called the *Crown*, reflecting the fact that criminal proceedings are brought by the state in the name of the Crown. This is why criminal cases are usually reported as *R* v (*Snodgrass*).

The appellant and the respondent

These are the parties in an appeal hearing. The appellant is the party who is bringing the appeal against the decision of the court below, in which the respondent won his or her case.

The common law

This has two possible meanings. The relevant meaning is usually clear from the context.

Case law as opposed to statute law

When the common law first began to develop in the early centuries after the Norman Conquest, there was no centralised legal system and there were great variations in the law across England. Judges appointed by the Crown had the task of welding together a system of law applicable (and therefore *common*) to the country as a whole. This law gradually emerged from principles developed and applied to cases which came before the courts. Common law in this context means judge-made law.

Case law and statute law as opposed to principles of equity

The civil law sometimes allows the court to exercise discretionary powers, which are based not just on the legal rights of the parties, but on what will produce a just and moral solution. These discretionary rules are part of the *law of equity*. They protect only those parties who are *morally* as well as *legally* entitled to a remedy.

Equitable principles govern the issue of court orders like injunctions and some contractual remedies which are described later in this book. They are the foundation of the law of mortgages and trusts, since they seek to protect the vulnerable parties to the transaction from the abuse of power by lenders and trustees respectively.

The law of equity has its origins in the fourteenth century; it was initially developed by successive Lord Chancellors to put right the defects that had become apparent in the common law system. Lord chancellors for many years were churchmen as well as lawyers, which gave this branch of the law the emphasis on moral principle which governs its operation in the civil courts today. Its principles coexist with other principles of common law (statute and case law in this context) and may come into play at the discretion of the court where the common law principle or remedy will cause injustice.

INTRODUCTORY STUDY TIPS

This section mainly is addressed to any reader who has not studied law before, but it may serve to refresh most memories.

Most readers will study law as one component of a course: it may be something that you might not have chosen to do. However, if you keep the following hints in mind you may find it both easier and more rewarding than you thought.

Get rid of your misconceptions

Law is probably much more interesting than you think. It is not primarily concerned with ancient, dry and precise regulations which you have to learn by heart; most of your studies are concerned with quite modern cases, which have come to court just because the law was not precise and consequently gave rise to the dispute. This book looks at how the law applies to real-life situations, which will help you to recall the legal principles on which it is based. Effective communication of your *understanding* of the principles is the main requirement for examination success.

Remembering all the cases by name and being able to quote statutes word for word is icing on the cake – impressive, but not essential.

Law is relevant to you

Remember that the law responds and develops as required by the society within which it operates. It affects you personally; studying this book will increase your knowledge of your rights as a consumer and of your responsibilities and rights as a business owner, employer or employee.

Widen your horizons

Your studies will be more rewarding if you do not consider law as something to be thought about only when you are in class or reading a textbook. The effects of many areas of the law are widely reported and discussed in the media. Such reports can help you to see how the law works (or doesn't work), as well as reminding you of what you have studied. Stay in touch with the news, try to look at a quality daily paper and look out for relevant TV and radio programmes. Some suggestions for resources appear in Appendix 1, including a list of websites. The Internet is an excellent research tool.

Make connections

The more you study, the easier it gets. Studying law is rather like doing a large jigsaw without the help of a picture – progress is initially slow while the framework is established, but patience is rewarded. Once the picture begins to reveal itself you can see how the different pieces fit together and the task gets easier and quicker.

Try not to think of each topic as a separate entity to be 'done' and neatly filed away in the memory. Exploit the links with other related topics; this aids both recollection and understanding. Exam questions may involve a problem, raising issues about a number of different topics; the ability to see connections is vital to an effective response. To help you do this frequent cross-references appear in the text.

Read and practice applying your knowledge

Somebody (not a lawyer) once told the author that law is a very 'paper-based subject'. This made it sound a bit like origami, but nevertheless contains some truth. Reading thoroughly and widely is essential; practising the written skills required by the examinations is also crucial.

It is hoped that you will find this book accessible, but if you are new to the study of law it would take magical powers to understand it all fully at a first reading. Be prepared to go back and re-read a section that you do not understand. Often it is better to try to get a general picture on the first reading, pressing on even if you do not understand it; you will get something from it, and on each subsequent reading it will become clearer.

Get all the writing practice that you can. Homework provides safe space to make mistakes; and it is much better to make them then rather than in the exam. Try the quizzes and assignments in this book. Hints on writing assignments, revision and examinations can be found in Chapter 28.

Quiz 1

1 What distinguishes law from other rules?

2 What does the court hope to achieve when imposing a criminal sentence?

3 What does a civil litigant hope to achieve by taking a case to court?

4 What are the likely legal consequences in the following case? Sparrow, who has had too much to drink, carelessly crashes his taxi into Finch's lorry. Sparrow's passenger, Wren, is injured and Finch's lorry is damaged. The incident is witnessed by PC Hawk.

Answers to all quizzes can be found in Appendix 2.

CHAPTER 2

Resolving legal disputes

INTRODUCTION

This chapter explains the institutions and processes which may be relevant to the resolution of a legal dispute involving a business. It aims to give you an overview of the workings of the legal system and primarily focuses on the operation of that system in relation to the areas of law covered in this book.

While it is important to understand the court structure and the procedures by which a civil action may be brought, the great majority of civil disputes are settled without resort to the courts at all, with private agreements being reached voluntarily between the parties. Such agreements are sometimes assisted by the use of an arbitrator.

THE COURT AND TRIBUNAL SYSTEM

The courts described below form a hierarchy. This means that they are positioned in a structure in which some courts are superior to others. Through the doctrine of binding precedent (explained in Chapter 3), the decisions of the superior courts are binding on the courts below.

The courts

The magistrates' court

Magistrates' courts are very busy courts in which approximately 95 per cent of all criminal offences are prosecuted. These are summary and hybrid offences. Summary offences are petty offences which can be tried only by the magistrates. Hybrid offences may be tried by either the Crown Court or the magistrates' court, usually at the choice of the defendant; they usually involve conduct which is capable of being viewed as either serious or relatively trivial, like theft or criminal damage.

All cases are usually tried by a bench of three justices of the peace (JPs). These act voluntarily and are not legally qualified, but they are advised on points of law by the clerk of the court. Exceptionally the case may be heard before a stipendiary magistrate who is legally qualified.

The magistrates' court is the usual venue for trial of most environmental health and other regulatory offences under the Trade Descriptions Act 1968, the Consumer Protection Act 1987 and the Health and Safety at Work Act 1974 (see Chapters 13 and 18). Most crimes against business owners, like shoplifting and criminal damage, are usually prosecuted in the magistrates' court.

Bail and legal aid applications are heard by magistrates.

The sentencing powers of the magistrates' courts are restricted. They may impose imprisonment for up to six months and a fine of up to £5000. A party tried for an offence carrying a potentially higher penalty may be sent to the Crown Court for sentencing.

With regard to civil and administrative jurisdiction, the Family Proceedings Court has wide jurisdiction over many aspects of domestic and matrimonial law and has significant powers under the Children Act 1989. The magistrates also have powers to license premises selling alcohol and to enforce payment of council tax and business rates, and charges for gas, water and electricity.

The Crown Court

These courts are found mainly in county and borough towns. The Crown Court is staffed by High Court judges, circuit judges and recorders. The seriousness of the offence determines the type of judge to officiate.

The Crown Court has criminal jurisdiction in the following circumstances:

1 *Trial of indictable offences*. These include those offences which are so serious that they must be tried in the Crown Court. For example, homicide, rape and grievous bodily harm. Trial is by jury if the accused pleads not guilty.

2 *Sentencing cases committed from the magistrates' court.*

3 *Legal aid and bail applications.*

4 *Appeals*. The defendant found guilty in the magistrates' court may appeal against conviction or sentence to the Crown Court. The appeal will be heard by a judge (usually a recorder) sitting with a bench of JPs.

The county court

There are over 400 county courts in England and Wales, staffed by circuit judges and district judges. The county court has an extensive and purely civil jurisdiction, including contract, tort, recovery of land, trusts, mortgages and partnerships, contested wills, divorce, bankruptcy and company insolvency.

Since the Courts and Legal Services Act 1990 (CLSA), almost any case which can be heard in the High Court can now be heard in the county court provided that it falls within specified and generous financial limits. For example, cases in tort and contract may be heard if the claimant is not suing for more than £50 000. The CLSA provisions aim to free the High Court from hearing all but the most complex, costly and specialist cases.

The following cases must generally be tried in the county court:

1 all actions worth up to £25 000;

2 any personal injury case worth under £50 000;

unless its specialist nature or complexity makes trial in the High Court appropriate.

Otherwise, provided that a case falls within the prescribed financial limits, the choice of venue is determined by:

1 the amount involved;

2 whether points of law of general public interest are involved;

3 the complexity of the case;

4 the procedures and/or remedies likely to be involved. Some are obtainable only from the High Court.

Cases which have been started in the High Court can be transferred to the county court at the request of a party or at the discretion of the judge. A successful party

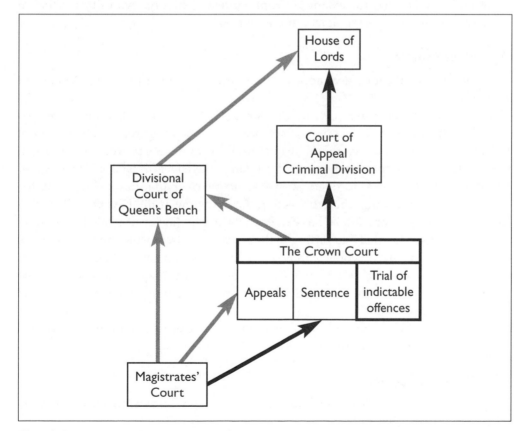

Figure 2.1 The criminal court structure

may not get the full costs paid if the judge believes the case should have been pursued in the county court.

The High Court

This court is staffed by High Court judges. The court's principal venue is The Royal Courts of Justice in London, but cases are also heard in provincial cities. It is divided into three divisions and primarily is concerned with the trial of civil cases outside the jurisdiction of the county court. The three divisions of the High Court are:

1 the *Queen's Bench Division*, which primarily is concerned with the trial of cases in contract and tort. It also contains the Commercial Court which hears cases between people in business arising out of issues like imports and exports of goods, insurance, banking and agency;

2 the *Chancery Division*, which tries cases in copyright, patents and design rights, bankruptcy and the dissolution of partnerships, sale of land, trusts, mortgages and disputed wills;

3 the *Family Division*, which deals with the most complex areas of family and matrimonial law arising, for example, from contested divorce, validity of foreign marriage and divorce, legitimacy and adoption.

Appellate functions

Separate divisional courts hear appeals from designated inferior courts. A bench of two judges is usual.

The *Divisional Court of the Queen's Bench* hears criminal appeals from the magistrates' court by either prosecution or defence, when the interpretation of a point of law is in dispute. (Note that this is distinct from the appellate powers of the Crown Court which hears appeals only by the defendant, where facts as well as law may also be in dispute.) It also has a supervisory jurisdiction over all inferior courts and tribunals exercised through the process of judicial review. If the Divisional Court is satisfied that a court or tribunal has exceeded its jurisdiction or has failed to conduct its proceedings impartially according to the rules of natural justice, an order may be issued overturning the outcome of those proceedings or preventing their continuance.

The *Divisional Court of the Chancery Division* hears appeals against decisions of the county court in bankruptcy cases, and in revenue law against the decisions of the Inland Revenue Commissioners.

The *Divisional Court of the Family Division* hears appeals from the magistrates' courts in domestic and matrimonial cases.

The Court of Appeal

This is staffed by Lords Justices of Appeal and has two divisions. Cases are heard by a bench of three or five judges.

The Civil Division of the Court of Appeal has jurisdiction to hear appeals against decisions of the county court and High Court. It also hears appeals from some tribunals, including the Employment Appeals Tribunal, concerning cases originally heard at employment tribunal level.

The Criminal Division of the Court of Appeal has jurisdiction to hear appeals from Crown Court trials. (Note that the Court of Appeal cannot hear an appeal from the Crown Court where that court has itself been exercising its own appeals jurisdiction regarding cases from the magistrates' court. The only further avenue for such appeals is the Queen's Bench Divisional Court.)

The House of Lords

This court is staffed by the Lords of Appeal in Ordinary (the Law Lords). It has jurisdiction to hear appeals from the Divisional Courts and the Court of Appeal, provided a point of law of public importance is involved. Cases generally concern statutory interpretation and are heard by a bench of three to seven judges.

Since the Administration of Justice Act 1969, an appeal may be made to the House of Lords directly from the High Court, bypassing the Court of Appeal (the 'leap-frog' procedure). This is permitted only where the point of law is already the subject of a Court of Appeal decision by which it and the High Court is bound. This measure was introduced to overcome the restraints of the law of precedent, but is very rarely used.

The tribunal system

Like the courts, the tribunal system provides a means of judicial resolution to a legal dispute. Tribunals usually consist of a panel of members with knowledge relevant to the specialist jurisdiction of the tribunal. The panel chair is generally legally qualified.

There are over 60 different kinds of tribunals, references to some of which are made in later chapters, including:

- *Employment Tribunals:* see below;
- the *Lands Tribunal:* compensation for compulsory purchase, planning appeals;
- the *Mental Health Review Tribunal:* appeals by mental patients against compulsory detention in mental hospitals;
- the *Social Security Appeals Tribunal:* appeals concerning income support and family credit applications;
- the *Comptroller of Patents:* appeals against refusal to register patents or trade marks.

Characteristics of tribunals

All tribunals have entirely different jurisdictions and powers, but they all have at least some of the following characteristics:

- statutory duties and powers;
- a very narrow jurisdiction;

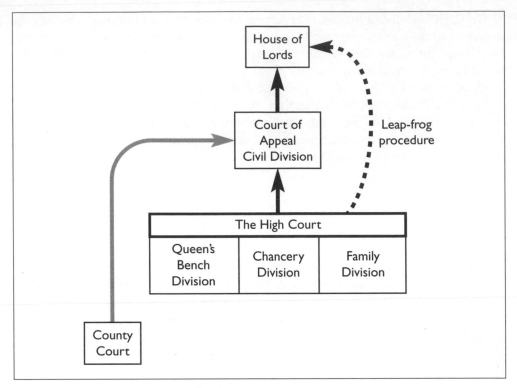

Figure 2.2 The principal civil courts and appeal routes

- chaired by a lawyer, with specialist lay panel members;
- open to the public;
- appeal procedures, which may include a superior tribunal, the court hierarchy or a senior official or government minister;
- sit at a number of locations.

The Employment Tribunal reflects all the above characteristics:

1 governing statutes include the Employment Rights Act 1996;

2 jurisdiction:

   (a) disputes between employers and employees concerning unfair dismissal, redundancy and sex and race discrimination at work;

   (b) appeals by employers against the imposition of improvement and prohibition orders by the Health and Safety Executive;

   (c) disputes between individuals and trade unions concerning exclusions and expulsion from closed shops;

3 it is chaired by a lawyer sitting with two other people nominated by bodies representing employers and employees respectively;

4 hearings are open to the public;

5 appeal structure: where a point of law is disputed, it is possible to appeal to the Employment Appeal Tribunal. The appeal is heard by a panel of three, being a High Court judge who chairs proceedings and two appropriately qualified lay people. Further appeal is possible to the Court of Appeal, the House of Lords and the Court of Justice of the European Communities;

6 it sits at 50 different locations.

Benefits of tribunals

Tens of thousands of cases are heard by tribunals every year and the system is seen as valuable to the parties using it. The main benefits of the tribunal system as compared with the courts are perceived to be:

1 *Cheapness*. Legal representation is not essential at a tribunal and the specialist knowledge of panel members makes it unnecessary to call specialist witnesses. The parties do not generally have to travel far to the hearing.

2 *Informality*. Procedures are usually less formal and adversarial than those of the ordinary courts, therefore a tribunal hearing is less intimidating.

3 *Speed*. A case may take years to come to court. Cases should reach tribunals within weeks or months of proceedings being started.

4 *Flexibility*. Tribunals are not bound by their own precedents (but they are bound by relevant decisions reached by the courts).

Criticisms of tribunals

Not everyone agrees that tribunals are as effective as they should be. There are a number of criticisms that can be raised regarding the operation of the tribunal system:

1 *No access to legal aid*. There is no state-funded representation for most tribunal hearings, which may unfairly prejudice the chances of the claimant. At employment tribunals the employer is usually able to afford legal representation, while employees may be unrepresented unless help is provided by their trade union or other pressure group. At the Social Security Tribunal, claimants have to dispute their cases with a body which has considerable experience of such hearings, and do not always receive the assistance they need from panel members.

2 *Proceedings have become legalistic and tend to be bound by the tribunals' own previous decisions*. Some tribunals have not maintained an informal and flexible approach and therefore may not be user-friendly to the average complainant. Employment tribunals have been particularly criticised on this ground.

3 *Urgent cases are not resolved sufficiently quickly*. Some tribunals, particularly Social Security and Immigration Appeals Tribunals, have very heavy caseloads. They try issues of great economic and personal concern to complainants. A delay of

several weeks, or sometimes months, before a case is heard is not uncommon, and is clearly unacceptable.

4 *Inconsistency of appeals rights.* Although appeal to the courts against a tribunal decision may be possible, there is no universal rule, and rights vary according to which tribunal is involved. The final appeal from some (like immigration appeals) may be to the relevant government minister. It is clearly undesirable that the person who makes the relevant rules and policy is also the final judge of the application.

Proposed reforms of the tribunal system

In 2001 the Leggatt Report made a number of recommendations for reform, concentrating on the needs of users:

1 Generally a more user-friendly approach should be adopted.

2 A coherent and more independent system should be developed, with a centralised entry point for claims which would be allocated to the appropriate tribunal.

3 More state funding should be provided to ensure quality advice for claimants and access to funded legal representation via the Community Legal Service on a case-by-case basis.

BRINGING A CASE IN THE CIVIL COURTS

The enforcement of legal rights is all too often perceived as a universal remedy, but there are many factors which can prevent a successful outcome. Many people who technically have a good claim in law may be unable to enforce it successfully for any of the following reasons:

1 their opponents do not have the necessary funds to satisfy the claim;

2 the lawbreaker cannot be traced, e.g. an offending company may have gone into liquidation;

3 the wronged party may not have the funds to pursue the claim. Litigation is a costly and protracted process, which may require expert assistance. Legal representatives do not simply send in a bill at the end of proceedings; regular payments are required pending the outcome of the case, and a party may run out of money even before the case comes to court. Rights to legal aid are means-tested and largely restricted to parties whose income does not exceed basic welfare benefit levels;

4 the losing side may be responsible not only for their own legal costs, but also for those of their opponents. This may discourage pursuit of a case where the outcome is unpredictable.

THE WOOLF REFORMS 1999

In 1993, Lord Woolf (Master of the Rolls) headed an inquiry into the civil justice system which was prompted by concerns that its procedures were neither efficient nor effective. The report drew attention to a range of problems for the would-be litigant including the undue and often disproportionate cost of litigation, compounded by the unnecessary complexity of rules and procedures. It also expressed concerns that abuse by lawyers of the adversarial system could lead to litigation being controlled more by the lawyers rather than the parties or even the judge. Implementation of recommendations in the report in April 1999 have resulted in radical changes to civil litigation. The new Civil Procedure Rules (CPR) are drafted in plain English, with an emphasis on clarity and avoidance of legal jargon, to make them user-friendly for the unrepresented litigant and more accessible to all.

Some materials like case reports, which you may use for wider reading, which were published before the new rules came into effect will use the old terminology, so you may like to note a list of the old terms with the CPR equivalent in Appendix 3.

SETTLEMENT OUT OF COURT

Litigation is time-consuming, costly and often emotionally draining for the parties. It is a step to be taken only when all alternatives have failed.

The huge majority of legal claims can be enforced without litigation, or even specialist help. Simple cases may be settled informally between the parties. A customer who is sold defective goods will usually obtain a refund from any reputable business without argument. A party who is unable to achieve a successful outcome may get a solicitor to reinforce the claim with a letter pointing out the relevant legal requirements. Sometimes the threat of litigation may produce the required result; if this fails proceedings may be started, but this does not commit either party to a court appearance. Most civil cases are settled before trial.

The Woolf Report stressed the importance of early settlement wherever possible and the CPR give judges a number of powers to encourage this. For example, if a judge believes that a party has acted unreasonably in pursuing or conducting the case, penalties may be imposed as regards costs.

PAYMENT INTO COURT AND OFFERS TO SETTLE

If proceedings have been started, the defendant may offer to make a payment into court. This represents the amount of compensation the defendant is prepared to pay. It is not in itself an admission of liability. The claimant does not have to accept this offer, but may feel pressured to do so. If the case proceeds, the claimant will be liable for the defendant's costs, even if successful, if the amount of damages awarded by the court is less than the amount offered by the defendant.

The CPR have also introduced rights for a claimant who makes an offer to settle for a certain sum. If the defendant refuses the offer and the claimant then wins the case and is awarded that sum or more, the court has the discretion to increase the amount of interest payable on damages from the date of the decision by up to 10 per cent. Strategies of this kind are aimed at encouraging early settlement with a consequent saving of cost to the litigants and time for the judge.

CIVIL LITIGATION PROCEDURES

Starting a civil action

1 Letters of claim and pre-action protocols

The CPR aim to encourage the parties to clarify the issues between them before any claim is issued. They will be expected to exchange letters indicating clearly their allegations and defences to forestall unnecessary legal action. Protocols requiring very detailed and specific information and documentation must be exchanged in certain types of cases, such as personal injury and clinical negligence; protocols for other types of case are being implemented.

2 Issue of claim

The claimant fills in the claim form with detailed particulars and submits it to the court where it is processed and served on the defendant.

3 The defendant's response

The defendant must either admit the claim or file a detailed defence within 21 days. Failure to respond may result in the claimant obtaining immediate judgment against the defendant for any sum specified in the claim.

4 The case is allocated to the relevant track

The Woolf Report stressed that the cost of and resources for litigation should be proportionate to the complexity and size of the claim. The CPR aim to achieve this by designating a case to one of three tracks with differing procedures relative to the value and difficulty of the claim.

The small claims track
This is for claims of £5000 or less and provides a relatively simple procedure aimed primarily at consumers who wish to bring a small and simple claim without the cost of paying a solicitor. However, a wide variety of cases are heard in this way and evidence suggests that it is equally useful to businesses as a means of debt enforcement against their customers.

The hearing before a district judge is informal and the normal rules of evidence do not apply. The CPR encourage an inquisitorial approach: the judge may question witnesses and limit cross-examination. The claimant may bring a friend to support him or her. A successful party may recover the costs incurred in issuing the proceedings, travel costs and a limited contribution to any expert-witness fees and loss of earnings. Legal costs are not recoverable for any money claim. This rule aims to discourage the use of lawyers but arguably loads the dice against a consumer since a business is likely to be represented.

The fast track
Cases involving £5000–£15 000 will usually be dealt with this way.

The judge will give directions to the parties to clarify the issues to be tried and a trial date not later than 30 weeks ahead will be announced. A party who is not ready by that point may have problems obtaining an extension; unnecessary delay may ultimately result in costs penalties.

The trial is limited to one day's duration and limits may be imposed on how long expert-witness evidence may take.

These rules reflect the Woolf Report's recommendations that time (and the litigant's money) should not be wasted during the preparation or conduct of relatively small and simple cases.

The multi-track
Any case over £15 000 will be allocated to this track.

The bigger and more complex the case, the greater will be the powers of the judge to manage its progress towards trial through case management conferences involving the litigants and their legal representatives. Such case management is a dominating characteristic of the Woolf reforms and is intended to ensure that time is not wasted by lawyers in pursuing irrelevant legal arguments and to constrain the legal representatives to make proper and full disclosure of evidence to their opponents. It also enables the judge to set time limits for the achievement of any necessary processes and organise the conduct of the trial in advance.

5 The interlocutory stages

This is the period between issue of claim and hearing when detailed preparations for the hearing are made. In multi-track cases there are likely to be a number of case conferences called by the judge.

At this time there may also be requests for information, disclosure, and the issue of interlocutory injunctions.

Requests for information: one party may require the other to provide further clarification of the particulars of his or her claim or defence.

Disclosure: the documentary evidence on which a party intends to rely must be made available at this stage. Third parties may also be required to give access to information.

Application to the judge may be necessary to obtain compliance.

In exceptional cases a search order may be required from the court which permits the claimant to get entry to the defendant's premises and seize evidence. An application for such an order may be made without notice to the defendant to prevent him or her from covering his or her tracks.

Issue of interlocutory injunctions: injunctions are orders from the court which may stop the defendant from doing something or require him or her to do something. An injunction is an equitable remedy, which means that a party has no right to them. An injunction is granted at the discretion of the court. The judge must be convinced that the claimant is morally entitled to the remedy and that it will not be unjust to impose it on the defendant. A freezing injunction may be required at the interlocutory stage to prevent the defendant from transferring assets abroad or otherwise concealing them so as to avoid compensating the claimant.

Exceptionally, an injunction may be required as a holding measure to prevent the defendant from causing or continuing to cause serious damage to the claimant prior to the trial.

THE TRIAL OF THE CASE

The court hears legal arguments from both parties, who will generally be represented by a barrister or a solicitor-advocate. Solicitors in general do not have the right to appear in the High Court, but under the CLSA they may do so if they obtain an additional advocacy qualification by relevant litigation experience and satisfactorily completing a training course. Witnesses may be called and questioned by both sides.

The judge who hears the case will decide who is the winner and explain why that conclusion has been reached. An award of damages is the usual remedy, but, where appropriate, an injunction or any other order within the jurisdiction of the court may be issued.

EXECUTING THE JUDGMENT

A claimant who is successful at trial has won a major battle but not the war. If awarded damages, the claimant has the status of a judgment creditor, but this does not in itself compel the defendant to pay – the claimant may have to return to the court to take steps to enforce the judgment. This may be done in any of the following ways:

1 *A writ of fieri facias (a 'fi fa' writ)*. This entitles the claimant to seize goods to the value of the debt from the defendant's premises. Bailiffs are usually employed for this purpose, at the claimant's cost.

2 *A charging order*. This prevents the defendant from disposing of any assets, including land, trust funds, shares and debenture stock and other financial securities, pending satisfaction of the claimant's action.

3 *Attachment of earnings*. The defendant's employer may be required to pay a proportion of the defendant's earnings to the claimant.

4 *A garnishee order*. This enables the claimant to gain control of funds belonging to the defendant but held by a third party (usually the bank).

5 *Insolvency proceedings*. If any debt (whether resulting from litigation or not) owed to the claimant is £750 or more, the claimant may institute insolvency proceedings against the debtor. This does not guarantee payment: if there are a large number of creditors the claimant will have to join the queue, and at best may recover only a proportion of the debt.

ALTERNATIVE DISPUTE RESOLUTION (ADR)

Given the cost and difficulties raised by taking a case through the courts, a happier outcome may be achieved through using an alternative method of dispute resolution. This may consist of any of the strategies set out below.

Arbitration

The parties voluntarily submit their dispute to a third party and agree to be bound by the resulting decision. Arbitration has been the most favoured method for settlement of commercial disputes for hundreds of years. Its value is recognised by the courts and it is governed by statute, which empowers arbitrators and regulates the process. More recently it has become a common method of resolving consumer disputes.

Commercial arbitration

It is common for an arbitration clause to be a term of contracts between businesses; the parties may subsequently agree to submit a dispute to arbitration. Any person acceptable to the parties may act as their arbitrator. In practice they will tend to choose somebody with skill and experience in the relevant field. The role of arbitrator has become professionalised and the Institute of Arbitrators regulates the standards of its members.

The Arbitration Act 1996 (AA) regulates to some extent the operation of arbitration procedures and the behaviour of the arbitrator. The stated purpose of the AA is to empower the parties and to increase their autonomy. It was always the case that if an arbitration agreement existed the courts would not hear the case until the arbitration procedure has taken place. Under the AA the powers of the court to intervene have been restricted further. It may determine a preliminary point of law arising in the course of proceedings. The court may, on the application of a party, revoke the arbitrator's appointment for failure to fulfil their duty to act with impartiality and fairness. Rights of appeal against the arbitrator's decision are limited. Appeal on a point of law underpinning the decision is possible unless the parties have previously agreed to exclude this right. It is also permitted on the grounds that the arbitrator exceeded his or her jurisdiction or committed a serious irregularity.

The advantages of the arbitration process are that it ensures privacy for the parties in dispute and it is more likely to ensure a friendly outcome between the parties than litigation. This may be valuable in a specialist business area where the choice of contracting parties is limited. The problem can usually be resolved relatively cheaply and speedily at a time and place convenient to both parties. The arbitrators' expertise in the business field enables them to understand the issues in dispute. There are possible disadvantages, though: arbitrators have fewer powers than the courts to obtain evidence from the parties and to expedite the proceedings; they may lack necessary legal knowledge, ultimately necessitating an appeal, which will increase the cost.

Commercial arbitration procedures are not necessarily appropriate unless the contracting parties are in a position of equal bargaining power. The Consumer Arbitration Act 1988 stipulates that an arbitration clause in a contract does not bind a consumer until a dispute arises, and only then if the consumer agrees in writing at that point. Consumers cannot be forced into arbitration.

Code arbitration

Some trade associations impose a code of conduct on their members and permit consumers to take disputes through an arbitration procedure run by the association. A well-known example is ABTA (Association of British Travel Agents). Similar codes govern dry cleaning, photographic processing, car sales and a number of other trades.

These codes, developed under the auspices of the Director General of Fair Trading, are aimed at the protection of consumer buyers. A fee is payable to initiate the arbitration process, but this will be refunded if the consumer wins. The arbitrator is appointed by the trade association from appropriately experienced members of the Institute of Arbitrators. All communication with the arbitrator is written only. If the trader is at fault, the association is responsible for enforcing any award.

A consumer can take this action only if the firm involved is actually a member of the relevant trade association. It is likely to be helpful only in relatively simple cases where the facts and evidence can readily be presented in documentary form.

Ombudsmen services

The organisations responsible for the supervision of legal, banking, insurance and financial services have each appointed officials called *ombudsmen* who have the power to investigate and resolve problems reported to them by dissatisfied customers.

Conciliation

A conciliator aims to assist the parties to a dispute to find a resolution. The conciliator may suggest a solution, but has no power to enforce it. Parties to a dispute which has been referred to an employment tribunal are offered the services of the Advisory, Conciliation and Arbitration Service (ACAS). The case proceeds to the tribunal only if the conciliation process is refused or is unsuccessful.

Mediation

A mediator assists the parties to communicate with each other and find their own resolution to their dispute. Mediation is becoming a popular means of sorting out property and custody issues when a relationship breaks down. Means-tested funding in such cases is provided by the Community Legal Service. Some health authorities use mediation to resolve complaints of clinical negligence. It increasingly plays a part in the pre-litigation process.

In 1995, the Lord Chief Justice issued instructions that legal representatives must check that their clients are fully aware of the possible use of alternative means of resolving the dispute before proceeding to take a case to the High Court. The Woolf Report stressed the importance of encouraging parties to use ADR, and under the CPR judges have the power to require parties to attempt to resolve some or all the issues of the case in this way.

Quiz 2

1 Where will the proceedings involving the following parties take place?

   (a) Wackford Squeers, on a charge of manslaughter of pupils at Dotheboys Hall.

   (b) Bill Sykes, who wishes to appeal against his conviction for murder.

   (c) Polly Peachum, who wishes to appeal against her conviction in the magistrates' court for soliciting.

   (d) Mr Micawber, from whom Uriah Heep wishes to recover a debt of £200.

   (e) Mr Dombey, who is claiming £75 000 against The Great Western Railway Company for injuries caused when he fell under one of its trains.

   (f) Newman Noggs, who is claiming that he was unfairly dismissed by Ralph Nickleby.

   (g) Mr Dorrit, regarding repossession of his house by The Benevolent & Warmhearted Building Society.

2 In what ways do tribunals differ from the ordinary courts?

3 What is the purpose of a freezing order?

4 What is the difference between arbitration, mediation and conciliation?

Assignment 1

'Lord Woolf was right to stress the importance of alternative dispute resolution in obtaining settlement of civil claims, since very few need to come to court.'

Discuss.

A suggestion solution for this assignment can be found in Appendix 2.

CHAPTER 3

How the law is made

INTRODUCTION

This chapter explains where English law comes from and how it is made. There are currently three important sources of law:

1 European law.

2 Parliament.

3 The courts.

Parliament and the European Union are the primary sources, but the courts also have a minor (though important) law-making role. The courts also have a crucial role in the interpretation of legislation.

EUROPEAN LAW

The law of the European Community has been a source of UK law since 1973, when the UK became a member of what was then called the European Economic Community (EEC). The 1992 Treaty on European Union (the Maastricht Treaty) officially changed the name to European Community (EC) to signify that the objectives of the Community are wider in scope than just economic. The Maastricht Treaty also created the European Union, which consists of three 'pillars'. In the middle pillar are the three existing Communities (i.e. the ECSC, Euratom and the EC). These three Communities are known collectively as the European Communities. On either side of this central pillar is the Common Foreign and Security Policy (CFSP) and Co-operation in Justice and Home Affairs (JHA). These three pillars support the overarching constitutional order of the Union. However only the central pillar, the EC, is governed by Community law. The CFSP and the JHA pillars are governed by intergovernmental co-operation. This means that they are outside the jurisdiction of the Community institutions, particularly the Court of Justice. Neither are any of the articles of the outside pillars enforceable, or challengeable, in national courts. Thus, although the Union is wider than the European Community it has its roots in the Community. EC law is an important source of business law and you will notice its impact in a number of topic areas such as product safety and employment law.

Under the European Communities Act 1972 (ECA), s 2, EU law is part of UK law. In the event of conflict EU law takes priority. Disputed points of EU law must be referred by the domestic courts for interpretation to the Court of Justice of the European Communities, or be decided in accordance with principles found in its existing decisions.

The institutions of the European Union

The Councils

In 1974, in Paris, it was agreed at a meeting of Community leaders to hold regular meetings at the highest political level within what became known as a 'European Council'. This European Council met regularly on an informal basis, until it was given a legal basis by Article 2 of the Single European Act. Its current basis is governed by Article 4 of the Maastricht Treaty, which states its composition and functions. Today it is more commonly known as the 'Council of Ministers'. The Council is the main legislative organ of the Community and it is within that body that the interests of member states find direct expression.

The Council of Ministers is made up of the heads of state or government of the member states and the President of the Commission. They are assisted by the minister of foreign affairs of each of the member states and by a member of the Commission. The European Council's function is to provide the Union with the necessary political impetus to define the general political guidelines for its development.

The European Council must meet at least twice a year. It is chaired by the head of state or government of the member state currently holding the presidency of the Council of Ministers. The membership of these Council meetings is made up of one minister per member state. For General Council meetings the member state representative is generally the foreign minister, otherwise meetings are attended by the ministers of state with the relevant portfolio. So, for example, a meeting will be made up of agriculture ministers when the Common Agricultural Policy is under discussion.

The European Commission

The Commission is composed of one nominee from each member state and is an executive and policy-making body with legislative powers. Most major decisions taken by the Council must be made on the basis of proposals from the Commission.

The European Parliament

This consists of 626 members directly elected by people with the right to vote in each member state (the UK returns 87 Euro-MPs). Parliament exercises democratic supervision over the Commission, with the appointment of the president and members of the Commission subject to its approval. The Commission is thus politically answerable to the Parliament, which can pass a 'motion of censure' calling for its resignation. Together with the Council, Parliament formulates and adopts legislation proposed by the Commission.

The European Court of Justice (ECJ)

The court is composed of one judge from each member state plus one extra. It has two functions:

1 to interpret any point of EU law referred by the courts of member states. It is mandatory for the highest appeal court of any member state to make a referral, if the meaning of a principle of EU law is unclear;

2 to decide the outcome of cases alleging breaches of EU legal obligations, brought by EU institutions, member states or individuals.

Once the court has reached its decision this is immediately effective. It takes precedence over any conflicting domestic legislation.

Individual states have responsibility for implementing the court's decisions by changing the relevant domestic law. Reluctance to comply may result in pressure from other member states. Since the Maastricht Treaty, a state which does not comply with a judgment may be subject to a penalty payment.

The sources of European law

The treaties

A number of treaties impose legal obligations on member states, including the Treaty of Rome 1957, the Maastricht Treaty 1992 and the Treaty of Amsterdam 1997. Some of these obligations are directly enforceable by individual citizens, regardless of whether the relevant member state has taken legislative action to implement them. Such directly enforceable obligations include those under Article 119 (now 141) of the Treaty of Rome, which relates to the equal treatment of men and women in employment.

Regulations

These are intended to impose uniformity of law throughout the Community. They take effect in all member states immediately on being issued.

Directives

This is the most prolific source of law in the EC. Directives apply to all member states; they are intended to lead to harmonisation of law between member states, making it similar but not identical. Directives set the aims which must be achieved but leave the choice of the form and method of implementation to each member state. Thus they have to be implemented by national parliaments. Implementation legislation may reflect the legal and social conventions of each member state.

States are required to implement directives within specified time limits, but sometimes drag their heels if a particular directive is unpopular. The Court of Justice may permit claims by individuals against an organ of a member state (though not an individual) for breaches of a directive which has not yet been implemented, provided that the wording of the directive is sufficiently clear and unconditional.

Decisions

A decision affects only particular member states, companies or individuals. It may empower the party to whom it is issued to do something, or prevent it from doing something.

The impact of EU membership on English law

The main impact so far has been felt in the areas of trade, industry, employment, the environment and provision of financial services. Membership of the EU has, therefore, had considerable influence in many areas of business law. A number of references to such developments will be found throughout this book.

As the scope of European law expands through new treaties, its impact on English law, politics and society at large increases. The Treaty of Amsterdam, which came into force on 1 May 1999, aims to place employment and citizens' rights at the heart of the Union, to remove the last remaining obstacles to freedom of movement within the Union and to strengthen security. This will have a considerable impact because of its emphasis on human rights. It requires the widening of the existing principles of non-discrimination legislation in relation to gender, race and ethnic origin to include religious belief, age and sexual orientation, in employment. Directives on all these issues have already been issued to member states (for details see pages 279 and 289–90 below).

The Treaty also seeks to promote privacy of citizens' personal data. The security issues within the Treaty will also have an impact on criminal law and procedure, since the Treaty requires the police and the judiciary of all member states to co-operate more closely in the fight against racism, terrorism, offences against children, drug trafficking, corruption and fraud.

PARLIAMENT

Most English law is today made by, or with the authority of, Parliament. Direct (parliamentary/primary) legislation comprises Acts of Parliament, created by the passage of a Bill through certain prescribed processes in the House of Commons and the House of Lords. Indirect (delegated) legislation is created by a body (usually a government department or local authority) which has been given the power to legislate by Parliament under an *enabling* Act.

How an Act of Parliament is created

Most legislation is proposed by government ministers, but backbench MPs have limited opportunities to put forward *private members' Bills*. These usually relate to non-party-political issues. In practice, few private members' Bills become Acts, because of the limited amount of parliamentary time available to them.

The pre-legislative stage

A government Bill is usually preceded by the issue of a *Green Paper* which sets out the legislative proposals for discussion. Consultation with relevant interest groups may take place. A *White Paper* is then issued, which lays down the principles on which the draft Bill is based.

Parliamentary procedure

The first stage of a Bill's journey through Parliament is *the introduction and first reading*. Most Bills are initially processed in the House of Commons and then go through the same procedures in the House of Lords. All important and controversial Bills, including all money Bills, must start off in the Commons. The first reading is a formality to announce the existence of the Bill and to set down a date for the second reading.

The *second reading* involves a full debate which starts with a speech from the minister who is proposing the Bill. This is answered by the relevant shadow minister. After contributions from any interested member, a vote is taken. Provided a majority is in its favour, the Bill passes on to the committee stage.

At the *committee stage* a standing committee of 25–45, appointed in proportion to party representation, usually examines the Bill clause by clause. Amendments may be proposed. (Some Bills require consideration by a committee of the whole House. They do not have a report stage, but progress straight to the third reading.)

Following the committee stage the committee reports on its findings (the *report stage*), debate takes place on proposed changes, and further amendments may be proposed to the Bill.

At the *third reading* of the Bill, a short debate concentrates on the main points of the Bill. In the Commons, only superficial changes (to grammar or syntax) will be made, though greater changes may take place in the House of Lords.

The processes discussed above are repeated when the Bill reaches the House of Lords (*transfer to the other House*). Note that under the Parliament Acts 1911 and 1949, the House of Lords cannot reject a Bill outright, although it may delay any Bill except a money Bill for up to a year: a money Bill can be delayed only for a month. The power to delay may give the Lords considerable power, as the government is likely to seek a compromise to enable it to pursue its policies.

Before the Bill can become an Act of Parliament and pass into law, it must receive the *Royal Assent*. By convention this is just a formality: hundreds of years have passed since the Crown took an active legislative role.

The date of implementation of the whole or any part of an Act of Parliament is usually specified in it.

Delegated legislation

This is indirect or secondary legislation made by bodies outside Parliament, through the exercise of legislative power delegated to them by Act of Parliament. You will come across examples of delegated legislation in later chapters of this book in connection with, for example, the Health and Safety at Work Act 1974 and the Consumer Credit Act 1974.

In practice, the bulk of law created every year is delegated, rather than direct. Such legislation is the means by which both central and local government agencies administer their policies. Over 2000 such regulations are enacted annually. These may, for example, limit benefit entitlements, raise the required hygiene standards in a fast-food business, and help to keep local parks free from noise pollution.

There are four main types of delegated legislation:

1 *Orders in Council*. The Emergency Powers Acts 1939 and 1984 give law-making powers to the Privy Council in times of national emergency.

2 *Statutory instruments*. These are created by government departments to execute general principles of policy set out in the enabling Act of Parliament. The Consumer Credit Act 1974 empowers the Secretary of State to make rules to safeguard users and potential users of credit facilities.

3 *Regulations to implement law from the EU*. The European Communities Act 1972, s 2, empowers ministers and government departments to implement directives and treaty provisions. For example, the Unfair Terms in Consumer Contracts Regulations 1999 were created under this power.

4 *Bye-laws*. These are made by local authorities and other bodies with statutory powers, like London Underground and Railtrack, to regulate the facilities which they provide.

The use of delegated legislation is somewhat controversial. In general, however, its practical advantages outweigh its disadvantages. The advantages of delegated legislation are:

1 *Saving of parliamentary time.* The parliamentary legislative process is slow and protracted. Parliament finds it difficult to complete its annual legislative schedule and does not have time to debate the fine details of the regulations necessary to execute government policy.

2 *Specialist knowledge*. The creation of many regulations requires specialist knowledge not enjoyed by the average MP. They are, for example, unlikely to understand the finer points of abattoir management, or appreciate the appropriate levels of pork to be found in a sausage.

3 *Flexibility*. Such rules may be easily and quickly introduced, altered, or extinguished, as and when appropriate.

4 *Legislation can take place when Parliament is not sitting*. This assists the smooth running of central and local government outside parliamentary sessions.

The disadvantages of delegated legislation are:

1 *Loss of parliamentary control*. Since details of policy administration are determined by the relevant government department, Parliament may be deprived of the

opportunity to question and debate them. Scrutiny of most delegated legislation is negligible. It is laid before Parliament, but most of it is subject to a 'negative resolution' procedure. This means that it will be implemented as it stands unless an objection is sustained within the specified time limit. Exceptionally, the enabling Act may require Parliament positively to approve the regulations.

2 *Bulk and frequent change*. The huge quantity of delegated legislation which is produced every year makes it very difficult – even for lawyers – to keep abreast of all changes. Adapting to changes may considerably add to the burdens of running a business, even where publicity materials are circulated by the regulating body.

THE COURTS

Creative powers

The law made by the courts is case law, sometimes described as common law. Until the nineteenth century the courts were the primary lawmakers, but were superseded by Parliament since social conditions required a different style of law-making. Case law evolves slowly and haphazardly, when relevant cases come before the courts with facts which justify further legal development. A point of case law may be very narrow in its effect since the courts can legislate only with regard to things that have already happened; they cannot legislate for what is to happen in future cases with different facts. This makes case law an inadequate form of law-making in a sophisticated industrial society, where blanket legislation is needed to regulate possible future problems.

Today the bulk of both civil and criminal law is statutory. New principles are most commonly developed in this way and much of the common law has been *codified* (converted into statutory form). The senior courts retain some limited creative powers, mainly in tort and contract law which are still not predominantly statutory. For example, the law of negligence, which is described in Chapters 10 and 11, has been, and mainly continues to be, developed by judges.

Interpretative powers

Since most law is now statutory, the courts are mainly concerned with the interpretation and application of points of law derived from Acts of Parliament and delegated legislation. When exercising this function the courts aim to give the meaning to a disputed point of legislation which will reflect what Parliament is thought to have intended.

The words used in the statute are the main focus of the interpretation exercise and limit the freedom of the court. If the statute has an apparent gap and consequently an injustice exists, the court is not free to create the law to fill that gap. All that the court can do is to recommend that Parliament amends the legislation.

Judges have a number of resources and tools which may assist their interpretative function.

1 Intrinsic aids

These are found within the statute itself. It is common for an interpretation clause to be included which explains any special meaning to be given to words within the statute. For example, the Occupiers' Liability Act 1957 defines 'premises' as any 'fixed or moveable structure' (see Chapter 12).

2 External aids

These are materials which are not part of the statute itself. They include the following:

(a) *The Interpretation Act 1978*. This gives guidance on terms and phrases commonly found in legislation.

(b) *Reports of the Law Commission or government inquiry*. These may indicate why legislation is needed and thereby indicate its meaning.

(c) *Parliamentary Reports*. Until 1993 the courts refused to admit evidence from Hansard Reports of parliamentary proceedings relating to the passage of the statute. There were three main objections:

- the legislative and judicial functions of the state would be confused;
- the cut and thrust of parliamentary debate was unlikely to provide objective explanations;
- the research required to check Hansard would also add considerably to the cost of litigation.

Pepper v Hart (1993, HL)

A majority of the House of Lords held that Hansard may be consulted by the courts if all the following circumstances exist:

- the disputed legislation is ambiguous or obscure, or the words taken at their face value produce an absurd result; and
- the Hansard extract consists of statements made by the relevant minister or other sponsor of the Bill; and
- the meaning of the extract is clear.

This new practice has been followed in a number of cases, but it is doubtful how far it will be useful. The disputed section of an Act may not have been debated. Even if it was, any comments made may in themselves be ambiguous and confusing.

3 Judicial principles of statutory interpretation

The judiciary has developed the following practices to assist the interpretative process:

(a) *The contextual approach*. Any disputed words must always be interpreted within the context of the statute as a whole. A vague, obscure, or even apparently meaningless word may become crystal clear when scrutinised in relation to the surrounding text. The *ejusdem generis* rule forms part of the contextual approach. General words, like 'other animals', 'other person', or 'other thing' are meaningless in themselves. Their meaning may be clarified by reference to any specific words which precede them. Thus, if the words 'other animals' were preceded by the words 'cats, dogs and guinea pigs', it would be reasonable to assume that they include any animal commonly kept as a domestic pet. Generous interpretations are sometimes made to assist the perceived purpose of the statute.

> ### *Flack v Baldry* (1988)
> An electric shock from a stun gun was held to come within the definition of 'any noxious liquid, gas or other thing' under the Firearms Act 1968.

(b) *The literal rule*. This approach requires the court to take words at their face value where there is no ambiguity and the meaning is clear, even if this produces an absurd result.

> ### *Fisher v Bell* (1961)
> A statute making it an offence to 'offer for sale' an offensive weapon was not breached by the display of flick knives in a shop window. In contract law, a display of goods is an 'invitation to treat' and not 'an offer for sale' (see Chapter 4).

The application of the rule in such a case has been justified by the courts on the ground that it is for Parliament to correct any practical problems arising from the statute. Any action by the courts is an unjustifiable interference with the parliamentary legislative function.

(c) *The golden rule*. This developed as a means of blunting the worst excesses of the literal rule. If the statute is ambiguous, the court will apply the least ridiculous meaning in order to avoid an absurd result.

Adler v George (1964)
A CND demonstrator who invaded a sentry post at an army base was charged with obstructing a member of HM Forces 'in the vicinity of a prohibited place' under the Official Secrets Act 1920. It was argued that since she had actually entered the base she was on it when the obstruction took place rather than in its vicinity. The court held that to dismiss the charge on the basis of a literal interpretation would produce an absurd result; 'vicinity' must be interpreted as including the place itself, not just its environs.

Smith v Hughes (1960)
A prostitute who, from her window, encouraged gentlemen passing in the street to avail themselves of her services, was successfully prosecuted for 'soliciting in the street'. The court held that the purpose of the legislation was to prevent annoyance to people in public places arising from the activities of prostitutes. Since the effects of the defendant's conduct were felt by people in the street, that conduct clearly fell within the purpose of the Street Offences Act 1959.

(d) *The mischief rule.* This sixteenth-century rule allows the court to adopt a meaning which will enable the statute to fulfil its intended purpose. The court examines the law before the Act to discover the problem (mischief) which the statute was intended to correct; then the statute can be given the meaning which resolves the problem.

This rule largely fell into disfavour with the rise of the literal rule, which dominated judicial decision-making in the nineteenth century and for approximately the first 70 years of the twentieth century.

(e) *The purposive approach.* This approach, which is somewhat similar to the mischief approach has come into use since the UK's entry into the EC. The courts of other member states have traditionally used this approach, as does the European Court of Justice. It requires the court to interpret the statute by looking beyond its words to determine the general purpose behind it. To do this the court may examine relevant extrinsic documentary evidence such as government reports proposing the reform. The House of Lords' decision in *Pepper v Hart* (see above at page 34) may be seen as enabling and encouraging this approach. While the literal rule is still used today, a purposive approach is common where this assists a just outcome in the public interest. The court may use it to complement the literal rule: looking at the purpose of the statute will assist correct choice of meaning of an ambiguous word or phrase. It may be more radically used to correct an anomaly or fill a small gap.

Although called 'rules' it is more accurate to describe these judicial principles as 'tools' of interpretation. They represent differing possible approaches to the interpretation process. They are not in any way superior or inferior to each other. Judges will choose what they view as the approach likely to produce the interpretation most beneficial to the public interest and which reflects current constitutional developments.

4 Judicial presumptions

The courts will presume in the absence of clear evidence to the contrary that a statute will not:

(a) impose strict liability, i.e. where it is not necessary to prove that the accused *intended* to commit the offence;

(b) operate retrospectively, i.e. be said to apply to offences committed before the statute came into force;

(c) change the common law.

These presumptions may be contradicted (*rebutted*) only by express wording in the statute, or by clear implication to that effect.

> **Sweet v Parsley** (1969, HL)
> Miss Sweet let out a house which was raided by the police who found cannabis in the possession of the tenants. Miss Sweet was charged with a statutory offence of 'being concerned in the management of premises' where the drugs were found. The court held that in the absence of a clear indication in the statute that she could be liable without reasonable knowledge of what was happening on her property, Miss Sweet was not guilty without proof of guilty knowledge. Strict liability was presumed not to have been intended.

The law of binding precedent

When exercising either their creative or interpretative functions, judges are bound by the law of binding precedent. This is a distinctive feature of the English legal system. In mainland European countries judges tend to follow each others' decisions in a similar way but are not obliged to do so. Their fellow judges' decisions are all *persuasive* but they are not *binding*. Under English law judges are not necessarily entitled to make their own decisions about the development or interpretation of the law. They may be bound by a decision reached in a previous case.

Two factors are crucial to determining whether a precedent (previous judicial decision) is binding:

1 the position in the court hierarchy of the court which decided the precedent, relative to the position of the court trying the current case. Inferior courts are bound by the decisions of superior courts. (The letters HL, CA and PC following the name of a case indicate that it involves an appeal in one of the higher courts.);

2 whether the facts of the current case come within the scope of the principle of law in the previous decision.

The court hierarchy

1 The House of Lords

This is the final court of appeal in the English court system. Its decisions are binding on all courts below. In the interests of preserving certainty, the House of Lords usually follows its own decisions. Since 1966 it has indicated that it is prepared to depart from existing decisions, if this is necessary to prevent injustice or unreasonable restriction of development of the law.

2 The Court of Appeal

(a) The *Civil Division* of the Court of Appeal is bound by the decisions of the House of Lords, and its decisions bind all the civil courts below. Subject to three exceptions laid down in *Young* v *Bristol Aeroplane Company* (1944), it is supposed to follow its own previous decisions. The exceptions are:

- two of its own previous decisions are in conflict: it must then choose which to follow; the one which is not chosen ceases to be good law;

- a previous decision conflicts with a decision of the House of Lords: the decision of the House of Lords must be followed;

- the previous decision was reached *per incuriam* (with lack of care): this means that the court's attention was not drawn to crucial statutory or case law, preventing a correct decision from being reached.

(b) The *Criminal Division* of the Court of Appeal is bound by the decisions of the House of Lords, and its decisions bind all the criminal courts below. It may depart from its own decisions where such flexibility is in the interests of justice.

3 The Divisional Courts

These are all bound by the House of Lords and Court of Appeal decisions. The decisions of the Divisional Courts are binding on those courts from which they hear appeals. They follow their own decisions subject to the same exceptions as the Civil Division of the Court of Appeal.

4 The High Court

Judges in the High Court are bound by the decisions of the House of Lords and Court of Appeal, but not by the decisions of their fellow judges. High Court decisions are binding on the Crown Court, county courts and magistrates' courts.

Decisions made in the Crown Court, the county courts and magistrates' courts are not binding in other cases or in other courts. Such courts are, of course, bound by the decisions of the relevant superior courts.

The relevance of the previous decision: the scope of the *ratio decidendi*

When judges have heard cases in the High Court or any of the courts above, they may deliver lengthy judgments. These explain their reasons for deciding in favour of one party rather than the other.

This statement of reasons, which refers both to relevant proven facts and to the applicable principles of law, is called the *ratio decidendi* (the reason for the decision). It is the *ratio decidendi* which forms the potentially binding precedent for later cases.

A later court, when hearing a case, has to decide whether that case's facts are sufficiently relevant to the principle of the *ratio decidendi* of a previous case. If so, the previous decision must be applied, provided it was decided by a relevant court. If there are material differences then the later case can be *distinguished* on its facts and the previous decision is not applicable.

Reversing and overruling decisions

An appeal court may decide to overturn a decision reached by a lower court. This may be on the ground that the case was incorrectly decided in the light of the current law. The lower court's decision is then said to be *reversed*. The victor at the previous trial is now the loser.

Reversing a decision does not in itself affect the validity of any precedent applied in the case. If the appeal court believes that a precedent which bound the lower court no longer represents the law, it may (subject to the rules explained above) *overrule* that precedent and restate the legal principle.

The importance of the law reporting system

No system of precedent can work unless there is an accurate and comprehensive collection of the key decisions of the superior courts readily accessible to all who have need of them. Authoritative reports compiled by legally qualified law reporters are produced primarily by the Council of Law Reporting. The courts may refuse to allow a non-authoritative report to be quoted in court.

Persuasive precedents

While a court may be bound to apply a precedent, other decisions called persuasive precedents are influential only. The court can choose to apply them. Persuasive precedents include:

1 *Obiter dicta*. In a judgment it is quite common to find statements of law relating to hypothetical facts. These are not part of the *ratio decidendi* and are called *obiter dicta* (*dictum* in the singular). These indicate how the judge thinks the law should develop in the hypothetical circumstances. They are highly persuasive if they come from the House of Lords or Court of Appeal, but a court still has a choice about applying them in a future case. Once applied, the *obiter dicta* become

39

binding principles of law. Some important principles of law have originated from *obiter dicta*. See *Central London Property Trust* v *High Trees House* (Chapter 5).

2 *The decisions of the Judicial Committee of the Privy Council.* The Privy Council, which is staffed by members of the House of Lords, hears appeals from the courts of some Commonwealth countries. As the decisions do not involve English cases they are of persuasive influence only, despite the status of the judges. The rules relating to remoteness of damage in negligence are derived from a case called *The Wagon Mound*, an appeal from the Australian courts (see Chapter 11).

The advantages and disadvantages of the binding precedent doctrine

Conflicting opinions exist about the value of the binding precedent system. The advantages are said to be:

1 *Certainty*. The system promotes valuable certainty in the law. A party can generally be given a reasonably clear prediction of the outcome of its case.

2 *Flexibility*. The necessarily firm rules are tempered by the ability of the higher courts to overrule their own decisions. A court's ability to distinguish or reconcile decisions on their facts also promotes flexibility.

3 *Practical nature*. Principles of pure case law can be developed in response to actual problems and tailored to solve them.

4 *Speed*. The law can be developed without waiting for Parliament to legislate in a new area.

The disadvantages of the system often appear correlative to the perceived advantages:

1 *Uncertainty*. The powers of the courts to distinguish and reconcile binding precedents often lead to confusing hairline distinctions and distorted applications of case law.

2 *Rigidity*. Certainty is preserved by rigid rules which arguably inhibit development of the law.

3 *Retrieval problems*. The vast amount of case law makes it easy for relevant precedents to be overlooked during preparation for litigation, and increases the time and therefore the cost to the client.

4 *Haphazard development*. A change in the law depends on a case with relevant facts reaching the appropriate court. This usually means the Court of Appeal or the House of Lords; litigants do not necessarily have the means to take their cases that far.

5 *Undemocratic*. The development of case law by judges (not interpreting statutes) is not appropriate since they are not democratically appointed.

THE HUMAN RIGHTS ACT 1998 (HRA)

This important statute, which came into force in October 2000, makes rights under the European Convention on Human Rights directly enforceable in the English Courts. It has the potential directly and indirectly to be highly influential on the content and interpretation of legislation and on the way case law is developed.

The legal and political background to the Act

The European Convention on Human Rights (the Convention) was drafted by the Council of Europe and came into force in 1953. It now has over 40 signatories, including the UK. It requires signatory states to uphold a number of fundamental civil rights, including freedom from arbitrary arrest, freedom of religion, expression, assembly and association. The rights to life, a fair trial and privacy and family life are also included. Until the HRA, none of these were directly and specifically enforceable in the UK courts. Individuals had to take claims that the UK had breached its duties under the Convention to the European Court of Human Rights (ECHR) at Strasbourg, if no remedy had been found to exist in their case by the UK courts under domestic law.

The Convention, even when not directly binding on the English courts, was used as an aid to statutory interpretation and to determine the scope of the common law. Decisions of the ECHR were used as persuasive precedents.

The Convention and the ECHR must not be confused with the law and institutions of the EU. They are different in their origins, membership and operations. However, the European Court of Justice, based at Luxembourg, which is responsible for upholding the law of the European Union, tends to reflect the principles of the Convention in its decisions.

The operation of the HRA

The direct effect

The Act gives an entirely new right of action against a *'public authority'* for alleged breaches of Convention rights. Public authorities are rather vaguely defined by the Act as exercising public functions. They may be pure or quasi-public bodies. Pure public authorities include central government and local authority departments, courts, tribunals and police forces. They are required to act compatibly with the Convention in regard to their public law and private law functions. For example, the Home Office public law functions include prison management and its private law functions include making employment contracts with prison staff. Quasi-public authorities like Railtrack must act compatibly with the Convention when exercising public law functions only.

A variety of powers are available to the court where a breach is proved, including damages and injunctions and other orders.

The indirect effect

This is likely to have a subtle but pervasive effect on the interpretation of statutes and development of case law as the Act requires the courts to decide all cases, whether concerning common law or statute law, compatibly with the Convention. The courts are also required to take case law from the ECHR into account when coming to a decision. Therefore, although a private body or individual cannot have an action brought against them under the Act, Convention principles are still capable of affecting the outcome.

To preserve parliamentary sovereignty, the Act does not permit the court to override a statute which it has found to be incompatible with the Convention. Instead, the Court has the power to issue a declaration of incompatibility to the relevant minister, who then has a discretion as to whether to ask Parliament to amend the legislation. In the first year of the operation of the Act only three such declarations were issued in a total of 56 successful claims under the Act.

> **R v Secretary of State (Home Department) ex parte Pearson and Martinez: Hirst v Attorney-General** (2001)
> It was held that the Representation of the People Act 1983, which states that prisoners do not have the right to vote, was not incompatible with Article 10 of the Convention (right to freedom of expression). The Convention right is not absolute and proportionate restrictions can be imposed by the state.

The impact of the Act

Contrary to many people's belief prior to implementation, the impact of the Act has not generally been a dramatic one. This is not surprising. Apart from the innate conservatism of the English judiciary, Convention rights are very broadly worded, giving judges flexibility to find compatibility. Almost all Convention rights are not absolute but are hedged around with qualifications. For example, the right to life (Article 2) may not be breached if a person dies while being lawfully arrested. The right to liberty (Article 5) may be limited in the interests of protecting the public through lawful arrest. Similarly, a person with mental illness may be detained against their will if necessary for their own or the public's safety.

The court, when determining a human rights claim, has to attempt to balance the interests of the parties to ensure neither suffers an undue limitation of their rights. For example, a claim to protect a right of privacy (Article 8) must not be decided in a way that unduly curtails freedom of expression of the other party, or which will unreasonably interfere with the public's right to information.

The Act has not directly generated large numbers of claims and most have not been successful. Between October 2000 and December 2001, 297 claims were heard and only 56 of them were upheld. However, the challenge under the Act affected the outcome, reasoning or procedure in 207 of them, which indicates that the Convention was highly influential This has also been evident in a significant number of cases over the last two years, which were not brought under the Human Rights Act but which required the court to interpret the relevant law compatibly with the Convention. In *A v B sub nom Garry Flitcroft* v *Mirror Group Newspapers Ltd* [2002, CA], the court refused to grant an injunction for breach of confidence to a professional footballer to prevent publication of the story of his extramarital one-night stand. The court in its decision balanced the claimant's right to privacy against the rights to freedom of expression and the public interest and found that these outweighed the claimant's rights. (More detail below at page 388.)

The Human Rights Act has clearly already had a significant impact on the development of the law and a human rights culture is beginning clearly to emerge. You will find a number of examples of relevant decisions in later chapters.

Quiz 3

1 Name the three main sources of English law.

2 Distinguish between EU regulations and directives.

3 Name the stages through which a Bill will pass in Parliament.

4 Name two kinds of delegated legislation.

5 Explain the difference between the literal rule and the mischief rule.

6 Explain how the *ejusdem generis* rule works.

7 When may a precedent be binding?

8 What is the difference in the potential effect of a *ratio decidendi* and an *obiter dictum*?

9 Why are law reports important to the operation of the law of binding precedent?

10 Why might the status of a decision by the Judicial Committee of the Privy Council be described as an anomaly in the law of precedent?

Assignment 2

Imagine that in 1985 the Court of Appeal decided in *Home* v *Dry* that bats were afforded protection under the Feathered Friends Act 1980. Your client, having shot a bat, has had damages awarded against him and is considering an appeal. You discover that in 1988 the House of Lords, while not referring to *Home* v *Dry*, held in *Over* v *Out* that the Feathered Friends Act 1980 was concerned solely with the protection of creatures wholly or partially covered in feathers (which a bat is not). Since then a number of Law Lords have given a clear indication that in their opinion *Over* v *Out* is wrongly decided.

(a) Explain whether the Court of Appeal is free to refuse to follow *Home* v *Dry*, and

(b) as to whether, in the event of the case coming before the House of Lords, it is likely that the House would overrule its own decision in *Over* v *Out*.

(ICSA Introduction to English Law: December 1993)

CHAPTER 4

The law of contract: offer and acceptance

INTRODUCTION

A contract is a legally binding agreement concerning a bargain which is essentially commercial in its nature and involves the sale or hire of commodities such as goods, services or land. Such contracts are known as *simple* or *parol* contracts, since they are usually enforceable without having to be put into writing. You probably make literally hundreds of contracts every year when doing everyday things like shopping, getting your hair cut, or having your shoes repaired. None of the legal paraphernalia that the words 'forming a contract' may bring to mind will have been involved in such transactions. They are legally binding without documents, signatures or witnesses. If the goods or services provided to you are defective, you have legal rights arising from the contract you made with the shop. To enforce those rights you will, of course, need to prove the existence of the contract. The receipt is handy evidence of this. However, if you have lost this, other evidence – like a credit card docket, or a cheque stub or the word of your Aunt Ada who was with you at the time – will be perfectly adequate.

Written evidence may well be useful proof that a contract was made. It is sometimes crucial to proof of your rights if the contract involves complex terms or future performance. While the law does not require a building contract to be in writing, most clients would not be very happy to have settled the terms only by word of mouth.

A minority of contracts *must* be written in order to be valid. These include contracts to sell land under the Law of Property (Miscellaneous Provisions) Act 1989, and contracts to obtain credit which are governed by the Consumer Credit Act 1974. Where such regulation applies, the written document comprises the contract. Without the contractual document the law will treat the transaction as if it does not exist, regardless of other available evidence.

Some transactions will be legally valid only if put in the form of a deed. You need not be concerned with such transactions, which do not necessarily involve bargains at all and do not come within the scope of the law of parol contract.

THE ESSENTIALS OF A BINDING CONTRACT

No contract can come into being unless the following features exist:

1 an offer;

2 an acceptance;

3 consideration (each party will contribute something of material value to the bargain);

4 intention to be legally bound.

This chapter considers the first two elements (offer and acceptance); consideration and intention to be legally bound are discussed in Chapter 5.

THE OFFER

This may be defined as a clear statement of the terms on which one party (the offeror) is prepared to do business with another party (the offeree). An offer may be bilateral or unilateral.

Most offers are *bilateral*, i.e. such an offer consists of a promise made in return for a promise. In a sale of goods contract, for example, the offeror (buyer) promises to take and pay for goods and the offeree (seller) promises to supply goods of an appropriate description and standard. A *unilateral* offer is a promise made in return for the completion of a specified act. An offer of a reward for the return of lost property falls into this category.

A legally binding offer will include:

1 clearly stated terms;

2 intention to do business;

3 communication of that intention.

These must all exist for a valid offer to have been made.

Clearly stated terms

A statement may be held to be too vague to comprise a valid offer.

> **Guthing v Lynn** (1831)
> The buyer of a horse promised to pay the seller an extra £5 'if the horse is lucky for me'. The court held that this was too vague to be enforceable.

An apparently vague offer may be capable of clarification by reference to:

1 *The parties' previous dealings and the nature of the relevant trade.*

> **Hillas v Arcos** (1932, HL)
> A contract to supply wood for one year contained an option permitting the buyer to buy more wood the next year, but it did not specify the terms on which the supply would be made. Clarification of this rather vague option could readily be gleaned from the previous business dealings of the parties, as well as from custom and practice in the timber trade. It was therefore a valid offer.

2 *Statutory implied terms.* For example, an offer to sell goods is valid even if no price is mentioned. Under the Sale of Goods Act 1979, s 8, if no price is stated, a reasonable price is payable.

3 *Arbitration clauses.* Sometimes the parties may purposely state terms vaguely and include provision for arbitration to settle disputes if and when they arise. This allows for later variations to take into account future needs, availability or price. Since the lack of clarity may be resolved, a binding offer exists.

> **Foley v Classique Coaches** (1934, CA)
> The Court of Appeal held that the arbitration clause in a long-term contract to supply petrol to a coach company 'at a price to be agreed in writing and from time to time', would enable any lack of clarity to be resolved as necessary.

Intention to do business

An offer represents the parties' 'last word' prior to acceptance. A statement which does not indicate commitment to be bound by its terms (if accepted) will not be interpreted as a valid offer.

Problems arise where a party, who believes that an offer has been made, communicates an 'acceptance'. The party then believes that a contract exists. However, if the original statement is not a valid offer, there will as yet be no contract, since a valid contract requires both offer and acceptance.

There are two types of statement which may be confused with a legally binding offer:

1 invitations to treat;

2 statements in negotiation.

An invitation to treat

Statements advertising goods or land or services for sale are not usually treated by the courts as indicating the necessary intention to form an offer. Such statements invite potential customers to make an offer. It is then up to the business proprietor to decide whether or not to accept. Without acceptance no contract exists, therefore, buyers have no rights to the goods, etc. they want to purchase.

Fisher v Bell (1961, CA)
The Court of Appeal held that goods in a shop window, even those bearing a price tag, represent an invitation to treat not an offer. Customers make offers by saying that they are prepared to do business at the price shown. Sellers then decide if they want to accept; only if they do does any contract result.

Pharmaceutical Society (GB) v Boots Cash Chemists (Southern) Ltd (1953, CA)
Goods displayed on the shelf in a self-service shop represent an invitation to treat. The customer makes an offer only when presenting the goods at the checkout.

Partridge v Crittenden (1968, HL)
The House of Lords held that a magazine advertisement saying 'Bramble finch cocks and hens 25 shillings each' was an invitation to treat. Any offers came from those responding to it and asking to buy the birds.

The same principle applies to catalogues, price lists, menus and circulars advertising so-called 'cheap offers' at local businesses.

The courts support this principle in the interests of business efficiency. In practice, this may mean what is efficient for the sellers rather than for the disappointed buyer whose request the shopkeeper is able to refuse. If statements currently treated as invitations to treat were interpreted as offers, shopkeepers would be forced to demolish their window displays to remove goods which customers had contracted for simply by expressing their wish to buy them.

(The Race Relations Act 1976 and the Sex Discrimination Act 1975 aim to prevent abuses of the right of a business to refuse a customer's offer. Misleading pricing notices may be an offence under the Consumer Protection Act 1987 (see Chapter 13).)

Statements made in negotiation

Lengthy negotiations may lead up to a contract. Problems may occur where one party assumes that a statement represents the other party's offer and claims to have accepted it. The court will have to decide whether the alleged offeror had by that point indicated a sufficient intention to be bound. In a potentially complex contractual situation where protracted negotiations would normally be expected, a statement made early in the negotiations is unlikely to be held to be a valid offer.

Harvey v Facey (1893)
The claimants were interested in buying land which the defendant had not advertised for sale. They sent a telegram asking the defendant to state the lowest price he would accept. When the defendant replied with a mere statement of price, the claimants attempted to accept. It was held that the statement of price was merely an early step in negotiations and did not amount to a valid offer.

The offer must be communicated to the offeree

The communication of an offer may be written or spoken, but it may often be by conduct, such as taking goods to the supermarket checkout, or putting money into a vending machine. An offer is most commonly made to an individual, but a unilateral offer may be made to the world at large. In such a case a contract will be made with all the people who can and do fulfil the terms of the offer.

Carlill v Carbolic Smoke Ball Co. Ltd (1893, CA)
The defendants published an advertisement which claimed that their product would prevent influenza, and promised that they would pay £100 to any person who, having used the product correctly, still caught influenza. The advertisement also stated that £1000 had been placed in a separate bank account to meet any claims.
   Miss Carlill bought a smoke ball from her local chemist. When she became ill with influenza despite regularly sniffing her smoke ball as instructed, she claimed £100 from the manufacturers. The Court of Appeal held that the advertisement was a unilateral offer by the manufacturers to the world at large, which would be accepted by any person who knew of it and who contracted influenza after using the product as directed.

The offeree must, therefore, know of the offer in order legally to be able to accept it. Coincidental performance of the terms of an offer, made in ignorance of its existence, does not create a binding contract.

Bloom v American Swiss Watch Co. (1915)
The claimant gave evidence to the authorities which led to the arrest of some jewel thieves. He then discovered that the defendant had previously advertised a reward for such information. The defendant refused payment. The court held that the defendant was not legally obliged to pay as no contract to do so existed between the parties, since the offer of the reward had not been communicated to the claimant prior to his giving the information.

Tenders

A tender is a competitive offer to provide goods or services. Many businesses and other organisations will invite tenders to ensure that they get the best value for money. Some, like local authorities, may be required to do so by law. Although the request for tenders is an invitation to treat, it may also be an offer by the advertisers to *consider* any offer submitted to them.

Blackpool & Fylde Aero Club v Blackpool Council (1990, CA)
The Aero Club was invited by the council to tender for a concession to provide pleasure flights for the summer tourist trade. Although the club delivered its tender before the deadline, the council, due to an oversight, failed to clear its letter box and so the tender did not reach the appropriate committee in time to be considered. The Court of Appeal held that as well as inviting tenders, the council's request also implicitly contained a unilateral offer to consider any tender submitted by the deadline. The council was therefore in breach of this contract with the Aero Club which had been deprived of its chance to be the successful bidder.

The termination of offers

An offer, if not accepted, can be brought to an end in a number of different ways.

Refusal and counter-offer

If an offer is rejected it ceases to exist. If offerees then change their minds and try to accept, they will in contractual terms be making a new offer. The same result is achieved by a counter-offer. This is an attempt to vary the terms of the existing offer to get more favourable terms, like a price reduction.

Hyde v Wrench (1840)
The defendant offered to sell his farm for £1000. The claimant at first said that he would pay only £950, but after a few days said he would pay the full price. He heard nothing from the defendant. It was held that there was no contract between the parties: the defendant had not accepted the offer from the claimant, who had destroyed the defendant's original offer by his counter-offer of a reduced price. The claimant's subsequent statement that he would pay the asking price could not revive the original offer. It was a new offer which the defendant never accepted.

If the offeree, while not accepting an offer, asks for further information, or tests out the ground to see if further negotiation is possible, this is not treated as a counter-offer; it, therefore, does not destroy the offer.

Stevenson v McLean (1880)
An offer to sell iron at a certain price was not destroyed when the offeree enquired whether delivery and payment might be made in instalments. This was merely an enquiry as to whether the terms might be varied, not a counter-offer of different terms, and therefore it did not destroy the original offer.

Lapse of time

An offer will cease to exist if not accepted within any specified time limit. Otherwise it will lapse if not accepted within a reasonable time.

Ramsgate Hotel Co. Ltd v Montefiore (1866)
The defendant applied to buy some shares in June but heard nothing more until November when the company informed him that the shares were his. It was held that the company's delay had made the defendant's offer lapse and the acceptance came too late to result in a contract.

Revocation

Offerors are entitled to change their minds and withdraw offers at any time right up to the moment of acceptance. If, at an auction sale, you place the highest bid and the auctioneer is saying 'going, going ...' you still have time to shout that you are withdrawing your offer, as it will not be accepted until the auctioneer's gavel hits the table (Sale of Goods Act 1979, s 57). However, if you do choose to do this, it might be a good idea to leave the auction room immediately.

Notice of revocation is crucial, it is not effective unless the offeree knows of it. Usually the offeror will personally notify the offeree, but this is not essential as long as the offeree knew or reasonably should have known that the offer had been withdrawn. For example, if you had offered to sell your grand piano to your neighbour who did not immediately accept, they would know of your revocation if someone was seen loading the piano into a van, later that day. Even reliable information from a third party, who is not acting on the offeror's instructions, may be sufficient notice.

Dickinson v Dodds (1876, CA)
The defendant made an offer to sell property to the claimant, but sold it to a third party before the claimant responded. A mutual acquaintance of the buyer and the claimant told the claimant of the sale. This was held to be adequate notice.

A *promise to keep an offer open* for a certain time or to give someone 'first refusal' will not be legally binding unless the offeree gave some payment to the offeror in return for the favour. Otherwise the offeror is making only a gratuitous promise: giving something for nothing. Such a promise is not a contractual one, since it lacks consideration (see Chapter 5). The offeror, while waiting for the offeree to make up his or her mind, might have sold the goods at a better price to someone else. The offeree could ultimately decide not to accept and the offeror could be left with the goods on his or her hands. The offeror is therefore free to withdraw (revoke) the promise at any time before the offer is accepted.

Routledge v Grant (1828)
The defendant offered to buy the claimant's house, promising that he would keep the offer open for six weeks. It was held that he could withdraw the promise at any time before the offer was accepted as his promise was merely gratuitous.

If the offeree does pay for the offer to be held open, a legally binding option is created. This means that the offeree has a contract that allows time to choose whether or not to accept the offer. This is different from putting down a deposit on goods or land. An option agreement gives you time to choose *whether* or not to buy: the deposit is evidence that a contract to purchase has been made.

It would obviously be unjust to apply the ordinary rules of revocation to *unilateral offers*, for two reasons:

1 *Notice*. A unilateral offer is often made to the world at large. If the offeror decides to revoke such an offer, it would be virtually impossible to notify everyone who saw it. Provided the offeror takes reasonable steps to give notice, this will be sufficient. Putting another advertisement in the same newspaper which carried the offer would clearly be adequate.

2 *Incomplete acceptance*. Acceptance of a unilateral offer always involves the performance of an act. If an offeree has begun but not completed the acceptance of a unilateral offer, it would be unjust to allow the offeror to revoke the offer. Revocation will therefore not be effective if the offeree is already in the process of accepting a unilateral offer.

Errington v Errington & Woods (1952, CA)
A father bought a house and promised his son and daughter-in-law that it would become theirs if they paid all the mortgage instalments. The Court of Appeal held that the father's promise was irrevocable as long as they kept up the payments. His offer would technically be accepted only when the last payment had been made. The son and his wife had embarked on performance by starting to pay; while they continued to do so it would be unjust for the offer to be revoked.

THE ACCEPTANCE

The offeree, by acceptance, agrees to be bound by all the terms of the offer. To be legally binding, such acceptance must fulfil three rules:

1 it must be a 'mirror image' of the offer;

2 it must be firm;

3 it must be communicated to the offeror.

Acceptance must be a 'mirror image' of the offer

The offeree must be agreeing to all the terms of the offer and not trying to introduce new terms.

Jones v Daniel (1894)
The offeree responded to an offer by submitting a draft contract which included some new terms. This response was held to be a counter-offer, not an acceptance.

Where two businesses are negotiating a contract, they may each wish to contract on their own standard terms (pre-set terms not open to negotiation). The offerors present their standard terms, but the offerees, instead of accepting on those terms, reply with their own set of standard terms. This is sometimes called 'the battle of the forms'.

Butler Machine Tools Ltd v Ex-Cell-O Ltd (1979, CA)
The claimants, on their standard terms, offered to sell machine tools to the defendants. These terms named a price but allowed the claimants to vary this on delivery. The defendants replied with their terms, which specified a fixed price and required the claimants to return an attached acknowledgement slip indicating that they were prepared to supply the defendants' order on these terms. The claimants did so, but when the goods were delivered they tried to claim that the price could be increased. The Court of Appeal held that the claimants' offer had not been accepted by the defendants: their reply was a counter-offer accepted by the claimants when they returned the slip. The contract was on the defendants' terms and only the fixed price was payable.

Acceptance must be firm

Conditional acceptance is not binding. In sales of land it is normal practice for a seller to accept an offer 'subject to contract'. The parties will not be legally bound to each other until exchange of contracts takes place. This is meant to assist buyers by giving them time to carry out surveys and searches before deciding to commit themselves. It can also mean that the seller is free to sell to another buyer who is prepared to offer more money in the meantime. Such 'gazumping' may cause financial loss to the first buyer, who may have spent money on legal and survey fees and is then left without means of redress against the seller, since there is as yet no binding contract with the seller.

Acceptance must be communicated

The law relating to communication involves a number of different rules.

Communication is effective only if made by an authorised person

> **Powell v Lee** (1908)
> The claimant was notified that his job application had been successful by a member of an appointments board which then decided to give the job to someone else. It was held that the person who had told the claimant of his success had not been authorised to do so and therefore acceptance had not been effectively communicated.

Acceptance may be communicated by speech, writing or conduct

> **Brogden v Metropolitan Railway Co.** (1877, HL)
> Mr Brogden had supplied coal to the railway company for some time, when the company suggested that they should regularise their arrangements with a new contract. The draft contract was sent to Brogden who added certain terms, including the name of an arbitrator. He then marked it 'approved' and sent it back to the company. He heard no more but the company continued to order coal, which Brogden supplied on the terms of the draft agreement. It was held that Brogden's amendments to the draft contract amounted to a counter-offer. The company had accepted this by conduct – either when it placed the first order, or when it accepted the first delivery. The House of Lords stressed that the company's intention to assent was in itself insufficient to be acceptance. It became sufficient only once Brogden knew of it.

Communication is, therefore, effective only when it reaches the offeror or the offeror's place of business.

Since acceptance is effectively communicated only when the offeror has received notice of it, acceptance by *telephone* is effective only on being heard by the offeror.

Entores Ltd v Miles Far East Corp. (1955, CA)
The Court of Appeal made it clear that acceptance by telex should be treated like acceptance by telephone: instantaneous and effective on being received.

Brinkibon Ltd v Stahag Stahl und Stahlwarenhandels GmbH (1983, HL)
The House of Lords suggested (_obiter_) that telex messages transmitted when the receiver's office was closed would be effective only once the office had reopened. (If you wish to refer to this case in your writing, calling it _Brinkibon_ is sufficient.)

Mondial Shipping and Chartering BV v Astarte Shipping Ltd (1995)
A telex message sent just before midnight on a Friday was held to have been communicated at 9 a.m. the following Monday when the receiver's office opened for business.

When developing such rules the courts are guided by the 'reasonable expectations of honest men' in the context of accepted commercial practice. In _Entores_ it was stressed that where it was the fault of the offeror that the message was not received, due perhaps to lack of ink in the teleprinter, the offeror would still be bound, as the offeree would reasonably expect successful receipt.

As yet there are no reported cases involving communication via fax, email, or answerphone. Using the reasonable expectations approach, faxes are likely to be treated like telex messages. Messages left on answering machines could be treated similarly, though it is more likely that they are not communicated until, like any telephone message, the recipient picks them up. Also it is immediately evident to the sender that the message is not going to be transmitted at once. Emails once communicated may well arrive instantaneously but delays may occur in transmission via the server, so perhaps here communication could be deemed to exist once the message hits the receiver's postbox, if constant monitoring of emails is to be reasonably expected in such a business.

Communication by post

Communication by post is an exception to the usual communication rule. In the nineteenth and early twentieth centuries the only method of communication for parties contracting at a distance from each other was the post.

Adams v Lindsell (1818)
It was held that once a letter of acceptance is posted, a contract comes into existence immediately.

The postal rules were later extended to cover telegrams.

Household Insurance v Grant (1879, CA)
Communication of acceptance by post is effective even if a letter is delayed in the post or fails to reach the offeror, as long as this is not due to the offeree's fault and the letter is properly stamped and addressed.

Only postal acceptance produces an instantaneous legal effect: a postal offer or revocation is effective only on receipt.

Byrne v Van Tienhoven (1880)

1 October:	The defendant posted an offer from Cardiff to the claimant in New York.
8 October:	The defendant changed his mind and posted a letter of revocation.
11 October:	The defendant's offer arrived and the claimant sent a telegram of acceptance.
15 October:	The claimant affirmed his acceptance by letter.
20 October:	The letter of revocation was received by the claimant.

It was held that a contract was formed on 11 October when the claimant mailed his telegram of acceptance. The revocation was not communicated to the claimant until 20 October and was, therefore, too late to be effective.

It has always been possible for offerors to avoid the postal rules either by specifying a different means of communication, or by stating that they would not be bound until receipt of an acceptance letter. Even where an offeror specifies nothing to this effect, the courts may be prepared to imply such an intention.

Holwell Securities v Hughes (1974, CA)
The offeror had granted an option to the offeree concerning the purchase of some land, which had to be exercised by 'notice in writing'. The claimant's letter of acceptance was posted before the deadline but failed to reach the offeror before the deadline expired, though this was not the claimant's fault. The Court of Appeal found that no contract resulted from the postal acceptance. The postal rule was implicitly excluded by the offeror, who, by requiring notice in writing, had indicated that for communication to be effective, it must actually receive the letter of acceptance.

Today the postal rules do not play an important part in the law of contract, though they continue to feature in exam papers. Parties contracting at a distance now have much faster and more reliable means of communication available to them. Even where the parties choose to use the post, it is very common for offerors to state that no contract will result until they receive an acceptance.

The offeror cannot waive the communication rule

Offerors cannot bind offerees by saying that they will assume acceptance unless the offerees tell them differently. The communication rule ensures that an offeree is not pressurised into acceptance.

Felthouse v Bindley (1862)
The claimant offered to buy a horse from his nephew, John, who was selling up all his farm stock. The claimant said that he would assume John's acceptance unless told otherwise. Intending to accept, John instructed the auctioneer to withdraw the horse from the sale, but by mistake the auctioneer sold it. The claimant sued the auctioneer in tort, but failed in his action because he was unable to prove that he was the horse's owner. Since John had not communicated his intention to accept to the claimant, there was no contract under which ownership of the horse could pass. The auctioneer had not disposed of the claimant's property. When the sale took place the horse still belonged to John.

The offeror may expressly require a particular method of communication

The court will usually be prepared to treat any reasonable method of communication as effective. Where no mode is specifically requested, the mode of offer and the nature of the subject matter of the contract may indicate suitable methods of response. For example, a telephone offer of perishable goods would necessitate a swift means of communicating acceptance.

Quiz 4

1 Does an offer exist in the following circumstances?

   (a) Joshua puts a teddy bear wearing a price ticket in his shop window.

   (b) Ruth distributes flyers stating 'Cheap Offer: 10% off the cost of all our pizzas'.

   (c) Mary advertises a reward of £50 for the return of her lost bracelet.

   (d) Martha returns Mary's bracelet and then discovers that a reward was offered.

(e) Peter offered to sell his car to Esther for £3000; Esther told him she would pay only £2500.

(f) Elizabeth offered to sell her fridge-freezer to Paul for £100. He asked her to give him three days to decide. On the next day she sold the freezer to Jacob.

2 Has a valid acceptance resulted in the following situations?

(a) John offers to sell potatoes to Thomas, who replies that he will take them if he can raise the money.

(b) Eve offers to sell apples to Matthew and tells him that she will assume that he wants to buy them unless he tells her to the contrary by ten o'clock on Saturday morning. The deadline has now passed but Matthew has not been in touch.

(c) Luke sent a letter to Michael offering to sell an antique clock. Michael replies accepting, but his letter is lost in the post.

(d) Susanna offered by telephone to rewire Antony's house. He accepted, but Susanna did not hear because the line went dead.

Assignment 3

Iris made an offer to sell her piano to Diana for £500 on Monday. Diana replied: 'I will buy it if I can raise the money.' Iris promised that she would not sell to anyone else before Saturday, and added that Diana could collect the piano any time before noon on Saturday. On Wednesday, Diana phoned and left a message with Iris's daughter, Athene, saying that she had got the money and would come to collect the piano on Saturday morning. Athene forgot to pass on the message. On Thursday, Iris was visited by Juno who said that she would pay £600 for the piano. Iris accepted this offer. Later that day Iris posted a letter to Diana telling her that she could not have the piano. Mercury, the postman, delivered it to the wrong address and Diana, who never received the letter, appeared with a hired van to collect the piano at ten o'clock on Saturday morning.

Advise Iris of her legal position.

(Some hints on answering problem questions, including an analysis of the above assignment, can be found in Chapter 28. A suggested solution can be found in Appendix 2.)

CHAPTER 5

The law of contract: consideration, intention and privity

INTRODUCTION

Contracts are essentially commercial agreements: they are about striking bargains, or achieving what is sometimes called 'mutuality'. Both parties stand to gain materially from the transaction: each receive a 'consideration'. Where one party agrees to do something for the other without anything being promised in return they are said to be making a 'naked' or 'gratuitous' promise. A legally binding contract cannot result from such a promise, only a moral obligation.

It is quite possible to find agreements in which the elements of offer, acceptance and consideration can be identified, but the agreement will not be binding as a contract unless that is deemed to be the parties' intention. When they entered into the agreement they may not have intended that failure to perform the agreement would make them liable to legal sanctions for breach of contract.

CONSIDERATION

Consideration has been defined by the courts in different ways. In *Currie* v *Misa* (1875) it was held to constitute a benefit to one party or a detriment to the other. Generally it is easy to analyse contracts on this basis. When you buy a video recorder from a shop, the benefit you receive is the video and the detriment is the money you pay the shop. The shop clearly enjoys a corresponding benefit and suffers a corresponding detriment in taking your money and parting with the video.

In *Dunlop* v *Selfridge* (1915, HL), the House of Lords defined consideration in terms of the price by which one party bought the other party's act or promise. This is also clearly reflected in the example of the sale of the video recorder.

Executory and executed consideration

Executory consideration

A binding contract may be formed by the exchange of promises which will be carried out at a later date. If you order goods which are to be paid for on delivery, a binding contract results on your order being accepted. Failure to deliver the goods to you would be a breach of contract. The consideration in such a contract consists of the mutual promises and is described as 'executory' because they have not yet been executed (performed).

Executed consideration

Sometimes no obligation to pay arises unless or until another party has executed their consideration. For example, if someone advertises a reward for the safe return of a lost cat, that person is making a unilateral promise to pay money that will become binding on the performance (execution) of an act (the return of the cat). The consideration provided by the person who returns the cat is called 'executed consideration'.

The rules governing consideration

Consideration must not be past

The act claimed to represent consideration for another party's promise to pay must not precede that promise, or it will be treated as past consideration and the promise will be merely gratuitous. This rule is illustrated by the following example.

> Archibald, knowing that his elderly neighbour, Bertie, is concerned about the state of his garden, offers to clear it up for him. This occupies Archibald for most of the day, and Bertie is so pleased with the result that he promises to pay Archibald £15 for his trouble. If Bertie fails to pay, Archibald will not be able to sue for breach of contract as Bertie's promise to pay was made after the work was completed. The work represents past consideration and, therefore, the promise to pay is merely gratuitous.

To be contractually binding it must be shown that a promise to pay preceded the act so that the promise and act form one undivided transaction. The principle is clearly illustrated in the following case:

> **Re McArdle** (1951, CA)
> A house was left by Mr McArdle to his wife for life. On her death it was to be sold and the proceeds divided equally between the children of the marriage. The wife of one of the children paid for home improvements at a cost of £488. When the work had been done all the children agreed that she should recover this sum from the proceeds of the eventual sale. After Mrs McArdle died the validity of this agreement was disputed. The Court of Appeal held that no valid contract existed since the home improvements were past consideration; they had been carried out before any promise to pay had been made.

There is an exception to this rule when a subsequent promise is enforceable. Valid consideration may be held to exist in the absence of an express prior promise to pay provided that:

1 the act was done in response to a specific request; and

2 the situation was one where payment would normally be expected.

Re Stewart v Casey (Casey's Patents) (1892, CA)
An employee contributed many hours of his own time to the development of an invention for his employers at their request. When the work was completed, the employers promised that they would pay him a share of the profits once the invention was patented. It was held that the employers were bound by the promise as the employee had done the work at their request, and the nature of their relationship implied that future payment would be made. The subsequent explicit promise in such situations is seen as an affirmation of an implied promise which accompanied the request that the work be carried out.

Consideration must move from the promisee

This common law rule prevents a party from enforcing a contract unless he or she has contributed consideration. However, considerable exceptions have been created by the Contracts (Rights of Third Parties) Act 1999 (see below at page 70).

Consideration must be sufficient

Consideration must be of material value, capable of assessment in financial terms. Usually the financial nature of the consideration is obvious where goods, land or money is involved. Any legal right has financial value. Settling a case out of court involves a contract under which one party agrees not to sue the other provided that the other pays an agreed sum of compensation. The consideration for the compensation is the promise not to sue.

Alliance Bank v Broome (1864)
A bank provided consideration for the defendant's promise to give security for a loan by promising not to take action to recover it.

White v Bluett (1853)
A son who agreed not to bore his father by nagging him to make a will in his favour had not provided valid consideration for his father's promise to release him from a debt. As he had no right to dictate how his father disposed of his property, he had not given up anything of material value.

Note that consideration *may be sufficient without being adequate*. Provided the alleged consideration is of financial value, it is irrelevant that it is not an adequate return. The courts are not interested in whether the parties have made a good bargain, but only in whether they have made a bargain at all. Therefore, proof of financial value, however minute, will be enough to make consideration sufficient.

Thomas v Thomas (1842)
A widow was promised a house in return for a ground rent and promising to keep the property in good repair. An annual rent of £1 was held to be sufficient consideration for the promise.

Chappell v Nestlé & Co. Ltd (1960, HL)
A promotion by Nestlé offered pop music recordings for a sum of money plus three chocolate wrappers; these were held to constitute part of the consideration.

Sufficiency usually involves taking on some *new obligation* in return for the other party's promise of payment. Performing an existing legal duty does not generally amount to sufficient consideration.

Collins v Godefroy (1831)
The claimant was a key witness at a trial and was under a court order to attend. Failure to do so would have made him guilty of the crime of contempt of court. The defendant was a party to the proceedings; because the claimant's attendance was important to him, he promised to pay the claimant if he would attend. The court held that the defendant's promise of payment was not contractually binding. The claimant had not provided sufficient consideration merely by promising to perform his existing legal duty.

In a case like this the claimant is effectively promising the defendant that if the claimant pays him money he will not commit a criminal offence, and such agreements are treated as being against *public policy*: not in the public interest.

Similarly, where two parties have made a contract, a subsequent promise of additional payment to encourage performance is not a binding contractual promise. The promisee is already contractually bound to perform and is therefore providing no fresh consideration.

Stilk v Myrick (1809)

Two sailors deserted from a ship in the course of a voyage. The captain promised the remainder of the crew that he would pay a bonus to each man if they got the ship home to England from Scandinavia. It was held that this promise was not binding. Crew members were required by their contracts to cope with the normal difficulties of a voyage, which in those days included crew shortages of this kind. Therefore, there was insufficient consideration to make the captain's promise enforceable.

The court's unwillingness to enforce promises of this kind generally results from a concern that the promisee has exerted economic duress – blackmailed the promisor into offering extra payment. This topic is explained in Chapter 7.

The court may take a more generous attitude if satisfied that the public interest is not adversely affected and that enforcing the promise would produce the fairest outcome. The court may justify such a decision in one of two ways:

1 *By finding that the promisee has exceeded the scope of their legal duty*. The excess represents the consideration.

Glasbrook Bros v Glamorgan County Council (1925, HL)

The defendant mine owners, fearing vandalism of their premises during an industrial dispute, promised that if the police authority provided a full-time guard, they would make a donation to a police charity. This promise was held to be binding as the police could have fulfilled their legal duty by periodic inspection of the premises: the full-time guard exceeded this and was therefore sufficient consideration.

Hartley v Ponsonby (1857)

The facts of this case are similar to those in *Stilk* v *Myrick*, but here the depletion of the crew and the length of the journey were so great that the crew's existing contract of employment was discharged. It was held that in getting the ship home the crew effectively were taking on a new set of duties and thus providing sufficient consideration for the captain's promise of more pay.

2 *By finding that the promisee in carrying out the legal duty has actually conferred a benefit on the promisor or enabled him to avoid some material disadvantage.*

Williams v Roffey Bros (1990, CA)
Roffey was a builder who had a contract to refurbish a building for a housing association. This contract contained a delay clause under which Roffey was required to pay substantial sums if the work was not finished on time. Roffey sub-contracted carpentry work to Williams, who later ran into financial difficulties and told Roffey that because of this he would be unable to continue. Roffey promised him payment of extra money to complete the contract on time. Roffey's promise was held to be binding, since by securing the completion of the contract he was obtaining a benefit, or at least avoiding a burden. He avoided having to pay the delay costs to the housing association. The Court of Appeal stressed that it was crucial that there was no evidence of any economic duress by Williams.

In making this decision the Court of Appeal was breaking new ground judicially, but the ruling reflects current commercial practice.

Stilk v *Myrick* is not overruled by *Williams* v *Roffey Bros*. It must be decided on the facts of a case which decision will apply. When you are answering examination questions on this area of the law it is probably wise to mention both cases.

Part payment of debt is not sufficient consideration

Pinnel's Case (1602)
A promise by a creditor to accept less than the full sum owed does not discharge the debtor from the legal obligation to pay the balance.

The rule in *Pinnel's* case is illustrated by the following example:

Marmaduke owes Josephine £50, but he is so hard up that he can pay her only £35 when the date of repayment arrives. She can still pursue him later for the £15 even if she agrees that she will take the £35 in full settlement. This looks unfair, but if you analyse Josephine's promise in terms of the rules of consideration you can see the legal logic, if not the moral justice, of the outcome. Marmaduke, by repaying only part of what he owes, obtains a benefit (£15) from Josephine but gives nothing in return. Josephine loses £15 from their agreement. Marmaduke is providing no consideration and so Josephine's new promise is not contractually binding; it is merely a gratuitous promise.

There are some exceptions to this rule. The debt will be discharged by part-payment if the creditor requests:

1 part-payment at an earlier date; or

2 at a different place; or

3 some goods or other material benefit to accompany the part-payment.

In these situations the debtor is providing some consideration by doing something different at the creditor's request. For example:

> Percy does building work at James's delicatessen for £1000. When payment is due James is unable to pay in full, so Percy agrees to take £900 plus £100's worth of smoked salmon for Percy's daughter's forthcoming wedding reception.

Part-payment by a third party in return for a promise from the creditor not to pursue the original debtor for the balance also discharges the whole debt. An agreement (*composition*) between creditors has a similar effect. It is common business practice for the multiple creditors of a debtor to agree that they will each accept a proportionate repayment of their debts. An individual creditor cannot renege on this contract to pursue the balance of their debt as this would be a fraud on the other creditors.

The cases of *Re Selectmove* (1995) and *Re C (A Debtor)* (1994), indicate that the Court of Appeal is not prepared to allow the principle in *Williams* v *Roffey* to validate agreements to pay *less* than the agreed sum, rather than *more*. This would otherwise undermine the rule in *Pinnel's* case.

Promissory estoppel

This is an equitable defence which may be relevant in part-payment situations. Under this principle, parties who gratuitously promise that they will not enforce existing contractual rights may lose their entitlement to do so if it would be unfair to allow them to go back on their promise; they are prevented (*estopped*) from breaking the promise. This defence was developed in the following case:

Central London Property Trust v *High Trees House* (1947)
The defendants owned a block of flats on land leased to them by the claimants. By September 1939, many flats had become vacant due to outbreak of war. Consequently, the defendants were having difficulties paying their ground rent. The claimants agreed that they would accept reduced payments. The defendants continued to pay the reduced rent even when the flats refilled and the war was over.

The claimants brought a test case claiming arrears of rent for the last two quarters of 1945 (by which time the war had ended). The claimants were found to be entitled to the arrears they claimed, but had they claimed for arrears prior to the end of the war this would have been refused. It would be unfair to allow them to go back on their promise on which the defendants had naturally relied. The claimants' gratuitous promise operated to suspend their rights to full payment while the extenuating circumstances in which the promise had been made continued to operate.

This *obiter dictum* (persuasive ruling) from a then youthful Mr Justice Denning, has been applied by the House of Lords:

Tool Metal Manufacturing Co. Ltd v Tungsten Ltd (1955)
A gratuitous promise, to suspend rights to royalty payments on a patent during the war, was held to be a good defence to a subsequent claim for such payments.

However, although this principle has been much discussed by the Court of Appeal and the House of Lords in subsequent cases, it has been used very little and its scope is far from clear. Two elements are certain:

1 *It can operate only as a defence.* In *High Trees* the defendants could not have sued on the claimants' promise, but it would have been a good defence against the claimants if they had tried to enforce their original contract rights for the period in which they had been suspended.

2 *It is an equitable principle.* The court will not grant an equitable remedy unless it will produce a just result for both parties; parties seeking such a remedy must show that they have behaved morally as well as legally.

D & C Builders v Rees (1965, CA)
Mrs Rees persuaded the builders, whom she knew to be in financial difficulties, to accept payment of £300 in full settlement of a debt of almost £483, by telling them that they would otherwise get nothing. Given that Mrs Rees had effectively forced the builders into accepting the reduced sum, it was held that it would not be equitable to allow their promise to be used as a defence against them.

INTENTION TO CREATE LEGAL RELATIONS

In determining whether the parties intend their agreement to be legally binding, the courts are guided by two presumptions:

1 parties to a domestic or social agreement do not intend to be legally bound;

2 parties to a business agreement intend to be legally bound.

These are presumptions only and can be rebutted (disproved) by sufficient evidence to the contrary.

Domestic and social agreements

The courts believe that family members and friends do not generally intend agreements, made merely for their mutual convenience, to be legally enforceable. Property rights between family members are generally adequately covered by other areas of the law. Unless there is clear evidence of a commercial transaction – for example, the sale of a car between family members – an intention to be contractually bound will not be presumed.

Balfour v Balfour (1919, CA)
No intention to create legal relations existed in an agreement under which a husband working abroad promised to pay maintenance to his wife in England.

The courts take a different view if the couple no longer intend to continue in the marriage:

Merrit v Merrit (1970, CA)
A contractual relationship was held to arise from a post-separation maintenance agreement.

Car pool agreements may involve the necessary intention:

Albert v Motor Insurers Bureau (1971, HL)
The House of Lords held that if lifts are provided on a regular and systematic basis under which drivers anticipate payment, an intention to create a legally binding relationship is present.

Even a 'fun' transaction may implicitly contain a more formal intention.

Simpkins v Pays (1955, CA)
Joint participation in a competition under which the parties agreed to share entry costs and potential winnings was held to give rise to a legally binding contract.

Exam tip: If the question describes parties in a problem as friends or family members, this may be to nudge you into mentioning the issue of intention to create legal relations.

Business agreements

In the world of business, an explicit indication of lack of intention to create legal relations is generally necessary.

Next time you see an advertisement for a competition, check the small print and you will usually find similar words being used to those in the following cases.

> **Rose & Frank Co. v J R Crompton & Bros** (1925, HL)
> The wording of an agreement stated that it was not 'a formal legal agreement and shall not be subject to legal jurisdiction in the law courts and excluded any intention to be legally bound'. The House of Lords upheld this clause.

> **Jones v Vernons Pools** (1938)
> Here, the court held that no legally binding contract was created between punter and pools company: the entry coupon stated clearly that the relationship between the parties was 'binding in honour only'.

PRIVITY OF CONTRACT

From your study of consideration earlier in this chapter, you may remember that parties who have not contributed consideration to a contract cannot usually sue on it if it is breached. This is because they are not full parties to the contract: in the rather archaic language still used by lawyers, they are not *privy to the contract*, or there is no *privity of contract* between the parties.

> **Tweddle v Atkinson** (1861)
> William Tweddle was engaged to marry Miss Guy. The fathers of the happy couple contracted that they would each put up a sum of money when the marriage took place, but Mr Guy died before making payment. It was held that William had no right to sue Mr Guy's estate for the money since he had provided no consideration for the promise and was merely a beneficiary of the contract. As a mere beneficiary, William was not *privy to the contract*: he was not truly a party to it because he was not contributing to the consideration.

Similarly, the burdens of a contract cannot be enforced against a party to whom no consideration has been promised.

> **Dunlop Rubber Co. Ltd v Selfridge** (1915, HL)
> Dunlop supplied tyres at a discount (less than list price) to Dew & Co., who agreed not to resell below list price to trade buyers unless those buyers also agreed not to resell below list price. Dew supplied Selfridge who breached the resale price agreement. Dunlop tried to take action against Selfridge. Dunlop could not sue Selfridge, as there was no privity of contract between them: Dunlop had given no consideration to Selfridge in return for the promise to stick to the resale price. (Any action could only be taken against Selfridge by Dew for breach of the contract between them.)

Exceptions to the rule of privity

To prevent injustice, a number of exceptions to the rule have been acknowledged:

1 *Agency*. Where agents make contracts on behalf of their principals with third parties, the principals may sue or be sued on those contracts as if they had made them themselves. (See Chapter 15.)

2 *Third-party insurance*. A third party may claim under an insurance policy made for their benefit, even though that party did not pay the premiums. For example: life assurance and third-party motor insurance.

3 *Assignment of contractual rights*. The *benefits* (but not the burdens) of a contract may be assigned to a third party, who may then sue on the contract. For example: selling debts. The original debtor may be sued by the new creditor to whom the rights to collect the debt have been assigned. The duty to perform a contract cannot be assigned.

4 *Trusts*. This is an equitable concept by which one person transfers property to a second person (the trustee), who holds it for the benefit of others (beneficiaries). The party who created the trust, which is often done by a will, lays down the rules under which it is to be administered. If these are not complied with the beneficiaries have the right to ask the court to enforce the trust for their benefit.

5 *Collateral contracts*. The performance of one contract between A and B may indirectly bring another into being between A and C.

> **Shanklin Pier Ltd v Detel Products Ltd** (1954)
> Detel advised Shanklin Pier Ltd that their paint was suitable for maritime use and would last for at least seven years. Shanklin Pier Ltd contracted with a decorating firm to paint the pier; a term of the contract required the decorators to buy

▶

Detel's paint for the purpose. The paint began to peel off within three months. It was held that Shanklin Pier Ltd could successfully sue Detel Products on a collateral contract which was linked to the main contract between Shanklin Pier Ltd and the decorating firm. Detel had made promises about the quality of their paint and Shanklin Pier had provided consideration for this promise by requiring the decorators to buy it.

6 *Contracts for the benefit of a group.* Where a contract to supply a service is made in one person's name but is intended to benefit a group of people, the members of the group have no rights to sue if the contract is breached; there is no privity of contract between them and the supplier of the service. The court may, however, take some of their losses into account when awarding damages to the buyer, on the grounds that the buyer should be compensated for the defects in the package which was purchased.

Jackson v Horizon Holidays Ltd (1975, CA)
Breach of contract by Horizon ruined the Jacksons' holiday. Mr Jackson, who had made the contract, was awarded damages which took into account the loss to the whole family resulting from Horizon's failure to deliver a holiday of the promised quality.

Statutory reform of the privity rule

In 1996 the Law Commission (Report No. 242) stated that reform was needed since the present law:

(a) prejudices third parties who may rely on contracts which they have no power to enforce;

(b) causes problems in commercial life;

(c) is out of step with other EU members and much of the common law world, including New Zealand and the USA.

Reforming legislation has been introduced.

Contracts (Rights of Third Parties) Act 1999

Section 1 gives third parties the right directly to enforce any contract which expressly permits this or where the purpose of the contract is intended to benefit them.

Section 2 further protects third parties by preventing cancellation or variation of the contract without their permission unless the contract expressly provides for this.

Quiz 5

1 Are the following promises legally binding or merely gratuitous?

   (a) Red returned Brown's lost tortoise. Brown promised him £5.

   (b) Green agreed to sell his vintage sports car to Black for 10p.

   (c) Scarlet promised her employee Orange that she would give him a £10 bonus if he arrived at work on time for a week.

   (d) Blue was owed £50 by Yellow, but agreed to take £45 in full settlement if Yellow made the repayment a week early.

   (e) Pink agreed that his tenant Turquoise might pay a reduced rent while he was out of work.

2 White told his tailor to make a wedding suit for White's nephew Grey, who chose the style and material. The cost was to be charged to White's account. When the suit was finished it did not fit Grey who had to hire one. Has Grey any rights against the tailor?

Assignment 4

(a) Consider to what extent, if any, a person provides consideration for a promise by doing or promising to do what he is already contractually bound to do.

(b) Albert rents a caravan from Bernard. Albert's wife, Wendy, is subsequently hurt in a road accident and has to give up work. After a discussion between them, Bernard promises that he will accept half the rent for the next 12 months. Three months later he is advised that Wendy will never work again. On learning this Bernard tells Albert that he wants full rent now and also the balance of the past 12 months' rent.

Advise Albert.

(ICSA Introduction to English Law: December 1993)

A suggested solution for this assignment can be found in the Lecturer's Guide.

CHAPTER 6

The terms of the contract

INTRODUCTION

A contract is made up of *terms*, offered by one party and accepted by the other. This chapter contains three topics concerning terms:

1 *The difference between express and implied terms*. The parties may be bound by terms which they have not expressly agreed.

2 *The relative importance of contractual terms*. Some terms are crucial to the existence of the contract; others are more trivial, and therefore different legal consequences flow from breach of them.

3 *Exclusion of liability*. Even if a party is in breach of contract, it may be protected from liability by an exclusion clause.

EXPRESS AND IMPLIED TERMS

The terms of a contract fall into three categories: conditions, warranties and innominate terms (explained fully below). These terms may be expressed or implied. Express terms are specifically communicated by the offeror. Other terms may be implied by statute, custom or the courts.

The sources of implied terms

Statute: the Sale of Goods Act 1979

Parliament safeguards the consumer by implying certain terms concerning the standard and quality of goods in most sale of goods contracts. The seller is in breach if the goods do not meet these standards, regardless of whether the seller gave any undertakings expressly to the buyer.

This statutory protection means that if you buy a personal stereo from a shop you can assume that it will work. If it is faulty the shop cannot avoid liability by claiming that it never promised you that the stereo would work. These terms are fully explained in Chapter 16.

Trade custom and practice

In many trades it is customary for certain practices to prevail in performance of a contract, or for risks to be allocated between the parties in a particular way. For example, in crane and plant hire contracts, it is generally implied that any damage to the equipment occasioned during the hire period will be the financial responsibility of the hirer, not the owner.

Business efficacy

The court is not generally sympathetic to parties who assume that they have rights under a contract which were not expressly promised to them. Exceptionally, though, a term may be implied if its lack is so obvious that the parties are considered (*deemed*) to have intended to include it in the contract. For example, if you asked the dairy to deliver you 'two pints of milk', it is unlikely that you would specify that the milk must be in a container rather than left in a puddle on your doorstep.

> **The Moorcock** (1889)
> A party who hired docking space at the defendant's wharf was entitled to assume that the ship's bottom would not be damaged by the state of the river bed adjacent to the dock.

THE RELATIVE IMPORTANCE OF CONTRACTUAL TERMS

The terms of a contract are not necessarily equally important. Breach of contract, therefore, gives rise to different rights according to the importance of the breached term. Generally terms can be classified as conditions or warranties. Whether terms are to be classified as conditions or warranties is determined by the parties' apparent intentions when they made the contract. An apparently trivial matter like a sea view from the hotel bedroom may be elevated to the status of a condition of the contract if its necessity is stressed before acceptance takes place.

Conditions

Conditions are the most important terms which form the main structure of the contract. For example, when you are booking hotel accommodation, the dates of your stay and the type of room (single/double) are some of the most crucial requirements. If particular details are crucial to one party, this must be pointed out to the other party before the formation of the contract is completed. If you are booking a double room, this may result in your being given single or double beds unless you stipulate which you prefer.

Breach of a condition gives the injured party the right to treat itself as free of any further contractual duties and to claim compensation.

Warranties

Warranties are more minor terms; they are *ancillary* to the contract rather than crucial to it. For example, when you are booking hotel accommodation, the promise of tea and coffee making facilities and colour TV will not be vital to the performance of the contract. Their absence does not stop you from getting most of the enjoyment that you expect from the holiday.

Breach of a warranty does not entitle the injured party to refuse to perform its side of the contract. That party is entitled only to compensation for consequential loss, i.e. loss *resulting* from the breach.

More information on conditions and warranties can be found in Chapter 16.

Innominate terms

Not all terms are clearly and immediately identifiable as conditions or warranties. Some, described by the courts as *innominate*, are worded broadly to cover a variety of possible breaches, some more serious than others. The court then has to decide whether a particular breach is to be treated as one of condition or warranty.

Hong Kong Fir Shipping Co. Ltd v Kawasaki Kisen Kaisha (1962, CA)
A contract stated that a ship would be 'in every way fitted for cargo service'. This term was capable of including many types of breach, from a large hole in the hull to a missing life raft which was unlikely ever to be required. Due to the incompetent engine room crew and a malfunctioning engine, the ship broke down and 20 weeks' use of the ship was lost from a two-year charterparty (hire contract). The defendants who had hired the ship abandoned the contract and the claimant owners sued them for breach. The Court of Appeal held that the breach of the term relating to the ship's fitness was not sufficiently serious to permit the defendants to terminate the contract. The court came to this conclusion by judging the importance of the term relative to the actual damage resulting from it. The damage caused did not strike at the root of the contract (the ship was still available for more than 18 months of the hire period), and therefore no breach equivalent to a breach of condition had occurred.

A later Court of Appeal decision indicates the criteria by which the courts may interpret the status of an innominate term (*Cehave NV* v *Bremer Handelsgesellschaft* (*The Hansa Nord*) (1975, CA)):

1 the express intention of the parties is paramount: if the contract specifies that a particular breach will entitle a party to opt out of the contract, that is conclusive. The use of the words 'condition' and 'warranty' to describe terms is of evidential value only, it is not conclusive in itself;

2 if a party has a statutory right to terminate the contract if a term is breached the term is a condition (for example, Sale of Goods Act implied conditions, see Chapter 17);

3 if any previous case decision on relevant commercial practice indicates that the innocent party has repudiation (rejection) rights in these particular circumstances, the term must be treated as a condition;

4 if the damage resulting from the breach is so extensive that it substantially deprives the innocent party of the benefits bargained for, that party may repudiate their obligations. The damage test is, in practice, used as a last resort.

EXCLUSION OF LIABILITY

Many contracts include a term by which one party seeks to limit financial claims against it in the event of loss or damage to the other party, or to exclude itself from legal liability altogether. For example, by a *limitation* clause a holiday firm's contract may restrict customers' claims in the event of delay, postponement and cancellation of flights to specified sums for meals and overnight accommodation. When you pay to use a car park, it is usual for the contract to include an *exclusion clause* stating that the proprietors have no legal liability for damage to or theft of or from your vehicle.

Such limitation of or exemption from liability may be a perfectly reasonable business practice, but is subject to control, both by the courts and statute, to prevent abuses. Without such regulation a business could avoid liability for flagrant negligence, or for gross and irresponsible breach of contract.

Before any exclusion clause can be effective it must satisfy three criteria:

1 it must be incorporated within the contract;

2 it must be clear and unambiguous;

3 it must not be rendered ineffective by statute.

Incorporation

In order for a term to be incorporated in the contract (be part of it), the party to be bound by it must have sufficient notice of it. Two factors are crucial to the issue of notice:

1 *The term excluding liability must be notified to the other party prior to that party's acceptance.*

Olley v Marlborough Court Hotel (1949, CA)
A notice in Mrs Olley's bedroom stated that the hotel proprietor would not be liable for theft of guests' property. The contract between Mrs Olley and the hotel had been concluded at the reception desk when Mrs Olley booked in, *before* she read the notice. The hotel was therefore not exempt from liability for the theft of her jewellery and furs from her room.

Thornton v Shoe Lane Parking (1971, CA)
A notice inside a car park stated that the proprietors would not be liable for injuries to customers. This was also printed on the ticket dispensed from the automatic barrier at the car park entrance. The Court of Appeal held that the exemption clause did not form part of the contract: by driving alongside the machine at the car park entrance from which the ticket was dispensed, the claimant had already communicated acceptance of the defendant's offer to supply parking space.

Note that a party may be _deemed_ to have implied notice from past contractual dealings where the court is satisfied that these have occurred on the same terms, sufficiently regularly, over a sufficient length of time.

Kendall v Lillico (1968, HL)
The parties had contracted 100 times in the previous three years on consistent terms. They, therefore, had adequate notice of an exemption clause in a 'sold note' which had accompanied every delivery previous to the one giving rise to the seller's breach.

Such an implication is unlikely to be made in a consumer contract.

McCutcheon v David McBrayne Ltd (1964, HL)
The claimant had shipped his car on a number of occasions on the defendant's ferry. Sometimes he had been been asked to sign a risk note with a clause exempting the ferry company from liability for damage to goods. On one occasion, when a note had not been supplied, the ferry sank due to the defendant's negligence and the claimant's car was lost. It was held that the exclusion clause did not protect the defendant; the claimant had not had notice of the exemption. The previous dealings between the parties had not been sufficiently consistent, as risk notes had not been supplied regularly.

2 _Generally a clause will not be binding unless the offeror has taken reasonable steps to draw it to the customer's attention._

Notice may be given by a written sign of some kind displayed at the place of business, or in a contractual document. It should have been clearly evident to customers before they committed themselves to the contracts. Similarly, where the notice is on a document received by a customer, this document will not form part of the contract unless it was transferred before acceptance.

Chapelton v Barry UDC (1940, CA)
The claimant, who wished to hire a deckchair at the beach, took one from a pile beside which there was a notice. This stated the hire charge and said that payment should be made to the attendant. When he paid, the claimant was given a ticket which stated that the council would not be liable for accidents arising from use of the chairs. Later the claimant was injured when the chair collapsed because it had been negligently maintained. The ticket was held not to be a contractual document but merely a receipt, which the claimant did not receive until he had accepted the defendant's offer (to supply the chair). If the exemption had been printed clearly on the hire notice, this would have been sufficient.

The more onerous the term, the greater the degree of notice required. Exclusion clauses contained in the body of a document should be printed in clear type, which may need to be underlined or otherwise highlighted.

Interfoto Picture Library Ltd v Stiletto Productions (1988, CA)
(Although this case did not relate to an exemption clause, the principle is relevant to any contractual term.) In a contract for hire of photographic transparencies there was a clause imposing a penalty of £5 per transparency per day. It was contained in the delivery note which comprised the contract. This was held not to be binding as the supplier had not done enough to draw the attention of the hirer to the clause. A special cover note was needed, or at least bold type on the delivery note.

The sufficiency rule does not cover signed documents. Customers have constructive notice of the contents of any contractual document which they sign; this means that they are deemed to have notice of its contents, whether they have read it or not. There is no obligation to alert the signer to the presence of an exclusion clause.

L'Estrange v Graucob (1934)
The claimant signed a 'sales agreement' without reading it. An exemption clause in the agreement protected the sellers from liability when the vending machine supplied to the claimant failed to work properly. Her failure to read the document did not prevent it binding her.

It is useless for customers to claim that they misunderstood the effect of the clause, unless the seller helped to cause the misunderstanding.

Curtis v _Chemical Cleaning & Dyeing Co._ (1951, CA)
The claimant took her wedding dress to be cleaned and was asked to sign a note exempting the cleaners from liability for damage to the dress. She queried this, but signed it when told not to worry as it was there only to protect the company if beads or sequins were damaged. The dress was returned to her badly stained. The clause which stated that the company was protected against liability for any damage was held not to be effective as the customer had been misled about its scope.

An exclusion clause is not effective if it is ambiguous

Where its wording is unclear, the court may apply the _contra proferentem_ rule to restrict the effects of an exclusion clause. The clause is construed _contra_ (against) _proferentem_ (the party who offered it); the meaning least favourable to the offeror is, therefore, adopted.

Andrews v _Singer_ (1934)
A contract expressly stated that new cars would be supplied. An exemption clause stated that the supplier would not be liable for breach of any condition or warranty implied by statute. When the cars were delivered one was secondhand. It was held that the buyer could reject the secondhand car: breach of an express term of the contract had occurred. The exemption clause referred only to _implied terms_.

Liability for fundamental breach

Where a breach of contract is so serious that it defeats the whole purpose of the contract, the courts may still be prepared to allow an exclusion clause to protect the party in breach. The nature of the contract and the type of breach will be evidence of what the parties are deemed to have intended. For example, in a travel contract the provider promises to take the customer to a particular destination at a particular time; such contracts usually include a clause to limit or completely exclude the liability of the provider in the event of cancellation of services in bad weather. Failure to transport the customer on time is not the fault of the provider in such circumstances, though it may defeat the customer's purposes completely. Such exclusions are likely to be treated as effective. The customer is deemed to have intended to accept the risk.

Issues of insurance are also relevant, and an exclusion clause will protect a provider where the court believes that insurance responsibilities were intended to remain with the other party.

> **Photo Production Ltd v Securicor Transport Ltd** (1980)
> While on duty at the claimant's premises, Securicor's employee intentionally
> started a fire. The contract stated that there would be no liability for such damage
> unless Securicor was negligent; the claimant did not allege negligence. This is a clear
> example of fundamental breach: Securicor was the cause of the destruction of the
> property which it had promised to keep safe. The court held that the clause pro-
> tected Securicor from liability for fundamental breach; the parties had bargained on
> equal terms that periodical visits should be made by a patrolman for a modest
> charge (26p) per visit. It was reasonable to leave the risk for fire damage with the
> claimant, who would be the most appropriate party to insure against such damage.

Statutory controls on exclusion clauses

The Unfair Contract Terms Act 1977

The Unfair Contract Terms Act 1977 (UCTA) applies only where the contract gives
rise to *business liability* (s 1(3)). It only applies to parties who seek to limit or exclude
liability incurred in the course of business. A private seller or supplier of goods or
services is not restricted by the Act in the use of exclusion clauses.

Certain types of contract are *expressly excluded*, for example, contracts of insurance
and contracts for the sale or lease of land.

Although the title of the Act refers to 'contract terms', the Act also regulates non-
contractual notices which attempt to restrict liability for negligence. For example, a
notice outside premises which states that people enter at their own risk is covered
by UCTA 1977.

The question of *exclusion of liability for negligence* is covered by s 2 of the Act.
Under s 2(1), liability cannot be excluded if death or personal injury is caused by
negligence. Damage to property through negligence is addressed by s 2(2). Under
that provision, negligence liability may be excluded if this is *reasonable* in the circumstances (see below).

By s 3 of UCTA 1977, liability for breach of contract may not be excluded where a
party enters into a contract made on the other party's standard terms (when no
negotiation will have been possible), or where the party deals as a consumer, unless
the exclusion is *reasonable*.

Liability for breaches of contracts involving the *sale or hire of goods* is governed by
ss 6 and 7 of the 1977 Act. In contracts concerning the sale or hire of goods, certain
conditions are implied under the Sale of Goods Act 1979 and related statutes to protect the buyer. The supplier implicitly promises that it has title to the goods (rights
of ownership) and that:

1 the goods match their description; and

2 are of satisfactory quality; and

79

3 are suitable for their purpose; and

4 correspond to any sample which has been provided.

These terms are fully explained in Chapter 16. UCTA 1977 restricts the extent to which such conditions may be excluded. Consumers enjoy special protection: these conditions cannot be effectively excluded where the customer is a 'consumer'. A consumer is someone not contracting in the course of a business (UCTA 1977, s 12). As far as non-consumer buyers are concerned, the condition regarding title can never be excluded; the others may be excluded if the clause is *reasonable*.

What is 'reasonable' for the purposes of UCTA 1977? Section 11 and Sch 2 of the Act provide guidance:

1 a contract term will satisfy the requirement of reasonableness if it is fair and reasonable with regard to all the circumstances which should have been considered by the parties when they entered the contract;

2 if the claim relates to a non-contractual notice, reasonableness is judged with reference to all the circumstances prevailing when the damage was caused.

Schedule 2 of the Act offers further guidelines.

1 *Imbalance of bargaining power*. The parties to a contract may not enjoy equal bargaining power. In a standard terms contract, one party is presented with a set of terms and given no opportunity to negotiate existing terms or add others. The buyer of goods or services may be heavily reliant on the technical knowledge and expertise of the seller, and that ignorance produces power imbalance.

2 *Inducements and choices*. If a customer is given an unfair inducement to accept the exclusion clause, this may make it unreasonable. If that party could have made a similar contract with another party without being subject to such a term, this may make the exemption reasonable.

3 *Prior knowledge*. If the customer should reasonably have been aware of the existence and extent of the term, taking into account previous dealings between the parties and trade custom, it may be reasonable to impose the exclusion.

4 *Special requirements*. If the goods were made or adapted to meet the customer's special requirements, an exemption may be binding.

The courts have also taken other factors into account, including the issue of insurance and whether the customer should have taken independent advice.

Smith v Eric S. Bush (1989, HL)
The claimant bought a house in reliance on a surveyor's report, prepared on the instructions of the building society. The report stated that it was issued without any guarantee of accuracy or acceptance of any legal liability. The surveyor negligently overlooked some serious defects which led to the chimney collapsing into

Mrs Smith's bedroom, and resulted in a large bill for structural repairs. The House of Lords held that the exclusion of liability was not effective as it was unreasonable:

1 *the parties did not have equal bargaining power:* Mrs Smith could not be expected to know if what the surveyor said was correct, because of her lack of special knowledge;

2 *the financial resources of the claimant:* it was not reasonable to expect Mrs Smith to go to the expense of getting a second opinion. She was a first-time buyer of a modest property and, like most such purchasers, pushed to her financial limits;

3 *the surveyor had failed in a simple task:* any reasonably competent surveyor ought to have spotted the defects;

4 *insurance cover:* this was readily available at modest cost to the surveyor, while the purchaser was unlikely to enjoy such protection.

Green v Cade Bros (1978)

A standard terms contract, which complied with the requirements of the National Association of Seed Potato Merchants, restricted the right of rejection of potato seed to three days from delivery; any compensation was limited to the return of the contract price. The potato seed supplied to the buyer was infected by a virus which was not detectable until the growing process had started. It was held that the three-day time limit was *not* reasonable given the type of damage suffered. The limit on compensation was reasonable: it was usual in the trade, the parties enjoyed equal bargaining power, and the buyer had received no inducement to accept the limitation. The buyer could have bought guaranteed seed for a higher price.

George Mitchell v Finney Lock Seeds Ltd (1983, HL)

The claimant ordered cabbage seed from the defendant which did not match its description. It was also inferior in quality. The claimant lost his entire crop, sustaining a £61 000 loss. The contract limited liability for breach to replacement of the goods or a refund of the price. The House of Lords held that this was not reasonable because:

1 the breach arose from the seller's negligence;

2 the seller could have insured against crop failure at a modest cost;

3 in the past the seller had settled claims in excess of the limitation sum; this indicated that the seller did not always consider the clause fair and reasonable.

St Albans City and District Council v International Computers Ltd (1996, CA)
Computer software, supplied and installed by the defendant company to provide a
database facility for the local authority, was defective. It caused errors in the estimation of the number of eligible poll-tax payers, and as a result the local authority
lost substantial funds. A limitation clause in the contract restricted the defendant's
liability to £100 000. It was held that the limitation clause was unreasonable
because:

1 the defendant was a multinational company with substantial resources;

2 the defendant carried product liability insurance of £50 million and the limitation
   of liability was too small relative to the possible risk and the loss actually suffered;

3 the claimant's specialist needs greatly limited its choice of providers;

4 it was fairer to put the risk on the defendant who stood to make a profit on the
   contract. If the risk lay with the local authority, its taxpayers would be unjustly
   burdened by the loss.

The Unfair Terms in Consumer Contracts Regulations 1999

These regulations implement an EC Directive (91/13 EC) and replace the 1994 Regulations of the same name. They protect consumers who have entered a contract
containing a non-negotiable term imposed by the seller or supplier of goods and
services, which is deemed to be unfair according to criteria laid down in the regulations. Such a term is *voidable* by consumers, i.e. they are not bound by it unless they
choose to comply, but the rest of the contract remains binding.

The scope of the regulations is as follows:

1 *The relevant contracts.* The regulations concern any contract for the supply of
   goods or services, including contracts for the supply of financial services. Terms
   in insurance contracts relating to the claims process are also regulated.

   It is not clear how far contracts concerning land are affected. It is unlikely that
   contracts for the sale of land or which create tenancies are covered.

   Contracts relating to employment, succession or family law rights are specifically excluded.

2 *Consumers.* Consumers are defined as human beings, making contracts for non-
   business purposes.

3 *Seller/supplier of goods or services.* The seller or supplier of goods or services must
   make the contract in the course of its business for the regulations to apply.

4 *Non-negotiable terms.* These will have been drafted before the contract was negotiated and the consumer will have had no influence on their contents. It is up to the
   seller or supplier to prove that such terms were non-negotiable.

5 *Unfairness.* A term is unfair if it fails to fulfil the requirements of *good faith* and this causes *a significant imbalance* in the parties' contractual relationship, which is prejudicial to the consumer's interests. In assessing whether the seller or supplier acted in good faith the court must have regard to all the circumstances relevant to the conclusion of the contract.

The regulations contain an illustrative list of terms which may be unfair. This includes terms to exclude liability for death or personal injury and other exclusion clauses covered by UCTA 1977; but terms other than exclusion clauses may be judged to be unfair. The given examples include terms which:

1 permit a seller unfairly to retain a deposit or to impose a penalty on the consumer in the event of non-performance;

2 bind a consumer who has not had sufficient time to study the term's implications before entering the contract;

3 permit the seller unilaterally to alter the terms of the contract or the characteristics of the relevant goods or service;

4 oblige consumers to perform all their obligations, while not placing a reciprocal responsibility on the other party.

The list is not intended to be comprehensive. It is up to the consumer to prove that the term was unfair, taking into account the nature of the subject matter of the contract, the legal and commercial context in which the contract was made and the reasonable expectations of both parties, and all the circumstances surrounding the contract are relevant to determining any imbalance. How the good faith principle is interpreted is well illustrated in the *DGFT* v *First National Bank* case below. Just because a term is not beneficial to the consumer and may come, as their Lordships commented, as 'a nasty surprise' does not necessarily indicate unfairness or breach of good faith.

Director General of Fair Trading v First National Bank (2001, HL)
Under the Consumer Credit Act 1974 (CCA), if a borrower defaults on a loan and judgment is obtained against him or her, the lender's full rights to interest on the future instalments are lost.

First National's loan terms stated that in such circumstances the Bank could claim remaining interest at the original contract rates. The DGFT claimed that this was an unfair term but the House of Lords said that it was not a breach of good faith. The CCA, despite being enacted to protect borrowers, did not forbid such agreement; without it the Bank would suffer an unreasonable loss. There was nothing unbalanced or detrimental to the borrowers in the term.

The regulations require written contractual terms to be expressed in clear and intelligible language. Any ambiguity is to be interpreted under the *contra proferentem* rule in favour of the consumer.

Enforcement of the regulations

The regulations may be used by consumers directly to enforce their contractual rights. The role of the Office of Fair Trading (OFT) is also crucial, since the 1994 Regulations empowered it to investigate complaints about allegedly unfair terms from consumers and trading standards departments. If the complaint is upheld, the OFT by legal action may require the offending business to change or withdraw the term. By the end of 1998, the OFT had investigated 3000 complaints, of which 1200 had been upheld. Other 'qualifying bodies' received enforcement powers under the 1999 Regulations. They include trading standards departments, the Director General of Water, Gas and Electricity Supply, and the Consumers Association. The *First National Bank* case above illustrates intervention by the Director General of Fair Trading.

A comparison of UCTA 1977 and the Consumer Contracts Regulations 1999

UCTA 1977

Scope

Renders ineffective certain types of exclusion clauses in a contract or non-contractual notice if the exclusion was issued in the course of business.

Protected parties

Not necessarily consumers or contracting parties.

Extent of protection

Some exclusions are automatically ineffective: for example, negligently caused death or personal injury.

Some liabilities can be excluded or limited if 'reasonable': for example, breach of a standard terms contract, or of any consumer contract.

The regulations

May render any term in a contract for the sale or supply of goods or services voidable by a consumer buyer, if the seller was acting in the course of business.

Consumers only: must be contracting parties.

An *unfair term* is one which does not fulfil the requirement of *good faith* by causing a significant imbalance of power between the parties to the *detriment of the consumer*.

Quiz 6

1 Distinguish between conditions and warranties.

2 What is an innominate term?

3 Are exclusion clauses incorporated in a contract when notified in the following ways:

   (a) in a notice on the counter of a shop?

   (b) in a signed document?

   (c) in a hotel bedroom?

   (d) in a receipt?

4 To what extent may negligence liability be excluded under UCTA 1977?

5 What special protection is given to consumers by UCTA 1977?

6 State the main differences between the effects of UCTA 1977 and the Unfair Terms in Consumer Contracts Regulations 1999.

Assignment 5

Widgets plc entered into a three-year contract with Crankit plc under which Crankit agreed to service Widgets' production line machinery. Widgets signed a document headed 'Service Agreement' consisting of 150 terms, including the following:

10. It shall be a condition of the contract that Crankit will attend in response to any call out request by Widgets within 24 hours.

36. Crankit will not be responsible to Widgets for any defect in quality of any spare parts supplied by Crankit when servicing customers' machinery.

142. Widgets agree to indemnify Crankit against any claims by Widgets or any other third party who may suffer damage to person or property arising from any failure properly to perform this service agreement.

Advise the parties how these terms will affect the outcome of a claim in the following circumstances:

(a) When carrying out the first annual service Crankit fit a new fuel pump. This malfunctions 48 hours later, causing an explosion. Injuries result to Jeremy who lives next door to the factory and the explosion also causes business interruption for three weeks.

(b) Twenty months into the contract Crankit are called upon by Widgets who report that a major mechanical failure has brought their production line to a halt. Crankit reply that due to a lack of staff it will be unable to attend for three days. Next day Widget tells Crankit that it is opting out of the contract as immediate servicing is obtainable from Best and Sons Ltd.

CHAPTER 7

Defects in the contract: misrepresentation, mistake, duress and undue influence

INTRODUCTION

A number of different defects may affect the validity of a contract. These have differing legal consequences and may render a contract void, voidable or unenforceable. It is important to grasp the difference between these concepts.

- *A void contract:* The defect is so serious that in the eyes of the law no contract ever came into existence. Even if both parties wish to enforce the contract this is not possible. If property has changed hands, ownership is not usually transferred and the property may be recovered.

- *A voidable contract:* The defect is not serious enough to make the contract void, but the party whose right is infringed *may* choose to opt out of the contract.

- *An unenforceable contract:* The contract is valid but is not enforceable against a vulnerable party (see Contractual Incapacity, page 113).

MISREPRESENTATION

During pre-contractual negotiations, statements (representations) may be made which induce a party to enter the contract. Such statements may, for example, be made by sales staff by word of mouth, or be included in catalogues or brochures. If untrue, they are called *misrepresentations*. A remedy in misrepresentation is available to the innocent party whether or not the statement became a term of the contract. If it is a term, an action for breach of contract provides alternative remedies.

Misrepresentation makes the contract *voidable*. The misrepresentee (the party to whom the statement was made) is entitled to avoid the contract or to persist with it.

An actionable misrepresentation is:

1 a statement of fact which

2 is a material inducement to enter the contract.

The principles have legal implications which it is important to grasp.

Statement of fact

This can be written, spoken or pictorial, and may also arise from other conduct.

Gordon v Sellico (1986)
The seller of premises who deliberately concealed dry rot was found guilty of misrepresentation to the buyer.

A statement of fact does not include *statements of opinion*.

Bisset v Wilkinson (1927)
The vendor sold land to the buyer, having told the buyer that, if properly worked, he estimated the land would carry 2000 sheep. Since the vendor had never used his land for sheep farming, he was voicing only an honest opinion when he told the buyer how many sheep he believed the land would support.

However, statements of opinion may be treated as statements of fact if the maker, with knowledge of the underlying circumstances, could not reasonably have held the opinion.

Smith v Land & House Property Corp (1884)
A vendor of a house described its tenant, Frederick Fleek, as a 'most desirable tenant', knowing that Fleek was in arrears with rental payments. This was held to be a misrepresentation given the known facts.

Statements of intention may be treated as statements of fact if at the time of making the statement the maker had no such intention.

Edgington v Fitzmaurice (1885)
A company prospectus said that the proceeds from the sale of debentures were to be used to improve buildings and extend the business; in fact the directors intended to use the money to pay off pressing company debts. It was held that a misrepresentation had been committed. Bowen LJ said: 'The state of a man's mind is just as much a fact as the state of his digestion ... A misrepresentation as to the state of his mind is therefore a statement of fact.'

More recent cases indicate a willingness by the courts to treat an estimation of future performance as a statement of fact, where it was reasonable for the other party to rely on it.

> **Esso Petroleum v Mardon** (1976)
> A sales forecast for a filling station, given by Esso's experienced manager to a prospective tenant of the garage, turned out to be radically incorrect and Esso was held to be liable for misrepresentation.

Statements of law are not usually regarded as statements of fact. Everybody is supposed to know the law and therefore to be aware when it is incorrectly stated. If the statement relates to existing civil law rights of the misrepresentor concerning the subject matter of the contract, it is likely to be treated as a statement of fact.

> **Lawrence v Lexcourt Holdings Ltd** (1978)
> A statement by a vendor that 'existing planning permission covers use of this building as an office' was treated by the court as a statement of fact.

Although there is a duty to answer questions truthfully, *failure to volunteer information* is generally not misrepresentation, even if the representee is clearly under a misapprehension.

> **Smith v Hughes** (1871)
> A race horse trainer believed that the oats he was buying were old oats, when actually they were new, but he did not ask the seller their age. He, therefore, could not claim that misrepresentation had occurred. The seller had said nothing about their age and it was irrelevant that he was aware of the importance of this to the buyer.

Liability for failure to disclose information may arise, however, in any of the following circumstances:

1 *Half truths.* A statement may be true as it stands, but still mislead because it is incomplete.

> **Nottingham Patent Brick & Tile Co. Ltd v Butler** (1886)
> A solicitor told the buyer of some land that he 'did not know' of any restrictive covenants upon it. In fact he had not checked to see if there were any. This was a misrepresentation.

Dimmock v Hallett (1866)
Land was described by the seller as being occupied by certain named tenants, but the buyer was not told that they had given notice. This was a misrepresentation.

2 *If circumstances change between making the statement and acceptance.*

With v O'Flanagan (1936, CA)
A doctor, who was selling his practice, gave the buyer correct information about its value. Before the buyer notified acceptance the value had considerably diminished, as many patients went elsewhere when the doctor became ill. His failure to notify the buyer of the drop in value amounted to a misrepresentation.

3 *A fiduciary relationship exists between the parties.* This relationship, involving a high degree of trust between the parties, exists, for example, between partners, solicitor and client, or doctor and patient. It is also relevant to insurance contracts, which are voidable unless full disclosure is made of all material facts – those 'which would influence the judgement of a prudent insurer' (Marine Insurance Act 1906).

Hood v West End Motor Car Packing (1917)
Failure by carriers to disclose that goods were to be carried on the deck of a ship rather than under cover, was a material fact which permitted the insurance company to avoid their contractual obligation to cover the risk.

It is irrelevant that the failure to disclose was not careless or intended to deceive. Some people have found that they were deprived of insurance cover because they quite innocently failed to reveal that their cars had modified features (e.g. alloy wheels and sun roof) which were not standard to a particular model.

The statement acted as a material inducement

The misrepresentation must be an important influence, but does not have to be the only reason why the misrepresentee entered the contract. The misrepresentee must both *know* of the statement and *rely* on it.

Re Northumberland & Durham District Banking Co., ex parte Bigge (1858)
A contract with a shareholder was not voidable: he was unable to prove that when he bought the shares he had already seen reports which had been issued about the company which later proved to be false.

Attwood v Small (1838)
The seller of a mine misrepresented its capacity. The contract was not voidable, however, because the buyer had not relied on the seller's statement, but had commissioned his own survey which also turned out to be inaccurate.

The misrepresentee is entitled to take the statement at face value and has no obligation to check the truth of the statement, even if the misrepresentor offers the opportunity to do so.

Redgrave v Hurd (1881)
A solicitor who was selling his practice gave information about its income and told the buyer that he could check the figures against relevant documentary evidence. The buyer did not choose to do so, and it was held that this did not prevent the contract from being voidable.

The remedies for misrepresentation

The remedies available to the misrepresentee depend on the perceived state of mind of the misrepresentor at the point at which the statement was made.

Fraudulent misrepresentation

Misrepresentation is fraudulent if the misrepresentor knows that the statement is untrue, or makes the statement recklessly, not caring whether it is true or false. The misrepresentee may sue in the tort of deceit and obtain damages and/or rescission of the contract. Rescission is an equitable remedy issued at the discretion of the court; it seeks to return the parties to their pre-contractual position. This enables the misrepresentee to recover any money paid.

In practice, deceit actions are rare, though fraudulent misrepresentation is common. It happens, for example, every time somebody obtains goods with a stolen credit card, thus fraudulently representing themselves as the card holder. In situations like these the misrepresentors quickly disappear and action against them is not possible. If action is taken, the burden of proof of intention is a very heavy one for the claimant to discharge. Cases are often unsuccessful.

Careless misrepresentation

Under s 2(1) of the Misrepresentation Act 1967, a representor who induces the claimant to enter into a contract, on the strength of a statement which the representor did not reasonably believe, may be liable in damages. Rescission may also be granted. It is up to the representor to prove reasonable belief in the statement.

Since a potentially fraudulent misrepresentor cannot be said to have had a reasonable belief in the truth of the statement, the victim may claim under s 2(1) instead of pursuing an action in deceit. This relieves the claimant of the burden of proof but gives access to an identical remedy.

The victim of careless misrepresentation may also have a remedy in negligence under the rule in *Hedley Byrne* v *Heller*, which is explained in Chapter 11. This is helpful where parties have been misled and suffer loss, but find out that the statement is incorrect before they enter the contract. It may also be used by someone who was misled by a third party. Such parties are not assisted by s 2(1) which relates only to misrepresentors who have actually succeeded in making the misrepresentee contract with them.

Wholly innocent misrepresentation

Even if a misrepresentation is made in good faith, with no intention to deceive and without carelessness, the contract is rendered voidable. Rescission is the usual remedy.

Damages may be an alternative remedy under section 2(2) of the Misrepresentation Act, which is applicable to any misrepresentation which is not made fraudulently. This gives the court the discretion to award damages instead of rescission. This discretion is likely to be used if the misrepresentation did not have a major impact on the contract and would, if it were a contract term, be classified as a warranty rather than a condition.

MISTAKE

Although it is common for a party to make a contract under a misapprehension, it is unusual for the resulting contract to be void. Such a contract may be voidable for misrepresentation; remedies for breach of contract may also be available.

An operative mistake makes the contract void

Exceptionally a mistake will be so fundamental that the contract will be rendered void. Such a mistake is said in law to be *operative* because it strikes at the root of the contract, effectively preventing any true agreement. In practice this is very rare.

Mistakes as to *quality* do not make the contract void. A mistake as to the attributes of the subject matter of the contract or of a party to it is never an operative mistake, even if the other party induces the mistake (misrepresentation), or fails to correct the mistaken party's false impression. If you ask to buy a food processor from a shop, under the mistaken belief that it has a juice-making facility, your mistake does not make the contract void. If the shop assistant told you that a juice maker was included, the contract is voidable for misrepresentation. If you were not actively misled, the contract is binding. The shop may be prepared to let you exchange the goods, or even give you a refund, but there is no legal obligation on it to do so. In sale of land contracts the courts were sometimes prepared to treat a contract as voidable under equitable principles. Rescission was sometimes granted if both parties made the same mistake. This was possible only if it produced the most just result. Similarly, the court would not allow a party to obtain a decree of specific performance, if this would permit a party to exploit a mistake unfairly. [This equitable doctrine was abolished by the Court of Appeal in *Great Peace Shipping* v *Tsavliris (International) Ltd* (2002).] (Full information about equitable remedies can be found at the end of Chapter 9.)

Solle v Butcher (1949)
The parties to a lease both mistakenly believed that the premises were subject to rent control. They accordingly agreed a rent which was well below normal market value. The Court of Appeal held that the landlord should be granted rescission of the contract, provided that he offered a new tenancy to the occupant at a reasonable rent.

Operative mistake may occur in the following circumstances:

Common mistake concerning the existence of the subject matter

Both parties reasonably but wrongly believe that the subject matter exists at the time they make the contract.

Couturier v Hastie (1856)
The parties made a contract for the sale of a cargo of corn. Unknown to either party, the corn had already been disposed of by the carrier, who was transporting it from abroad. The House of Lords held that as the contract was one to buy specific goods, there was no possibility of a contract coming into being if the goods did not exist at the point when the parties reached agreement.

However, the contract may not be void if one party has responsibility to check that the subject matter exists.

McRae v Commonwealth Disposals (1951)
The parties entered a contract under which the defendant gave the claimant rights to salvage a wreck, which the defendant said would be found on a reef at a given map reference. The defendant was found liable for breach of contract when it turned out that neither reef nor wreck existed. It was clear that the defendant had been careless in promising the existence of the wreck.

Mutual mistake concerning the identity of the subject matter

Both parties operate under different misapprehensions. Such cases are rare, but occasionally the long arm of coincidence strikes.

> ### *Raffles v Wichelhaus* (1864)
> Two ships called *Peerless* were both carrying cotton from Bombay. The parties contracted for the sale of such a cargo. The buyer believed that he was buying one consignment while the seller was disposing of the other. This mistake prevented any agreement coming into being and therefore the contract was void.

Unilateral mistake by one party regarding the identity of the other

One party is mistaken to the knowledge of the other. Although mistaken identity is very common, it is very unlikely to make a contract void, particularly if the parties have contracted face to face.

Mistaken identity usually arises from a fraudulent misrepresentation, which enables a fraudster (commonly called 'a rogue' in law books) to take possession of the victim's property. The resulting contract, between claimant and rogue, is voidable for misrepresentation. Ownership of the goods passes to the rogue, under what is called a *voidable title*. Unless the claimant takes steps to avoid the contract made with the rogue *before* the goods are sold on, the party who buys the goods from the rogue becomes the legal owner. Since the victim of the fraud cannot usually contact the rogue directly, giving information about the swindle to the police has been held to be sufficient to avoid the contract (*Car & Universal Finance* v *Caldwell* (1964)).

In practice, the victim is usually unable to avoid the contract with the rogue before the goods are sold on, so an innocent third party becomes owner of the goods. The only hope for the victim is to persuade the court that the contract is void for mistake, since this would mean that the goods have not become the property of the party who bought from the rogue and could be recovered. The problem for the court is how best to do justice between two innocent parties – the rogue's victim (the claimant) and the person who bought the goods from the rogue in good faith (the defendant). Generally the courts are more likely to sympathise with the defendant, unless the claimant is able to prove that it was entirely reasonable for the claimant to be duped by a virtually waterproof deception by the rogue. The rationale for this approach is that it is fair that the original seller carries the risk of the buyer not being creditworthy by letting the buyer remove the goods.

A contract will not be void for mistaken identity unless the claimant can prove that:

1 *The claimant intended to deal with some other person than the contracting party.* The claimant must be mistaken not merely as to the attributes (quality) of the other party, but also as to that party's actual identity. Therefore, the claimant's case will collapse unless he or she can prove that there are *two persons* – one with whom he or she contracted and one with whom he or she *intended* to contract.

King's Norton Metal Co. v Edridge, Merrett & Co. (1897)

A rogue represented himself to the claimant company as the agent of a successful business enterprise which did not actually exist. The claimant entered into a postal contract which was not held to be void since the claimant clearly intended to make a contract with somebody and the only entity with whom this was possible was the rogue.

Compare:

Cundy v Lindsay (1878, HL)

A rogue, Blenkarn, represented himself as Blenkiron & Co., a reputable company already known to the claimant and trading from an address in the street where the rogue had set up his premises. The resulting postal contract, under which the claimant supplied linen handkerchiefs to the rogue, was held to be void. This meant that the claimant could recover the goods which been sold on to the defendant.

2 *The other party was aware of the claimant's mistake.* This is not generally a problem, since usually the other party is bent upon deception.

3 *When the contract was made the issue of identity was crucial.* The claimant will have to satisfy the court that he or she intended to contract only with the person whom the rogue claimed to be. In practice, the courts are often unwilling to accept this where the contract was made face to face and may place a heavy burden of proof on the claimant, who must show that it was reasonable to place reliance on the rogue's representations. Otherwise it is presumed that the claimant intended to contract with the person before them.

This is judged objectively with reference to the conduct of the parties.

Phillips v Brooks (1919)

The claimant jeweller contracted to sell a ring to a rogue who claimed to be Sir George Bullough. The claimant checked this name and address in a street directory and was satisfied by this flimsy evidence. It did not demonstrate any real link between the rogue and the person he claimed to be. It proved nothing more than that a Sir George Bullough did live at a particular address. It was held that the contract was not void; the issue of identity was not crucial to the claimant, who consequently was unable to recover the jewellery which had been pawned to the defendant.

Ingram v Little (1960, CA)
A rogue offered to buy a car from three elderly sisters. They initially refused to take a cheque so the rogue claimed to be P.G.M. Hutchinson who he said was a successful businessman. He also supplied an address. While two of the sisters kept the rogue talking, the third went to the post office and checked the particulars in the telephone directory and found that the name and address given by the rogue were correct. This, of course, proved nothing except that the rogue knew the given name and address but the sisters agreed to sell. The cheque was not honoured and the rogue sold the car to the defendant, a car dealer.

It was held (by majority) that the contract was void and therefore the car was recoverable from the defendant. The test was whether the rogue should reasonably have believed at the time of entering the contract that the offer from the seller was to the person they represented themselves as being. The sisters had intended to deal only with Hutchinson as was evidenced by their initial refusal to accept the cheque until they had checked the phone book. Every case in these circumstances must be determined on its facts and *Phillips v Brooks* could be distinguished as the jeweller had agreed to sell before he checked the street directory.

While it is difficult to see any material difference between the facts of the two cases above, the decision in *Ingram* v *Little* may be justified as reflecting the customary approach of protecting the more vulnerable party at the expense of the business party. Remember it was a dealer who bought the car from the rogue.

Lewis v Averay (1971, CA)
The claimant sold his car to a rogue, who had claimed to be Richard Green, a film actor well known for portraying Robin Hood in a popular TV series. Before the sale was agreed, the rogue showed the claimant a chequebook in the name of R.A. Green, and a pass to Pinewood Studios. The pass bore an official stamp, the name Richard Green and the rogue's photograph. This was not held to be convincing evidence of the rogue's identity. It showed that the rogue's name was probably Richard Green and that he worked at Pinewood. 'Green' is a common name and there are many jobs at film studios which do not involve leading acting roles. The contract with the rogue was not void and therefore the defendant purchaser of the car had acquired ownership.

The court by majority refused to apply *Ingram* v *Little* and instead applied the *Phillips* v *Brooks* decision. *Ingram* v *Little* was perceived as anomalous as the facts of all three cases were indistinguishable.

In a recent and rather surprising decision the Court of Appeal revived the *Ingram* v *Little* approach, although with the result that the vulnerable party was not protected.

Hudson v Shogun Finance (2002)

A rogue using a stolen driving licence to back up his false identity obtained a car on hire purchase from the claimant finance company which had made very limited identity checks. He later sold it to Hudson. The finance company succeeded in their claim for damages against Hudson as the contract between it and the rogue was deemed void.

It was held (by majority):

(a) Identity was a crucial issue for the finance company. In these circumstances the rogue would reasonably believe that the offer was being made not to him personally but to the person named on the driving licence.

(b) This was not a face-to-face contract as the car dealer was not acting as agent of the finance company when dealing with the rogue. Therefore the presumption that the claimant intended to deal with the person before him did not apply.

(c) The face-to-face presumption should only have to be rebutted by the claimant in oral contracts, not in written contracts like the one in question.

This case was also argued on the grounds that Hudson had obtained title to the car under s 27 of the Hire Purchase Act 1964. (More detail on this aspect of the case can be found below at page 250.)

This decision appears to weaken the position of the vulnerable party in mistaken identity cases. All the judges hearing this case commented on the confusing state of the law in this area and the need for statutory reform to enable a clear and fair system of loss distribution in such cases. The fact that greater minds than ours find it problematic may be of some comfort to us lesser mortals as we struggle to understand this rather intractable area of the law.

Unilateral mistake regarding the terms of the contract

Parties will not usually be able to treat a contract as void by claiming that they were mistaken about the terms on which the contract was based. Exceptionally, the contract will be treated as void if the error would have been clearly evident to the other party, who will not be allowed to rely on it.

Hartog v Colin & Shields (1939)

A written contract to sell hare skins stated that the price would be calculated by the pound. It should have stated that the goods would be sold by the piece. This had been agreed orally between the parties and reflected the customs of the trade. It was held that the buyer was not entitled to take advantage of this clerical error in the contract which must be treated as void.

Wood v Scarth (1858)
The defendant's written offer to let premises did not include a premium of which the claimant was not informed when he concluded the contract with the defendant's agent. The contract was not invalidated by this mistake, since the claimant could not reasonably be expected to have anticipated that a premium would be payable.

The equitable remedy of rectification

The court may be prepared to amend a written contract which contains a mistake, provided that there is clear evidence that as it stands it does not represent the intention of the parties and that injustice would result from enforcement of the written document in its existing form.

Documents signed by mistake

The courts are generally very unsympathetic to people who try to avoid the effect of a mistakenly signed document. It is usually binding, unless misrepresentation or undue influence makes it voidable. Exceptionally, a plea of *non est factum* (this is not my deed) may be applicable.

The House of Lords has specified certain proof points for this plea, which if satisfied will result in the mistakenly signed document being void. Signers must prove that:

1 the document signed is radically different in its effect from what they believed they were signing;

2 the signers were not careless. The standard of care exercised by a signer is judged subjectively taking into account age and physical and mental capabilities.

Gallie v Lee (Saunders v Anglia Building Society) (1970, HL)
Mrs Gallie, who was 78, had poor sight and had mislaid her spectacles, signed a document without reading it. She assumed it to be a deed of gift assigning her house to her nephew, Wally. She had previously agreed to give him the house so that he could raise money on it for a business venture, provided that she would be able to continue living there. In fact, the document presented to her for signature by Lee, Wally's friend and business colleague, actually assigned the house to Lee for £3000. He never paid Mrs Gallie the money, but mortgaged the house to the building society. He then failed to make any repayments and so the building society attempted to repossess the house. By the time the case reached the House of Lords, Mrs Gallie was dead and the parties to the case were her executor and the building society.
The House of Lords held that the plea of *non est factum* failed.

> **1** The document was not sufficiently different in purpose from what Mrs Gallie believed she was signing: it transferred the ownership of the house, which was what she intended. It was irrelevant that it transferred the house to a different person, by sale not gift.
>
> **2** Mrs Gallie had not taken sufficient care before signing. She should at least have checked the contents of the document by asking someone to summarise it for her if she was not able to read it for herself.

The courts have shown great reluctance to allow a plea of *non est factum* to succeed in most of the cases where it has been raised.

DURESS AND UNDUE INFLUENCE

The essence of a contract is that it is a voluntary agreement. Evidence that a party entered a contract under compulsion may make it voidable.

Duress

Duress is a common law doctrine, under which threats or use of violence to force a party to make a contract may make it voidable. In practice, physical duress is very rare.

> ***Barton v Armstrong*** (1975, PC)
> B successfully claimed that he had been coerced by A's threats against his person, into selling his large shareholding to A on very favourable terms.

Traditionally the doctrine of duress encompassed only threats and violence against the person, but the courts, in the latter half of the twentieth century, extended the doctrine to cover *economic duress*. Such duress usually consists of threats by one party not to perform the contract with the other party unless the terms of the contract are varied in favour of the coercive party. In the past the courts have tended to treat such variations as void in law because of an absence of consideration, but increasingly they are tending to hold them voidable because of economic duress.

The following criteria are relevant to deciding whether the contract is voidable:

1 The extent of the pressure employed. This must exceed acceptable levels of pressure normally to be expected in commercial dealings.

2 The level of protest evidenced by the aggrieved party.

3 Did the aggrieved party have any real choice about complying with the other party's threats?

4 Was independent advice available to the aggrieved party?

Altas Express Ltd v Kafco Importers & Distributors (1989)
The claimants had contracted to transport goods for the defendants at a certain price calculated (by the claimants) on the basis of an estimated size of load. The first load was actually much smaller than was economic. The claimants then said that they would not make any further trips unless the price was renegotiated with a raised minimum cost per load. The defendants felt obliged to accept this as there was not time to find another carrier; they were also heavily dependent on a current order to Woolworths, where the next delivery was to be made. The court held that where a party is forced to renegotiate terms to its disadvantage and has no alternative but to accept the new terms offered, economic duress has occurred.

Undue influence

This is an equitable doctrine, applicable where one party abuses his or her personal influence or authority over another, to make that other party enter a transaction. If the influence is effective the transaction is voidable.

Williams v Bayley (1866, HL)
A father was told by his bankers that his son would be prosecuted, unless he (the father) paid back money that the son had fraudulently obtained from the bank by forging his father's signature. The resulting contract was held to be voidable against the bank by the father because he had not entered into it freely.

Avon Finance v Bridger (1985, CA)
An elderly couple were buying a retirement home; their son was making the financial arrangements and was providing part of the money. To do this he obtained a loan from the claimant, but did not tell his parents who signed a legal charge as security that it related to their home. The son then failed to keep up the repayments and the claimant took action to possess the house. The security agreement was held to be voidable for undue influence by the son which was attributable to the claimant. The son was in effect acting as the claimant's agent. The claimant should have been aware that the son would exercise influence over his parents who had not received independent advice.

Where there is *no fiduciary relationship* between the parties the burden of proof of undue influence is on the complainant. He or she will have to satisfy the court that, but for the influence to which he or she had been subjected, he or she would not have entered the transaction. Proof that the complainant had no independent advice before entering the transaction may be evidence that he or she did not act with free will.

Where a *fiduciary relationship* exists between the parties undue influence is presumed, provided that the complainant can prove that the resulting transaction was disadvantageous to him/her. The transaction will be voidable unless the other party can prove that the complainant was not prevented from exercising freedom of will. Evidence that the complainant had access to independent advice will be proof of this.

A fiduciary relationship is deemed in law to exist automatically in some situations. These include:

1 doctor and patient;

2 solicitor and client;

3 principal and agent.

However, the court may be prepared to acknowledge that particular circumstances give rise to a fiduciary relationship in the case before them.

Re Craig (1971)
A secretary companion who persuaded her frail and elderly employer to make gifts to her from the bulk of his savings, was held to be in a fiduciary relationship to him. He was both physically and emotionally dependent on her. She had to repay the money to his estate.

Goldsworthy v Brickell (1987, CA)
The claimant, who was elderly, owned a large and valuable farm which had become very run down. He came to rely heavily on the defendant (his neighbour) for advice. Within a few months the defendant was effectively managing the farm. The claimant then gave the defendant a tenancy of the farm on very favourable terms to the defendant, but took no independent advice. A fiduciary relationship was held to exist and undue influence therefore was presumed. The tenancy was voidable.

In general, the courts have not often been persuaded to find a fiduciary relationship to exist between husband and wife, even if the relevant transaction was for the benefit of the husband.

Barclays Bank v O'Brien (1993, HL)
The facts of this case are set out below. The House of Lords indicated that a more generous approach may be appropriate where a wife stands surety for a husband's debts:

1 the informal nature of business dealings between spouses raises a substantial risk that the husband might fail accurately to inform his wife of the extent of the liability she was undertaking;

2 many wives placed trust and confidence in their husbands' judgement in financial matters.

3 Similar principles would apply to transactions between cohabitees where there was an emotional relationship, whether heterosexual or homosexual.

Occasional exceptions are made but no fiduciary relationship is usually acknowledged to exist between a bank and its customers. The bank does not even have a duty to ensure that a customer takes independent advice prior to entering into a transaction with it. However, failure to do so may prevent the bank from enforcing a contract in its favour, if it is perceived as having constructive notice of undue influence or misrepresentation which led the customer into the transaction. Such notice may be given by the nature and substance of the agreement and the relationship between the customer and any other party involved in or benefiting from the transaction.

Barclays Bank v O'Brien (1993, HL)
Mr O'Brien persuaded his wife to sign a mortgage on the jointly-owned matrimonial home, as security for the overdraft for her husband's company in which she had no interest. He told her that the overdraft was limited to £60 000 for a period of three weeks. In fact it was unlimited in both respects. When it rose to £154 000, the bank sought to enforce the mortgage. The branch where Mrs O'Brien had entered the transaction had failed to carry out instructions from head office to make sure that both parties were fully aware of the nature of the transaction and to recommend independent advice. It was held that if the circumstances surrounding the transaction should have put the bank on notice that a wife had been subject to undue influence or misrepresentation, she could avoid the transaction, unless the bank had warned her in confidence of the need to take independent advice. Mrs O'Brien was entitled to avoid the transaction as the bank had been put on notice of her husband's likely misbehaviour and had not taken adequate steps to safeguard her.

Later cases indicate that it is hard to persuade the court that the bank did have constructive knowledge unless the circumstances are exceptional.

Credit Lyonnais v Burch (1997)

The defendant was a junior employee in a small company and a family friend of the owner, who was also her boss. She was persuaded by him to take out a second mortgage on her flat and to give the bank an unlimited guarantee of the company's debts, to enable the company to increase its overdraft from £25 000 to £270 000. Neither he nor the bank ever revealed to her the heavy state of indebtedness of the company. The bank urged her to take legal advice before signing the relevant documents but when she refused, in a letter clearly written in consultation with her employer, it allowed her to enter what it knew to be a precarious contract. The court held that the bank had constructive notice of the influence her employer was capable of exercising over her and of the lack of legal advice and, therefore, could not enforce the mortgage and guarantee against her.

In the majority of cases the court has generally held that the bank does not have constructive notice once the vulnerable party has been advised to take independent advice. The courts have usually interpreted the concept of independent and adequate advice in favour of the bank. However, in the *Etridge* case (below) the House of Lords restated and clarified some of the issues and has revived a little of the spirit of the *O'Brien* decision. Nevertheless, there are still concerns about whether the surety is sufficiently protected with regard to the issue of independent legal advice. As the law now stands the surety's only remedy in most cases may be an action in negligence against the solicitor, rather than being able to avoid the transaction with the bank.

Royal Bank of Scotland v Etridge No. 2 (2001, HL)

The House of Lords held that:

(a) The bank is automatically put on notice when the surety is not acting in the course of business.

(b) The bank must reasonably ensure that the surety has understood the consequences of what they are signing, has been warned of the risks in non-technical language and freely chose to sign. However, the bank need not personally meet with the surety. Confirmation from the solicitor advising the surety will normally be sufficient.

(c) Independent advice may be supplied to the surety by the borrower's solicitor. That solicitor must determine whether there is any conflict of interest which indicates that the surety should be separately advised.

(d) Once the bank was informed that the surety had been advised, the bank could assume that the advice had been delivered competently.

The only remedy for undue influence is *rescission*. This is an equitable remedy and, therefore, available only at the discretion of the judge. The right to avoid the transaction may be lost in the following circumstances:

1 *Affirmation*. The complainant performs the contract with no complaint once freed from the other party's domination.

2 *Delay*.

Allcard v Skinner (1887, CA)
Miss Allcard joined a religious order and made large gifts to it. She stayed in the order for eight years. It was not until six years after she had left the order that she tried to recover the money she had given. It was held that there was evidence of undue influence, but Miss Allcard's claim to avoid the gifts came too late.

3 *A third party has acquired bona fide rights over the contract property*. If property was transferred under a contract voidable for undue influence and sold on before the complainant had time to avoid the contract, the right to rescind is lost.

Quiz 7

1 What effect does a successful claim of **(a)** misrepresentation, **(b)** mistake, **(c)** duress, **(d)** undue influence, **(e)** *non est factum*, have on a contract?

2 On what grounds may the following contracts arguably be defective?

(a) Crockford sold his house to Wisden, having placed a large and heavy bookcase to conceal subsidence cracks in the wall.

(b) Kelly contracted to sell Bradshaw 1 tonne of jelly babies, which both parties believed to be in a warehouse in Scunthorpe. Earlier the same day, a massive fire had destroyed the contents of the warehouse.

(c) Chambers told Webster that he was Pears, the famous flute player. As a result, Webster agreed to sell him his antique flute.

(d) Whittaker, who is frail, elderly and heavily dependent on his son, Moore, sold Moore valuable shares for a fraction of their market price, because Moore threatened that otherwise he would go and live abroad.

Assignment 6

(a) Explain the remedies for misrepresentation.

(b) James sold his car privately by cheque to a rogue who represented himself as Robert Gould whose cheque book and bankers card the rogue had recently stolen. For additional proof of identity the rogue showed James a travel pass in Robert's name onto which the rogue had put his own photograph. The rogue then sold the car on to a secondhand car dealer called Harry. The cheque bounced when James presented it and he has traced the car to Harry's showroom.

Advise James.

Would it make any difference to your answer if James had become suspicious shortly after selling the car and had notified the police?

A suggested solution for this assignment can be found in the Lecturer's Guide.

CHAPTER 8

More defects: illegality and incapacity

INTRODUCTION

In the law of contract, the word 'illegal' has a wider meaning than that understood by lay people. It includes not only contracts which are actually *prohibited* by law, but also contracts to achieve a *purpose which is against the law*, as well as contracts seen to be *against the public interest* but which do not actually break the law. A contract found to be illegal is *void*.

In general, any person is legally *capable* of making a contract and may, therefore, sue or be sued on any contract to which he or she is a party. However, some types of person have *limited contractual capacity* and will not necessarily be bound by all the contracts which they make. Special rules apply to incorporated bodies which are explained in Chapter 22. This chapter examines the rules concerning two categories of people whose capacity is limited to protect them against exploitation – minors and mentally impaired persons.

ILLEGALITY

The rules governing illegal contracts are found in statute and common law.

Contracts illegal by statute

These are numerous and include the following:

1 under the Resale Prices Act 1976, collective agreements between manufacturers to regulate the resale price of goods are prohibited;

2 under the Gaming Act 1845, gaming and wagering contracts are void. The Act does not prohibit gambling as such, but effectively prevents a party to such a contract from having any rights to pursue gambling debts through the courts.

Contracts illegal at common law

The court determines the existence and extent of the illegality by reference to public interest considerations, sometimes described as 'the public policy'. Contracts invalidated for public policy reasons fall into two categories.

1 *Illegal contracts.* Here the parties agree to do something which is directly or indirectly against the law. The following types of contract are illegal:

(a) *A contract to commit a crime, a tort or a fraud.*

Everet v Williams (1725)
Two highwaymen agreed to rob a stagecoach and share the proceeds. Not surprisingly, the court refused to allow one to sue the other for his share of the proceeds.

(b) *A contract which is damaging to the country's foreign relations.*

Regazzoni v Sethia (1957, HL)
India's export regulations prohibited exports from India to South Africa. To avoid the prohibition, the claimant and defendant contracted that the goods for which they were contracting would first be exported to Italy. From there they would be sent on to South Africa. The buyer sued for breach of contract when the seller failed to deliver. It was held that the contract was illegal since its performance would breach the law of India and was likely to endanger its friendly relationship with Great Britain.

(c) *A contract for a sexually immoral purpose.*

Pearce v Brooks (1866)
The claimant coach builders supplied a carriage to the defendant, knowing that she would use it to ply her trade as a prostitute. It was held that the contract was illegal. The coach builders could neither recover payment from the defendant nor repossess the carriage. They had effectively aided and abetted soliciting.

The illegality taints the whole contract, rendering it void. A party may find themselves indirectly penalised for making the contract. For example, if a party was aware of the illegal purpose before entering the contract, he or she will not generally be able to recover any property which has changed hands. This can be seen as a deterrent to discourage parties from making such contracts.

2 *Contracts which are merely void.* These are contracts which the courts believe are against the public interest though they do not involve breaking the law. The parties will not be penalised by the courts for making them. Property which has changed hands is always recoverable. The contract will be enforceable as far as it is not void. The most important type of such contracts are those said to be in restraint of trade.

Contracts in restraint of trade

These are commonly a feature of the following agreements:

1 *Contracts of employment.* Employees may be required to give undertakings not to reveal trade secrets or to compete with their employers on leaving their service.

2 *Contracts for the sale of a business.* Where a business is sold as a going concern, the seller may undertake not to set up in competition with the buyer.

3 *Solus agreements.* A seller of a particular product may agree to deal with only one supplier in return for a discount or some other financial benefit. This is very common in contracts for the supply of petrol. The owner of a filling station obtains a discount price, or financial assistance to develop a site from the supplier, in return for a promise to sell only that supplier's brand.

The use of such restraints is not generally regarded as being in the public interest, because they tend to hamper competition and freedom of movement of labour. All such restraints are said to be prima facie void – i.e. they will initially be treated as against the public interest – but will be enforced if proved reasonable. This means that the court will not give a remedy (like an injunction) to help a party enforce the restraint, unless there is evidence that in the particular circumstances the restraint is reasonable.

Three questions are relevant to determining reasonableness:

1 Is the business interest one which can legally be protected? Such interests are limited to trade secrets and influential relationships in employment contracts. If the contract concerns the sale of a business, the goodwill may be protected.

2 How long is the restraint intended to last?

3 How wide a geographical area is covered by the restraint?

Provided that a legally recognised business interest is found to exist, the issues of time and geographical area are determined in the light of the particular facts of the case. The courts have exceptionally upheld lifelong or worldwide restraints. In practice, however, most restraints operate only within a very limited time and area.

Restrictive covenants in employment contracts

An employer may seek to impose restrictions on employees who have moved to a new employer.

With regard to *trade secrets*, an employer may restrain employees with access to unique information concerning the manufacturing process or composition of goods from revealing this information to others or using it for their own purposes.

Forster & Sons Ltd v Suggett (1918)
The employee had access to secret bottle-glass manufacturing processes invented by his employer. It was found to be reasonable to restrict the employee from being involved in such a trade for five years after he stopped working for the employer, anywhere in the UK.

Business connections created by an employee through close relationships forged with customers during the relevant employment may also be protected. This is to prevent an ex-employee from poaching customers.

Fitch v Dewes (1921, HL)
A solicitor's managing clerk could reasonably be restrained from working as a solicitor for the rest of his life, within a seven-mile radius of Tamworth town hall, as he had dealt confidentially with many clients within his employer's practice. They might follow him if he were allowed to practise locally.

Employees who have learnt skills and obtained business knowledge from their employment cannot be legally prevented from using these elsewhere, unless trade secrets were imparted or close relationships with customers resulted.

Morris v Saxelby (1916, HL)
A draftsman and engineer could not be restrained from working in the crane components manufacturing business. Knowledge about the way in which his ex-employers organised a similar business was not an interest which could be protected.

Eastham v Newcastle United Football Club (1964)
Football Association rules stated that players who left a club at the end of a contract could be placed on a retainer list. This prevented them from seeking employment with any other club in the UK or abroad, for as long as their ex-club paid them 'a reasonable wage'. It was held that this was not binding since no legitimate trade interest was protected by it.

Faccenda Chicken Ltd v Fowler (1986, CA)
The claimants sold frozen chickens door to door. Mr Fowler was their sales manager but had no direct contact with customers. He left Faccenda's employment and
set up a similar business in the area, using his ex-employers' customer lists. Eight of
the claimants' other employees left to work for him. It was held that Fowler could
not be restrained from this activity: the information he had used was not a trade
secret and he was not breaching his ex-employers' confidence by using it. He was
at liberty to offer jobs to any person that he thought suitable.

The issue of reasonableness must be determined in the way most likely to produce
a fair outcome for both parties. In each of the three cases above, the employer
was merely trying to prevent legitimate competition by an ex-employee. This
would have unduly restricted the employee selling his labour, or setting up in
business elsewhere.

The courts recognise that employees do not usually share equal bargaining power
with their employers. The wording of a contract is therefore strictly interpreted to
prevent unreasonable restraints upon employees. The court must, however, balance
the parties' interests. The court may not always take the literal meaning of the
words if this would allow an employee to abuse the employer's legitimate interests.
Instead, a purposive approach may be adopted. The contract is interpreted in the
way which prevents the employee from avoiding a reasonable degree of restraint.

Home Counties Dairies v Skilton (1970)
Skilton's employment contract required him not to sell milk or dairy products to
any person whom he had served during his time with the dairy, for one year after
leaving the dairy's employment. The object of the clause was found to be to prevent
the dairy's loss of customers from Skilton's old milk round, not to prevent him from
taking up work, for example, in a grocery shop selling butter and cheese. It would
be valid insofar as it prevented him from poaching his ex-employer's customers
when working as a milkman.

Littlewoods Organisation v Harris (1978, CA)
The claimant, who had planned the contents of Littlewoods' mail order catalogue
for the next year, left to work for Littlewoods' main competitor, Universal Stores.
His contract with Littlewoods stated that he must not work for Universal Stores
for one year after leaving Littlewoods. The Court of Appeal held that this very generally drafted restraint, if interpreted literally, would prevent Harris working in any
capacity for Universal Stores. It must be interpreted with implied reference to

▶

Harris's very high degree of access to crucial trading information in the mail order market sector. Once this was taken into account the clause became reasonable as it protected Littlewoods' secret information.

Restraint on the seller of a business

Buyers of the goodwill of a business may protect themselves against loss of customers by restraining the sellers from setting up in a similar business too close and too soon. The only business interest which can be protected here is the existing custom enjoyed by sellers: they can be restrained only from running a business of *exactly the same kind* as they are selling.

BRC Engineering v Schelff (1921)
Schelff sold his business, which was concerned with the sale of loop concrete road reinforcements. The contract of sale contained a clause that attempted to restrain him from being involved in the sale or manufacture of *any type* of concrete reinforcement. It was held that the only business interest that could validly be protected here concerned the sale of loop reinforcements. Any wider restraint was unreasonable as it related to business interests that were not being sold.

Nordenfelt v Maxim Nordenfelt Guns & Ammunition Co. Ltd (1894)
Nordenfelt sold his arms manufacturing business to the Maxim Nordenfelt Co. The contract restrained him from being involved for 25 years in any way with the armaments trade. No geographical limit was mentioned. Given the wide scope of the business (a large variety of armaments were manufactured by Nordenfelt) and the very small number of customers involved (state governments), this was held to be a reasonable restraint.

Solus agreements

These most commonly arise in contracts between petroleum companies and retail petrol outlets.

Esso Petroleum v Harper's Garage (Stourport) Ltd (1968, HL)
Two solus agreements were made between Harper's and Esso: agreement 1, which was to last four-and-a-half years, was made in return for a price discount on the petrol; agreement 2, which was to last 21 years, was made in return for a mortgage loan of £7000 from Esso secured on the filling station and which was repayable

▶

111

over that period. Agreement 1 was held to be reasonable and binding. Agreement 2 was held to be unreasonable in relation to its time span. It was longer than necessary to allow Esso to protect their business interest in maintaining stable levels of distribution. It was irrelevant that it had been agreed in relation to a mortgage.

Notice that in the above case Harper's already occupied the land at the point that they took the mortgage. They were giving up their freedom to trade from there with whomever they chose. The restraint rules do not apply where a party agrees to a restraint *as a condition* of being given possession of land.

Cleveland Petroleum v *Dartstone Ltd* (1969, CA)
The defendants took a lease of a garage from Cleveland. The lease stated that they could sell only Cleveland's petrol for the duration of the lease. It was held that since the defendants had not previously been in occupation of the land and had taken on the tenancy with full knowledge of the restriction, it was not an unreasonable restraint of trade.

The same principle applies to tied pubs.

The consequences of a void restraint

The fact that a restraint is void does not prevent the rest of the contract from being valid. A party can sue successfully for breach of a contract of employment or sale of a business, as long as the alleged breach does not relate to the void restraint.

The court may be able to sever (cut out) the unreasonable part of a restraint. The remainder of the restraint can then be enforced.

Goldsoll v *Goldman* (1915, CA)
The defendant sold an imitation jewellery business situated in London. Much of the business was conducted through mail order in the UK. In the contract of sale he undertook that he would not for two years be involved in the sale of real or imitation jewellery in any part of the United Kingdom, France, the USA, Russia, or within 25 miles of Berlin or Vienna. This was clearly too wide to be reasonable as regards:

1 *business interest*: the claimant was buying an imitation jewellery business only, and could restrict the defendant's trading only in that respect;

2 *the geographical area covered by the restraint*: this was wider than reasonably necessary to protect a business interest where sales had previously been limited to the UK.

It was held that the reference to real jewellery would be severed, as would the geographical references apart from the UK.

Severance means what it says – cutting out; the court does not take it upon itself to rewrite a restraint to make it reasonable.

Even if severance is not applicable, the purposive approach adopted by the courts in cases like *Home Counties Dairies* v *Skilton* (described above) may enable a widely drafted restraint to be interpreted reasonably.

CONTRACTUAL INCAPACITY

Minors

Minors (people under the age of 18) are legally capable of making most kinds of contracts and may take steps to enforce them against the other party. The law protects minors by restricting the extent to which their contracts may be enforced against them. Some – like a contract to lend money to a minor – are never enforceable by the creditor; others are binding only to a limited extent.

Contracts capable of binding a minor

Contracts to purchase necessaries are capable of binding a minor. 'Necessaries' are defined by s 3 of the Sale of Goods Act 1979, as 'goods suitable to the condition in life of the minor ... and to his actual requirements at the time of sale and delivery'.

There are two issues here:

1 Are the goods capable of being necessaries? The lifestyle and social standing of the minor may be relevant.

Peters v Fleming (1840)
A watch chain was held to be capable of being a necessary to the defendant undergraduate, and his social standing could make it reasonable for it to be a gold one.

2 Were the goods necessary to the minor's requirements at the time of sale and delivery?

Nash v Inman (1908)
The claimant supplied clothing to the defendant minor, a Cambridge undergraduate. The clothing included 11 fancy waistcoats. It was held that as the defendant was already amply supplied with clothing appropriate to his station in life the clothing purchased could not amount to necessaries and the action must fail.

The concept of necessaries also, by analogy, covers services. All the following are capable of being necessaries: food, clothing, lodgings, transport to work, legal advice, education.

A minor's liability in a contract for necessaries is limited to payment of a *reasonable* price. The minor is not necessarily bound by the price specified in the contract. Section 3 of the Sale of Goods Act 1979 states that a 'reasonable price' is payable for goods 'sold and delivered'. The court may require the minor to pay less than the price agreed with the seller. The words 'sold and delivered' suggest that the minor has a duty to pay only when delivery of the goods has been made.

A *harsh or onerous contract* will not be enforced at all.

> ### Fawcett v Smethurst (1914)
> A contract for hire of a car made the minor liable for any damage sustained to it whether caused by the minor or not. It was held that this contract for necessaries was void as it posed an unreasonably heavy burden on the minor.

Beneficial contracts of employment are also capable of binding a minor. These include training and apprenticeship contracts, but not trading contracts. The contract is binding on the minor if overall it is for the minor's benefit, but not if it is unduly burdensome.

> ### De Francesco v Barnum (1890)
> Under a dancing-apprenticeship contract, a girl of 14 promised that she would not marry during the apprenticeship, or accept any engagements, without her master's permission. He was under no obligation to find her engagements, or to pay her if she was unemployed. When employed her pay was very poor (9d per night) even by the then existing standards. The contract was held to be void; it was onerous and unfair to the minor who was at the total disposal of the claimant.

Voidable contracts include a number of different types of contracts which create continuing obligations. Tenancy agreements, partnership agreements and contracts for the purchase of shares are examples. A minor can opt out of such a contract at any time before majority, or within a reasonable time after, but is liable for any obligations (rent, calls on shares) which accrued before then.

Contracts which are not enforceable against a minor

All contracts which do not fit into the categories discussed above are not binding on minors. The commonest unenforceable contracts are for loans of money or the sale of non-necessary goods and services.

Historically, parties who did business with minors did so at their peril, and often found themselves out of pocket. Today they may be able to obtain payment or recover goods under the Minors' Contracts Act 1987, which aims to redress the sometimes excessive immunity enjoyed by minors:

1 *Guarantee of minors' debts*. Under s 2 of the Act, contracts by a third party to guarantee payments by minors under contracts not enforceable against them are binding on the third party.

2 *Restitution orders against minors*. This is an equitable remedy available at the court's discretion whereby a minor may be required to return to the other party any property acquired under the contract (Minors' Contracts Act 1987, s 3). This remedy was available prior to 1987 and was sometimes granted in cases of fraud, where minors obtained property under a contract by lying about their age. The court may also order minors to hand over the proceeds of sale of any goods supplied to them (*Stocks* v *Wilson* (1913)). It does not generally enable a creditor to recover a money loan, since the actual coins or notes supplied are no longer recoverable from the minor, having been spent (*Leslie* v *Sheill* (1914)).

3 *Ratification of debts contracted during minority*. Section 1 of the 1987 Act provides that if on attaining majority persons ratify debts transacted in their minority, this ratification (confirmation) is binding on them.

Mentally impaired persons

The contractual capacity of a person who is mentally impaired is limited in two situations:

1 *Where the other party knew of the impairment*. If the other party to the contract knew or reasonably should have known of a party's mental impairment, the contract is voidable by the impaired party, i.e. the impaired party can choose to opt out of it. If the other party was not aware of the impairment, the contract is valid and enforceable.

2 *Contracts for necessaries*. Under s 3 of the Sale of Goods Act 1979, a mentally impaired person is obliged to pay a reasonable price for necessaries when they are supplied by a seller who is aware of that person's mental state. The court will not interfere with the price if the seller was not aware of the buyer's mental state.

Quiz 8

1 How does illegality effect the validity of a contract?

2 Why may the following contracts be illegal?

   (a) a contract to rob a bank;

   (b) a contract to make a pornographic film;

   (c) a contract by an English firm to supply arms to terrorists in the United States.

3 Are the following contracts enforceable against Algernon who is 17?

   (a) to buy a suit to wear at job interviews;

   (b) to buy 50 Christmas cakes which he intends to distribute to local old people's homes;

   (c) to work for Busby Ltd as a packer in their dispatch department;

   (d) to borrow £50 pounds from Jemima.

Assignment 7

Boffin is employed by Sweeties Ltd and has learnt secret toffee-making processes exclusively used by Sweeties in the UK. His contract states that if he leaves Sweeties he must not be involved in the manufacture of toffee or any other confectionery in the UK or the USA for one year.

1 Is this restraint lawful?

2 If unlawful, is it capable of being made lawful?

CHAPTER 9

Discharge of the contract and remedies for breach

INTRODUCTION

Contractual obligations do not last forever and may be discharged in any of the following situations:

1 *Performance.* A contract is discharged when its terms have been performed.

2 *Agreement.* The parties may agree not to go ahead with the contract which is then discharged, provided that this agreement is, in itself, a valid contract.

3 *Frustration.* If the contract becomes impossible or futile to perform due to events outside the parties' control, this defeats the parties' intentions and ends the contract.

4 *Breach.* Not every breach of contract is capable of ending the contract, but the breach of a major term (condition) may have this effect.

This chapter examines these concepts and also describes the remedies available at common law and equity for breach of contract.

DISCHARGE OF CONTRACTS

Discharge by performance

The general rule: A party is discharged only when he or she has completely performed all his or her obligations under the contract. A party's failure to perform may make him or her vulnerable to an action for breach of contract by the other party, who may also be entitled to withhold payment. Although it may generally be fair to hold someone to the letter of a bargain, this rule is capable of producing some unjust results.

Cutter v Powell (1795)

The defendant, Captain Powell, engaged Lieutenant Cutter as part of his crew for a voyage from Jamaica to Liverpool. The contract stated that payment was due only on completion of the voyage, but the Lieutenant died 19 days before the ship reached Liverpool. It was held that his widow, who sued on behalf of his estate, could not claim any part of his salary since payment of it was not due until the voyage had been completed.

Exceptions have been developed to prevent injustice.

Divisible contracts

The contract made by Lieutenant Cutter was an *entire* contract; he was obliged to perform one whole obligation in order to be able to claim payment – complete the voyage from Jamaica to Liverpool. The outcome for Mrs Cutter would have been happier if this obligation had been *divisible* – broken down into smaller units (for example, weeks), on completion of each of which payment of a proportion of his wages would have been due. She would have been able to claim for three weeks' wages.

Ritchie v Atkinson (1808)

A contract stated that goods would be shipped at a cost of £5 per ton. When only part of the agreed cargo was transported, the owners claimed that they were not bound to pay. Since the obligation was divisible, payment was owing for each ton of the cargo which had been carried.

Contracts of employment are divisible, with payment due on a weekly or monthly basis. Building contracts are another example; specified sums become payable on completion of performance of specified portions of the work.

One party prevents the other from completing performance

Grand opportunities for fraud would occur if parties could claim that they were not bound to pay contract prices when they themselves had prevented the other parties from completing the necessary work. To prevent such injustice, the party who prevents performance is deemed to be in breach, which releases the other party from the obligation to tender complete performance.

Planché v Colburn (1831)

The claimant entered into a contract to write a book for the defendant publisher and was to be paid £100 when the book was completed. He had researched and written part of the book when the defendant told him that it would not be required. He was held to be entitled to a sum to represent the value of the work he had done towards completion of the contract.

Acceptance of part performance

Where the contract is entire, part performance does not discharge a party's obligation. However, part performance, if *voluntarily* accepted by the party to whom it is offered, discharges the other party. The accepting party must then pay an appropriate price. The accepting party must have a genuine choice to accept or reject the part performance. A buyer can refuse to take delivery of a consignment of goods, but may have no real choice in a contract to supply goods and services if materials have become part of their own property.

Sumpter v Hedges (1898)
The claimant contracted to build a barn for the defendant, but then abandoned the project when it was only half completed. It was held that no payment was due since the defendant, who had completed the barn himself, had no choice but to accept part performance and make the building safe by finishing the work. The defendant did have to pay for materials which the claimant had left behind and which the defendant had *chosen* to use to complete the building.

Substantial performance

Provided a party has received the bulk of what was agreed, payment is due, even if final performance deviates marginally from the letter of the contract. The payer is then entitled to a discount to cover the minor failure to perform. The court has to decide whether the performance is sufficiently substantial to discharge the obligations. Compare the following two decisions.

Bolton v Mahadeva (1972)
A contract to install a central heating system was not substantially completed: fumes escaped into the house, which was also substantially less warm than was promised as a condition of the contract.

Hoenig v Isaacs (1952)
A contract to decorate and furnish a flat had been substantially performed since the defects (repairs to a bookcase and replacement of a wardrobe door) were superficial and easily remedied. The total cost of the contract was £750 and the cost of the defects £55.

Notice that none of these exceptions would have helped in the *Cutter* v *Powell* case:

- Lieutenant Cutter's contract was an *entire* obligation; payment was made on the basis of completion of the whole voyage, not on a weekly or daily basis;
- the captain did not *prevent completion* of the contract: fate intervened;
- the captain had *no choice but to accept part performance*;
- performance was not *substantial*; Cutter had not performed more than about two-thirds of what was required of him.

Today a remedy would be provided under the Law Reform (Frustrated Contracts) Act 1943 (see pages 120 and 125).

Discharge by agreement

Having formed a contract, the parties to it may agree not to go through with it. This agreement (which is in effect a secondary contract) will be binding as long as the necessary requirements of a valid contract are satisfied. The issue most likely to be problematic is consideration.

Bilateral discharge

Where the first contract is still wholly or partially executory (neither party has performed all his or her obligations), consideration will consist of each party's promise not to insist on the other party's performance of those obligations. Each party is giving up legal rights under the first contract.

Unilateral discharge: accord and satisfaction

Where one party has completely performed his or her obligations under the original contract and the other party wants to be released from their obligations, a promise by the first party to allow this is binding only if the other party promises some material benefit in return. Such a transaction is described as accord (agreement) and satisfaction (consideration). A promise to pay a sum of money, or to provide some other consideration in return for the other party giving up their rights will immediately discharge the contract.

Discharge by frustration

If, between formation and performance of the contract, events outside the parties' control render further performance impossible or futile, the contract may be discharged. The party claiming that the contract has been frustrated must satisfy the court that the supervening events have radically changed the nature of the contractual obligation. This doctrine was developed in the nineteenth century to prevent injustice where a party is prevented from carrying out a contract through no fault of his or her own.

Frustration may discharge the contract in the following situations:

1 destruction of the subject matter;

2 the death or illness of one of the parties;

3 supervening illegality;

4 government intervention;

5 the event on which the contract is based fails to occur.

Destruction of the subject matter

Taylor v Caldwell (1863)
A contract to let a music hall was found to be frustrated when the hall was destroyed by an arsonist.

Death or illness of one of the contracting parties

This affects contracts involving a service which can be performed only by the relevant party. Illness does not necessarily frustrate the contract. The average employment contract is not frustrated by an employee having a week off with influenza. Relevant factors to consider include the length of the illness relative to the length of the contract and whether the essential nature of the contract is threatened by the loss of performance. A seven-year contract with an actor in *The Mousetrap* will not be frustrated by one night's laryngitis, but this would prove fatal to a contract for a one-night performance by a famous soprano at The Royal Opera House.

Condor v The Barron Knights (1966)
Condor, drummer with the The Barron Knights pop group, became ill with nervous strain. His doctor said that he should perform no more than four nights a week. His contract was held to be frustrated, since such restraint was incompatible with the nature of such work. In the music business, performance dates might not arise at regular intervals. It might involve performance seven nights a week at busy periods.

Supervening illegality

A contract which is completely legal when formed may become illegal by a change in the law occurring before performance. A contract with a foreign national will be made illegal if Britain subsequently declares war against that person's country.

Government intervention

This has often arisen in wartime due to the internment or conscription of personnel and requisitioning of property.

Morgan v _Manser_ (1947)

The conscription in wartime of a comedian frustrated his contract. At the point when he received his call-up papers there was no indication of how long hostilities would last.

Other exercise of power by government agencies may have the same effect.

Shepherd v _Jerrom_ (1987)

The imposition of a prison sentence was held to frustrate a contract of apprenticeship.

The event on which the contract is based fails to occur

Here the letter of the contract can usually still be performed, but such performance has become futile and in no way reflects the object which the parties intended to achieve.

Krell v _Henry_ (1903)

A contract for the one-day hire of a room for the purpose of viewing Edward VII's coronation procession, was frustrated when the coronation was postponed due to the King's illness. It would have been possible for the hirer and his party to have sat and watched the traffic on the booked date, but this clearly was not what the parties had intended.

If part of the purpose of the contract can still be achieved, however, the contract will not be frustrated.

Herne Bay Steamboat Co. v _Hutton_ (1903)

Hutton hired a boat to take a party of guests to view the fleet and watch the naval review on coronation day. The contract was held not to be frustrated by the cancellation of the review since the fleet could still be toured.

The limitations of the frustration rule

The courts do not willingly free parties from their contractual obligations. An event which should have been foreseeable when the contract was made will not frustrate the contract because its occurrence was outside the parties' control. The court will take the view that this eventuality should have been covered by the contract.

It is also irrelevant that subsequent events have caused mere inconvenience or delay, or made the performance of the contract more expensive than was planned.

Davis Contractors v Fareham District Council (1956, HL)
Davis had contracted to build houses for the council and had specified a fixed price. Due to bad weather, and lack of materials and manpower because of post-war shortages, the contract took much longer to complete than the builders had expected and was much more costly. The House of Lords held that frustration had not occurred. Inconvenience and expense were not sufficient: frustration occurs only where the end result of the contract is radically different from what the parties intended. (If the contract had been frustrated, the council would have had to pay a price truly in line with the cost to the builder.)

Tsakiroglou & Co. v Noblee Thorl GmbH (1961, HL)
Closure of the Suez Canal did not frustrate a shipping contract although it added to the length, and therefore to the cost, of the journey.

Force majeure clauses

The parties in these last two cases could have spared themselves involvement in litigation by ensuring that the contract was drafted more carefully. A *force majeure* clause determines the rights of the parties in the event of specified circumstances outside their control. It can be useful in two ways:

1 To exempt a party from or limit its liability for breach of contract to cover situations where failure to perform arises from circumstances which are unlikely to be treated as frustrating the contract. Hazards which commonly prevent performance are deemed by the courts to be foreseeable and therefore incapable of frustrating the contract. For example, bad weather is a common cause of delay in the performance of transport, travel and construction contracts. These may also be interrupted by trade union action, or through outbreak of civil or national hostilities. Remember that exemption and limitation provisions are subject to the controls which you studied in Chapter 6.

2 To avoid the contract being discharged by events which would normally frustrate it. This will be effective only if the court is satisfied that the parties really intended to keep the contract alive in the circumstances which are now threatening its existence.

Metropolitan Water Board v Dick Kerr & Co. (1918)
A contract made in July 1914 for the construction of a reservoir within six years contained a provision that the time limit could be extended in the event of delay arising from difficulties, delays or impediments, however caused. On the outbreak of war the following September, the work was halted by government order. It was held that the clause did not prevent the contract being frustrated, since the delay occasioned by interruption of the work appeared likely to be much more lengthy than the parties could have contemplated when they made the contract.

Self-induced frustration

The courts are not sympathetic to a party who causes the allegedly frustrating event.

Maritime National Fish Ltd v Ocean Trawlers Ltd (1935)
The defendants hired a trawler equipped with an otter trawl which required a licence. The defendants applied for five licences, to cover their own ships and the hired ship, but only four were granted. The defendants, therefore, used these to license their own ships. They claimed that the lack of a licence for the claimant's ship frustrated the contract of hire by making its performance illegal. The contract was held not to be frustrated as the defendants had chosen which ships to license and could have licensed the hired ship instead of one of their own.

The difference between frustration and mistake

It is important to note the difference between a contract which is void for mistake and one which is frustrated due to destruction of the subject matter. The distinguishing feature is one of time, as you can see from the two examples outlined below.

1 Stephen agrees to sell a consignment of teddy bears to Matilda. He believes that they are safely stored in a warehouse at his factory, but unknown to both parties the warehouse has caught fire after being struck by lightning and the goods have ceased to exist before Stephen makes his offer. Here no contract ever came into existence. It was void from the outset, as it was based on non-existent subject matter. It was impossible for a contract to result.

2 If the facts are altered, so that destruction of the teddies occurred after Matilda had accepted Stephen's offer, the contract is frustrated. The contract was formed with reference to goods which existed at the time the contract was made, but these were destroyed before it was performed.

(For operative mistake, see Chapter 7, page 93.)

The consequences of the contract being frustrated

When a contract is discharged by frustration, it ceases to exist from that moment on. Rights that have already arisen with regard to a party remain that party's property, but the party loses any rights which are due to arise (accrue) later. This means that a party who has received property is entitled to retain it; a party with no entitlement to claim payment before the contract was frustrated, loses its right to do so under the contract. Prior to 1943 such loss was said to 'lie where it fell'. There was no means by which a party could recover prepaid money, or payment for services rendered in preparation for performance of the contract.

Appleby v *Myers* (1867)
The claimants contracted to install machinery on the defendant's premises. Payment was to be made on completion of the work. The defendant's premises were destroyed by fire prior to completion. It was held that the claimants were unable to recover any of the cost of their labour and materials.

While the common law still determines the situations where frustration may occur, the rights of the parties to a frustrated contract are now regulated by statute. Under the Law Reform (Frustrated Contracts) Act 1943, once the contract has been frustrated all prepaid sums are returnable to the payer. Any sum that was already due ceases to be payable. However, the payee can retain or claim such prepaid or prepayable sums to cover the actual costs of work done so far (s 1(2)). This enables the court to prevent unjust enrichment by either party. A payee who has obtained money but not yet done any work towards performance of the contract, will have to return a prepaid sum. If the payee has incurred expenses in preparing to perform the contract, the court has powers to apportion the loss between the two parties, if it is just to do so. The payee may be allowed to hold on to some or all of a prepaid sum, or to claim a sum that had come due. Thus, both parties may have to carry some loss.

A party who, prior to the frustrating event, has conferred a valuable benefit on the other (apart from the payment of money) may claim its value, if it is just to do so (s 1(3)). This right exists as an alternative to or in addition to the rights conferred under s 1(2). Unfortunately the 1943 Act does not define what is meant by a 'valuable benefit'. Some guidance was given in the next case, which also illustrates how a just sum should be calculated.

BP Exploration Co. v *Hunt* (1982, HL)
Hunt owned an oil concession in Libya. His contract was with BP, under which it was to explore the concession to see if it was commercially viable and if so develop it. This would be done at BP's risk and cost. If oil were found in commercial quantities, BP would be repaid out of Hunt's share. A substantial oil field was developed

▶

and went into production, but the contract was frustrated when the Libyan government withdrew the concession. BP claimed that the oil Hunt had received was a valuable benefit.

It was held that the Act must be interpreted purposively to prevent either party obtaining an unfair financial advantage.

The valuable benefit was the end product of the service as opposed to the service itself. Hunt had been given his share of the oil and, therefore, received a valuable benefit from BP's performance of contractual services.

The value of the benefit must be determined at the moment the contract was frustrated. This represented the upper limit of any award. The value of Hunt's share of the oil so far was £85 million, but this must be reduced to take into account gains made by BP so far and the terms of the contract.

The just sum to be awarded to BP was £35 million, since it had already recovered £62 million of its £85 million development costs but had also paid Hunt £10 million. The fact that BP bore the main risks attached to the contract was also relevant to determining this sum.

It cannot be said that in *Appleby* v *Myers* the defendant (under today's law) would acquire a valuable benefit from incomplete and, as yet, useless machinery. If he were able to use the equipment to a limited extent, that would represent a valuable benefit.

The Act, therefore, always protects a payee who has asked for some prepayment. The payee will be covered, whether or not he or she has actually provided any valuable benefit.

It is instructive to see how the doctrine of frustration would affect the outcome of *Cutter* v *Powell*, which was explained at the beginning of this chapter. Today, Lieutenant Cutter's contract would be frustrated by his death. By serving on the ship, he would have provided a valuable benefit to his employer prior to his death.

Discharge by breach

Not every breach of contract is capable of resulting in its discharge. The distinction between conditions and warranties, which you studied in Chapter 6, is important here:

1 *Breach of warranty*. The innocent party has the right to claim damages if he or she has suffered any actionable damage or loss. The breach is not capable of bringing the contract to an end.

2 *Breach of condition*. Where a term has the status of a condition and, therefore, is crucial to the contract, the innocent party is entitled to refuse further performance of his or her obligations; he or she may recover any property transferred under the contract and obtain damages. Notice that the innocent party, in theory at least,

has a choice. An innocent party can free himself or herself from his or her obligations if he or she wishes, or may attempt to hold the other party to the bargain. In many cases no real choice exists, as the breach will be so ruinous to the contract that the injured party will be only too glad to be able to avoid his or her obligations. A breach of condition may consist of a refusal to perform, or arise from performance which is so inadequate that the innocent party is effectively deprived of the bargain. It may occur before, or at the date of performance.

Anticipatory breach

So-called anticipatory breach of a contract occurs where one party indicates, *before the time for performance is due*, either that he or she does not intend to perform or that he or she intends performance different from that set out in the contract.

> ### *Hochster v De La Tour* (1853)
> The parties made a contract in April, under which the defendant agreed that the claimant should act as his courier on a foreign tour, due to begin on 1 June. On 11 May, the defendant informed the claimant that his services would not be required. It was held that the claimant could sue for damages immediately: he did not have to wait for the performance date.

Victims of an anticipatory breach are, therefore, entitled to repudiate their contractual obligations as soon as the other party indicates his or her refusal to perform. The party in breach must know of the innocent party's intention, but notice may be implied from the conduct of the parties and/or commercial practice.

> ### *Vitol SA v Norelf* (1996, HL)
> The buyer of a cargo wrongly repudiated the contract because of unfounded fears about delay in loading and notified the seller, by telex, of what he was doing. The seller took no further action to perform the contract and, therefore, did not send the buyer the bill of lading which would, in this sort of contract, normally be sent once the cargo was loaded. Their Lordships held that the absence of the bill of lading should have made the buyer aware of the seller's intentions. The seller's behaviour in the context of trade practice 'clearly and unequivocally' evidenced intention to treat the contractual obligations as discharged by the buyer's breach.
> Formal communication of notice is not necessary and may be effective even if it comes from an unauthorised third party. The issue is whether a reasonable person would have believed that the innocent party was opting out of further performance.

Alternatively, the innocent party may wait for the performance date in the hope that the other party will, after all, perform. Three consequences may follow from doing this.

1 *The innocent party may have no duty to mitigate any loss before the date when the other party's obligations become due.* The innocent party's duty to take reasonable steps to avoid adding to the loss arising from the breach, may not arise until he or she acknowledges the breach or until the date of performance, whichever comes first. The innocent party may continue with his or her performance, where this can be done without the co-operation of the other party, and claim his or her full costs.

White & Carter (Councils) Ltd v McGregor (1962, HL)
Mr McGregor, who owned a garage, was persuaded to advertise it through White's advertising plates, which the company contracted to display on council litter bins for three years. McGregor's obligation to pay arose only once the plates were installed. He attempted to cancel the contract the same day that he had made it, but the company refused to accept his repudiation. It was able to claim the full sum, having performed its obligations. As the company had not chosen to repudiate the contract, no duty to mitigate arose, i.e. the company was under no obligation to look for another advertiser so as to avoid losing money.

The facts of the above case were exceptional since performance was completely within White & Carter's control and the product was only any use to McGregor. The House of Lords stated that such a claim should not be successful unless the innocent party had a legitimate interest in keeping the contract alive.

Clea Shipping Corpn v Bulk Oil International (1984)
The charterers of a ship wrongfully repudiated the contract before the charter was due to commence. It was held that the owners had no legitimate interest in maintaining the ship in readiness for the charter period. They should have mitigated their loss by seeking another charterer.

2 *The contract remains alive for the benefit of both parties.* The innocent party is not discharged from his or her duties under the contract until he or she repudiates the contract. If he or she does not repudiate, but fails to perform obligations as they fall due, the innocent party could be liable for breach.

3 *If the contract is frustrated before the performance date, the innocent party loses any rights to sue for breach.*

Avery v Bowden (1855)
The claimant hired a ship to the defendant at a port in Russia. Before the hire date the defendant told the claimant that he would not be able to fulfil the contract, but the claimant chose to wait to see if he would change his mind. The outbreak of the Crimean War then frustrated the contract and the claimant no longer had any right to sue. The contract from which his rights had been derived had ceased to exist.

Actual breach

This occurs when performance is due, or in the course of performance. It takes one of two forms: a failure to tender any form of performance, or performance which is so inadequate that it largely destroys the purpose of the contract. An example of the latter occurred in December 1994, when passengers on the *QE2* were transported to New York while the ship was still in the process of refitting; the ship resembled a construction site rather than a luxury liner. Although the passengers were delivered to their destination on the correct date, the conditions under which they had travelled were so appalling that their contractual expectations were largely defeated. There is little doubt that a court would treat such poor performance as amounting to a breach of condition. A very high standard of comfort, with access to the facilities to be expected on such a trip, is central to such a contract. Cunard immediately offered all the passengers a full refund of their fares. (See *Jarvis* v *Swan Tours*, below at page 133.)

REMEDIES FOR BREACH OF CONTRACT

The most common remedy for breach is damages, but some equitable remedies are sometimes appropriate.

Damages

The purpose of damages is to compensate the injured party for loss or damage arising from the breach. The court awards a sum which is aimed at putting the injured party in the financial position which he or she would have enjoyed if the contract had been performed. To do this the court must assess the damage alleged to result from the breach and decide whether any of it is too *remote*. It may not be justifiable to blame defendants for *all* the results of their actions, which may be knock-on effects of the breach. Having decided how much of the damage is attributable to the defendant, the court must decide on the *quantum* of damage, i.e. determine how much money the damage is worth.

Remoteness of damage

Hadley v Baxendale (1854)
The defendant contracted to carry the claimant's mill shaft from Gloucester to London, where it was to be used as a pattern to construct a new one. Due to the fault of the defendant, there was a considerable delay in the return of the shaft. The claimant claimed damages for his lost profits due to the mill being out of action. It was held that the defendant was not liable for this loss because it was too remote. There was nothing to alert him to the problem, since the claimant had not indicated that failure to return the shaft within the promised time limit would produce this result.

In *Hadley* v *Baxendale*, the court distinguished between the two types of damage that might follow a breach: usual and non-usual damage.

1 *Usual damage.* The damage that anybody might reasonably anticipate would arise from a contract of the relevant kind. For example, breakage is an obvious hazard in a contract to transport china.

2 *Non-usual damage.* Damage which arises because of particular circumstances which will not necessarily be known to the other party, unless these are drawn explicitly or impliedly to that party's attention before the contract is made. For example, in a contract to transport china, failure to disclose that the delivery time is crucial to a highly profitable sale would prevent a claim for more than normal profits in the event of a late delivery.

The following cases illustrate how these principles may be applied.

Victoria Laundry v Newman Industries Ltd (1949, CA)
Victoria Laundry, wishing to extend its business, asked the defendant to deliver a boiler by a stated date in June. Delivery did not take place until November, due to damage caused by the defendant. Due to this delay, the claimant was unable to take on some particularly lucrative dyeing contracts. The defendant knew that expansion of the business would be delayed if the boiler was not promptly delivered. It was, therefore, held liable for the profits that would have resulted from the use of the boiler between June and November. However, the defendant knew nothing about the dyeing contracts, so it was not liable for those losses.

Koufos v Czarnikow Ltd (The Heron II) (1969, HL)
The defendants contracted to carry a cargo of sugar for the claimants. They knew that the claimants were sugar merchants and that there was a sugar market at the destination port. Due to delay caused by the defendants, the sugar was sold at a

loss. It was held that the claimants were entitled to recover their lost profits because of the defendants' knowledge of the nature and purpose of the contract. This should have alerted them to the consequences of delay.

The remoteness rule in contract is more stringent than the reasonable foreseeability test in tort, because of the parties' relationship to each other. When negotiating a contract, the parties have the opportunity to discuss risk allocation, and may refuse to do business if this cannot be resolved satisfactorily.

Quantum of damages

When establishing the financial value of the claimant's loss, the court is governed by a number of criteria:

1 the loss must be financially quantifiable;

2 agreed damages will not be altered, but penalty sums will not be enforced:

3 the injured party has a duty to mitigate any loss;

4 contributory negligence may reduce the amount of damages.

1 Quantifiable damage

It must be possible to assess the loss to the injured party in financial terms. This is easy where goods are damaged, since the costs of repair or replacement are easily verified. The usual measure of damages for breach of a building contract is usually the cost of reinstatement (correcting the defect) rather than the diminution in value of the end product, but this is subject to exceptions in the interest of producing a just result.

Ruxley Electronics & Construction Ltd v Forsyth (1995)
A contract to build a garden swimming pool specified that it would be 7 foot 6 inches at its deepest part, but on completion it was found to be 9 inches shallower and 18 inches shallower at the point where diving would take place. It was held that reinstatement damages were unreasonable here as they would be 'out of all proportion to the benefit to be obtained'. Ruxley was entitled to £2500 for loss of amenity.

Claims for loss of profit are common in contract. Under s 50 of the Sale of Goods Act 1979, a buyer who refuses to take delivery of goods may be liable to the seller for any loss on the resale of the goods due to fluctuation of the market price.

A party may also recover *reliance losses*: expenses incurred while preparing to perform a contract which never takes place due to the breach of the other party.

Anglia TV v Reed (1971)

Christopher Reed, who unlawfully repudiated a contract to appear in a film, was held liable for the costs Anglia TV had incurred in preparing for the production.

Other damages are less easily quantifiable. Where a party suffers personal injuries, his or her resulting financial losses may also often be calculated with reasonable accuracy. There are, though, some rather arbitrary rules which exist to enable the court to compensate for non-financial losses like physical pain and suffering.

Until recently, the courts were reluctant to award damages for mental distress, hurt feelings and disappointment.

Addis v Gramophone (1909, HL)

It was held that damages were not available to compensate for the claimant's hurt feelings and distress at being wrongfully dismissed, nor for the fact that the mode of his dismissal made it difficult for him to obtain future employment.

This principle was for many years deemed to apply to all contracts but a number of distinctions and exceptions have gradually developed.

Damages may be awarded for loss of reputation:

Aerial Advertising Co. v Batchelors Peas (1938)

The defendant had contracted to advertise the claimant's product by flying an aircraft with a suitably worded banner over a number of locations. In breach of the contract, the defendant flew the aircraft over Salford during the two-minute silence on Remembrance Day. People were so scandalised by this disrespectful behaviour that Batchelors suffered a boycott of their product and damages were awarded for the damage to their reputation.

The House of Lords recently developed the concept of *stigma damages*.

Malik v Bank of Credit & Commerce International (1998, HL)

The defendant bank went into liquidation after its dishonesty and corrupt dealings emerged. The claimant, an ex-employee, was awarded damages for the losses he incurred, caused by a continuing difficulty in securing employment, because of the misdeeds of his previous employer.

The House of Lords held that *Addis* did not apply here. This was not a distress claim. Malik's claim could succeed on the grounds that the bank were in breach of

▶

the employment contract. Employer and employee have a mutual duty of trust and confidence. Failing to conduct business honestly was a breach of this. (See Chapter 18 below at page 265.)

Distress losses are now recoverable in contracts with *consumers*, where the *purpose* of the contract is to provide *peace of mind and freedom from distress*, but where the breach which has occurred has produced the opposite result.

Jarvis v Swan Tours (1973, CA)
When he bought a skiing holiday package, Mr Jarvis was promised a houseparty atmosphere with full bar facilities, a welcome party, afternoon tea and cakes, and a yodeller evening. There were only 13 guests in the first week. During the second week Mr Jarvis was the only guest. The yodeller turned up in working clothes, and sang only a few songs. The afternoon tea consisted of crisps and dry nut cakes. The bar was open on one evening only and the skiing facilities were very poor.

Mr Jarvis was held to be entitled to damages for his disappointment at the absence of all the promised facilities which were central to the contract's performance, and recovered the full cost of his holiday.

Heywood v Wellers (1976)
The claimant contracted with the defendant solicitor to obtain an injunction to prevent her ex-boyfriend from harassing her. Due to the solicitor's negligence the procedure failed and she continued to be molested. Damages were awarded for her distress since the entire purpose of the contract was to prevent this occurring.

Even where the court is not prepared to categorise a contract as one for peace of mind, it may award damages for distress directly resulting from physical inconvenience caused by the breach.

Perry v Sidney Phillips (1982, CA)
The defendant, who was under contract to the Perrys to survey premises they wished to buy, overlooked roofing faults and a defective septic tank. Once they moved in the need for repairs became evident, especially as the smell from the septic tank was causing nuisance to the neighbours. The court refused to categorise an ordinary surveyor's contract as one for peace of mind and freedom from distress. However, damages were awarded for the distress arising from the physical inconvenience of the execution of the repairs.

Cases since the late 1990s generally indicate greater readiness by the courts to recognise peace of mind obligations in contracts. In *Farley* v *Skinner (No. 2)* below the House of Lords held that the particular circumstances of the contract should determine whether it placed such obligations on the surveyor.

Farley v Skinner (No. 2) (2001, HL)
The claimant specifically requested the defendant to advise whether the property he was interested in buying was badly affected by aircraft noise from Gatwick airport.
    The claimant was awarded £10 000 when the surveyor's favourable report proved inaccurate. It was sufficient that a major or important part of the contract was to give peace of mind, pleasure or relaxation, for recovery of such damages to be permissible.

2 Liquidated damages and penalties

It is quite common for a contract to specify that in the event of a breach, a sum of agreed or *liquidated* damages will be payable. If the court is satisfied that this sum represents a genuine attempt by the parties to determine a reasonable pre-estimate of the loss likely to result from such a breach, that sum will be awarded *whether or not* it represents an appropriate level of compensation. If the sum is not adequate, the injured party cannot claim more, since it contractually agreed to accept it. If it is more than necessary, the injured party does not have to return the difference. However, the court is *not* prepared to enforce a sum that is held to represent a *penalty*, i.e. a punishment to be suffered by the guilty party if it fails to perform its obligations, rather than an appropriate level of compensation. The object of awarding damages in contract is to compensate an injured party, not punish the defaulter. If the court decides that the sum represents a penalty, this will be disregarded; instead a sum will be awarded which is representative of the injured party's actual loss. In the following case, Lord Dunedin proposed the following tests to distinguish between liquidated damages and penalties:

1 the words used to describe the sum are evidence of what the parties intended but are not conclusive;

2 the sum should be treated as a penalty, if grossly disproportionate to the greatest damage likely to result from the breach;

3 where the breach consists of a failure to pay money, the prescribed sum is a penalty if it exceeds the sum payable;

4 where one sum is payable in the event of the commission of any of a number of different breaches, some of which are trifling and some of which are more serious, it is probably a penalty;

5 even if accurate pre-estimation is almost impossible, this does not prevent a sum from being treated as liquidated damages, as long as it represents a genuine attempt to make a reasonably accurate assessment.

Dunlop Pneumatic Tyre Co. Ltd v New Garage & Motor Co. Ltd (1915, HL)
Dunlop had a clause in its contract of sale which attempted to impose a minimum price restraint on resales of its tyres by New Garage. It stated that breach of this term would make New Garage liable to pay '£5 by way of liquidated damages for every tyre, cover or tube'. Their Lordships held that this sum was liquidated damages. It was impossible to forecast precisely the damage resulting from each sale in breach of the agreement and there was no reason to suspect that this was not a genuine bargain to assess damages. (Application of criterion 5 above.)

Since £5 was quite a substantial sum in 1915, this seems a rather surprising decision. Perhaps the House of Lords felt such a restraint was appropriate to the development of a new area of the market.

3 The duty to mitigate

The injured party cannot claim the cost of damage which it could reasonably have avoided. It is up to the party in breach to prove that the damage was avoidable.

Brace v Calder (1895)
A clerk with a fixed contract of employment with the defendant's partnership lost his job when the partnership was dissolved. He attempted to claim the wages which would have been payable had his contract run for its remaining two years, but failed. The partnership had been immediately reformed and the partners had offered him a job on his old contractual terms, which he had refused. He had been given a perfect opportunity to mitigate his loss and had failed in his duty to do so.

Compare _Brace_ v _Calder_ with the following decision:

Pilkington v Wood (1953)
It was unreasonable to expect the claimant to take legal action against the seller of land to correct a defect in title which the defendant solicitor had negligently failed to notice when acting for the claimant during the purchase of the land.

4 Contributory negligence

It is possible that this may reduce the amount of damages awarded by the court. The Law Reform (Contributory Negligence) Act 1945, which regulates this defence in the law of tort, does not refer to contract liability. It is arguable whether in its current form it can legitimately be extended to cover contractual situations. The courts have been prepared to reduce damages where claimants' own lack of care has aggravated their loss. This appears to have been restricted to cases where a defendant is in breach of an obligation to act with reasonable care and skill which would entitle the claimant to sue in tort or contract. In 1993, the Law Commission recommended a new statute explicitly extending the defence to claims arising from any breach of a contractual duty to act with reasonable care and skill. So far Parliament has not implemented this recommendation.

Equitable remedies

A dominant characteristic of such remedies is that they are *discretionary*. The court has a choice whether or not to award them, unlike damages, which must be awarded if a party proves its case. A party may be refused access to an equitable remedy unless the court believes that it is just to *both* parties. The party claiming the remedy must show that:

1 damages would not be an adequate remedy;

2 he or she acted completely honestly: dishonest, though legal, behaviour will defeat a claim.

For example, the seller of a house has no legal duty to declare its defects unless asked. If, however, a seller knowingly failed to disclose such defects, a decree of specific performance would not be awarded against a buyer who discovered the defects later and refused to perform his or her contractual obligations.

Imposition of the equitable remedy must not be unnecessarily oppressive to the other party.

The victim of a breach of contract may find the following remedies helpful:

1 rescission;

2 specific performance;

3 injunction.

Rescission

The court sets the contract aside and restores the parties to their pre-contractual positions. Note that the courts are more generous to a breach victim than to a party who claims rescission on other grounds, like misrepresentation. Rescission may be granted in a breach action even though the party at fault cannot be restored to his or her pre-contractual position, for example, where the victim of the breach has consumed the goods.

Specific performance

The court orders a party to perform their contractual obligations. Specific performance is rarely granted except in relation to contracts for the sale of land. It will never be granted to enforce a *contract of employment*; it would be an unreasonable restriction of personal liberty to enforce such a contract. It is also unlikely that the outcome of such enforced performance would be satisfactory. A sale of goods contract concerning a unique item, like a rare antique or a work of art, might attract the remedy. Generally damages are regarded as adequate, as the buyer can obtain similar goods elsewhere.

Cohen v Roche (1927)
A contract to sell a set of Hepplewhite chairs was held not to be specifically enforceable since the chairs were regarded as 'ordinary articles of commerce'.

Specific performance is unlikely to be granted to enforce a *continuing obligation* which requires continuing supervision.

Ryan v Mutual Tontine Association (1893)
Specific performance was held not to be appropriate to enforce a requirement in a lease relating to the provision of a janitor in full-time attendance at a block of flats.

Specific performance has been used to enforce a *debt owed by a third party* to the estate of a third party.

Beswick v Beswick (1968)
A contract between Peter and John Beswick, under which John promised Peter that he would pay an annuity to Peter's wife after Peter's death, was enforceable by Peter's widow as she was the administrator of her husband's estate. (As she was not privy to the contract between Peter and John, she had no rights to sue on it on her own behalf: see Chapter 5.) Although the estate itself had suffered no loss through the breach, the court awarded specific performance of the contract to prevent John from getting away with the breach.

Injunction

This is a commonly requested remedy for breach of restraint of trade contracts (see Chapter 8). It will not be granted to force one party to employ or work for another, as this would amount to specifically enforcing a contract of employment.

Page One Records v Britton (1968)
An injunction would not be granted to restrain The Troggs (a pop group) from employing a new manager, since this would force them to go on employing the claimant.

But compare *Page One Records* v *Britton* with the following case.

> **Warner Bros v Nelson** (1936)
> The film star, Bette Davis (Nelson), breached her contract under which she had agreed not to act on stage or screen for anybody except Warner Bros for one year, by agreeing to make a film with a UK company. An injunction was granted to restrain Bette Davis from making films for the rival company. The contract restrained her from acting for anyone other than Warner, but did not prevent her from earning her living in other ways. The injunction did not force her to perform the contract if she was prepared to earn her living in a less profitable way.

Quiz 9

1 Is Flannel discharged from his contractual obligations in the following circumstances?

  (a) He delivers 50 kilos of turnips to Denim who had ordered 70 kilos, and:

    (i) the turnips were costed at 50 pence per kilo, or

    (ii) the turnips were costed at £250 for 50 kilos, but Denim agrees to take the smaller order.

  (b) He contracts to decorate Wool's house. When the work is half complete, Wool refuses to let him in.

2 On 1 May, Chambray contracted to hire his vintage Rolls-Royce to Linen on 30 May. On 15 May, Chambray tells Linen that he is not prepared to supply the car on the due date. Linen says he will wait and see if Chambray will change his mind. On 29 May, Chambray's chauffeur writes off the car. What is the legal position? What difference would it make to your answer if the accident had already happened at the point Chambray and Linen made the contract?

3 Distinguish between the concepts of remoteness and quantum of damage.

4 When may the court refuse to award a decree of specific performance?

Assignment 8

What is the legal effect of the following clauses in General Terms and Conditions?

(a) Neither party shall be liable for failure to perform its obligations under this contract if such failure results from events beyond the control of that party, and which could not have been foreseen by either party.

(10 marks)

(b) Where there is any delay of the goods, the purchaser reserves the right to cancel the contract, and in such an event, to charge the seller by way of liquidated damages, 20% of the purchase price.

(15 marks)

(CIPS Legal Applications: May 1992)

CHAPTER 10

Tort liability for defective goods

INTRODUCTION

A tort is a civil wrong independent of contract. The law of tort imposes duties at civil law in respect of a wide range of behaviour relevant to business activity. This area of the law has a particular importance for consumers and those doing business with them.

Rights in contract are not sufficient to protect all consumers. The law of contract protects only the buyer of the defective goods or services. Other people harmed by defects in the goods will not be able to sue in contract because of the lack of privity of contract between themselves and the seller. Even a buyer may not be adequately protected if it has effectively become impossible to recover from a seller who has gone out of business.

Both the buying and non-buying consumer may be protected by the law of tort, as may any other person adversely affected by a product. This chapter is concerned with situations where parties suffer loss or damage due to defective products, and explains their rights in negligence and under the Consumer Protection Act 1987.

NEGLIGENCE LIABILITY

The tort of negligence gives rights to persons who have suffered damage to themselves or to their property, as against a party who has failed to take reasonable care for those persons' safety. Negligence is the commonest tort claim and is relevant to the whole gamut of accidental injury situations: for example, road accidents, illness and injuries caused by workplace conditions and harm arising through medical treatment. It also plays an important part in product liability: a person who suffers damage because of defects in a product caused by the carelessness of the manufacturer or other party responsible for the state of the goods, may have a right to sue in negligence.

To be successful in a claim of negligence the claimant must prove that:

1 the defendant owed the claimant a duty of care; and

2 failed to perform that duty; and

3 as a result, the claimant suffered damage.

The duty of care

The claimant must be able to show that he or she is someone who, in the circumstances, the defendant should have had in mind when embarking on the course of conduct which led to the alleged damage (or the accident). This concept was established by the House of Lords in the following key case.

> ### Donoghue v Stevenson (1932, HL)
> Mrs Donoghue and a friend stopped for refreshment at a café one hot afternoon. The friend purchased from the proprietor some ginger beer manufactured by the defendant. This was supplied in stone bottles which were opened at the table. Having happily consumed a glassful, Mrs Donoghue tipped the bottle to make sure nothing was left; to her horror the decomposing remains of a snail slithered into her glass. She consequently became ill with gastro-enteritis and sued Stevenson (the manufacturer) in negligence. By a majority, the House of Lords held that the manufacturer did owe Mrs Donoghue a duty of care. As she was the user of its product, she was somebody who reasonably foreseeably would be affected by the way the manufacturer processed its product.

This case established a general principle of product liability in negligence. Under the 'neighbour principle', manufacturers of goods owe a duty of care to the 'ultimate consumer' of the product. Mrs Donoghue is the perfect example of an ultimate consumer – the actual user of the defective goods who is harmed by the defects, but who is not necessarily the buyer. Had the House of Lords not found that Mrs Donoghue had a right to sue, she would have had no right to take any legal action; she could not have sued the café proprietor since she had no contract with him. Her friend could have sued him in contract, but would have obtained damages only for the loss she herself suffered, namely the cost of the ginger beer.

It is not just a manufacturer who owes a duty of care. Anybody who services goods before sale, or a supplier with responsibility for testing or checking goods, may be liable.

Consumers need not have been actually using the goods at the point of suffering injury. If the use was reasonably likely to affect them, they will be owed a duty, since the supplier should have taken their needs into account.

> ### Barnett v Packer (1940)
> A shop assistant laying out chocolates for display was injured by a wire protruding from them. It was held that anybody handling the chocolates could have suffered injury from this foreign body, therefore, the manufacturer owed a duty of care to the shop assistant, as well as to people who ate the goods.

Even a bystander with no relationship to a party to the original transaction may come within the neighbour principle.

> **Stennett v Hancock** (1939)
> The claimant, a pedestrian, suffered a leg injury when he was hit by a piece of a wheel which came off a passing lorry. He was held to have been owed a duty by the garage which had recently fitted the wheel.

The product includes the packaging and instructions. The goods may be perfectly safe but become dangerous because not appropriately packaged, or because they do not carry correct instructions or a warning.

The limits of the duty of care

> **Marc Rich & Co. AG v Bishop Rock Marine** (1995, HL)
> The House of Lords held that when deciding whether a duty of care exists in any negligence action, the court must take into account whether the following criteria are satisfied:
>
> 1 reasonable foreseeability
>
> 2 proximity
>
> 3 justice and reason.
>
> These factors are interlinked and interdependent.

1 *Reasonable foreseeability.* No duty of care will exist unless it is *reasonably foreseeable* that the particular claimant was vulnerable to the risk created by the defendant. For example, in *Stennett* v *Hancock* (above) it was reasonably foreseeable that if the lorry wheel was not securely fitted, an accident endangering any pedestrian in the vicinity might result.

2 *Proximity.* There must be a close enough relationship between the defendant's acts and the claimant at the time of the wrong complained of. As Lord Atkin said in *Donoghue* v *Stevenson*, the claimant must be 'closely and directly affected' by the defendant's actions. In the following circumstances such *proximity* is lacking.

   (a) *The goods are not under the control of the defendant.* The control of the defendant ceases if, prior to use, the goods have been tampered with or examined in such a way as to be likely to cause or reveal a defect. Tampering or inspection may be carried out by a third party or the claimant. Remember that in *Donoghue* v *Stevenson* the ginger beer was supplied to Mrs Donoghue in an opaque bottle which was opened in Mrs Donoghue's presence. There was no possibility that its unwanted inhabitant could have got there through the intervention of a third party. The bottle arrived at the table in the same state as when it left the manufacturer. The stone bottle prevented the hazard from being detected by a third party.

(b) *Too much time has elapsed since the product left the defendant.* Whether the goods have been used or not, it would be unfair to place the manufacturer under a duty for an indefinite time.

Evans v Triplex Glass (1936)

Mr Evans bought a new Vauxhall car fitted by the manufacturer with a windscreen made of toughened safety glass manufactured by Triplex. One year later he and his family were injured during a car journey when the windscreen shattered and disintegrated. It was held that Triplex did not owe Evans a duty of care because:

- too much time had elapsed between the product leaving their control and the accident – the glass could have been weakened in use;

- a defect might have been detectable on inspection by Vauxhall prior to fitting. Any weakness might have been caused by Vauxhall when fitting the windscreen.

(c) *The claimant has failed to take reasonable precautions prior to or when using the product.* A claimant must be able to show that the product has been used appropriately, in accordance with instructions.

3 *Justice and reason.* A duty will exist only when it is believed to be in the *public interest.* In *Donoghue* v *Stevenson*, public health considerations made it desirable to impose a duty, as well as the fact that Mrs Donoghue had no other legal rights to pursue. It is not usually regarded as just and reasonable to impose a duty of care where the defect results in *pure economic loss.* Such loss, which is derived from the goods being defective rather than dangerous, merely causes the claimant to be out of pocket. Such losses are seen by the courts as contractual only. This is not helpful to a party who did not buy the goods in the first place. These principles are clearly illustrated by the following example:

Horace was given an electric blanket for Christmas by his Aunt Betty. Due to a design defect, it set fire to his bedroom on Christmas night and caused damage to carpets and furniture. Horace was made ill due to smoke inhalation. He is entitled to claim damages from the blanket manufacturer for:

1 the pain and suffering caused by the smoke inhalation;

2 any loss of earnings while he recuperated and the cost of replacing furnishings and decorating his bedroom. These are the knock-on costs of the damage caused by the defendant's negligence and are described as *consequential economic loss*.

Horace would not be entitled to recover the cost of replacing the defective electric blanket, which is categorised as pure economic loss; *the defect* does not of itself give rise to liability of the manufacturer in negligence. It is *the physical damage to person or other property* which imposes the duty. The lack of *quality* in the goods does not in itself give rise to negligence liability.

This issue is illustrated by the following case.

Muirhead v Industrial Tank Specialities Ltd (1986)
The claimant, who ran a lobster farm, was supplied through a contract with a third party with oxygen pumps manufactured by the defendant. They proved to be unsuitable for use with the English electricity system and kept cutting out. The claimant's lobsters died and he was unable to restock for a substantial period of time while he attempted to work out what was wrong. It was held that he was entitled to recover the cost of restocking the lobsters and for the loss of profits on those that died. He was *not* entitled to recover for profits lost during the time that lobster production was suspended, or the cost of replacing the pumps since these were pure economic losses only.

Exceptionally, the claimant might be able to claim for pure economic loss if it can be shown that the claimant obtained the goods after having personally and directly consulted the manufacturers and placed reliance on their expertise.

Junior Books v Veitchi (1982, HL)
Junior Books made a contract for the construction of a warehouse. They told the building contractor that they wanted flooring to be supplied by the defendant, who was consequently a nominated sub-contractor. The defendant had no contract with the claimant. The flooring was so defective that the warehouse was unusable until the floor was replaced. It was held that the claimant's reliance on the defendant's expertise was sufficient to bring the parties into close proximity, and so a duty of care existed.

Veitchi was not applicable in the *Muirhead* case as Muirhead had not nominated the manufacturer to his supplier. The court usually takes the view that a contract between the claimant and supplier provides the appropriate route to compensation.

The supplier should have been able to negotiate terms to give himself or herself adequate protection, or if this is not workable, to insure against possible pure economic losses, such as business interruption.

The claimant must prove breach of duty

The claimant must prove that by objective standards the defendant failed to take reasonable care, i.e. did not provide a reasonable level of protection against reasonably foreseeable accidents. This includes taking into account the particular needs of a target group and giving adequate warning or instructions about the use of the product. For example, a soft toy manufacturer must consider that small users of its teddy bears may indeed literally try to consume them; it must ensure that non-toxic materials are used and that the bears' eyes and noses are very firmly attached.

The claimant must prove consequential damage

The claimant must prove that it was the defendant's breach of duty which actually caused the damage suffered. In the story of Horace and the electric blanket outlined earlier, Horace would not be successful despite proof of a defect in the blanket making it a fire risk, if there was evidence that the fire was actually caused by defective wiring in Horace's house.

Defendants are not necessarily liable for all the consequences of their behaviour: some may be deemed *too remote* from their original act. In negligence a defendant is generally liable for all reasonably foreseeable damage, but not for highly improbable or fluke results.

These issues are explored in greater depth in the next chapter.

THE CONSUMER PROTECTION ACT 1987 (PART I)

The Consumer Protection Act 1987 (CPA), which was enacted to implement the EC Product Liability Directive (374/85/EC), has introduced a measure of strict liability for defective products.

The difference between fault and strict liability

Most torts, including negligence, are based on fault liability. The claimant has to prove not only that the defendant's behaviour broke the law and caused damage, but also that the defendant either intended to cause harm to the claimant, or was blameworthy in overlooking the risk to the claimant.

Strict liability is exceptional in tort. Where it exists the claimant is relieved of the need to prove any intent or carelessness on the part of the defendant; the claimant merely has to prove the causal link between the defendant's tortious behaviour and the damage suffered. This may increase the claimant's chances of a successful claim, as proof of failure to take care is often problematic.

Cases involving injuries caused by the side-effects of drugs like Thalidomide raised public perception of the problems caused by fault liability and encouraged recommendations for reform from the Pearson Commission of 1978, as well as from judges and pressure groups. These recommendations were ignored by successive governments and change came only after intervention by the EC prompted the enactment of the CPA.

Part I of the Act is concerned with civil liability. Part II, which is concerned with criminal liability, is discussed in Chapter 13.

The main provisions of Part I of the Consumer Protection Act

The potential claimant: s 5

Any person hurt or suffering damage to his or her *private* (not business) property may claim under the Act.

Methods of supply: s 46

The goods may have been supplied by way of sale, barter, hire, prize or gift. The supplier must have been acting in the course of business.

Potential defendants: s 2

Section 2(1) provides that 'where any damage is caused wholly or partly by a defect in a product', the following persons shall be liable:

1 *The producer*. This includes the manufacturer and persons responsible for winning or abstracting a product, for example mineral water or electricity.

2 *The marker*. Where goods are marketed under an 'own brand' label (like many supermarket goods) the company or firm whose name appears on the label is treated as a producer.

3 *The importer*. The party who initially imported the product into the EU may be liable. (This is not necessarily the party responsible for the goods entering the UK.)

4 *The supplier*. Suppliers are liable only if they fail, on request from the injured party, to identify the manufacturer, producer or importer.

The meaning of 'product': s 1

This includes packaging and instructions and potentially covers a huge variety of products.

1 *Manufactured products*. This includes components of another product.

2 *'Substances won or abstracted'*. This includes things like electricity and water.

3 *Things which owe their 'essential characteristics' to an 'industrial or other process'*.

Agricultural products, which were not originally covered by the Act unless they had been subjected to an industrial process, have been included since a 1999 EU Directive was implemented in the UK.

A and Others v National Blood Authority (2001)
Blood and blood products supplied by the defendant were 'products' within the meaning of s 1 and had been subject to an industrial process.

It is unclear whether the Act covers intellectual property, such as books and computer programs. It would be possible for information transmitted in this form to cause harm through its defects. A book on fungi might incorrectly describe a species as edible, with disastrous consequences. There is medical evidence which suggests that some computer games may trigger fits and migraine. Unless and until such matters are conclusively determined by the courts this will remain an uncertain area.

Defective means dangerous: s 3

The product is not defective unless it is unsafe: there is no liability unless it actually causes damage to the consumer or the consumer's property. The standard of safety under the Act is that which people 'generally are entitled to expect'. The following factors are relevant in deciding whether this standard has been met:

1 *The packaging and any warnings or instructions.* A medicine may be perfectly safe in and of itself, but rendered dangerous because it lacks clear instructions or a warning that it is unsuitable for people with certain medical conditions.

2 *The normal uses of the product.* The needs of the relevant class of consumer must be taken into account in deciding whether the manufacturer has rendered the product safe. Toys marketed for use by small children require different safety standards, in relation to things like sharp edges, non-toxic materials and the size of removable parts, than goods for the entertainment of adults. If the consumer is harmed by use of the product for purposes which are not normal, liability does not arise. By indicating the purpose of a product and the age group for which it is intended, the manufacturer may limit the 'normal use' of the product.

3 *The time when the product was issued.* This is relevant to issues like shelf life, or situations where the product met appropriate standards of safety when issued but current research now indicates that those standards were not high enough.

Actionable damage: s 5

This covers death, personal injuries and damage to property (including land) which the claimant is *not* using for business purposes. A claim for property damage must be for at least £275.

Area of law	Contract	Tort	Tort
	Sale of Goods Act 1979 (SGA) Supply of Goods and Services Act 1982 (SGSA)	Negligence	Consumer Protection Act 1987
Who can sue?	Buyer only	Injured party (ultimate consumer)	Injured party
Who can be sued?	Seller	Manufacturer of goods Servicer of goods Supplier – if duty to inspect	Producer of product Manufacturer Own-brand labeller Importer Supplier
What must be proved?	Goods – breach of ss 13, 14, 15 SGA 1979 Goods and services – breach of s 4 & s 5 SGSA 1982 Goods – like SGA Services – lack of reasonable care and skill, reasonable timeliness and reasonable charging	(i) Duty of care (ii) Breach of duty (iii) Consequent damage	(i) Product defective and unsafe (ii) Damage suffered as result
Damage compensated	Any loss or damage to buyer as long as not too remote, including purchase price	Any loss or damage to injured party as long as not too remote; excluding purchase price and other pure economic loss	Death/personal injuries Damage to land, goods (over £275)
Liability	Goods – strict Services – fault Civil only	Fault Civil only	Strict Criminal liability also possible

Figure 10.1 Liability for defective products

Since pure economic loss is not recoverable, the cost of replacing or repairing the defective item cannot be claimed. The same principles apply here as in negligence.

Causation and liability: s 2

The claimant must prove that the defect was the cause of the damage claimed. *Liability is strict*: the claimant does not have to prove that the defendant was careless, merely that the product comes within the statutory meaning of defective.

Defences

Under s 4 of the Act, the defendant will have a defence if able to show the following:

1 The goods comply with EC or UK safety standards and the defect is attributable to compliance with those standards.

2 The goods became defective after they were supplied. The defendant is liable only if the defect is present when the goods are put in circulation. If it arises later due to use or abuse by the consumer or a third party, the defendant is not liable.

3 The 'state of the art/developments risk' defence. This is a special defence under the Act which potentially undermines the strict liability element. The defendant will not be liable if it can be shown that when the product was released the defendant had done all that was required to fulfil safety standards in accordance with current research and technological expertise, and in consequence the defect was not discoverable.

   This defence is meant to be a safeguard for manufacturers of new products. It is argued that without it important new product development, with great potential benefit to the public, might be restricted by manufacturers fearful of litigation.

4 That the defendant did not at any time supply the product to another in the course of business.

Contributory negligence and consent are also relevant. These are examined at the end of Chapter 12.

Time limits

Under the Limitation Act 1980, s 11A, claimants must take action within three years of the date when they first became aware of the damage, the defect, and the identity of the defendant. There is a final cut-off date of ten years from the date on which the product was supplied to the claimant and no action can be started after that time.

The impact of the Consumer Protection Act

As cases emerged some commentators perceived that the way in which the law was being interpreted seemed to provide no more protection for claimants than an action in negligence. This was a concern since the Product Liability Directive had indicated that its purpose was to enable claimants to avoid the need to prove fault by the defendant, thus overcoming one of the main obstacles to a successful claim. The Act (s 1) stated that it was intended to comply with the Directive.

European Commission v UK (1997, EC)
The Commission claimed that the UK was failing in its obligations to implement the purpose of the Directive with respect to the concept of a defective product and the scope of the state of the art defence.

The European Court of Justice stressed the need for the Act to be construed in accordance with the purpose of the Directive and that the Directive must prevail in the event of conflict.

Two subsequent judgments since this case clearly reflect this approach.

Abouzaid v Mothercare (UK) Ltd (2001, CA)
The claimant who was 12 years old was blinded in one eye while attempting to attach the defendant's product (a Cosytoes sleeping bag) to his little brother's push chair. An elastic fastening strap sprang from his hand and the attached buckle struck his eye.

It was held that the product was defective under s 3. The reasonable expecta-tions of the public that the product was safe to use were not satisfied, given the vulnerability of the eye and potential seriousness of such injuries. There was a risk attached to use of the product but no warning was given to the user to avoid the risk. The fact that no injuries had previously been reported and the unlikelihood of serious damage to the face, indicated that the defendants were not negligent. How-ever, this was irrelevant to a claim under the Act where proof that the product was defective was what was needed to establish liability.

In the next case the judge constantly referred to the Directive for assistance in inter-preting the meaning of defective product and the scope of the state of the art defence.

A and Others v National Blood Authority (2001)
The claimants contracted Hepatitis C after being given transfusions of contami-nated blood products supplied by the defendant.

It was held that the product was defective under the Act. The claimants did not have to prove fault or negligence, merely that the product did not meet the reason-able expectations of the public to be safe for any foreseeable use. A reasonable person would expect that blood used for transfusion would not be infected.

> Both the Act and the Directive required the court to take into account 'all the circumstances attendant upon the reasonable person's expectations of safety'. These did not include the questions of whether the defendant could have avoided the danger, nor whether this would have been impracticable, costly or difficult.
>
> The state of the art defence should be narrowly interpreted in order to avoid defeating the purpose of the Directive. It only protects the defendant against unknown risks in the context of the most advanced available knowledge which should have been accessible to the defendant.

These cases provide a more level playing field for the consumer, the party the Directive was aiming to assist. It can also be seen as a sensible loss distribution system since the losses of the claimant are made the responsibility of the manufacturer who sought to make a profit from their product. The manufacturer is not unreasonably burdened as the losses are insurable and that cost passed on to the consumers.

Quiz 10

1 What must a claimant in an action for negligence prove?

2 In an action for negligence, what factors are important to proof of duty of care?

3 What circumstances may bring a duty of care for defective goods to an end?

4 Basil buys a pork pie from Tarragon Stores. The pie was manufactured by Marjoram Foods. Basil shares the pie with Rosemary and they both become ill. What are the civil law rights of Basil and Rosemary?

5 What are the main differences between liability for negligence and liability under the Consumer Protection Act 1987?

Assignment 9

Handyman plc is a recently established company which specialises in manufacturing and selling goods in the 'Do It Yourself' range. Consider its liability in tort, including Part I of the Consumer Protection Act 1987, in the following, alternative circumstances. In all cases it may be assumed that Handyman has exercised all reasonable care:

(a) Handyman manufactures and supplies a wood preserving fluid which causes skin cancer in a number of users. It is accepted that this side-effect is utterly unpredictable in the state of scientific knowledge at the time of supply.

(b) Handyman buys in some ladders, importing them from a Far East manufacturer and selling them through its retail outlets, labelled 'Produced for Handyman'. One such ladder collapses and injures its user, Peter.

(c) Handyman manufactures and sells washing machines. One such washing machine, which is virtually new, is being used in a luxury residential property belonging to Max, who also owns the machine, when it fails, causing water to flood down into Paul's flat which is situated immediately beneath. The flat requires extensive decoration and Paul's personal computer, which he uses in his professional capacity as an architect, is damaged beyond repair. The washing machine costs £75 to repair.

(ICSA English Business Law: December 1993)

A suggested solution for this assignment may be found in Appendix 2.

CHAPTER 11

Tort liability for defective services

INTRODUCTION

Any third party reasonably likely to be affected by the workmanship of a service provider is clearly owed a duty of care in negligence if he or she suffers personal injury or damage to property. A central heating engineer will, therefore, owe a duty to people in a building who suffer carbon-monoxide poisoning from the system which the engineer negligently installed.

Sometimes there may be a large pool of potential claimants. The garage which services your car owes a duty of care to carry out the work safely not only to you, but to your passengers as well as other road users and pedestrians in the vicinity of your vehicle when it is in use. However, the law is unwilling to make defendants vulnerable to every possible claim of damage resulting from their negligent behaviour. Liability in negligence is greatly restricted by the courts in some situations. The problem of recovering pure economic loss was mentioned in the preceding chapter. There are also a number of other problematic duty situations relating to negligent statements, shock-induced injuries and damage caused by third parties. These may be relevant to the delivery of services and are explained below.

PROBLEMATIC DUTY SITUATIONS

In claims for damage outside the traditional scope of negligence, the three criteria relevant to existence of duty (reasonable foreseeability, proximity, justice and reason) may be stringently applied.

Pure economic loss

Negligence liability does not usually arise from the poor quality of a service, but from the physical damage to people and property caused by it. Any purely financial loss arising from defective performance is not generally recoverable.

Spartan Steel Alloys v Martin Ltd (1972, CA)
Early one morning the negligent operation of a power shovel outside the claimant's steelworks resulted in a power cut which put the furnace out of action for the rest of that day. The metal which had been in the furnace when the power was cut off was spoilt and no further consignments could be processed that day. The claimant successfully claimed for the cost of the spoilt metal and the proceeds which would normally have been made on its sale in good condition. Its claim for the lost profits on the melts which could not be processed that day was rejected, as it concerned pure economic loss: it did not result from any damage to the claimant's property.

Murphy v Brentwood Council (1990, HL)
The claimant's newly-built house subsided when the foundations turned out to be defective. As a result he had to sell the house for £35 000 less than its proper market value. He claimed that the local authority had been negligent in its checks on the foundations. The House of Lords held that the house was defective, but no personal injuries had been caused to Mr Murphy and none of his property had been damaged. The local authority did not owe a duty of care to the claimant, since his only loss was purely economic. There was insufficient proximity between the parties, since it was not reasonably foreseeable to the council that Mr Murphy would place reliance on its checks. It also was not just and reasonable to burden local taxpayers with homeowners' financial losses in such circumstances.

A different approach was used to justify imposing a duty of care in *White* v *Jones* (below).

White v Jones (1995, HL)
An elderly man, after a quarrel with his two daughters, cut them out of his will. Three months later he forgave them and informed his solicitor that he wished to make a new will under which the daughters were each to be given a legacy of £9000. Two months after giving his instructions he died, before the solicitor completed the necessary work. Due to this negligent delay, the daughters did not receive their inheritance. They successfully sued the solicitor. It was held that he was brought into a special relationship of close proximity with them. By agreeing to draft the will, he was deemed voluntarily to have accepted the responsibility for ensuring the creation of a valid will. It was reasonably foreseeable that the daughters would suffer pure economic loss if he failed to do so.

Note the different but equally valid criteria applied by the House of Lords for determining proximity in these cases:

- *Murphy* v *Brentwood Council*: reasonable reliance by the *claimant*;
- *White* v *Jones*: voluntary assumption of responsibility by the *defendant*.

In some cases both factors may be present (see, for example, *Hedley Byrne* v *Heller* below). The *White* v *Jones* approach is more realistic, where the defendant is asked by a third party to do something which affects the well-being of a claimant, who is unaware of the request and so cannot realistically be said to be placing reliance on the defendant.

Negligent statements

In principle, there is no difference between liability arising from negligent statements and from negligent acts. A party may suffer damage by reliance on incorrect advice just as he or she may be injured by other negligent conduct (see *T* v *Surrey County Council*, below). In practice, the duty is generally limited, because a negligent statement is likely to have more far-reaching effects than a negligent act. One snail-infested bottle of ginger beer will poison only one or two people, but a negligent statement may affect thousands and its effects may last a long time. The courts are not willing to make the defendant liable to potential claims from a large and unidentifiable class of persons, for an indefinable period of time.

Where a duty exists between the parties, there is liability for all forms of damage including pure economic loss. The duty arises from the claimant's close relationship to or reliance on the defendant. This relationship must satisfy the three-stage duty test.

Proximity

The parties must have been brought sufficiently into a close relationship with each other. A high degree of trust will be involved. In *Hedley Byrne* (below) it was described as 'quasi-fiduciary' and 'akin to contract'.

1 *The statement is made directly to the claimant by the defendant*

Hedley Byrne v Heller (1963, HL)
An advertising agency was given a reference from a client's bank which incorrectly represented the client's creditworthiness. The House of Lords held that there could be a duty not to make a statement carelessly which causes economic loss.

2 *The statement is made to a third party who passes it on to the claimant*

Smith v Eric S. Bush (1989, HL)
The defendant surveyors' valuation report prepared for a building society was shown with their knowledge to the claimant buyer. It was held that the defendants owed a duty of care to the claimant.

3 *The statement may be made to a third party who relies upon it thus causing consequent loss to the claimant*

T v Surrey County Council (1994)
T was injured by the actions of a childminder negligently recommended to his mother by the defendant council. It was held that the council owed a duty of care to T.

Reasonable foreseeability

Defendants will not be liable unless they should reasonably have foreseen that the claimant would reasonably rely on the statement and voluntarily assumed responsibility for it. The House of Lords has indicated criteria helpful to establishing this (*Hedley Byrne* v *Heller*, 1963):

1 *The defendant's ability to give reliable advice.* Specialist knowledge, professional qualifications or other expertise are all relevant.

2 *The circumstances in which the advice was given.* Specialist advice cannot reasonably be relied on when given off the cuff, or on a purely social occasion. Even if given in a business context, it may not be reasonable to rely on it if it is given without proper checks on relevant data.

3 *Disclaimer or condition.* If the defendant indicates expressly or impliedly that the advice should not be relied upon, this may make the claimant's reliance unreasonable and, therefore, not reasonably foreseeable. The Unfair Contract Terms Act 1977 makes it impossible to exclude liability for negligence for death or personal injuries. Liability for negligence may be excluded for other damage or loss if reasonable.

In *Caparo* v *Dickman* (1990), the House of Lords tightened the rules to prevent a defendant from being potentially liable to a large and unascertainable group of people. This is an important safeguard where information is released into the public domain:

1 when the advice was given the defendant must reasonably have anticipated what it would be used for;

2   the defendant must reasonably have known the destination of that advice – a specific (not necessarily named) individual, or a member of a clearly ascertainable group;

3   the defendant must reasonably have anticipated that the advice would be acted upon without the claimant seeking further clarification or independent advice.

It must be just and reasonable to impose a duty

While glad to assist a vulnerable consumer without many financial resources, the courts do not wish to encourage a lack of responsibility in parties with access to independent advice, particularly when pursuing a speculative deal with high stakes.

If alternative legal remedies are available, a right of action in negligence may be seen to be redundant, even though the other remedies may not be applicable to the particular claimant.

The following cases illustrate the operation of some of these criteria.

Caparo v Dickman (1990, HL)
The claimant company owned shares in Fidelity plc. The defendants were the accountancy firm which had audited the annual accounts. These negligently stated that Fidelity had profits of £1.3 million; it had actually made a loss of over £465 000. The claimant increased its shareholding and later made a successful takeover bid. It then discovered that its acquisition was much less valuable than it had been led to believe by the accounts. The House of Lords held that no duty of care was owed to the claimant. The purpose for which the information was given was crucial here. The accounts were to enable shareholders to decide how to vote at the annual general meeting, not to give them personal investment advice.

McNaughten (James) Paper Group Ltd v Hicks Anderson & Co. (1991, CA)
No duty was owed by accountants to a company director for whom they prepared draft accounts for consideration prior to a takeover bid. It was not reasonably foreseeable that the claimant would rely on the draft accounts, particularly as he had access to expert advice to evaluate them.

Compare these two decisions with the following:

Morgan Crucible Co. plc v Hill Samuel Bank (1991, CA)
The claimants' takeover bid was made in reliance on a profit forecast issued to them by the defendant company. The defendant accountants and bank stated that this had been made in accordance with the company's accounting procedures, after

▶

full and careful enquiry. It was held that the defendants were liable. They had intended the claimants to rely on the information when making the bid, which they had done. The claimants' reliance was reasonable since, although they had independent advice, much of the information was available only to the defendants and could not be independently verified.

See also *Smith* v *Eric S. Bush* (1989) which is described at page 156.

Most of the reported cases on negligent statement concern pure economic loss; the next one concerns a personal injuries claim.

T v Surrey County Council (1994)
T was a small baby. His mother consulted the council to check on the suitability of a registered childminder. The council failed to tell T's mother that previously a small baby had been brain-damaged while in the minder's care and, although there was no conclusive evidence against her, it had been suggested that she should in future only look after children over two years old. T subsequently suffered severe brain damage when shaken violently by the childminder. It was held that the council owed a duty of care to T since it had given advice directly relevant to his safety and created a relationship of sufficient proximity. The council should reasonably have foreseen that the advice, which came from one of their professional officers with special knowledge, would be relied upon. If incorrect, it would clearly jeopardise T's safety.

Interesting questions of liability are raised by specialist information on financial and legal issues broadcast to the public on radio programmes and in some periodicals. There are also books which claim to help you to do your own conveyancing, or to make a will. Here the large class of potential claimants which exists might make the courts unwilling to entertain claims. On the other hand, such publications often encourage reliance on the given information by offering help and suggesting that this will be provided by experts.

Nervous shock

A duty of care readily exists where the claimant has suffered physical injury from the defendant's careless behaviour. It may be harder to establish a duty of care when the claimant suffers illness induced by acute shock or distress caused by the defendant. *Damages are not recoverable for the actual shock or distress*; liability arises from the medically recognisable illness or condition triggered by it. Such illness could be physical, like a heart attack, but many claims concern psychiatric conditions like post-traumatic stress syndrome.

In *Page* v *Smith* (see below) the House of Lords held that the rules determining duty of care are different according to whether the claimant is categorised as a primary or a secondary victim of the accident caused by the defendant. Primary victims were defined as those directly involved in the accident, including rescuers and involuntary participants. Secondary victims are not so closely involved; stricter rules are necessary to limit the duty to them, as large numbers might claim and it would not be fair, just and reasonable to make the defendant responsible for them all.

Primary victims

Since the defendant has caused a dangerous situation to arise, the duty is largely based on reasonable foreseeability of some physical or psychiatric injury to the claimant.

Page v *Smith* (1995, HL)

The defendant's negligent driving caused his car to collide with that of the claimant. Minor damage resulted to the vehicles but the claimant appeared unhurt. Shortly afterwards, however, he suffered a recurrence of ME (myalgic encephalomyelitis) from which he had enjoyed a lengthy remission. It was held that the defendant owed the same duty of care to the claimant as he would to any other fellow road user, since it was reasonably foreseeable that he would be physically harmed if the defendant drove negligently. It was not necessary for the claimant to prove that psychiatric damage might result. The distinction between physical and psychiatric injury was irrelevant in these circumstances.

Involuntary participants

The claimant who is made to feel responsible for the accident, although it is the defendant's conduct which is the real cause, is also treated as a primary victim.

Dooley v *Cammell Laird* (1951)

The claimant was operating a crane which had been negligently maintained by his employer. The crane cable snapped and he saw the heavy crate attached to it hurtle into the hold. His shock at the anticipated fate of his workmates (who miraculously escaped injury) induced an acute nervous breakdown. The court held that the employer was liable since the claimant's response was prompted by his feelings that he had helped to cause the accident, and fear for his colleagues was reasonably foreseeable.

Rescuers

Chadwick v British Rail (1967)
The claimant became acutely clinically depressed after spending a gruelling night giving first aid and comfort to severely injured and dying victims within the compacted wreckage of a horrific train crash. The court held that it was reasonably foreseeable that volunteers would render assistance and might suffer psychiatric injury as a result and, therefore, a duty of care was owed to the claimant.

The duty of care to rescuers was restricted by the House of Lords in *White* v *Chief Constable of South Yorkshire*. It was held that a duty of care to rescuers exists only if the rescuer was actually in danger or reasonably believed that they were.

White v Chief Constable of South Yorkshire (1999, HL)
At Hillsborough football stadium 95 people were killed and hundreds injured in the crush resulting from the failure of senior police officers adequately to control admission to the stadium. The claimants, who were junior police officers, claimed for post-traumatic stress syndrome resulting from the harrowing scenes in which they had been heavily involved for many hours as rescuers. The claims all failed, since the claimants had not been exposed to or feared danger and therefore no duty of care was owed to the claimants by their employers.

This decision can be justified on policy (public interest) grounds. The House of Lords was concerned to limit the increasing number of claims for compensation from members of the emergency services whose employment as a matter of course involves potential exposure to harrowing, though not necessarily dangerous situations. The cost of settling such claims could, if not checked, undermine the provision of the services themselves and put an unreasonable burden on the taxpayer.

Secondary victims

These merely witness the accident or, if involved, are not in danger or reasonable fear of it.

Alcock v Wright (1991, HL)
The 16 claimants had loved ones who had perished in the horrific occurrences at the Hillsborough stadium. None was successful because they did not fulfil the necessary criteria laid down by the House of Lords, which restrict the concepts of reasonable foreseeability and proximity applicable in such circumstances.

▶

It was held that claimants must be able to prove that:

(a) *they have suffered some medically recognised illness or condition as a result of a sudden and immediate attack upon their senses.* This rules out claimants who do not suffer a quick and sudden trauma, but whose illness is caused by a build-up of stress and fear;

(b) *it was reasonably foreseeable that they would react in this way: there must be a close bond of love and affection between them and the accident victim.* This is presumed only between spouses and parents and children, all other claimants must prove that the bond exists in the relevant circumstances. (Not all the *Alcock* claimants could satisfy this test.) Their reaction must be that of a reasonably brave person given the level of trauma that they witnessed;

(c) *they were sufficiently proximate to the accident.* Proximity is measured both in terms of time and space. The claimant must be present at the scene when the accident occurs, although seeing the build-up to it and/or the immediate aftermath may be sufficient. The claimant must have witnessed the accident directly with his or her own senses and not have had the scene interpreted for him/her by a third party. (This ruled out some of the *Alcock* claimants, who had seen events unfold through a simultaneous TV broadcast, or who had identified a body at the mortuary eight hours after the accident.)

The following case, which was approved in *Alcock*, illustrates how proximity may be derived from witnessing the immediate aftermath of an accident.

McLoughlin v O'Brian (1982, HL)
The claimant suffered acute depression and personality change from the shock of witnessing injuries caused to her husband and children by the defendant's negligent driving. Although she was not present when the accident occurred, it was held that what she witnessed at the casualty department an hour afterwards was sufficiently horrific to make her sufficiently proximate, and her response reasonably foreseeable.

This is a complex and controversial area of the law of negligence. The rules often seem arbitrary and may sometimes produce apparently unjust results for both primary and secondary victims. In practice very few claims by secondary victims succeed. However, as regards primary victims this may be a costly area of liability for service providers. This is evidenced by the Kings Cross fire, where London Transport was liable for a number of successful claims. Others arose from the Zeebrugge ferry disaster and the sinking of *The Marchioness* pleasure boat.

Omissions to act and liability for damage caused by third parties

Omissions

The law of tort is concerned with compensating acts by a defendant which have actively damaged the claimant, rather than with the defendant's failure to act for their benefit. Consequently it is rare for a duty of care to result from an omission to act. It is important here to distinguish between moral and legal duties as the two do not necessarily overlap.

For example, you would not be liable in negligence or any other tort if you failed to stop a blind person, for whom you had no previous legal responsibility, from walking into a road in front of an oncoming bus. If, however, you did intervene, a duty of care would be created and you would be liable for resulting damage if your rescue operation was bungled.

Acts of third parties

The law does not generally impose a duty of care on one party for the wrongful acts of another. (However, an employer may be held *vicariously* liable for the negligence of its employees: see below at page 190.)

> ### Smith v Littlewoods Organisation (1987, HL)
> Vandals started a fire on unoccupied premises belonging to the defendant. It spread to the claimant's premises. The claimant alleged that the defendant had a duty to prevent this damage by making the premises secure against trespassers. It was held that the defendant was not liable as the vandals' behaviour was not reasonably foreseeable.

Occupiers do not generally have a duty to secure their premises in order to safeguard neighbouring premises unless alerted by evidence that they represent a risk. If the defendant's premises have previously been subject to trespass and vandalism, this would make the damage to the claimant reasonably foreseeable.

A duty may arise if:

1 the defendant had a responsibility to control the third party's behaviour because of a pre-existing relationship with the party.

> ### Home Office v Dorset Yacht Co. Ltd (1970, HL)
> The Home Office was held liable when the claimant's yacht was damaged by improperly supervised Borstal trainees who had escaped from a nearby work camp.

2 the defendant's pre-existing relationship to the claimant makes the defendant responsible for preventing the damage.

Stansbie v Troman (1948, CA)
Stansbie was a decorator who was left in sole charge of Mrs Troman's house. He left it unlocked when going out to buy wallpaper and was held liable for the loss arising from the burglary which took place in his absence.

Public authorities and statutory discretion

Public authorities like local government, the fire brigade and the police operate in the context of statutory duties and powers. A duty is mandatory but is often widely drafted, leaving a large element of discretion to the authority about how it is implemented. For example, a local authority must provide full-time education for children in its catchment area, but how it does so is left largely to its discretion. The authority decides, for example, whether single-sex education shall be an option and determines the selection methods if any for transfer to secondary schools. Such choices are made with regard to the perceived needs of the particular community and may be limited by budgetary concerns. The statutory duty exists to benefit the public at large through the provision of services relevant to local needs.

The courts have traditionally been unwilling to permit a duty of care in negligence to be owed by a public authority to individual members of the public who claim to be harmed by the way the authority has used its discretion. There is particular reluctance where an omission to exercise the power is the alleged cause of the damage or where a third party is actually responsible for the harm. The court has in the past generally struck out such claims, without any further hearing on the grounds that there are no legal grounds for the claim.

X v Bedfordshire County Council (1995)
A claim against the local authority for failing to take the claimants into care to prevent them from being abused by their parents must be struck out. No duty of care existed in such cases or social services departments would be unduly constrained. They might be inclined to act defensively and unnecessarily take children into care.

Cases against the police also provide good examples of the courts' approach. While the police authority will be liable in the same way as any other employer for negligent driving by its officers or failure to protect a person in custody from coming to harm, the court has refused to impose liability where the police have apparently been negligent in preventing crimes occurring. It was perceived that this would unduly restrict discretion in an area where much flexibility is needed and could lead to defensive behaviour by the police which would be prejudicial to the public.

> **Osman v Ferguson** (1993, CA)
> A schoolmaster who became obsessed with a pupil harassed him and his family, carried out acts of vandalism against their property and tried to ram their car while it was being driven. The police were informed and interviewed the man but did not take steps to arrest him. He continued his campaign of harassment which culminated in his shooting both father and son, killing the former and injuring the latter.
>   An action in negligence was taken against the police.
>   It was held that the action must be struck out. Arguably there was sufficient proximity between the police and the victims of the shooting to give rise to a special relationship. It was not fair, just and reasonable to impose a duty of care by the police to the victims of crime. It would not improve standards and could dangerously divert police resources from the general investigation and suppression of crime necessary to protect the public.

This case seemed to indicate that the police enjoyed complete immunity from litigation concerning policing discretion.

However, the courts have been compelled to take a less prescriptive approach since certain decisions of the European Court of Human Rights (for example, *Osman v UK* (1999) and *Z and A* v *UK* (2002)). In order not to breach the right of the claimant to a fair trial (Article 6) the courts now take the view (*Barrett* v *Enfield Borough Council* (1999)) that such claims must be tried to determine whether a duty of care exists. This, of course, does not mean that a duty will necessarily be held to exist, but the claimant will have the opportunity to have their own case considered.

BREACH OF DUTY

It is up to the claimant to prove that the defendant failed to take reasonable care in performing the duty of care. What is reasonable is measured objectively against the standards of the so-called 'reasonable man' in the circumstances of the particular case. Certain criteria exist to guide the court.

The seriousness of the risk

The greater the likelihood of an accident the more care the defendant may need to take. The court will need to be satisfied that the incidence of risk was reasonably reduced. It need not be completely removed for the standard to be met.

Bolton v Stone (1951)
The claimant was injured by a cricket ball hit from the cricket club grounds controlled by the defendant. The boundary fence was 17 feet high and the ball had travelled over 80 yards from the wicket. There was evidence to show that such a hit was a very rare occurrence.

It was held that the defendant had taken reasonable care to reduce the chances of such an occurrence.

However a similar accident occurring in different circumstances gave rise to liability for the defendant.

Hilder v Associated Portland Cement (1961)
Children were known to play football on some land belonging to the defendant which was close to a road and bordered by a wall less than three feet high. A motorcyclist was killed when a ball was kicked into the road.

It was held that the defendant had not taken reasonable care to reduce the chances of a very likely accident.

The extent of the potential harm

The greater the extent of the likely damage the more the defendant is expected to do to reduce its risk.

Paris v Stepney Council (1951)
It was held that the defendant should have supplied goggles for use by a claimant who had only one eye. It was irrelevant that the work he was doing would not necessitate use of goggles by a normally-sighted person. The consequences of injury to his eyes was much more serious than to other employees, as an accident could make him totally blind.

The practicability of taking precautions: risk–benefit analysis

The court when determining reasonable care seeks to impose a standard of care that gives reasonable protection to the claimant while not unduly burdening the defendant. This may be described as *a risk–benefit analysis*. A risk-free environment cannot ever be fully guaranteed.

Withers v Perry Chain Ltd (1961)
The claimant who was allergic to grease, employed in a factory where contact with grease was involved at every stage of the production process, was moved by her employer to the most grease-free job that fitted her capabilities, but the allergy persisted.
   It was held that the defendant had done everything that they could reasonably be expected to do and were therefore not in breach of their duty.

Latimer v A.E.C. (1953)
A factory floor was slippery after a flash flood. The defendant spread sawdust over most of the walkways in the factory and issued warnings to employees. The claimant, who was injured when he slipped in an area which had been sawdusted, argued that the building should have been closed until it had dried out.
   It was held that the extent of the risk and likely injury did not justify this. The precautions taken were all that was practicable in the circumstances.

The defendant's resources and the nature and size of the business may be relevant factors for the court to take into account. However, the greater the risk and danger the less relevant the cost factor to the defendant. This is an area of the common law where standards have been influenced by statutory developments in health and safety regulation (see Chapter 18 at page 259 below). This commonly requires prior risk assessment for certain activities. Provided evidence of such a process indicates that it was sufficiently comprehensive, this often indicates that reasonable care has been taken. Risk assessment is becoming accepted practice even where it is not statutorily required.

The qualifications claimed by the defendant

Defendants will be held liable if they fail to act with the reasonable degree of care and skill to be expected from a person with the qualifications which the defendants claim to have – *Bolam* v *Friern Hospital Management Committee* (1957) (see below).

Phillips v William Whitely (1938)
The defendant jeweller who pierced the claimant's ears was not liable for the abscess which resulted. He had used the level of care and skill to be expected from a person with his training. The standards of a surgeon could not be expected of him.

Only the level of qualification is relevant. Lack of experience is not taken into consideration: the same standards are expected of a newly-qualified professional or craftsperson as of one with considerable experience.

> **_Wilsher v Essex Area Health Authority_** (1986)
> The Court of Appeal held that it was irrelevant that the doctor who treated the claimant was newly qualified and had been working excessively long hours when she treated the claimant.

This extends to learner drivers, who are required to demonstrate the same standard of care as one who has passed a driving test (see *Nettleship v Weston* (1971, CA)). This is to prevent insurance companies avoiding liability to third parties.

Good practice

Conformity with accepted and current good practice may be indicative of reasonable care.

> **_Thompson v Smiths Ship Repairers Ltd_** (1984)
> Failure to provide ear protectors was held not to amount to a failure to take reasonable care until employers had been alerted to the necessity by government circular.

There may be more than one type of good practice: both claimant and defendant may produce expert witnesses with conflicting views. The judge does not have the relevant professional skill to decide whose procedure was correct. The claimant must prove, on the balance of probability, that the defendant was in breach. If there is proof that what the defendant did would also have been done by another similar professional in compliance with good practice then the claimant fails.

> **_Bolam v Friern Hospital Management Committee_** (1957, CA)
> The claimant, who suffered a fractured pelvis when undergoing electro-convulsive therapy, brought expert evidence that his limbs should have been restrained during treatment. However, the hospital was able to prove that its practice of cushioning limbs was equally well accepted in respected medical circles and therefore there was no proof of a failure to take reasonable care.

The House of Lords approved the *Bolam* principle in *Bolitho* v *City and Hackney AHA* (1997), but stressed that it is not enough to show that other professionals subscribe to the practice: an expert witness must be able to justify its use in the circumstances of the particular case, having weighed up its risks and benefits.

Unhappy outcomes

In *Bolam* v *Friern Hospital Management Committee* Lord Justice Denning neatly summarised the nature of reasonable care when he said 'the doctor does not promise to cure the patient nor the lawyer to win the case'. All reasonable care may be taken but the claimant may still suffer damage. Proof of damage to claimant or even proof of a mistake by the defendant does not necessarily prove that the defendant has failed to take reasonable care.

> **Luxmoore May v Messenger May Bakers** (1990, CA)
> The defendant auctioneers claimed to be expert picture valuers. They failed to judge correctly the potential of two paintings owned by the claimant, who consequently obtained only a tiny fraction of their true value when they were sold. The Court of Appeal held that the defendants had not been proved to have acted without reasonable care. A competent valuer could have made the same mistake.

PROVING CONSEQUENT DAMAGE

The claimant must prove the necessary link between the defendant's failure to take reasonable care and the damage which they have suffered. Two elements are involved:

1 Causation in fact

The defendant's failure to take care actually caused the damage. Claimants must show that they would not have been injured *but for* the defendant's behaviour.

> **Barnett v Chelsea & Kensington Hospital Management Committee** (1969)
> A man died from arsenic poisoning which the hospital negligently failed to detect. The hospital was not liable, however; according to expert evidence he would still have died even if the hospital had diagnosed the problem and treated him appropriately.

The 'but for' principle works well as long as there is only one likely cause of the damage. Where there are multiple causes the burden on the claimant may be insuperable.

Wilsher v Essex Area Health Authority (1988, HL)
Failure by the hospital to give the claimant, a premature baby, the correct oxygen mixture was alleged to be the cause of his becoming visually impaired. He lost his case however as he was suffering from a number of other conditions, any of which could have caused the same damage. It could not be proved on the balance of probability that the oxygen mixture was a material cause.

It was held that the claimant could not succeed since the 'but for' test had not been satisfied.

In a previous case the House of lords had adopted a different approach.

McGhee v National Coal Board (1972, HL)
The claimant worked in very hot and dirty conditions in a brick kiln. No showers were provided and he could not get clean until he had cycled home from work. He contracted dermatitis. He could not prove that showering before leaving work would have prevented the dermatitis but as the medical evidence indicated that lack of showers greatly increased his chances of developing the condition, the court held that the NCB was liable.

In *Wilsher* v *Essex Area Health Authority* the House of Lords described the *McGhee* approach as 'robust and pragmatic': correct on its facts but not a principle of law. This cast doubt on the standing of *McGhee*, and produced a puzzling distinction for many students. However, the House of Lords has now clarified the law:

Fairchild v Glenhaven Funeral Services (2002, HL)
The claimants in this case all contracted mesothelioma (a form of invariably fatal cancer) from being exposed to asbestos fibres at work. There was clear evidence of flagrant breach of safety standards by all the employers. Causation was problematic, however, as all the claimants had been employed by more than one employer. It was impossible for the claimants to prove which one was the source of the disease as only one fibre may have triggered it.

It was unanimously held that the claimants should succeed. It was fair and just to use the less stringent *McGhee* rule here, as by breaching safety standards all the employers had materially increased the claimants' chances of contracting the condition. The facts could clearly be distinguished from those in *Wilsher* where a number of possible causes, apart from the oxygen, could have led to the claimant's disability. In *Fairchild* asbestos was the only possible cause. The House of Lords in *Wilsher* was incorrect in failing to acknowledge *McGhee* as establishing a new principle of law.

The *Fairchild* decision is important as it firmly establishes the *McGhee* approach as a principle of law. It is also a good example of a public interest or 'policy' decision. Had the employers escaped liability others would be encouraged to ignore safety standards in similar situations, secure in the knowledge that the causative link could not be established. Insurers, too, would unjustly profit.

The development of an alternative principle always attracts the criticism that the law has been made uncertain. The House of Lords by drawing distinctions on the *Wilsher* facts has clearly defined the scope of this alternative principle. Certain law is not necessarily just in all circumstances. If it is likely to encourage irresponsible behaviour and appears unfair to the public, flexibility for the courts is desirable.

2 Causation in law

The damage was not too remote. The defendant is not held legally responsible for all the results of the breach. The damage caused to the claimant by a non-intentional tort must be of a reasonably foreseeable type.

The Wagon Mound (1961, PC)
The defendants were held not to be liable for fire damage to the claimant's dock caused when a spark from a welding torch being used on the dockside ignited oil which the defendants had negligently discharged into the harbour. It was held that the chance of fire breaking out in such circumstances was not reasonably foreseeable by the defendants.

Provided that the *type of damage* is reasonably foreseeable, the defendant will be liable. It is irrelevant that the defendant might not have been able to foresee its cause or its severity.

Hughes v The Lord Advocate (1963, HL)
The defendant telephone engineers left an inspection hole covered only by a tent and surrounded by lighted paraffin lamps. The child claimant was severely burned when he fell down the hole carrying a lamp which exploded as it hit the ground producing a fireball. The defendants were held liable as they should reasonably have foreseen that a child would be attracted by the lamps and might be burned when playing with them. It was irrelevant that they could not have foreseen the explosion or the severity of the burn damage.

The *'eggshell skull rule'* is an exception to the *Wagon Mound* principle: the defendant must take the claimant as he or she finds him or her. If the claimant has some particular weakness that makes him or her susceptible to a type of harm which is not reasonably foreseeable, the defendant will nevertheless be liable. In *Page* v *Smith* (1995, HL) the House of Lords held that the eggshell skull principle applied to both mental and physical conditions.

> **Smith v Leech Brain & Co. Ltd** (1962)
> Due to the defendants' negligence, an employee suffered a minor burn to his lip which would normally have caused only superficial damage. However, pre-cancerous cells in his lip which might otherwise have remained dormant were activated and he died. It was held that the defendants were liable for their employee's death although such serious damage was not foreseeable.

THE HUMAN RIGHTS ACT 1998: AN ALTERNATIVE TO NEGLIGENCE CLAIMS?

An action under the Human Rights Act in cases involving a public authority is now possible. It may well be more appropriate than an action in negligence and more likely to be successful, where the claim involves omission to act, failure to prevent damage by a third party or negligent exercise of a statutory discretion. In *Z and A* v *UK* (2002) the claimants (two of the children involved in *X* v *Bedfordshire County Council* (1995) above at page 163) successfully claimed that the council had breached its duty under Article 3: failure to protect children from prolonged and serious ill-treatment and abuse was cruel and inhuman treatment. Article 8 (right to respect for family life) was breached in respect of another child who was wrongly taken into care. Her mother also succeeded with an Article 8 claim.

Quiz 11

1 May a duty of care exist in the following circumstances?

   (a) To Ruby, who was wrongly advised by Turquoise on the value of her antique clock?

   (b) To Sapphire, by Beryl Electrical Appliances, the manufacturer of an electric kettle which was given to her for Christmas and which did not work?

   (c) To Emerald, who witnesses a horrific accident caused by Diamond in which Emerald's daughter Crystal was killed?

   (d) To Amber, who suffered theft from her premises; the thieves gained access to her premises through a hole in the next-door fence which belongs to Garnet?

2 What is the relevant standard of care against which the defendant will be judged in a negligence action?

3 What is the eggshell skull rule?

 ## Assignment 10

Alice bought a small bakery business. It was surveyed by George, for Happy Homes Building Society which provided Alice with the mortgage. Alice paid Happy Homes for a summary report from George. This stated that there were no major structural problems and that the premises were worth the asking price. It concluded: 'This report is for valuation purposes only and will not give rise to any legal liability'.

Alice contracted with Industrial Kitchen Fitters Ltd (IKF) to refit the kitchen. They installed a new oven manufactured by Cinders plc.

On moving in Alice discovered severe and large-scale dry rot when she fell through a storeroom floor and broke her leg. Her injuries and the eradication of the dry rot delayed the opening of the premises for several months.

A week after the business eventually opened, the new oven malfunctioned. As a result a wedding cake was badly burnt, leading to a claim for damages for breach of contract against Alice, by the bride's father.

IKF have gone out of business. Advise Alice of the possible liability in negligence of George and Cinders.

CHAPTER 12

Tort liability for premises

INTRODUCTION

This chapter explains the duties imposed by the law of tort on occupiers in relation to the maintenance and use of their premises. Occupiers have a duty to maintain the premises safely for the benefit of third parties on or outside the premises. They must also ensure that the use of premises does not cause unreasonable inconvenience to other people. This is obviously of great relevance to business occupiers, whose premises are often visited by large numbers of people, or whose business activities are potentially hazardous or disruptive to other people.

THE OCCUPIER'S LIABILITY TO PEOPLE ON THE PREMISES

Negligent activities

Occupiers who carry out activities on their land without taking reasonable care may be liable under the general principles of negligence which you studied in the previous chapter.

> *Ogwo v Taylor* (1987, HL)
> The defendant negligently set the roof space on fire while using a blowtorch to burn off paint from weatherboarding on his house. The claimant, a firefighter, was injured in the ensuing conflagration. The defendant was found liable as the claimant's injuries were a reasonably foreseeable consequence of the defendant's negligent behaviour.

Dangerous premises

Occupiers have a legal duty to maintain the structure of their premises in a reasonably safe condition. If, for example, you run a hotel, you must take care to avoid harm to your guests from over-polished floors, low beams or slippery tiles. This part of the law is covered by statute.

The Occupiers' Liability Act 1957

The 1957 Act covers the liability of an occupier to what the Act calls 'visitors', i.e. those people who are on the premises with the occupier's consent – family members, employees, customers, the window cleaner and the meter reader are obvious examples.

Who is the occupier?

In *Wheat* v *Lacon* (below) it was held that the person *in control of the premises* at the time of the accident is the 'occupier'. If you abandon your premises during radical refurbishment, the builder, shopfitter or plumber who is the cause of the hazard, will be liable to the injured person rather than you. There may be more than one occupier at a time.

> **Wheat v Lacon** (1966, HL)
> The licensee and brewery owner of a pub were both held to be the occupiers of a pub since, under the lease, the brewery was responsible for repairs.

What are premises?

Premises are widely defined and cover not only buildings and open spaces but also 'any fixed or moveable structure', and include 'any vessel, vehicle or aircraft' (s 1(3)). This has been held to include a wide variety of things, including scaffolding (*Kearney* v *Eric Waller* (1966)) and a large excavating machine (*Bunker* v *Charles Brand* (1969)).

The extent of the occupier's duty

The occupier must ensure that the visitor is reasonably safe for the purposes for which the visitor is on the land (s 2(2)). Notice that the occupier's duty is limited to making the visitor reasonably safe only *for the purposes of that visit*. The occupier's consent to a visitor's presence is limited by the purpose of the visit. If visitors stray into a part of the premises where they are not reasonably expected and suffer injury, the occupier is unlikely to be liable under the 1957 Act. There may be liability instead under the Occupier's Liability Act 1984 which covers duty of care to trespassers (see *Tomlinson* v *Congleton Borough Council* (2002) below).

The standard of care

As in negligence, there exists a duty to take *reasonable* care. The occupier is not liable just because the accident happens; the injured visitor will have to prove that the occupier failed to take reasonably adequate precautions to prevent it. What is reasonable is determined with reference to all the circumstances.

Cunningham v Reading Football Club (1991)
Due to the club's failure to maintain its terraces, loose lumps of masonry provided handy missiles for the use of football hooligans. As a result the claimant, a policeman on duty at the ground, was injured and successfully sued the club.

The type of hazard, the nature of the premises and the needs of the visitor are all relevant. Each case has to be decided on its own facts.

Murphy v Bradford Metropolitan Council (1991)
A school keeper had twice cleared snow from a notoriously slippery path before 8.30 a.m. on the morning when the claimant was injured by a fall. It was held that reasonable care had not been taken: the nature of the path, the numbers of people using it and the severity of the weather demanded the use of grit, not just regular clearance.

An occupier whose premises are open to the public must take account of the needs of a wide cross-section of people, including children, the elderly and those with disabilities, since it is reasonably foreseeable that such people may form part of the clientele. The 1957 Act refers specifically to two categories of visitor: children and visitors with special skills.

1 *Children*. An occupier must expect children to be less careful of their own safety than adults; consequently a higher standard of care may be needed (s 2(3)(a)). Things which present no hazard to an adult may be a dangerous allurement to a child.

Glasgow Corporation v Taylor (1922, HL)
The corporation was held liable for the poisoning of the child claimant by attractive berries on a tree in a public park.

An occupier is not liable for all accidents to children: the standard of care required of an occupier is no greater than that of a reasonably careful parent. It may be reasonable for the occupier to assume that very small children will be appropriately supervised by an accompanying adult.

Phipps v Rochester Corporation (1955)
An occupier was held not to be liable to a five-year-old child who fell into a trench on a building site on the corporation's land. Devlin J said that 'responsibility for the safety of little children must rest primarily upon the parents'.

2 *Visitors with special skills.* An occupier is not liable to contractors carrying out a service on the premises for accidents arising from job-related hazards, since the contractors should be aware of these given their trade skills and experience (s 2(3)(b)).

> ### *Roles* v *Nathan* (1963, CA)
> The claimants were asphyxiated by fumes when they carried out flue repairs in a boiler room while the boiler was alight. It was held that the occupier was not liable for their deaths: their knowledge and experience of this kind of work should have made them extinguish the boiler before starting work.

Under s 2(4) of the 1957 Act, the occupier is not generally liable if a visitor suffers damage arising from construction, repair or maintenance work carried out by an outside firm, provided that the occupier took reasonable precautions to select a competent firm and checked the completed work. Here the visitor must take action against the contractor.

Discharging the duty

The duty of care may be discharged in a variety of ways. Ideally the hazard should be removed – you can carpet your shop entrance if the floor is slippery on a wet day. However, removal of the hazard may not always be practicable, either immediately or in the long term – if you remove the low beam in your quaint old tea shop the roof may fall in, presenting much greater risks to your customers than the occasional bruised head. It may be possible to protect visitors adequately by the erection of suitable barriers, or even warning notices.

Under s 2(4) of the 1957 Act, occupiers may be found to have taken reasonable care of their visitors by giving *adequate warning* of the hazard. To be adequate the warning must be sufficient to allow the visitor to be reasonably safe. Such notice must be given in sufficient time and with sufficient clarity to enable the visitor reasonably to avoid the hazard. It should indicate the nature of the hazard ('take care: wet floor') and give an indication, where appropriate, of how it should be safely avoided ('please use other exit'). Written warnings are not effective for those who cannot reasonably be expected to read or understand them, for example children or the visually impaired.

Actionable damage

Under the 1957 Act, the damage giving rise to liability is damage to the person or to goods.

Excluding liability

It is possible to exclude liability for breach of the duty imposed by the 1957 Act (s 2(1)), subject to the Unfair Contract Terms Act 1977. Business liability cannot be excluded if the visitor dies or suffers personal injuries from the occupier's failure to take reasonable care.

Liability for damage to property may be excluded if this is judged to be reasonable in the circumstances. For example, if the damage is caused by a third party who is not subject to the occupier's control.

The Occupiers' Liability Act 1984

This Act regulates the duty of an occupier of premises to trespassers. Not surprisingly, the occupier owes only a very limited duty of care to trespassers hurt by the dangerous state of the premises. It would not be in the public interest to encourage a burglar to claim damages after falling down the stairs of the house which he was rifling. An innocent trespasser, straying onto premises containing highly dangerous plant or machinery, clearly deserves some protection. This is illustrated by the following case, which preceded the 1984 Act but was based on similar principles.

> **British Railways Board v Herrington** (1972, HL)
> The claimant, a child of six, was injured when he strayed onto the railway from a public park through broken fencing belonging to the railway, whose drivers had reported trespassers on the line. The House of Lords held that the Board was liable for the child trespasser's injuries since it knew of the possibility of trespassers and could have avoided the risk at 'small trouble and expense' (i.e. by mending the fence).

When is the duty owed?

Under s 1(3) of the 1984 Act, the following criteria must all be satisfied:

1 the occupier must have reasonable knowledge of the danger;

2 the occupier must know or reasonably suspect that trespassers are in the vicinity of the premises or are reasonably likely to come into the vicinity;

3 the risk is one against which, in all the circumstances, it is reasonable for the occupier to offer some protection.

The courts will take account of the resources of the occupier relative to the likelihood of trespassers and the extent of the danger. A lake in a remote hill area presents much less of a danger than an electrified railway running through a heavily populated locality.

The extent of the duty

The occupier's duty under the 1984 Act is limited to taking such care as is reasonable to see that the trespasser *does not suffer injury* from the relevant danger (s 1(4)). It is interesting to compare this with the *positive* duty owed to the lawful entrant under the 1957 Act whereby the occupier must ensure that visitors are *reasonably*

177

safe. The occupier's responsibility to the trespasser is a *negative* one: to take reasonable steps to prevent harm.

Performing the duty

Such a minimal duty can be performed by taking reasonable steps to keep trespassers out. A sufficiently explicit warning clearly displayed will generally be enough for the adult trespasser, while properly maintained boundary fencing should be a sufficient deterrent to children.

The following case illustrates how these principles are applied.

> ### Ratcliff v Harpur Adams College (1998, CA)
> The claimant was a student at the college. One night he entered the grounds of the college pool by climbing over a 7 ft wall. He was paralysed when he broke his neck after diving into the pool where the water was too shallow. The Court of Appeal held that the college was not liable. Even if it should have been aware that students trespassed in this manner, it was not in breach of its duty. Their duty did not extend to warning adult trespassers against evident risks, or to lighting the premises at night to make them safe for trespassers.

However, each case is determined on its own facts. This may lead to different outcomes in cases which may at first sight appear similar.

> ### Tomlinson v Congleton Borough Council (2002, CA)
> Mr Tomlinson dived into shallow water in a lake in a public park. He was paralysed when he struck his head on a rocky outcrop. The lake was a flooded quarry and signs beside it clearly prohibited swimming and warned that it was dangerous.
>
> Under s 1(3) a duty was owed if the danger was one against which it was reasonable to expect the occupiers to offer some protection. A duty existed here since there was a continuing risk of grave injury.
>
> It was breached because the warning signs had proved to be inadequate as they were frequently ignored. Landscaping the area and planting vegetation to keep people away had been recommended prior to the accident. Implementation of the scheme had been undertaken after the accident and had been effective.
>
> The damages were reduced by two-thirds to take account of the claimant's negligence.

The Court of Appeal seems to be taking a very hard line against the occupier in the above case. It may be argued that in the public interest of maintaining high standards on premises open to the public, it was reasonable to require the occupier to erect physical barriers to areas to which public access was not permitted, when notices clearly did not work. There was also the issue of danger to children who could not be expected to observe notices.

Actionable damage

Liability under the 1984 Act is restricted to death and personal injuries only (s 2(9)).

DUTIES OF AN OCCUPIER TO PEOPLE OUTSIDE THE PREMISES

An occupier owes a variety of duties in tort to people who are not actually on the premises. Where physical damage to people or their property occurs which is caused by failure to take reasonable care, action may be taken in negligence.

A heavier burden of liability, based purely on the reasonable foreseeability of damage, is imposed through the law of nuisance. This imposes liability not only for tangible harm, but also for unreasonable levels of inconvenience arising from the occupier's use of premises. This is composed of two separate torts (private and public nuisance) which have some characteristics in common.

Private nuisance

This protects an occupier of land against unreasonable interference with the enjoyment of their premises caused by the state of a nearby occupier's land or activities taking place on it. A nuisance is usually caused unintentionally, indirectly and as a by-product of an ongoing state of affairs on the defendant's land.

Proof of liability

The claimant must prove, first, that the defendant has caused *damage*. This includes:

1 *Damage to the structure of the claimant's premises.*

> **Davey v Harrow Corpn** (1957, CA)
> Mr Davey successfully sued the Harrow Corporation for subsidence damage caused by tree roots spreading under his house from the corporation's land.

2 *Damage to goods on the claimant's land.*

> **British Celanese v Hunt** (1969)
> Metal foil stored on the defendant's premises blew onto power cables causing a cut in the electricity supply to the claimant's factories. The defendant was liable for damage to machinery and components.

Liability for personal injury may also exist, though generally the courts have not usually imposed this unless the injury was caused by the defendant's negligent or intentional conduct.

3 *Amenity damage.* Liability may arise where the defendant's behaviour has unreasonably reduced the comfort and convenience of use of the claimant's premises. This may accompany or exist independently of property damage; it can cover a wide range of annoying activities, commonly including noise, smells, smoke and vibrations.

Secondly, the claimant must show that the defendant's activities caused *an unreasonable level of interference.* Most of us would claim to suffer disturbance from our neighbours' activities; few of us, however, would have a successful claim in private nuisance, because we would not be able to persuade the court that the level of interference was unreasonable. The law aims to maintain a fair balance of interest between parties and requires a certain amount of give and take. While your shop is being refitted your next-door neighbour may be somewhat inconvenienced by noise or dust, but provided you are doing what you reasonably can to keep it under control, you are within your legal rights. In six months' time, when your neighbour is having major work done, you will be expected to show a similar understanding.

Halsey v Esso Petroleum (1961)
Pungent and nauseating smells escaping from Esso's works pervaded the claimant's premises. At night, noise from Esso's boilers made the claimant's doors and windows vibrate, preventing him from sleeping; all day heavy goods vehicles caused a high level of noise. Esso was held liable to the claimant.

Where amenity damage only is claimed, it is usually harder to prove unreasonable interference. Proof of tangible damage, however, is likely to point to unreasonable behaviour by the defendant. Each case is decided on its own facts, but any of the following criteria may be relevant:

1 *Locality.* In *Sturges v Bridgeman* (1879), Thesiger J declared, 'What would be a nuisance in Belgrave Square would not necessarily be so in Bermondsey'. No doubt Mr Justice Thesiger was glad to live nearer Belgrave Square than Bermondsey, but you can see the common sense of his pronouncement. If you live in an industrial and commercial area with a high density of population, the level of peace and quiet is bound to be reduced. Similarly, agricultural activity is to be expected in a rural area and some level of related smell or noise must be endured. Locality is relevant only in a claim restricted to amenity damage. It is not appropriate where some tangible loss has been caused to the claimant.

St Helen's Smelting Co. v Tipping (1865, HL)
Fumes from the defendant's chemical works damaged the claimant's trees. It was held that this damage indicated an unreasonable interference with the claimant's enjoyment. It was irrelevant that the defendant's activities were not out of keeping with the locality.

2 *The timing, level, duration and frequency of the nuisance.* Night-time noise is more likely to be actionable than noise during the day. See, for example, *Leeman v Montague* (1936) on the nocturnal crowing of cockerels. The more substantial the inconvenience to the claimant the less important is lengthy duration or frequency.

3 *The practicability of preventing the nuisance.* Defendants who can prove that they have taken all reasonable precautions to avoid causing annoyance will probably not be liable for intangible, as opposed to tangible, damage. Note that it is up to the defendant to prove this: the claimant does not have to prove failure to take precautions.

Moy v Stoop (1909)
The claimant complained about the noise of children crying in the defendant's day nursery. It was held that the noise was an unavoidable consequence of the defendant's activity. It was not caused by neglect by the defendant of the children's welfare, and therefore the defendant was not liable.

Andreae v Selfridge (1938)
The defendant was held liable in nuisance through failure to take reasonable steps to reduce the noise and dust arising in building operations.

4 *The defendant's motive.* Most nuisance is caused by unthinking behaviour, but occasionally the defendant may actually be trying to cause distress to the claimant. If the claimant can prove such motivation, this may cast new light on the defendant's behaviour, rendering potentially reasonable behaviour unreasonable.

Hollywood Silver Fox Farm v Emmett (1936)
Believing that the presence of the claimant's farm was inhibiting the sale of building plots on his own land, the defendant carried out intensive shooting operations on his land throughout the silver fox breeding season. He knew that this would disturb the animals and thus cause damage to the claimant's business. It was held that his malicious intentions made his behaviour unreasonable.

5 *The claimant's sensitivity.* The claimant will have to prove that the level of nuisance is higher than that which the average person could reasonably be expected to endure. A sensitive claimant cannot impose a heavier duty on the defendant to accommodate his unusual need.

Robinson v Kilvert (1889)
The defendant installed a boiler in his basement. This caused a rise in temperature and a drop in humidity in the claimant's adjoining basement. Most people would have been pleased, but the claimant complained because the previous conditions were essential for the storage of paper which became damaged by the warmer and drier air. It was held that the defendant's behaviour was not a nuisance; the claimant's damage arose from the peculiar sensitivity of his goods.

Reasonable forseeability

The burden of proof is easier for the claimant to discharge in nuisance than in negligence, since in nuisance the claimant does not need to prove that the defendant failed to take reasonable care. The claimant need show only that the type of damage caused was a *reasonably foreseeable consequence to a person in the defendant's position*. The state of the defendant's knowledge is crucial.

Defendants will naturally be expected to anticipate the consequences of their own actions. Where the nuisance arises from a state of affairs created by a third party like a previous occupant or a trespasser, a defendant will not be liable unless they should reasonably have known about this and of the risk to the claimant.

Sedleigh-Denfield v O'Callagan (1940, HL)
A ditch ran across the boundary of the defendant's property. The local authority installed a culvert (drainage pipe) in the ditch near the point where the ditch left the defendant's land. The end of the pipe extended into the defendant's property and a grid should have been placed near the end of the pipe. The workman, however, left it on top of the pipe where it was completely useless. The defendant had not given permission to the local authority which was therefore trespassing. The defendant was aware that there was a danger of flooding when debris was washed against the end of the pipe and blocked it. Usually the defendant kept the pipe clear, but once this job was overlooked and rubbish built up causing a flood on the claimant's property during heavy rain.

It was held that the defendant was liable in private nuisance as it had failed to take reasonably practicable steps to remove a known hazard from the land. It would have been very easy to put the grid into place and the flood would not have occurred.

The courts have extended this principle to cover entirely naturally-occurring events.

Leakey v The National Trust (1980, CA)
The claimant owned a house at the foot of a steep hill in the care of the National Trust, which had been alerted by him to evidence of minor landslips which occurred due to drought. A major slippage then occurred and large quantities of debris landed in the claimant's garden. It was held that as the Trust knew of the risk of such damage, it would be liable as it had failed to take reasonable steps to prevent landslips.

The House of Lords applied these principles in:

Marcic v Thames Water Utilities Ltd (2001, CA)
Overburdened sewers, which had been installed by a previous water authority, overflowed during periods of very heavy rainfall into Mr Marcic's premises. This caused structural damage to his house. Many customers were in a similar position to Mr Marcic and £1000 million was necessary to correct the problem. Thames argued that it was operating a points system under which work was being gradually undertaken with priority for the most urgent cases.

It was held that Thames Water was liable in nuisance. It was in the same position as any other occupier of land and must do everything reasonably practicable to deal with a known hazard whether caused by the act of a third party or by natural causes. The points system was not fair in its operation and the authority must have the necessary financial resources to deal with the problem. An injunction was refused and damages for future losses are not permitted by the common law.

Damages were recovered by Mr Marcic under the Human Rights Act 1998. This aspect of the case is explained below at page 186.

Who may sue in private nuisance?

Private nuisance protects the right to peaceable enjoyment of land and has traditionally been seen in law as the exclusive right of the owner, occupier or tenant. Other residents do not have the right to sue in private nuisance.

Malone v Laskey (1907)
The claimant was hit on the head by a lavatory cistern which became detached from its fixings due to the vibration of machinery on adjoining premises, but her claim was unsuccessful because she was 'a mere licensee' and had no proprietary rights over the premises. Her husband's employer permitted them to live on the premises but had not granted them a tenancy.

The principle was upheld by the House of Lords in *Hunter* v *Canary Wharf* (1997), which disapproved the Court of Appeal's decision in *Khorasandjian* v *Bush* (1993) to extend the right to sue to members of the occupier's family.

Who may be sued?

The current occupier is the most usual defendant, but the party who caused the nuisance (for example, a previous occupant) may be sued. A landlord who lets premises knowing that their use will create a nuisance is also liable.

The defence of prescription

Defendants will not be liable if they can prove that they have been causing the nuisance for *20 years* without anybody taking action against them. It is not enough to show that an activity has been carried on for that length of time; the court will have to be satisfied that it caused a nuisance to the claimant or his predecessors for the whole of that time.

Sturges v Bridgeman (1879)
A confectioner had a workshop in premises adjacent to the claimant dentist. Noisy equipment in the workshop had been in use for over 20 years, but caused no problems until the dentist built a new consulting room in his garden, near the boundary wall where the noise was highly audible. The court held that the defendant was liable in private nuisance since the noise level was unreasonable. Prescription was not an appropriate defence as it was the activity rather than the nuisance which had continued for 20 years. It was irrelevant that the claimant had moved into the noisier environment.

Public nuisance

The scope of liability

The tort of public nuisance resembles private nuisance as it may arise from similar situations, including the escape of noise, smells, dust and vibration. However, the scope of public nuisance is wider, covering any activity which unreasonably interferes with the comfort and convenience of the public. This includes the obstruction of highways or waterways. It even extends to the sale of impure food and running a brothel.

Behaviour giving rise to a public nuisance always involves criminal behaviour. Today there are a large number of statutory offences to protect public health, covering pollution of all kinds and regulating businesses involved in the preparation and marketing of food. Until the twentieth century, these activities were prosecuted under the umbrella of public nuisance.

Tort action may be taken to protect the public at large and an injunction may be sought, by the Attorney-General or by a local authority. Individuals are entitled to take action only where they have suffered special damage greater than that suffered by the public at large.

Mint v Good (1950, CA)
A garden wall belonging to the defendant collapsed onto the pavement and injured the claimant, who successfully claimed damages. Blockage of the pavement was a public nuisance: any members of the public passing by would be inconvenienced. The claimant who was injured physically clearly suffered special harm.

Proof of liability

To establish public nuisance, the following points must be satisfied:

1 *The nuisance must be capable of affecting 'the public'.* The nuisance must potentially affect too many people to make it reasonable to expect any one person to take action to stop it.

2 *The level of inconvenience must be unreasonable.* Similar criteria are relevant here as apply to private nuisance.

3 *Damage must result.* This includes physical damage to the person, land or goods, as well as amenity damage. Pure economic loss may also be actionable.

Lyons & Co. v Gulliver (1914)
The defendants were held liable for causing loss of custom to the claimant's tea shop, access to which was blocked by long queues outside the defendants' theatre.

4 *The damage must be reasonably foreseeable to the defendant.* As in private nuisance, the claimant is not required to prove any failure to take reasonable care. Defendants may avoid liability by showing that they took all reasonably practicable precautions to prevent reasonably foreseeable damage. A very high standard is required where the nuisance occurs on the highway.

Who may be sued?

The person who created the nuisance, or the current occupier of land from which a nuisance emanates may be sued in public nuisance.

Who may sue?

Any person who is caused special damage by the nuisance may sue, otherwise action will be taken by the Attorney-General or a local authority to obtain an injunction to protect the public.

Notice that, unlike private nuisance, claimants are not required to have any occupational rights to the land where they suffer damage to entitle them to sue. Sufficient geographical proximity to the nuisance is all that is required.

Dollman v Hillman (1941)
The claimant was awarded damages for injuries caused by slipping on a piece of fat, which had been dropped on the pavement outside the defendant's butcher's shop.

Remedies

In claims in both public and private nuisance, the remedies are damages and/or an injunction.

The impact of the Human Rights Act

The courts have acknowledged the relevance of the Human Rights Act in some recent nuisance cases.

Marcic v Thames Water No 2 (2001)
(For facts see above at page 183.)
The defendant was held liable under the Human Rights Act for breach of the claimant's rights under Article 8 (right to respect for privacy and family life) and Protocol 1 Article 1 (right to peaceful enjoyment of possessions). At a second hearing to determine the measure of damages, it was held that he should recover the amount necessary under the HRA to compensate him for the damage to his property to date plus a sum to cover future interference.

The next case indicates the possibility of development in common law rules where these are in conflict with the ECHR.

Nora McKenna v British Aluminium Ltd (2002)
The claimants were all children from over 30 families who claimed nuisance by British Aluminium in permitting a factory to emit fumes and noise which had caused them mental distress and physical harm. They argued that this breached their rights under Article 8 and under Protocol 1 Article 1 of the ECHR.
British Aluminium argued that the claims should be struck out as none of the children had the necessary proprietary interest in the land to enable them to sue in nuisance. The judge refused to strike out the action and said that there were strong ▶

arguments supporting the claim. Potentially the law of nuisance was in conflict with the Convention rights and arguably needed to be developed compatibly. Otherwise a person living in his home where enjoyment of property was interfered with would be unable to protect his Convention rights unless he also had propietary rights. The matter could only be decided at trial.

Note that the *McKenna* case does not in itself change the law of nuisance. That can only happen after a full trial decision which might well result in appeal to the House of Lords. However, it does indicate the potential for development in the light of the Human Rights Act.

DEFENCES IN TORT

Even if a claimant can satisfy the court that the defendant's conduct does amount to a tort, the defendant may be able to prove that there are mitigating circumstances which remove, or at least reduce, liability. The following defences may be relevant to any of the torts covered in this book.

Consent

If the claimant expressly or impliedly consented to the defendant's behaviour, the defendant is not liable. The claimant must make the decision with full knowledge of the likely outcome and be free to make a choice.

Smith v Baker (1891, HL)
The claimant quarryman was injured by rocks falling from overhead machinery. He had protested about the danger, but continued to work after being ordered to do so. The House of Lords held that the claimant had not consented to the risk of injury as, although he knew of the danger, he had never freely consented to the risk.

Rescue cases

If the claimant is injured rescuing somebody from a hazard created by the negligence of the defendant, the claimant is not considered to have consented to the risk, provided that:

1 *There was no legal or moral duty to intervene.* The nature of the claimant's job may impose a legal duty to assist in an emergency: firefighters and the police are obvious examples; a schoolteacher supervising children on an outing would also qualify. Most people seeing a third party in danger could be said to be under a moral duty to take some action.

Legal area	1957 Act	1984 Act	Public nuisance	Private nuisance
Potential defendant	Person(s) in control of premises	Person(s) in control of premises	Owner/tenant/creator of nuisance	Owner/tenant/creator of nuisance
Potential claimant	Lawful entrants	Trespassers	Any member of public suffering special damage	Occupiers of adjacent premises
Where damage occurred	On defendant's premises	On defendant's premises	Anywhere outside defendant's premises	On premises occupied by claimant
Type of damage	Personal injuries, damage to goods	Personal injuries only	Personal injuries, damage to property, interference with enjoyment of premises	Damage to property, interference with enjoyment of premises, possibly personal injuries
Cause of damage	State of premises	State of premises	State of premises and activities taking place there or obstructing highway	State of premises and activities taking place there
Nature of liability	Failure to take reasonable care of visitor's safety	Failure to take reasonable care to avoid causing injury to trespassers	Failure reasonably to foresee damage to claimant	Failure reasonably to foresee damage to claimant

Figure 12.1 The occupier's civil legal liability for premises

2 *The method of intervention was reasonable in the circumstances.* The greater the danger and the more able the rescuer, the more reasonable it will be to take risks. Nobody expects a non-swimmer to plunge into deep water, though such a person may have a moral duty to throw a lifebelt and summon assistance.

Haynes v Harwood (1935, CA)
A policeman was injured when attempting to stop bolting horses which were pulling a van in a busy street. The defendant was held to be liable for the police-man's injuries; the policeman had not consented to the risk and his intervention was a natural and foreseeable result of the defendant's negligence in failing to secure the horses.

Sylvester v Chapman (1935)
The claimant, while visiting a travelling menagerie, attempted to extinguish a ciga-rette end which he noticed was smouldering near straw bales beside a leopard's cage. To do so he climbed a safety barrier. The leopard, displeased by the distur-bance, reached out between the bars of the cage and clawed him. It was held that the claimant had consented to the risk. There was no need for him to do more than alert the staff to the fire risk.

Consent to negligence

It is not generally in the public interest to allow defendants to avoid liability for their careless behaviour. Where claimants have clearly acted recklessly, though, without regard for their own safety, or have willingly participated in the careless behaviour, the defendant may be provided with a defence.

ICI v Shatwell (1964, HL)
The claimant shot firer was injured when helping to carry out a controlled explo-sion. The claimant was experienced in the work and had encouraged the team leader to use inappropriate equipment. It was held that the claimant had consented to the risk of injury.

Ratcliff v Harpur Adams College (1998, CA)
A student, who was paralysed after breaking his neck when trespassing in his col-lege swimming pool outside opening hours, was deemed to have consented to the risk of diving into shallow water. (See above at page 178.)

Contributory negligence

Under the Law Reform (Contributory Negligence) Act 1935, the court may reduce the damages payable by the defendant if the claimant has failed to take reasonable care for his own safety and so aggravated the damage suffered.

Sayers v Harlow UDC (1958, CA)
The claimant visited the defendant's public lavatory and was trapped when the lock jammed. After trying to attract attention for 15 minutes, she attempted to climb out over the partition. Unfortunately she fell when the toilet roll, which she was using as a foothold, rotated and threw her to the floor. The Court of Appeal found that the claimant's escape attempt was reasonable, therefore, she had not consented to the risk of injury. Her choice of foothold, however, involved an unreasonable risk and so the damages payable by the defendant would be reduced by one quarter.

Stone v Taffe (1974, CA)
The claimant's husband was killed when, after a party hosted by The Royal and Antediluvian Order of Buffaloes, he catapulted himself down the unlit staircase in the defendant's pub. The claimant's wife and a friend who had preceded him had completed the descent safely. It was held that damages should be reduced by 50 per cent to take account of the lack of care taken by the deceased for his own safety.

VICARIOUS LIABILITY

Usually we are liable only for our own torts, but in certain situations we may be sued for the torts of others for whom we are said to be vicariously liable. This most commonly arises in relation to employers, who may be vicariously liable for the actions of their employees.

Employees and independent contractors

When you run a business you will employ your own staff but may need to bring in others to carry out some essential services. For example, if you run a shop you may employ sales assistants; window cleaning would be done by an outside firm. You are vicariously liable for any torts committed by the shop assistants because of the relationship arising from the *contract of service*. Such a relationship does not exist between you and the window cleaner, who is your independent contractor and works for you under a *contract for services*. The window cleaner is an accessory to your business rather than integrated within it.

This distinction may be difficult to make in big workplaces, where services like catering and cleaning may be contracted out to other firms. The distinction between the staff of the contractor and the 'real employees' is not immediately apparent; determining those employees for whose actions the owner of the workplace is vicariously liable may be problematic. The terms of the contract provide crucial evidence of the intention of the parties. The employee who provides plant, tools and materials and undertakes financial risks in carrying out a job will be deemed to be an independent contractor, even though the employer may exercise considerable control over the contractor's business enterprise.

Ready Mixed Concrete v Ministry of Pensions and National Insurance (1968)
Drivers employed by Ready Mixed Concrete were held to be independent contractors. They had to buy their own vehicles from a supplier nominated by Ready Mixed and paint them in Ready Mixed livery. They could not use the vehicles for their own purposes, and had to make them available whenever required by Ready Mixed, with a substitute driver if necessary.

The extent of the vicarious liability

As long as the activity which gave rise to the tort was sufficiently closely connected with carrying out designated contractual duties, the employer is liable, even if the employee was negligent or disobeying orders concerning the execution of those duties. This may seem hard on the employer, but the law takes the view that employers are obliged to supervise their workforce properly.

Bayley v Manchester, Sheffield & Lincolnshire Railway (1873)
Mistakenly believing that Mr Bayley had boarded the wrong train, the defendant's porter hauled him from it when it had begun to move away, causing him injuries. It was held that the porter had been carrying out his duties, although in a bungling and incompetent manner, and the railway company was vicariously liable.

Century Insurance v The NIRTB* (1949, HL)
While discharging petrol from a tanker the defendant's employee was smoking, which was forbidden under work rules. His employer was nevertheless held liable for the resulting explosion. His behaviour was an unauthorised way of carrying out his duties.

* Northern Ireland Road Transport Board

If, however, the employee's behaviour is not sufficiently coincidental to his job, the employer is not vicariously liable.

Beard v London Omnibus Co. (1900)
The company was not liable for injuries caused to Mr Beard when a bus conductor tried his hand at reversing the bus at the terminus: he was not employed to drive the bus.

Warren v Henlys Garage Ltd (1948)
A pump attendant challenged Mr Warren, believing that he intended to drive off without paying for his petrol. Mr Warren then said he would report him to the manager for insolence; the attendant, in response, hit him on the chin. It was held that the employer was not vicariously liable; the attendant had not been acting to protect his employer's interest when he hit Mr Warren, but to avenge himself.

The application of the doctrine of vicarious liability is increasingly dictated by policy. Where the court believes that the employer should be publicly accountable it will be generous when interpreting the issue of close connection, even where on the face of things the employee has acted only to further his own interests. This is well illustrated by the next case.

Lister (and Others) AP v Hesley Hall Ltd (2001, HL)
A warden of a care home sexually abused boys for whom he was responsible.
   The House of Lords held that the employer was vicariously liable because there was a very close connection between the acts of abuse by the warden and the work he was employed to do.

Liability for independent contractors

Although a person who employs an independent contractor is never *vicariously* liable for the contractor's torts, there are circumstances where the employer may be held *personally* liable for damage resulting from the contractor's work. Such liability arises where a non-delegable legal duty is imposed: the law attaches particular responsibility to the employer, which cannot be transferred to anybody else.
   Examples of situations where the employer will be personally liable are as follows:

1 *Public nuisance affecting the highway*. If scaffolding used by building contractors working on your premises causes an obstruction, you will be personally liable.

2 *Injury to a servant.* Employers have a non-delegable duty to provide a safe working environment for their servants (employees, etc.) and will be personally liable for injuries caused by contractors' work. This is covered in more detail in Chapter 18.

Quiz 12

1 What is the likely tort liability of Red Leicester in the following circumstances?

  (a) Mrs Double Gloucester is hit by a can of paint dropped from the top of a ladder into the street by Cheddar, who was up the ladder painting Red's shop front.

  (b) Stilton slipped on a spillage while climbing the stairs in the shop. A notice at the bottom of the stairs said 'Take care: wet floor, please use other stairs'.

  (c) Lymeswold, aged seven, went through a door in the shop marked 'Private' and cut himself on some broken glass in a storeroom.

  (d) Sage Derby, Red's next-door neighbour, has discovered wet rot in his premises caused by condensation from an unlined boiler flue on Red's premises.

2 What defence may be open to Cheshire, whose car collided with Wensleydale who was riding his motor bike and not wearing a crash helmet?

3 What is the difference between an employer's liability for the torts of employees and for those of independent contractors?

Assignment 11

Healing plc recently opened an anti-stress clinic on the edge of the village of Much-Dozing-in-the-Dell. Farmer Oswald's arable farm is immediately adjacent to the clinic's premises, which include a swimming pool. For three weeks during the summer, Grinders Farming Contractors Ltd are employed by Oswald to bring in the harvest. The work involves daily use of huge machines. The noise of the machinery upsets the clinic's patients, many of whom cancel expensive courses of treatment. The dust and dirt from the harvesting process forms a thick film on the swimming pool making it unusable, and clogs the filter causing it to break down and require expensive repairs. Ned, one of Grinders' employees, drops a cigarette end which starts a fire in the field. It spreads into the clinic's grounds and destroys a summer house.

    Advise Healing plc about its possible rights in tort.

A suggested solution for this assignment can be found in the Lecturer's Guide.

CHAPTER 13

Criminal law protection for the consumer

INTRODUCTION

The law seeks to protect consumers not only by giving them civil law rights in contract and tort, but also by the regulation of the conduct of business through the criminal law. The prevention of undesirable business practices cannot be achieved through the civil law alone. Individual consumers may not be sufficiently aware of their rights, or may not have the confidence to pursue them. Wrongs against the consumer may involve dishonesty, as well as activities which, being dangerous to life and limb, come within the scope of the criminal law. Criminal statutes regulate a wide variety of conduct relating to manufacturing, sales and marketing practices in the fields of environmental protection, public health, product safety and the description of goods and services. Powers of enforcement primarily lie with the trading standards and environmental health departments of local authorities. Businesses may be inspected and monitored to try to ensure compliance with the law. Prosecution of offenders may lead to undesirable publicity as well as the threat of a fine, confiscation of stock or, in extreme cases, business closure.

This is a complex area of the law and a detailed study is outside the scope of this book. Criminal offences relating to the provision of credit services are mentioned in Chapter 14. This chapter examines, in outline, two of the most important areas for consumers and retail businesses:

1 *The control of misleading descriptions of products.* The Trade Descriptions Act 1968 and Part II of the Consumer Protection Act 1987 contain measures aimed at preventing the consumer from being deceived about the nature, quality or value of goods or services.

2 *The regulation of product safety.* Part III of the Consumer Protection Act 1987 imposes a general safety requirement on suppliers of all consumer goods. It is also an enabling Act under which the Department of Trade and Industry is empowered to issue special safety regulations concerning certain types of goods. Breach of any of these duties is a criminal offence.

MISLEADING DESCRIPTIONS: THE TRADE DESCRIPTIONS ACT 1968

This Act covers false descriptions of goods and services. These are examined separately as the rules of liability are different.

False descriptions of goods

Section 2 of the 1968 Act explains the types of description which are regulated by the Act:

1 *Quantity, size, gauge.* For example: '35 mm camera lens'; 'Carpet 10 ft × 25 ft'.

2 *Method of manufacture, production, processing, or reconditioning.* For example: 'Hand-knitted jumpers'; 'Stone-ground flour'; 'Factory-fitted sun roof'; 'Pasteurised milk'.

3 *Composition.* For example: 'Pine shelving'; 'Silk shirts'; 'Goats' milk cheese'.

4 *Fitness for purpose, strength, performance, behaviour, accuracy.* For example: 'Machine washable'; 'Waterproof'; '40 miles to the gallon'; 'Very low mileage'.

5 *Any other physical characteristic not covered above.* For example: '1 free video tape with every new VCR'.

6 *Testing by any person and/or the result.* For example: 'Full MOT'.

7 *Approval by any person/conformity to an approved type.* For example: 'Meets British standards'.

8 *Place, date of manufacture, production, processing, or reconditioning.* For example: 'Cornish clotted cream'; '1993 Ford Escort'.

9 *Person by whom the goods were manufactured, produced, etc.* For example: 'Heinz Baked Beans'; 'Clarks Shoes'.

Not every false description is a criminal offence. Section 3(1) provides that it must be false 'to a material degree', which means that the description must be sufficiently influential to induce a purchase.

> **Donnelly v Rowlands** (1970)
> (This relates to a very common occurrence in the sale of milk.) The defendant dairy put some of their milk in bottles which were embossed with another dairy's insignia, but which also had caps clearly displaying the name of the defendant's dairy. It was held that nobody buying the milk would do so in the belief that it had come from the dairy whose name was on the bottle rather than on the cap. In these circumstances the bottle name merely indicated the provenance of the bottle, not that of its contents.

A statement may be found to be false even if the statement is true as far as it goes, but is incomplete and is consequently misleading to potential customers.

> **Routledge v Ansa Motors Ltd** (1980)
> A car which had been manufactured in 1972 but neither registered nor used until 1975 could not truthfully be described as a 1975 model. Such a description would lead the average customer to believe that the car had been manufactured in 1975.

Two offences are created by the Act:

1 *applying* a false description to goods;

2 *supplying* goods which carry a false description.

These offences have four characteristics in common:

- they can be committed only by someone who makes a statement *in the course of a business*. A private seller cannot be prosecuted under the 1968 Act;
- the statement need not be made to a *consumer*;
- no sale need have resulted;
- they are strict liability offences. Intention to deceive need not be proved.

The offence of applying a false description to goods (s 1(1)(a)) can only be committed actively; the defendant must be responsible for the creation and circulation of the description. The description may appear on packaging or labels, or in literature accompanying the goods. The offence also includes notices displayed in a shop, advertising in any form (including catalogues and circulars) as well as oral descriptions given by sales staff.

While descriptions are generally expressly made, they may also be implied – as when a car odometer is 'clocked' by a dishonest dealer who winds it back to make it appear that the car has done a smaller mileage.

The offence of supplying or offering to supply goods which have been falsely described (s 1(1)(b)) can be committed passively. The defendant need not have applied the description personally; in practice this usually happened before the goods came into the defendant's possession.

'Supplying' means selling, but 'offering to supply' includes not only exposing the goods, making them accessible to potential customers, it also covers a seller who has the relevant goods in its possession and intends to sell them. (Note the wide definition of 'offering' which includes situations which in the law of contract would be described as invitations to treat.)

Both these offences give rise to strict liability. Once the prosecution have proved that the necessary supply or application elements are satisfied, the defendant is liable unless protected by the 'due diligence' defence (below). The prosecution do not have to prove that the defendant intended to lie or was reckless or careless in issuing the description.

The due diligence defence (s 24) protects any defendant who can satisfy the court that it was not careless in issuing the statement. This may be possible if the defendant can prove that:

1 the statement was made with all reasonable care and the defendant reasonably believed it to be true; or

2 the false statement was applied by a third party and there were no circumstances (such as expert knowledge) which should have alerted the defendant to its falsity.

In practice, this defence is most likely to be successful when used by suppliers and other middlemen who merely pass on goods to which a third party (usually the manufacturer) has attached a description.

False descriptions of services

Under s 14 of the 1968 Act, it is an offence for a person in the course of business knowingly or recklessly to make a false or misleading statement concerning the supply of services. The statement does not necessarily have to have been made to a consumer.

Liability is not strict. The prosecution have to prove that the statement was made intentionally. The defendant need not have actually intended to tell a direct lie: it is sufficient to prove that the defendant acted recklessly and failed to give sufficient consideration to whether the statement was true or false.

Liability depends on the defendant knowing of the falsity of the statement at the time it was communicated to the customer. Liability may arise if a statement subsequently becomes untrue due to a change of circumstances which occurs after the statement was made and before it was communicated to the customer.

Wings v Ellis (1984)
A brochure from Wings, in good faith, described a hotel as having air conditioning. The company later discovered that this was untrue and issued a memo to its staff to correct the brochures. Mr Ellis was supplied with a brochure which had not been updated. This made Wings liable, since at the point Ellis was given the information the company was aware that it was untrue.

Not all incorrect statements attract liability under the Act. False and misleading statements concerning services give rise to liability in the following circumstances:

1 *The provision of services, accommodation and facilities*. The statement must be made in the course of business and relate to current provision. 'Opening shortly' announcements are therefore not covered. 'Services' must involve more than merely supplying goods. 'Accommodation' is intended to cover hotels, bed and breakfast establishments and holiday cottages; it does not apply to housing in general. Misleading statements in the sale or rental of dwellings may be covered by the Property Misdescriptions Act 1991. 'Facilities' covers provision for

optional use by a customer. This would include a hotel swimming pool, a car park or tea-making facilities.

2 *The nature of any services, accommodation and facilities.* The quality of the services etc. must be to the standard indicated in the statement. In *R v Clarksons Holidays* (1972), a hotel was falsely described as providing a 'good efficient service'.

3 *The timing or mode of the service or the nature of personnel.* For example: 'Two-hour photographic printing service'; 'Permanent security guards'; 'All our nursery staff have NNEB qualifications'.

4 *Examination, approval by authorised body.* For example: 'Our hotel is recommended by the RAC'; 'Approved by the Association of British Insurers'.

5 *Location and amenities.* This is designed to cover misleading statements that might not be covered by any of the other categories. For example: 'Three minutes from the beach'; 'In the centre of town'.

Section 25 of the Act provides an 'innocent publication' defence. Newspapers or magazines which carry advertising placed by manufacturers or suppliers are liable under the Trade Descriptions Act 1968 for any false statement in the advertisement only if they should have been aware of its falsity. The newspaper will be expected to recognise obvious falsity and to make checks if appropriate.

MISLEADING STATEMENTS CONCERNING PRICE:

THE CONSUMER PROTECTION ACT 1987 (PART III)

Under s 20 of the Consumer Protection Act 1987, it is an offence to issue *in the course of business* a misleading indication to a *consumer* regarding the *price* of goods, services, accommodation and facilities. The statement must be made in the course of business: statements by private sellers do not give rise to liability.

Liability is strict and rests upon the business which makes the relevant statement to potential customers.

R v Warwickshire County Council, ex parte Johnson (1993)
The employer or owner of the business with responsibility for the pricing policy is the appropriate person to sue, not the employee who merely passes on the statement in the course of employment.

Denard v Burton Retail (1997)
It is no defence for the retailer to claim that the misleading price tag was attached to the goods by the company which supplied the goods to the retailer.

No liability arises unless a consumer has actually been made aware of the statement. It must therefore have been displayed where a consumer would be likely to see it and there must also be evidence that they were actually misled by it, although no purchase need have resulted.

> **Gloucestershire County Council v Toys "Я" Us** (1994)
> The price marking on some of the defendants' goods was different from that on the bar codes for the same products. The defendants had a policy that if such a conflict arose the lower price would always be charged.
>
> It was held [on appeal] that, since there was no evidence that this policy was not adhered to, there was no evidence that any customer had actually been misled and therefore the defendants' conviction was dismissed.

The statement may be made orally, or appear on price tickets, shelf markings, notices, circulars, catalogues, as well as in advertisements in the media.

A price indication may be misleading in the following situations:

1 *The stated price is less than what is actually being charged*. For example, the customer is informed at the point of sale that a price tag is incorrect and that the actual price of the goods is higher.

2 *A special price depends on facts of which the customer has not been made aware*. For example, a sandwich bar runs a promotional offer for cheap snacks and does not indicate that it is not available between noon and two o'clock.

3 *The stated price appears to be inclusive but an additional charge is payable*. For example, quoting a price for a holiday without indicating that a singles supplement is payable.

4 *A false suggestion that the price of goods has been reduced or is likely to rise shortly*. For example, 'Further reductions'; 'No budget increase until 31 May'.

5 *Misleading comparisons with another price*. For example, advertising a 'reduced' price for goods which were never sold at the higher price.

Similar defences to those under the Trade Descriptions Act 1968 may assist a defendant:

1 due diligence and reasonable care (s 39);

2 bona fide advertising by the media of a third party's products (s 24(3));

3 bona fide media statements not in the form of advertising. This would protect consumer rights programmes like the BBC's *Watchdog* or *Which?* magazine.

A DTI code of practice was issued in 1988 under powers delegated by s 25 of the Consumer Protection Act 1987. It is intended to provide guidance on good trading practice and assist traders to fulfil their statutory obligations. Failure to comply with the code is likely to be treated as evidence of an offence, while compliance will usually prevent liability from arising.

PRODUCT SAFETY: THE CONSUMER PROTECTION

ACT 1987 (PART II)

Chapter 10 covered the issues of civil liability contained in Part I of the 1987 Act. This is largely reinforced by Part II of the Act, which imposes criminal law regulation of the safety of most types of goods intended for private use. Note that food, medicines and motor vehicles are not within the scope of the Act but are regulated under other statutes.

The Act lays down a general safety requirement covering all goods relevant to the Act. In addition, it enables special safety regulations to be issued at the discretion of the Secretary of State relating to particular types of goods. A large number of such regulations have been created imposing specific safety requirements on a wide range of consumer goods, including toys, furniture, night wear, protective hats for horse riders, vehicle accessories and condoms. EC law is also influential in this area. In 1994, the General Product Safety Regulations came into force; these implement the Product Safety Directive 1992.

Detailed information about the content of these regulations is outside the scope of this book. The remainder of this chapter focuses on the scope of liability under the general safety requirement and the powers of enforcement given to trading standards departments in the event of breach of this or of any of the special safety regulations.

The general safety requirement

Under s 10 of the 1987 Act, goods sold for consumer use must be reasonably safe, and it is a criminal offence:

1 to supply, or to offer or to agree to supply any consumer goods which do not meet the general safety requirement; or

2 to expose or possess such goods with the intention of supplying them.

An offence may therefore be committed without any actual sale of goods having taken place. Putting goods in the shop window, or merely having them in your storeroom may give rise to liability if they are intended for sale.

The goods conform to the safety standard as long as the risk of their causing death or personal injury is removed or kept to a reasonable minimum. Therefore, danger to people rather than property must be eliminated as far as is reasonably possible. It may be impossible to remove all risk from the use of some products, like ladders or kitchen knives. Despite high production standards and appropriate warnings, some people will still manage to fall off the former or cut themselves on the latter.

The general safety requirement is relevant only to the safety of people, not their property. Goods may threaten the safety of property while posing no risk to anybody's personal safety: paint leaking from a defective tin might damage your clothes, but would not generally pose any danger to your health.

The duty is breached only where the goods are actively dangerous. Therefore, goods which are merely defective but not dangerous do not breach the requirement. An electric iron which will not work is defective, but it may not pose any threat to life or limb.

Any person involved in the manufacturing, selling or supplying process may be liable.

Goods may be unsafe because of manufacturing defects in the product itself. However, s 19 of the Act also states that goods may be unsafe because of their packaging, or through lack of proper instructions or indications of the extent of their shelf life.

Sanctions

Prosecution

Trading standards departments may prosecute an offender in the magistrates' court, which may impose a fine of up to £5000 or a sentence of imprisonment of up to six months.

Suspension notices

The trading standards department may issue an order which forces the trader to hold on to the offending goods and which prevents their display or sale. This may be issued when a prosecution is pending.

Forfeiture notice

If the trader is found guilty, the court may issue an order requiring the trader to hand over goods which have been proved to be unsafe. The trading standards department may then destroy the goods.

Defences

Under s 39 of the Act, a due diligence defence is available to any defendant. A retailer who could not reasonably have known that the goods did not reach the approved standard at the time of supply or possession will not be liable.

HOW WELL DOES THE CRIMINAL LAW PROTECT

CONSUMERS?

There is no shortage of regulation, breach of which may lead to prosecution. Fines and imprisonment may result and powers exist under which offending goods may be confiscated and destroyed. In extreme circumstances premises may be closed. The legislation sets standards likely to be met by reputable businesses and which may act as a deterrent to some dubious trading practices.

Legislative controls are fully effective only if adequately enforced. Cuts in public spending have led to a reduction in the staffing levels of trading standards and environmental health departments of local authorities. Consequently, it is arguable that an appropriate level of inspection has become impossible to maintain, enabling many offences to escape detection.

Quiz 13

1 Consider which offences may have been committed by Dragon in the following circumstances:

   (a) He puts an advertisement in the local newspaper stating that he is selling '100% silk shirts' at his shop. The shirts are in fact made of a silk/linen mixture.

   (b) His storeroom contains overcoats bearing a manufacturer's label stating incorrectly that they are 'genuine Harris tweed'.

   (c) He displays a notice in his shop which says 'Two-Hour Alterations Service'. Minotaur, who wants his trousers shortened, is told that they will not be ready until the next day, as Gryphon, the alterations assistant, is on sick leave.

   (d) Basilisk wishes to buy a jacket marked '£50'. At the till he is told that the price ticket is incorrect and that the real price is £70.

2 What is the difference between 'applying' and 'supplying' a misleading description under s 1 of the Trade Descriptions Act 1968?

3 What is the difference in liability between offences under s 1 and s 14 of the 1968 Act?

4 When may an offence be committed under s 20 of the Consumer Protection Act 1987?

Assignment 12

Scribe has been engaged as a company secretary to a garage business which sells and repairs cars. He has been asked by the proprietor to draft a memorandum explaining how the Trade Descriptions Act 1968 impinges on the two aspects of the business. Discuss the main points which such a memorandum should contain.

(ICSA English Business Law: June 1994)

CHAPTER 14

Credit facilities and the consumer

INTRODUCTION

A wide variety of credit facilities are readily available to consumers: credit cards are in common use, many people automatically fund any large-scale purchases through a personal loan or by entering a hire-purchase contract. Such facilities are helpful to both consumers and businesses. Customers are able to obtain immediately goods or services which they may not currently be able to afford and spread the cost of repayment: the business they are dealing with is able to make a sale. During a recession the provision of credit facilities may help to maintain a crucial turnover of stock, which is beneficial to the national economy. There are, however, dangers inherent in easy access to credit. Provision is made on the lender's terms and, therefore, there is danger of exploitation of the borrower. The law consequently provides a variety of safeguards through the Consumer Credit Act 1974, which comprehensively regulates consumer credit provision.

The Act aims to safeguard users of credit facilities by ensuring that:

1 providers of the services are reputable;

2 advertisements for credit services are not misleading;

3 potential borrowers are fully informed about the nature and terms of the credit agreement prior to acceptance;

4 the terms of the contract adequately protect the borrower against abuse of power by the creditor.

This chapter gives an overview of the most important areas of the Act and illustrates its application, primarily in the area of purchase of goods and services. All statutory references are to the Consumer Credit Act 1974 unless the contrary is stated.

THE REGULATION OF CREDIT SUPPLIERS

Licensing

A licence is required by any person or business engaged in the provision of credit (s 21); it is an offence to engage in business without one (s 39). Licences are granted by the Director General of Fair Trading provided the applicant is deemed to be a fit and proper person to run a consumer credit business (s 25). The Director General keeps a register of licence holders. A licence is initially issued for a ten-year period and can be renewed subject to the approval of the Director General. A licence may be revoked or suspended at any time if the licence holder is guilty of conduct which would normally be grounds for refusal of a licence (s 32). A credit agreement made with an unlicensed dealer is unenforceable against the debtor (borrower) without the leave of the Director General (s 40).

Controls on advertising

The content of advertisements is controlled by regulations made by the Secretary of State. The Act (s 44) requires that advertising conveys reasonably full and fair information about the credit facilities offered and the true financial cost to the user. Section 46 and the Consumer Credit (Advertisements) Regulations 1989 make it a criminal offence to put a false or misleading advertisement into circulation.

> **Mersoja v H. Norman Pitt** (1989)
> Cars were advertised for sale on interest-free credit. To finance the deal the garage charged several hundred pounds more for cars bought on hire purchase than for those bought by cash buyers. It was held that the advertisement was misleading as what was advertised as an interest-free deal actually carried a hidden credit charge.

Credit reference agencies

These agencies are used by businesses to check whether customers' previous financial records suggest that they will repay their debts. Reference agencies maintain databases containing the names and addresses of people alleged to have defaulted during previous credit agreements, or to have failed to satisfy a judgment debt. Unfortunately the information may be misleading; for example, somebody who lives in a house divided into flats may find credit refused because a bad debtor once lived in an adjoining flat.

Applicants who are refused credit because of a bad credit reference are entitled under ss 157–159 to request the name of the agency from the business which has refused credit. They may then apply to the agency for a copy of the relevant file. A small fee is payable to the agency, which must then supply a copy of the file and amend it if necessary, within 28 days. Failure to comply is a criminal offence.

REGULATED AGREEMENTS

If a credit agreement has the status of a 'regulated agreement' under the Act, debtors have greater protection than is given by the common law. For example, they are entitled to full written information about the terms of the contract and its financial implications. They also have the right to cancel or terminate the contract in certain situations, and the creditor's (lender's) rights to recover goods supplied under a hire-purchase agreement are to some extent limited. Section 8 defines a regulated agreement as:

1 a personal credit agreement

2 by which an individual

3 is provided with credit not exceeding £15 000.

Although the section refers to personal credit and the title of the Act refers to consumer credit, regulated agreements may be made by persons on behalf of their small businesses, not just for their private and domestic purposes. 'Individual' is defined by the Act as including partnerships and other unincorporated bodies. A company is, therefore, excluded from making a regulated agreement.

The amount of actual credit being provided to the debtor is what determines whether an agreement is or is not regulated. The money with which debtors part in performing their obligations under a regulated agreement is not all credit payment. The deposit, if any, interest and any other charges for credit (like insurance costs), are not computed as being part of the £15 000. The credit payment represents the sum which is being lent.

Exempt agreements

Certain agreements which fulfil the criteria for regulation are fully or partially exempt from the control of the Act (s 16). These include:

1 loans for house purchases made by reputable lenders (these are completely exempt);

2 loans between friends and not made in the course of business; and

3 'small agreements' (except for hire-purchase or conditional sale) where the amount of credit does not exceed £50. Such agreements are subject to reduced regulation and can be made with less formality than is generally required.

Hire-purchase, conditional sale, and credit sale agreements

Some of the commonest agreements regulated by the Act are those by which a party obtains the immediate use of goods on credit and pays for them by instalments. There are three types of contract by which this can be achieved and they all have different legal consequences.

Hire-purchase contracts

When buyers enter a hire-purchase contract they become the hirer of the goods with an option under the terms of the contract to buy the goods when the hire payments have all been made. They are not bound to keep the goods once these payments have been made, though generally this is what happens. They do not become the owners of the goods until they exercise the option. Up to this point the ownership of the goods remains with the creditor.

Conditional sale agreements

The buyers in such contracts commit themselves to buying the goods on entering the contract, but do not become the owners of the goods until they have paid off all the instalments.

Credit sales agreements

Both ownership and possession pass to the buyers on delivery. Payment may be made by instalment. Since the buyers are the owners, they are entitled to dispose of the goods to a third party at any time even if they have not yet finished paying for them.

In such agreements the credit facilities are often not provided directly by the supplier of the goods, but by a finance company. In such circumstances the hirer/buyer's contract is with the creditor only. If the goods are defective, the creditor is liable for breach of contract rather than the supplier. This is because there is no privity of contract between the supplier and buyer. Exceptionally the supplier may be liable on a collateral contract (see Chapter 5).

The types of credit and credit agreement defined by the Act

The 1974 Act has its own jargon concerning the definition of different types of credit and the agreements by which they may be supplied; you need to be able to distinguish between these different concepts as sometimes they have different legal consequences, which are referred to later in this chapter. The person who obtains credit is called the *debtor*, while the provider is (not surprisingly) called the *creditor*. Where the credit agreement involves obtaining goods on credit, a *supplier* may also be involved; suppliers provide the goods but the credit comes from a separate source, like a credit card or finance company.

Credit

Credit falls into one of the following two categories: running account credit and fixed-term credit.

1 *Running-account credit*. The debtor is provided with credit for an indefinite time, up to a specified maximum, and may use it to obtain cash, goods or services. Interest is payable only if and when the debtor uses the credit facility. Running-account credit may be obtained from agreed overdraft arrangements and credit cards.

2 *Fixed-term credit*. Any credit which is not running-account credit is fixed-term credit. This includes the credit provided by personal loans from a bank or other lending institutions, or by a hire-purchase agreement.

Credit may be for restricted or unrestricted use. Where credit is for restricted use, it can be used only for limited purposes determined by the creditor who is paymaster. The debtor has no direct control over the credit funds. *Restricted use credit* exists in the following situations:

1 the debtor obtains goods or services under a contract with the creditor and pays for them in instalments over a pre-arranged period of time. For example, hire-purchase agreements;

2 the debtor obtains goods or services under a contract with a supplier and the creditor pays the supplier direct when requested. For example, purchases by credit card. Card holders are restricted in their choice of supplier to those who have already agreed to deal with the relevant card company;

3 re-financing agreements: the debtor, who already owes money to a number of other people, makes an agreement with a creditor to borrow sufficient funds to discharge all the existing debts. The creditor pays off the debts directly.

With *unrestricted use credit*, the creditor gives the debtor the means of controlling the money, either by handing it over or by paying it into the debtor's bank account. Personal loans from the bank fall into this category. It seems odd to describe such a loan as for unrestricted use, since it is not usually given unless the bank knows what the customer intends to do with it. It is defined as unrestricted use credit because the debtor has control of the funds and pays them out personally. The debtor may put the loan to entirely different purposes than those for which it was granted.

Credit agreement

The credit agreement falls into one of two categories: DCS and DC agreements.

1 *A debtor, creditor, supplier (DCS) agreement (s 12).* There is a pre-existing credit arrangement between supplier and creditor and the debtor has dealings with both of them. For example, credit card purchases and hire-purchase agreements where the supplier customarily uses the services of a particular finance company. There is a crucial difference between the relationship of the debtor and the supplier in these two situations. In a hire-purchase situation there is no contract for sale between supplier and debtor; the debtor's only contract in relation to the goods is with the creditor. With a credit card purchase the debtor has two contracts, one for the purchase of the goods and a pre-existing one with the credit card company (see Figures 14.1 and 14.2).

2 *Debtor and creditor (DC) agreements (s 13).* In such agreements no supplier may be involved at all (as in re-financing agreements). Where a supplier is involved there will not be any pre-existing connection between the creditor and supplier and they may never have any connection with each other at all: for example, a personal loan to enable the debtor to buy a new kitchen. DC agreements also occur where buyers make their own hire-purchase arrangements and do not use those available through the agency of the supplier.

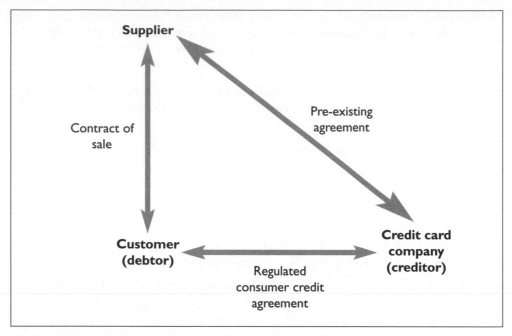

Figure 14.1 Contractual relationships in credit card sales

A *regulated agreement* is thus:

1 either a DCS or DC agreement,

2 with restricted use or unrestricted use credit,

3 which provides either running-account or fixed-term credit.

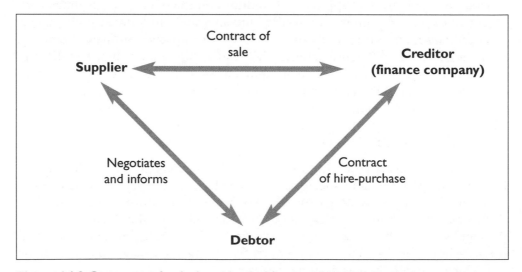

Figure 14.2 Contractual relationships in hire-purchase contracts

In the quiz at the end of this chapter there are some examples of credit arrangements for you to analyse according to these criteria. Here is an example to get you started.

A credit card agreement is:

- a DCS agreement
- for restricted use and
- provides running-account credit.

When you use your card, you do so to obtain goods or services from a limited number of suppliers who are in a pre-agreed relationship with the credit card company. For as long as you obey the terms of your contract with the card company (pay your monthly bill and do not exceed the credit limit), your account will continue and the credit company will service bills sent in by the businesses you have dealt with. You can run up your credit card bill as much or as little as you like up to the pre-agreed limit.

Protection for the debtor in a regulated agreement

Pre-contract information

The Act aims to ensure that potential borrowers will not be misled by false or misleading advertisements or quotations and will be given appropriate information to enable them to be aware of the implications of any financial commitment.

The form of the agreement

Section 60 and the Consumer Credit Regulations govern the form and content of the agreement. As far as the *form* of the agreement is concerned, it must be written and readily legible. Tiny print which could not be comfortably read by a ordinarily sighted person would not fulfil this requirement. With respect to the *content*, the creditor must ensure that certain information is contained in the contract including:

- the nature of the agreement (personal loan, hire-purchase, etc.);
- names and addresses of the parties;
- a description of goods and their cash price (hire-purchase, conditional and credit sales only);
- the amount of credit;
- the amount of any deposit;
- the total charge for credit;
- amounts and times of repayment;
- the APR (annual percentage rate of interest);
- the credit limit (in running-account credit agreements only).

The information required in the contract enables the debtor to appreciate the extent of the commitment and its full cost, and to be able to compare the difference between the cash and credit price of any goods to be supplied. The agreement is not executed (legally effective) unless it is *signed by both creditor and debtor*.

Unless the agreement is readily legible, contains the relevant information and is signed, it may be unenforceable against the debtor. This encourages the creditor to comply, since failure to do so can prevent it from enforcing its rights against a defaulting debtor.

Entitlement to copies of the agreement

Debtors are entitled to a copy of the agreement for reference. The point at which they must receive it depends on how the agreement is made. If the agreement is presented to a debtor personally for signature (not sent by post), the debtor must be given a copy immediately. If the creditor does not sign the agreement at the same time as the debtor, the agreement, while 'made' when the debtor signs, is not 'executed' until the creditor signs it. The debtor is entitled to a copy of the agreement within seven days of the contract being made.

Cancellation rights

At common law, once parties have accepted an offer they are contractually bound, and if they try to back out they will be in breach of contract. A limited class of debtors is given some statutory cancellation rights to protect them against hard-sell tactics by pushy sales staff visiting the debtors in their own homes.

Under s 67, a debtor may cancel the agreement within *five days*, provided that:

1 it was not made on trade premises; and

2 it resulted from prior negotiations made face to face with the debtor or a member of the debtor's household. Therefore, postal or telephone negotiations are excluded.

The five-day cooling off period runs from the day the debtor receives notice of the cancellation rights, which the creditor is required to supply either as part of the executed agreement or under separate cover (s 64).

The consequences of cancellation are as follows:

1 the debtor may recover any money already paid under the agreement, like a deposit for goods (s 70);

2 the debtor cannot be required to pay any outstanding payments;

3 any goods supplied are returnable (s 72).

The debtor is not personally responsible for returning the goods, but must keep them safe and make them available for collection by the creditor at any reasonable time.

Rights against the creditor for defects in goods and services

A creditor is vicariously liable for the supplier's misstatements. In any DCS agreement, the supplier, when negotiating with the debtor, is treated as the agent of the creditor (s 56). This means that if the supplier during pre-contract negotiations makes a misrepresentation, the creditor may be held liable to the debtor as if the creditor had made the statement personally. Section 54 is particularly helpful for the debtor in a hire-purchase or similar contract who is not in a contractual relationship with the supplier and who therefore has no means of taking action against the supplier.

A credit card user may sue the card issuer or supplier. Where defective goods or services are paid for by credit card, the debtor may sue the card issuer or the supplier provided that the cash value of the relevant item is at least £100 and not more than £30 000 (s 75). In such transactions the debtor enters into a contract with the supplier and pays for the goods by using the card. If the supplier commits misrepresentation or breach of contract the debtor has rights to sue the supplier. In addition, under s 75 the debtor has a 'like claim' against the credit card company, provided that the sale falls within the financial limits.

This can be very useful to a card customer who finds a defect in the goods after the supplier has gone out of business. It also applies to goods purchased abroad, though the card companies have recently pressed for a change in the law to remove this liability. It will be unfortunate for the consumer if the companies are successful; taking action against an overseas supplier is not a financially practicable measure for the great majority of consumers.

Rights to terminate the contract

A debtor is not bound to continue with the credit agreement until the end of its specified time span. There are two principal situations where termination rights come into play:

1 *The debtor wants to pay off the loan early (s 94).* Having taken out a loan or a hire-purchase agreement to buy a new car, kitchen, or state-of-the-art computer system, the debtor's financial circumstances miraculously change for the better. In this happy situation the debtor may immediately end the credit agreement under s 94, which entitles a debtor to terminate the agreement ahead of time by giving notice to the creditor and paying off the remainder of the debt. As the debtor is paying early a cheaper deal may be available as not so much interest will be payable; the debtor may receive a rebate on outstanding interest.

2 *The debtor wants to abandon the agreement (s 99).* Here the debtor falls on hard times and is unable to continue to finance a credit agreement. Not all agreements can be terminated voluntarily in these circumstances as this would be unfair to the creditor: for example, in a personal loan contract. However, s 99 enables the debtor to terminate a hire-purchase or conditional sale agreement by giving notice to the creditor, who is protected by his/her rights of title in the goods. The debtor is obliged to pay any outstanding instalments and hand back the goods. However,

the court may give the debtor the option of paying for the goods instead. Section 99 can be very beneficial to a creditor if the termination occurs near the end of the repayment period and the debtor cannot afford to exercise any option granted by the court.

Minimum payment clauses

To protect against loss from early termination, the creditor may include a minimum payment clause requiring payment of a specified sum on termination, in addition to any arrears. Section 100 restricts oppressive use of such clauses. A debtor cannot be required to pay in total (including all instalments paid or due at the date of termination) a sum greater than half the value of the purchase price of the goods. The following example illustrates how this will work in practice.

The total cost of a television set, the subject of a hire-purchase contract, was £600. At the point when the debtor terminated the agreement, he was up to date with his payments and had already repaid £300. He cannot be required to pay any sum in excess of this as this represents half the price of the goods. However, if at the point of termination, even when instalments are paid up to date, the debtor has paid only £270, the court has the discretion to order him to pay another £30.

The rights of the creditor when the debtor defaults

Default in this context means that the debtor has committed a breach of contract. The exercise of a debtor's rights of voluntary termination is not a breach of contract, since it is an exercise of a statutory right in relation to a regulated agreement. Where the debtor defaults, the creditor has the following rights.

The right to recover unpaid instalments

Failing to pay an instalment at the required time is clearly a breach of contract entitling the creditor to sue to recover the debt.

The right to repudiate the contract

If the debtor's breach is serious enough to be treated as a breach of condition, this entitles the creditor to refuse further performance of the contract. Such a breach would occur, for example, if a debtor in a hire-purchase contract disposed of the goods or damaged them, or wilfully failed to make a number of payments. A default notice must be issued *before* the creditor can take action to repudiate (s 87). Thus, the debtor in a regulated agreement enjoys privileges not available to a party governed by common law rules which permit the innocent victim of the breach immediately to terminate its side of the contract and start proceedings.

Under s 88, the notice must:

1 specify the nature of the breach;

2 indicate what needs to be done to correct it;

3 give a date by which this must be done (at least seven days from the issue of the notice);

4 state what will happen if it is not complied with: usually this would be repossession of the goods and termination of the agreement.

Provided that the debtor fulfils the requirements of the notice, the debtor is freed from liability for the breach and the contract continues to bind both parties (s 89). Only if the debtor fails to meet the deadline is the creditor able to embark on the repudiation process.

Limits to the right to recover goods

Even when the debtor fails to comply with a default notice, the goods are not automatically recoverable: they may enjoy protected status under the Act. If so, they can be recovered from the debtor only by the use of a court order (s 90). An order may well be refused by the court if it seems more appropriate to make a time order under which the repayment period under the contract is extended.

Goods are protected under s 90 if:

1 the debtor is in breach of the agreement; and

2 has paid more than one third of the total price of the goods; and

3 the title to the goods has remained with the creditor.

Note that the goods are protected only if the debtor has defaulted: if the debtor has voluntarily terminated the agreement under s 99 the goods must be handed back, regardless of how much the debtor has paid, although the court has a discretion to allow the debtor to pay the balance instead (s 100). A debtor may be better off waiting for the creditor to take action on default rather than voluntarily terminating the agreement, or agreeing on request from the creditor to hand back goods which would otherwise have had protected status.

If the creditor repossesses protected goods (takes them against the will of the debtor) without obtaining a court order, this automatically terminates the agreement (s 91). This not only releases the debtor from all liability under the agreement, but also entitles the debtor to recover all sums paid from the creditor.

The right to recover damages

In addition to recovering any arrears, the creditor is entitled to claim damages for other losses resulting from the debtor's breach. The debtor may therefore be liable for loss resulting from failure to take delivery of the goods, failure to take care of them where they remain the creditor's property, or to cover expenses due to refusal to comply with a lawful demand to give up the goods.

The powers of the court

These powers may all be exercised by the county court.

Enforcement orders

The court will not necessarily allow the creditor to enforce the contract. The form and content of the agreement will be scrutinised to check whether it contains irregularities. Under the Act, some irregularities are classified as fatal and make the contract automatically unenforceable against the debtor (s 127). These include failure of the debtor to sign the agreement, failure to include the prescribed terms in the agreement and failure to supply notice of any cancellation rights.

Non-fatal irregularities discharge the agreement at the discretion of the court if it is just to do so, taking into account the behaviour of the creditor and the damage, if any, suffered by the debtor.

If the court is satisfied that the agreement is enforceable it has a discretion as to whether to enforce it as it stands, or to enforce it subject to variations being made.

Time orders

Under s 129, the court may grant a debtor extra time to pay or to rectify a breach which is the subject of a default notice. While a time order is in operation, goods cannot legally be recovered from the debtor.

The power to investigate extortionate credit agreements

Any credit agreement (not just a regulated one) may be investigated on application to the court, on the grounds that it is extortionate (s 139). Section 138 defines as extortionate any credit bargain which requires a debtor to make grossly 'exorbitant' payments, or which 'otherwise grossly contravenes ordinary principles of fair dealing'. It also lays down factors to be considered when determining whether the bargain is extortionate. These include:

- the interest rates prevailing at the time the bargain was made;
- personal factors relating to the debtor such as age, health and business capability;
- the degree of risk to the creditor;
- the relationship of the parties;
- whether an inflated cash price was quoted to the debtor which concealed the interest or cost of credit.

Very high rates of interest may be justified in some circumstances.

Ketley v Scott (1981)
A 48 per cent interest rate was held not to be extortionate given the high risk of lending to K, who was already overdrawn and required the loan at short notice which precluded full enquiries being made.

Quiz 14

1 What are the characteristics of a 'regulated agreement' under the Consumer Credit Act?

2 What is the main difference between a hire-purchase contract, a conditional sale and a credit sale?

3 Indicate whether the following agreements are DC/DCS and explain what sort of credit is involved:

   (a) a credit card agreement;

   (b) a bank loan;

   (c) a hire-purchase agreement.

4 Advise Scarlet of her rights in the following circumstances:

   (a) She has entered a hire-purchase agreement to buy double glazing from Gable Windows. She signed the agreement at home where she had been called upon by Rhett, a sales representative from Gable.

   (b) She is unable to keep up the payments under a hire-purchase contract under which Ashley Motor Finance are supplying her with a car, and is considering giving it back.

Assignment 13

(a) Where goods are supplied under a hire-purchase contract and they are not fit for their purpose the hirer has long since had important rights against the hire purchase company. More recently, similar rights have existed where goods are acquired by using a credit card. Discuss.

(b) Alan acquires some secondhand stereo equipment from his local Ghettoblaster Shop. The cost of each item is no more than £75, but the total cost of the system is £320. He uses his Lowcost credit card in payment. Soon after setting up the system a fault develops in one item. The system bursts into flames and Alan's lounge is damaged. The cost of redecoration is £1000. Alan seeks your advice as to who may be liable to compensate him. Advise Alan.

(ICSA Business Law: December 1994)

A suggested solution for this assignment can be found in the Lecturer's Guide.

CHAPTER 15

The law of agency

INTRODUCTION

An agency relationship may arise in any situation where one party (the principal) authorises another person (the agent) to act on his or her behalf. Any contract made by the agent on the principal's behalf is binding by or against the third party with whom the agent negotiated. The agent may also be liable to the principal if the agent acted negligently or in breach of any contract of agency.

You will already be aware of a number of situations where an agent may be employed – when you want to buy a house you may employ an estate agent; you may have obtained insurance through an insurance broker or bought shares through a stockbroker; an employer may choose to obtain staff through an employment agency; in many sale of goods situations, agents may be employed by sellers or buyers to obtain customers or to arrange transport for international trading deals – in all these situations the principal (the person employing the agent) uses the agent in order to capitalise on the agent's expertise in the relevant business area.

An agent is not necessarily a professional, engaged for commercial purposes. An agency relationship may arise where a person agrees to handle the affairs of a friend who is currently unable to act personally, because of being abroad or in ill health.

This chapter explains:

1 how an agency relationship may be created;

2 the rights and duties of the agent;

3 the rights and duties of the principal;

4 how the agency relationship may be terminated;

5 the nature of some particular types of commercial agency relationships.

THE CREATION OF AGENCY

The authority of the agent is the keystone of the agency relationship. Provided an agent has legal authority to do business on the principal's behalf, any resulting contract is binding by and against the principal.

Such authority normally arises from agreement between the parties, but exceptions exist in the interests of commercial efficiency. The relationship may be deemed to exist to avoid injustice to a third party or the agent. Sometimes a principal can create authority retrospectively to allow it to take advantage of an unauthorised transaction.

Agency by agreement between the parties

An agency relationship is most commonly created by an agreement between the parties under which the agent is given *actual authority* by the principal. The agency agreement may be made in the following ways:

1 *Formally by deed*. This gives a *power of attorney* to the agent. This is essential where an agent is appointed to act on behalf of a person who has became incapable of managing his or her own affairs. More detail on this topic appears at the end of the chapter.

2 *Informally by written or spoken agreement*. No particular written formalities are generally required: it is possible to appoint an agent by word of mouth. The parties may choose to evidence the agreement in writing, but this does not necessarily include all the terms binding the parties.

Chaudhry v Prabhakar (1988, CA)
An agreement between friends, under which one who claimed knowledge of cars agreed to find a suitable secondhand model for the other, was held to have created an agency relationship.

3 *By implication*. The relationship of the parties may give rise to an implied agency agreement. This commonly arises from the employer and employee relationship. It may also exist between a cohabiting husband and wife since the wife has implied authority from her husband to pledge his credit (run up bills) to satisfy household requirements. However, despite some recent progress towards equality between the sexes, the husband cannot do the same.

The agency agreement may exist without any contractual relationship between principal and agent. An agency may be purely gratuitous, with the agent receiving no payment for his or her services. If a colleague asks you to buy a lunchtime sandwich for her, in law she is appointing you as her agent, but neither of you will anticipate that payment will be made for performance of the service. However, if you are trying to sell your house through an estate agent, a contract exists between you. Under its terms, the agent is entitled to payment of commission from you if a sale takes place with a buyer introduced by the agent.

Where the agency is created by agreement the agent has actual authority. Actual authority is divided into two kinds: express and implied.

1 *Express*. The power is conferred by the principal's explicit directions.

2 *Implied*. The principal is unlikely to spell out every detail of what he or she wants the agent to do. The principal is, however, deemed to have impliedly given the agent authority to accomplish anything necessarily incidental to the performance of the principal's directions.

The extent of implied authority is indicated by all the circumstances in which the agency arose, such as the relationship between the parties, the usual authority of the agent in the relevant area of business and the nature of the principal's orders. For example, if you ask an estate agent to find you a buyer, you give the agent actual authority to do so. You also impliedly authorise the agent to photograph your house and use this for advertisement purposes. In *Real and Personal Advance* v *Palemphin* (1893), the matron of a hospital was held to have implied authority to contract in her employer's name to buy essential supplies for the hospital.

Agency by estoppel

In certain circumstances a third party may presume that a person has the authority of an agent. If the principal's behaviour reasonably appears to give this impression, the third party may enforce a resulting contract against the principal. Provided there was nothing to alert the third party to the true facts, the principal is *estopped* (prevented) from denying that the relationship exists. The agent in such circumstances has *apparent or ostensible authority*.

Apparent authority may exist in the following situations.

1 An agency relationship has ceased to exist but the principal has failed to give notice of this to third parties. For example, if a wife leaves her husband she no longer has the right to pledge his credit. If she continues to do so, traders unaware of the couple's estrangement may still claim their money from the husband, unless he took adequate steps to notify them.

2 No agency relationship has ever existed, but the 'principal' allows a third party to believe the 'agent' was acting on the principal's behalf.

> ***Barrett v Deere*** (1828, HL)
> Payment of a debt to a rogue, who was in the creditor's counting house and appeared to be responsible for transacting business there, was held to discharge the debt. It was reasonable for the debtor to believe that the creditor had authorised the rogue's actions since the creditor had the right to control all transactions taking place on the premises.

3 An agency relationship exists and the principal allows a third party to believe that the agent's authority is greater than it is.

Todd v Robinson (1825)
A principal employed an agent to buy goods on credit from the claimant and told him not to pay more than £31. The agent bought goods from the claimant to the value of £45 and made off with them. It was held that the claimant could claim £45 from the principal as there was nothing to suggest to him that the agent's authority was limited.

Agency arising from necessity

An agency relationship may arise in an emergency situation, where one party spontaneously takes steps to preserve somebody else's property interests. This enables that party to avoid liability for the reasonable costs of the intervention on the owner's behalf.

Such agency may arise if *all* the following conditions are satisfied:

1 while one party has possession of another party's goods an emergency occurs; and

2 this forces that party to take action regarding the goods *for the benefit of their owner*; and

3 it is impossible to communicate with the owner first.

Such an agent has authority to take such reasonable and prudent steps as are necessary in the best interests of the owner of the property.

Sachs v Miklos (1948)
The defendant gratuitously stored the claimant's furniture. During the war he wanted the space it was occupying, but was unable to contact the claimant. He sold the goods. It was held that no agency of necessity arose here because there was *no emergency* justifying the sale and the claimant was acting *for his own benefit*. Therefore, the defendant was liable to the claimant in the tort of conversion (unlawful disposal of the claimant's goods).

In the past such agency often arose in situations where carriers were forced to make decisions to pay for the food and accommodation for livestock (*Great Northern Railway* v *Swaffield* (1874)) or to dispose of perishable goods. Such circumstances are unlikely to occur today given that generally it is possible for a carrier to communicate directly with the owner and obtain emergency instructions.

If agency of necessity exists:

1 the agents may claim their expenses;

2 agents have a defence if sued for trespass for disposing of the goods;

3 a third party who has acquired goods from such an agent gets good title to the goods.

Agency by ratification

Even if a party had no authority or exceeded the given authority to act for another when making the contract, authority can be given subsequently if the other party wants to adopt the transaction. This *ratification* creates antecedent authority for the agent: the law treats the agent as having had authority from the outset.

For ratification to be valid the following requirements must be fulfilled:

1 the agent must expressly or impliedly indicate that it is acting as someone's agent;

2 the principal must both exist and have the capacity to make the contract when it was made (promoters of a company making pre-incorporation contracts are not acting as company agents as the company as yet has no legal existence: see Chapter 22);

3 ratification must be within a reasonable time;

4 the ratification must be complete: the principal must agree to all, not part, of the contract with full knowledge of what is involved;

5 notice of ratification must be communicated: this may be done by conduct, such as retaining goods which have been delivered.

The consequences of ratification are as follows:

1 the agent is freed from any liability for acting without authority;

2 the agent is entitled to remuneration from the principal where appropriate;

3 a third party obtains title to any property which has been transferred under the contract;

4 a contract made by the agent on the principal's behalf is retrospectively binding on the principal.

The disclosed and undisclosed principal

Disclosed principal

When agents enter into contracts on behalf of principals, they usually name the principals or at least indicate that they are acting as agents. Here the principal is said to be disclosed even if not named. In auction catalogues, goods may be described as 'property of a gentleman/lady'.

In general, the disclosed principal is liable on any resulting contract and the agent is not. Exceptions may arise where words, conduct or surrounding circumstances indicate that the agent and principal are jointly liable, or that the agent is to remain solely liable. Thus, if an agent signs a deed without indicating that he or she is signing as an agent, he or she will be personally liable.

Undisclosed principal

Sometimes the agent behaves as if no principal is involved, although in fact one is; here the principal is undisclosed. The contract will be binding by and against the principal if:

1   the agent was acting under the principal's actual authority at the time the contract was made;

2   the terms of the contract do not preclude the existence of the principal.

> **Humble v Hunter** (1848)
> An agent signed a charterparty so that he appeared to be sole owner of the ship involved. It was held that the principal could not enforce the contract.

However, if the third party can show that it intended to do business only with the agent personally, the principal cannot enforce the contract against the third party.

> **Collins v Associated Greyhound Race Courses Ltd** (1930)
> A contract to underwrite a share issue involved exclusive reliance on the agent's business reputation and integrity. The principal was held to be excluded.

THE RIGHTS AND DUTIES OF THE AGENT

Rights

To payment

The agent does not have an automatic legal right to payment. Such a right exists only where the agency agreement indicates such an intention. If the agency is gratuitous, no payment is intended. Even if the agency is contractual, payment is due only if the terms of the contract governing payment are fulfilled. Payment may be conditional on a particular result being achieved.

> **G.T. Hodges & Sons v Hackbridge Residential Hotel** (1939)
> The owner of a hotel asked an estate agent to find a buyer. A representative from the War Office was introduced by the agent and began negotiations which then lapsed. Some months later the War Office announced that it would compulsorily purchase the hotel. It was held that this compulsory sale did not entitle the agent to their commission as this was not the sort of sale which had originally been contemplated by the parties.

Where the agency is contractual, the agent may sue for breach if the principal fails to make appropriate payment. The agent may also be entitled to exercise a lien (legal right to retain) over any property still in their possession which was purchased for the principal and for which the agent has not yet been paid.

To indemnity

Whether the agency is gratuitous or contractual, an agent is entitled to recover any expenses incurred or losses suffered, if these are sufficiently incidental to the agent's authorised conduct.

> **Anglo Overseas Transport Ltd v Titan Industrial Corpn** (1959)
> An agent was engaged to make arrangements for shipping of the principal's goods. The principal was late in delivering the goods to the port, which by the customs of the trade, made the agent liable for losses incurred by the shipowner. It was held that the principal must indemnify the agent for its loss.

A gratuitous agent may request the court to order the principal to pay restitution.

Duties

The agent is in a fiduciary relationship with the principal: he or she enjoys the trust and confidence of the principal, and consequently has a number of legal duties which must be performed whether the agency is contractual or gratuitous.

Performance

An agent must carry out the principal's orders within the limits of the agent's authority. Generally the agent is required to perform the duties personally and without delegation because of the agent's confidential relationship with the principal. Delegation may be permissible, however, if the principal consents, or if delegation is in keeping with trade practice. For example, if a case is being handled by country solicitors but it is to be heard in London, it is normal for some tasks to be delegated to a London firm. It may also be allowed if the delegated tasks require no exercise of special skill or discretion by the agent. Thus solicitors may delegate claim-form-serving duties to their clerks.

Reasonable skill

Agents must perform their duties with reasonable care and skill and may be liable in breach of contract, or negligence, if they fail to do so.

An agent with trade or professional skills is expected to act with the level of skill reasonably to be expected of a person from such a trade or profession.

Where a contract of agency exists, failure to perform duties appropriately will be a breach of contract.

Chaudhry v Prabhakar (1988, CA)
The defendant was a friend of the claimant and claimed to be knowledgeable about cars. He was asked by the claimant to find a car for her which had not been involved in an accident. He found what he claimed was a suitable vehicle, although he noticed that the bonnet had probably been replaced and that it came from a garage which did crash repairs. Within a few months it turned out to be unroadworthy because of previous crash damage. The defendant was liable to the claimant in negligence as he had not exercised the level of care and skill to be expected from somebody with the level of expertise he had claimed to possess and on which the claimant had reasonably relied.

Arensen v Casson Beckman Rutley & Co. (1977)
A professional share valuer placed too low a valuation on his principal's shares and was consequently held liable for breach of his duty to act with the degree of skill to be expected from a person with his level of professional experience.

Accountability

The agent must account for any profits resulting from the exercise of authority and transfer to the principal any monies or financial benefits received from performance of the agent's duties. This duty is closely related to the agent's duty to avoid conflict of interest.

Avoidance of conflict of interest

The agent must ensure that the principal's interests take priority over the agent's, and must not exploit the relationship for the agent's own profit.

Armstrong v Jackson (1917)
A principal instructed his agent to buy shares in a particular company. Unknown to the principal, the agent owned some shares in the company and sold these to the principal instead of obtaining them elsewhere. It was held that the agent had failed to avoid a conflict of interest and must pay the principal the profit obtained on the sale.

An agent who takes a bribe is in flagrant breach of the duty to avoid a conflict of interest. If an agent accepts payment from a third party in return for making a contract with that party in the principal's name, the contract is voidable for fraud. The principal is entitled to dismiss the agent without payment, and recover the amount of the bribe. The principal may also repudiate the contract with the third party and claim damages for any loss which has resulted from the contract being made.

THE RIGHTS AND DUTIES OF THE PRINCIPAL

In relation to the agent

The principal's rights and duties largely mirror the duties and rights of the agent. Therefore, the principal is entitled to the benefits to be derived from the agent's performance of their fiduciary duties. In return the principal must make any necessary payment to the agent.

In relation to third parties

Contractual duties

Any contract made by the agent with a third party is binding on the principal provided that it was made within the limits of the agent's apparent authority. The principal is therefore liable for any misrepresentation or breach of contract, even though this was caused by the agent.

Tort liability

A principal may be vicariously liable for any torts committed by the agent in the exercise of the agent's apparent authority. (More information about vicarious liability can be found in Chapter 12.)

The Commercial Agents (Council Directive) Regulations 1993

The common law rights and duties between agent and principal have been put on a statutory footing, but only in commercial agencies for the sale of goods. The regulations give the parties additional protection, including a right to a written contract and to a minimum period of notice if the agency contract is to be terminated. The agent is given rights to commission. This must be paid within specified time limits. The agent is entitled to check the principal's books to ensure that he or she has been paid at the correct rate.

TERMINATION OF AGENCY

The agency relationship may come to an end either:

1 by operation of law; or

2 by the acts of the parties.

By operation of law

Death

Since the relationship of principal and agent is a confidential one, the death of either party brings the agency to an end.

Mental incapacity

If a person's mental condition precludes him or her from having a reasonable level of understanding, he or she will be treated as no longer having the ability to be a party to a contract. If either party to an agency agreement becomes mentally incapable, this usually terminates the relationship. However, where the agent has been granted an irrevocable or enduring power of attorney, a principal's mental incapacity does not discharge the agency. (See further below.)

Bankruptcy

The bankruptcy of either party terminates the agency, since the bankrupt's property passes into the control of the trustee in bankruptcy to enable payment of creditors.

Frustration of the agency agreement

Any event rendering further performance of an agency contract illegal, impossible or futile will terminate the agency. (See Chapter 9.)

By the acts of the parties

Performance

Once the object of any short-term agency has been achieved the agency ends.

Agreement or revocation

Both parties may agree to terminate the relationship. One party may revoke the agreement regardless of the other party's wish to continue. If the agency is contractual this revocation may be a breach of contract entitling the other party to claim damages. No notice period is required, except where principal and agent are also in an employer/employee relationship.

Exceptionally an agency cannot be revoked. An irrevocable agency exists in the following circumstances:

1 *The agent's authority is linked to the agent's own interest.* The purpose of this agency is to provide security for some pre-existing interest which the agent has with the principal. The agency cannot be revoked until the interest (usually the principal's debt with the agent) is discharged. For example, a debtor who currently is unable to repay a creditor may authorise the creditor to liquidate some of the debtor's assets in order to raise the funds to repay the debt. Such an agency will be terminated by operation of law, however, if the principal subsequently becomes bankrupt or insane, unless the agent has obtained an irrevocable power of attorney.

2 *The agent has been granted an irrevocable power of attorney*. Under the Powers of Attorney Act 1971, s 4, an irrevocable power of attorney may be granted by the principal (donor of the power) to the agent (donee), which prevents an agency relationship from being terminated by the death, incapacity or bankruptcy of the principal. Similarly, if the principal is a corporate body the agency will survive its dissolution or winding up. An irrevocable power of attorney will be granted only to a donee who can prove that it is necessary to assist the donee to preserve a pre-existing interest in the principal's property. An irrevocable power of attorney exists for the *benefit of the agent* and must be distinguished from an enduring power of attorney.

3 *The agent has been granted an enduring power of attorney*. As was explained at the beginning of this chapter, it is common for parties to grant a power of attorney to other parties, enabling them to take care of the first parties' affairs if they are currently unable to do so themselves. The donee of such a power becomes an agent. Like any other agency relationship, this will be terminated by the subsequent mental incapacity of the principal unless an enduring power of attorney has been granted under the terms of the Enduring Powers of Attorney Act 1985. Where such a power exists, the agent manages the principal's affairs under the supervision of the Court of Protection to prevent the agent abusing their authority. An enduring power of attorney is primarily for the protection of the principal's interests.

SOME COMMON TYPES OF SPECIALIST AGENTS

Estate agents

Estate agents act for the seller of a property; their function is to find a buyer. They are regulated by the Estate Agents Act 1979, which requires estate agents to be insured against the loss of any deposits which they may be required to handle. They must also inform the seller of their commission charges before agreeing to act for them. Commission is payable only if a sale takes place to a purchaser whom they have introduced.

Auctioneers

The auctioneer initially acts as the agent of the seller, with the authority to sell to the highest bidder unless any reserve price is not reached. Once a sale has taken place the auctioneer becomes the agent of the buyer too.

An auctioneer is not authorised to transact a sale by credit. The buyer must pay immediately after the sale has taken place, although a cheque is acceptable instead of cash.

Brokers

There are a number of different types of brokers, all of whom act primarily as intermediaries between two parties, one of whom has something to sell – like stocks and shares, insurance or commodities – which the other party is interested in buying. The broker effects the introduction and may assist in the formation of the contract in return for commission. Unlike factors (see below), brokers do not generally have physical possession of the property which is being sold. Brokers' authority may be defined by customs relating to their particular trade.

Factors

The Factors Act 1889, s 1, defines a factor as 'a mercantile agent having in the customary course of his business as such agent authority either to sell goods or to consign goods for the purpose of sale or to buy goods or to raise money on the security of goods'. A factor, therefore, not only has apparent authority to sell goods – which any agent may have apparent authority to do – he or she also has apparent authority to pledge goods or the documents of title to goods. Such pledges are very commonly used to raise money on imports of commodities like cocoa or wheat.

A factor is given physical control of the goods. The sale or other disposition of the goods within the factor's apparent authority to a purchaser acting in good faith is binding on the owner, even if the factor has disregarded orders and exceeded their actual authority.

Quiz 15

1 Under what types of authority do the following agents act?

   (a) North, who was asked by South to take South's shoes to be repaired.

   (b) East, who was asked to drive West's car to the airport to collect West's business client and had to buy petrol as the tank was almost empty.

2 Port, while in Starboard's employment, had collected stationery supplies from Compass once a week. He is sacked by Starboard, but the following week collects the supplies from Compass, who has not been told that Port has been sacked. Port made off with the stationery. Is Starboard bound to pay?

3 When is a third party not bound by a contract with an undisclosed principal?

4 When is an agent entitled to delegate performance duties?

5 When will mental incapacity not bring the agency relationship to an end?

Assignment 14

(a) In a leading modern case it has been said that:

'Ostensible authority comes about where the principal, by words or conduct, has represented that the agent has the requisite actual authority, and the party dealing with the agent has entered into a contract with him in reliance on that representation. The principal in these circumstances is estopped from denying that actual authority existed.'

Explain and illustrate this principle of ostensible authority.

(b) Max runs a local estate agency business, employing a junior negotiator, Nick, whose main job is to show clients around houses which Max has for sale. Max has explained that when he took two weeks' holiday in March 1993 he left Nick with a general instruction to 'Keep things ticking over for me and contact me if there are any major developments'. He has further explained that during his absence Nick has signed a form of agreement for a long-term contract to hire a photocopier. A sales representative had called at the premises and Nick had given the impression that he was the owner of the business. Max now seeks your advice, saying that he has no need of such equipment.

Advise Max on the relevant principles of the law of agency which apply to these facts.

(ICSA English Business Law: June 1994)

A suggested solution for this assignment can be found in Appendix 2.

CHAPTER 16

Sale of goods: the contract and its terms

INTRODUCTION

A large number of contracts involve sales of goods; they are essential to healthy national and international trade. Statute has played a crucial role in the development of special rules of law in this area since the first Sale of Goods Act in 1893. This was primarily concerned with the needs of commercial buyers and sellers. In the twentieth century the interests of consumers became increasingly recognised, and this is reflected by the Sale of Goods Act 1979. This Act, amended by the Sale and Supply of Goods Act 1994, contains the current legislation.

The formation of sale of goods contracts, the elements which may invalidate them and, to a large extent, their discharge, are all still largely regulated by the common law. The Sale of Goods Act 1979 (SGA) primarily focuses on the contractual elements which are particularly crucial to the needs of the buyer and seller of goods, like the terms governing the nature and quality of goods sold, the transfer of ownership, performance obligations and means of enforcement. This chapter examines:

1 the meaning and scope of the statutory definition of the sale of goods contract;

2 the terms implied by the SGA 1979 into every sale of goods contract.

THE SALE OF GOODS CONTRACT

This is defined 'as a contract by which the seller transfers or agrees to transfer the property in goods to the buyer for a money consideration called the price' (s 2(1)). Two types of contract are contained in this definition:

1 a contract of sale;

2 an agreement to sell.

A contract of sale

Here the 'property in the goods', which means the title or ownership, is transferred immediately upon the contract being made. This is what usually happens when you buy goods over the counter in a shop: you immediately become the owner in possession of the chocolate bar, sandwich or socks handed to you by the sales assistant.

A contract of sale exists only if the goods already exist and are in possession of the seller and allocated to the contract; they must be *specific goods* which have been *identified and agreed upon at the time of sale* (s 61(1)). If they do not fulfil these criteria, ownership in them cannot be transferred by the seller and the parties will have formed an agreement to sell only.

An agreement to sell

An agreement to sell (s 2(5)) is a binding contract which will become a contract of sale once the goods exist and are specific in the eyes of the law so that the ownership of them is capable of being transferred. This is commonly the situation when you buy a new car; you do not become the owner until you are notified that the car is ready for delivery to you.

The buyer does not obtain ownership of the goods immediately upon agreeing to buy them, since the goods are not *ascertained*, because either:

1 the transaction concerns 'future goods', i.e. goods which have not yet been manufactured or acquired by the seller (s 61(1)); or

2 the goods have not yet been made specific. This occurs, for example, when the buyer wants to buy six tons of potatoes from the seller's bulk stock of 80 tons. Here the goods are described as *unascertained*. They will become specific only when irrevocably earmarked for the buyer.

Price

Section 8 of the SGA 1979 clarifies the term 'price' in s 2(1). The consideration provided by the buyer must be money, but the actual sum need not be specified in the contract (s 2(1)). If it is not specified, this does not invalidate the contract, since the statute says that a reasonable price is payable. What is reasonable is an issue of fact and must be decided according to the relevant circumstances.

Goods

Under s 61 of the Act, 'goods' in s 2(1) includes all personal property (chattels) capable of physical possession and control, but not property interests like shares in a company, or intellectual property such as a trade mark or copyright. Land (real property) is not goods; its transfer is governed by an entirely distinct set of rules. However, crops and other things attached to the land which are to be severed before sale or under the contract of sale come within the definition of 'goods'.

Contracts outside the 1979 Act

From the above definitions you can see that not all contracts involving goods come within the SGA 1979. The following types of contract all involve goods but do not come within the Act.

Goods and services contracts

Here the sale of goods is incidental to the provision of a service. For example, having double glazing installed, or getting new brake pads fitted to your car. Such contracts are regulated by the Supply of Goods and Services Act 1982. Some more information about these contracts can be found at the end of this chapter.

Hire-purchase contracts

Such contracts are regulated by the Consumer Credit Act 1974 and the Supply of Goods (Implied Terms) Act 1973. Under a hire-purchase contract, the person supplied with the goods is, in the eyes of the law, the hirer not the buyer. The contract gives the hirer possession of the goods, but not ownership. The hirer is entitled to exercise an option to buy the goods, but only when all the instalments have been paid. The hirer becomes the owner of the goods if and when the option is exercised. This topic is covered more fully in Chapter 17.

Hire contracts

These are regulated by the Supply of Goods and Services Act 1982. Possession, but not ownership, of the relevant goods passes to the hirer.

Contracts of barter

These are regulated by the Supply of Goods and Services Act 1982. In a bartering situation the parties exchange goods or services; even if goods are involved, it is not a sale of goods contract as no money changes hands. A part-exchange contract is generally treated as a sale of goods contract under which the buyer is given the option to tender goods in part satisfaction of the contract price.

A 'free' gift linked to a sale contract

Such transactions are probably regulated by the Supply of Goods and Services Act 1982, since this covers contracts not regulated elsewhere under which title to goods will pass.

Goods supplied in return for trading stamps

These contracts are regulated by the Trading Stamps Act 1964.

All the buyers and hirers in the above contracts enjoy similar protection to the buyer in a sale of goods contract if the goods are defective.

THE TERMS IMPLIED BY THE SALE OF GOODS ACT 1979

Under ss 12–15 of the SGA 1979, a seller automatically assumes certain obligations to the buyer as a result of terms which are automatically implied in every contract regulated by the Act. The seller is required by statute to promise that:

1 the seller has lawful authority to transfer ownership of the goods;

2 the goods will match their description;

3 the goods will be of satisfactory quality;

4 the goods will be suitable for any purpose specified by the buyer;

5 the goods will match any sample shown to the buyer prior to the contract being made.

These terms apply to all sales of new or secondhand goods, apart from terms 3 and 4 which apply only to sellers who are acting in the course of a business.

Breach by the seller of any of these terms puts the buyer in a strong position because:

1 *These terms all impose strict liability on the seller.* The seller is liable for breach of contract without the buyer having to prove that the seller is at fault. Indeed, it is irrelevant for the seller to prove that it is blameless and that it was not aware of the alleged defect in the goods. The seller will still be liable.

2 *All of these terms are defined by the Act as being conditions of the contract.* Breach of a condition enables victims to refuse further performance of their contractual obligations and enables them to recover any money or other property which they have tendered. (See Chapter 6.)

These implied terms are now examined in more detail.

Title: s 12

In a contract of sale, the seller implicitly promises that they have the right to sell the goods (to transfer title in them to the buyer) or, in an agreement to sell, the seller implicitly promises that they will have such a right at the time when the property is to pass. The seller can fulfil this promise only if he or she has ownership (title) himself or herself, or is acting with the real owner's permission, at the time of transfer.

Rowland v Divall (1923, CA)
The defendant had bought in good faith a car which had in fact been stolen. The thief could not pass good title, and neither could the defendant when he sold the car on to the claimant. After the claimant had used it for four months the real owner turned up and took the car back. It was held that the claimant was entitled to recover the full purchase price from the defendant. No discount was allowed against his four months' use, as he had never received what he had contracted to buy – full ownership of the car.

Description: s 13

Almost all goods are sold by description, and the seller is in breach of contract if this is inaccurate.

The form of the description

The description may be given by word of mouth ('these boots are waterproof'), or by a written notice put in place by the seller ('silk shirts'). The seller is also responsible for any descriptions which the seller personally did not attach to the goods but which came from a manufacturer or other source, for example labels attached to the goods or wording on the packaging ('produce of Spain', 'machine washable').

   In practice, the huge majority of sales involve the use of some kind of description. In a self-service situation, where the goods are picked out by the customers, the customers rely on the label on the tin to tell them whether they are buying baked beans or sweetcorn. Some selling situations (like catalogue or mail order sales) are entirely reliant on descriptions of goods which the buyer will not see before making the contract.

Sales by sample and description

Where the sale is by sample as well as by description, the seller will be in breach of s 13 even though the goods match the sample if they do not match the description. Many selling situations involve sample and description. You may examine a carpet sample, but gain knowledge of its composition only from an accompanying notice. If this information is incorrect, a breach of contract exists even though in all other respects the carpet meets the statutory requirements.

The relationship of description to quality

The seller's obligations concerning quality and description may overlap. Stating the age of a car can be said to involve a description and also a reference to its quality; the two factors are inextricably interlinked. This may be advantageous to the buyer, as s 13 obliges all sellers to be accurate in their descriptions, whether or not they are selling by way of business.

Beale v Taylor (1967, CA)
A car was described in good faith by the seller as a 1961 Triumph Herald convertible, but turned out later to be two halves of two different cars welded together. Only the rear half conformed to the seller's description. The defendant, a private seller, was liable only for breach of s 13. He could not have been sued under s 14 on the ground that the car was not of satisfactory quality, as this applies only to commercial sellers.

Description may be a completely separate issue from quality. Goods can be rejected on the ground of incorrect description even though they are not defective in any other way.

> **Arcos v Ronaasen** (1933)
> An order was placed to buy wooden staves, described by the seller as 'half an inch thick'. When delivered the width of the staves varied from between half an inch to nine-sixteenths of an inch. It was held that the goods could be rejected as they did not match their description. (But see the effect of s 15A on non-consumer sales below at page 254.)

Liability depends upon reliance

If the buyer did not know of the description or did not rely upon it (having checked it with a third party), the sale is not by description. Examination of the goods does not automatically preclude reliance by the customer. The average customer does not have sufficient knowledge to spot that the description is inaccurate. In *Beale* v *Taylor* (above) the fact that the buyer had examined the car prior to purchase did not prevent his being held to have relied on the seller's description of it. However, if a buyer with expert knowledge buys from a non-expert seller, that buyer is not likely to be held to have relied on the seller's description.

> **Harlingdon & Leinster Enterprises Ltd v Christopher Hill Fine Art** (1990, CA)
> An art dealer who, to the buyer's knowledge, was not an expert on German impressionist painting, offered to sell two paintings which he claimed were by a famous German impressionist. After inspecting the pictures the seller bought them. The description later turned out to be incorrect. It was held that the buyer had relied on his own skill and judgement when deciding to buy, so sale was not by description.

The goods must be of satisfactory quality: s 14(2)

Where goods are sold in the course of business, there is an implied condition that the goods are of satisfactory quality. The words 'satisfactory quality' were introduced by the Sale and Supply of Goods Act 1994 which amended the SGA 1979. They replaced the rather archaic phrase 'merchantable quality'. Arguably, the new statutory definition, which is given below in s 14(2A) and (2B), does little more than spell out factors which were always relevant to the courts when determining whether goods were of 'merchantable quality'.

The meaning of 'satisfactory quality'

The goods must meet the standard which a reasonable person would regard as satisfactory, taking into account all 'relevant circumstances', including price and any description attached to the goods (s 14(2A)). The court objectively assesses the quality of the goods with reference to the expectations of the average buyer. Section 14(2B) gives examples of some factors which might be 'relevant circumstances':

- whether the goods are fit for the purposes for which such goods are normally used;
- appearance and finish;
- freedom from defects;
- safety and durability.

Section 2 of the Sale and Supply of Goods to Consumers Regulations 2002 [implemented on 31 March 2003] amended s 14(2) to give additional protection to consumers. The Act now states (s 14 (2D)) that 'relevant circumstances' include 'public statements' about the product by the 'producer or his representatives', such as advertising or labelling. The seller can only avoid liability for the statement if he can prove that he or she did not know or was not reasonably aware of the statement, or before the relevant contract was made, the seller (s 12(2E)) had publicly corrected, or withdrawn the statement.

How liability arises under s 14(2)

Goods which are physically dangerous, or which do not work at all, are clearly not of satisfactory quality, whether they are expensive or cheap, reduced in a sale, new or secondhand. A buyer of secondhand goods may, however, be expected to put up with some defects in finish or performance. If you buy a car which is five years old, you must expect the upholstery to be showing some signs of wear and anticipate that the engine will be noisier than in a newer model. Even with new goods, you are entitled only to get what you pay for. The finish and durability of a cheap item will not be the same as that to be expected at the luxury end of the market.

The buyer merely has to prove the defect, not how it happened or that the seller was in any way at fault. If the seller is found liable, they can recover their losses from the party who supplied the goods.

Godley v Perry (1960)
A six-year-old boy bought a plastic catapult from a stationery and toy shop. When he attempted to use it, the handle shattered and a piece hit him in the face causing him to lose an eye. It was held that the seller was liable for breach of s 14(2). It was irrelevant that the defect was caused by a design or manufacturing fault over which he had no control.

235

Liability may arise from goods which are of satisfactory quality in themselves but are contaminated by foreign bodies, since these impurities prevent normal use. In *Chaproniere* v *Mason* (1905), a bun made of otherwise normal ingredients contained a stone and was held not to be of appropriate quality.

Wilson v Rickett Cockerell Ltd (1954)
A delivery of coal included fragments of detonators. This resulted in an explosion when the coal was burnt, which caused serious structural damage to the buyer's house. It was held that the coal was not of satisfactory quality, being inseparably contaminated with the explosives.

The goods include their *packaging and instructions*. Defects in these may render the goods defective or dangerous. Liability may arise even if the packaging remains the property of the seller.

Geddling v Marsh (1920)
The seller of mineral water was liable for failing to supply goods of satisfactory quality when the returnable bottle, in which the water was supplied, exploded and hurt the buyer.

The limits to liability under s 14(2)

Section 14 applies only where the sale arises *in the course of business*, not where sale is by a private seller.

The seller is not liable if *the buyer knows about the defects* (s 14(2C)). Such pre-sale notice may be acquired in two ways:

1 *Notice of the defects may be given by the seller*. Such notice must explicitly describe the defects. For example, a notice might be displayed on a washing machine saying 'instruction manual missing' or 'dents in casing at rear'. Only those defects are covered by the notice. If the motor was faulty the seller would be liable for breach of s 14 even if the fault was traced to the accident which caused the dents.

2 *Inspection by the buyer*. Buyers are not generally under any obligation to inspect the goods; but if they do they cannot claim that the seller is liable for any defects which should have been reasonably evident, given the level of inspection to which they subjected the goods. Thus, a superficial inspection can reveal only superficial defects, but latent defects will not generally be revealed even by thorough inspection. The buyer's level of skill and expertise is relevant: a lay car buyer looking at a car engine would not be expected to spot the clues that would alert a professional dealer.

If the buyer *fails to follow the instructions supplied* with the goods, the seller is not liable for any resulting damage. The seller will also not be liable for damage caused by the buyer's *mistreatment* of the goods.

> **Aswan Engineering Establishment Co. Ltd v Lupadine Ltd** (1987, CA)
> The sellers supplied waterproofing material in plastic pails. These collapsed spilling their contents, having been stacked by the buyer in piles six pails high in bright sunshine and temperatures up to 150°F for several days. It was held that the sellers were not in breach of their duty. The packaging was appropriate for normal storage practices.

The buyer is expected to take any precautions which would normally be employed when using the relevant type of goods.

> **Heil v Hedges** (1951)
> A pork chop, which would have been safe to eat if properly cooked, caused tape worm infestation to the buyer. It was held that the chop was not unsatisfactory in quality. The buyer's problems were caused by his own failure to cook the chop for long enough.

A buyer is expected to take only ordinary precautions if no special processes are spelt out by the seller.

> **Grant v Australian Knitting Mills** (1936, PC)
> Woollen underwear bought by the claimant caused him skin irritation due to a residue of chemicals left in the garments by the manufacturing process. No warning of this risk was supplied with the goods. It was held that the goods were not of appropriate quality. It was irrelevant that if the buyer had washed the pants prior to use, the defect would have been removed. The usual practice is to wash underwear after wearing it, not before.

The goods must be suitable for their purpose: s 14(3)

Where goods are sold in the course of business they must be reasonably suitable for any purpose for which such goods are normally sold. They must also fulfil any special purpose which the seller claims for them, provided that the buyer reasonably placed reliance on the seller's skill.

The buyer will only succeed with a claim if it can be shown that the buyer placed reliance on the seller. Such reliance may be implicit or explicit.

Implicit reliance

Such reliance occurs where the buyer neither knowledgeably inspects the goods to check their suitability, nor asks any questions about them. The condition will be breached if the goods turn out to be unsuitable for the usual purposes of such goods, or for any particular uses specified by the buyer. If you buy a sandwich you can assume that it is suitable for human consumption; if you buy a shampoo, the label of which says that it is suitable for use on small children, you can assume that it is suitable for them. If the buyer does not specify particular needs, the seller is not liable if the particular needs of the buyer exceed what is normally required.

> **Griffiths v Peter Conway** (1939)
> The buyer of a fur coat suffered an allergic reaction due to her particularly sensitive skin. It was held that since she had not advised the seller of her exceptional needs, there was no breach of contract: the goods were not unsuitable for their purpose.

Explicit reliance

The buyer may question the seller about what the goods may be used for, or ask the seller to recommend the goods which will best suit the buyer's purposes. If you visit a sports shop and ask to buy a watch suitable for use when diving, what you are sold should not leak or respond unfavourably to changes in water pressure.

The goods must correspond with their sample: s 15

Many types of goods are sold by sample, including carpets, wallpaper, perfume and some types of make-up and toiletries. It is an implied condition in a contract for sale by sample that:

1 *The bulk will correspond with the sample in quality.* The buyer will have to show that any defect complained of in the bulk of the goods was not present in the sample.

> **Godley v Perry** (1960)
> A shopkeeper was able to show that he had tested a sample catapult for strength by pulling back the elastic. It was held that this was sufficient to check that the sample was not defective.

2 *The goods will be free from any defect rendering them unsatisfactory which would not be apparent on reasonable examination of the sample.* Therefore, buyers cannot reject the goods for defects that they should have spotted in the sample, but can reject if other defects are present.

Generally a sale by sample will also be a sale by description, so these requirements need to be studied in conjunction with those concerning s 13 (above).

The right to reject the goods

Breach of any of the above terms is a breach of condition, which means that buyers are entitled to reject the goods and recover the price from the seller. Buyers have a limited time to exercise this right. If they delay too long they will be deemed to have accepted the goods regardless of defects. In that situation they will be entitled to be compensated for the defects, but cannot reject the goods. Once acceptance has taken place, the breach becomes one of warranty rather than of condition (see page 253).

IMPLIED CONDITIONS IN OTHER ACTS

Similar implied conditions and rights of rejection are found in other statutes and regulations.

The Supply of Goods and Services Act 1982

The following terms, which are designated as *conditions* under the Supply of Goods and Services Act 1982, apply to all goods supplied under a contract of hire or a contract for goods and services:

- title: s 2
- description: s 3
- satisfactory quality and suitability for purpose: s 4
- sample: s 5.

The following terms are implied in all contracts involving a supply of services:

- the work will be performed with all reasonable care and skill: s 13
- the work will be carried out within a reasonable time: s 14
- the price charged will be reasonable: s 15.

Note that the 1982 Act specifies that these are *terms* only: they are not designated as conditions or warranties. Their status depends on what, if anything, was agreed in the contract. Sometimes the amount of damage caused by the breach will be used as evidence of their importance. They are a good example of *innominate terms*. (See Chapter 6.)

Many contracts involve delivery of both goods and services, for example fitting a new central heating system. If the system fails to work properly, this may be due to defective goods or defective workmanship. The buyer will have to prove which of these two possibilities is causing the problem. If the goods are defective, the buyer may repudiate the sale and refuse to pay since liability under ss 2–5 is strict. If the problem arises from the standard of workmanship, the buyer must prove failure to carry it out with reasonable care and skill. Even if this can be done, the buyer will not be able to refuse payment unless the breached obligation amounts to breach of a term with the status of a condition. If the contract does not make that clear, then the extent of the damage may be indicative. If the damage was caused by one dripping radiator which has stained part of your carpet, you will be entitled to compensation only, which will be discounted against the price. If there has been a major flood involving collapsed ceilings and ruined furniture, carpets and fittings, you will be able to refuse payment.

The Supply of Goods (Implied Terms) Act 1973

The same conditions concerning goods are implied in hire-purchase contracts. The Sale and Supply of Goods to Consumer Regulations 2002 amended these two Acts. They now give the same protection to the buyer regarding public statements as that enjoyed by the buyer under s 14(2D) of the Sale of Goods Act 1979 (see above at page 235).

The Unfair Contract Terms Act 1977

Liability for breach of implied terms as to *title* in a sale of goods contract, or a supply of goods and services contract or a hire-purchase contract, cannot be excluded or limited at all. Liability for breach of implied terms concerning description, quality and purpose cannot be excluded in any *consumer sale*, but may be excluded in sale or hire to a person buying in the course of a business if this is *reasonable* (see also pages 79–80).

The Unfair Terms in Consumer Contracts Regulations 1999

The regulations are also relevant to all the above contracts if the buyer is a consumer and the seller a business. For further details, see Chapter 6.

Quiz 16

1 What is the difference between a contract of sale and an agreement to sell under s 2 of the SGA 1979?

2 Why is a hire-purchase contract not a sale of goods contract?

3 Explain the rights of the following parties under the SGA 1979:

   (a) Ash, whose supplier promised him a TV manufactured by Sunny but delivered one manufactured by Prickle.

(b) Birch, who has discovered that the fridge he has just bought from a shop warms things up instead of keeping them cool.

(c) Poplar, who finds that the carpet which he has just purchased is a paler colour than that which he was shown in the shop.

(d) Oak, who got frostbite on a mountain climbing trip while using a sleeping bag which the shopkeeper had assured him was appropriate for rugged outdoor use in winter.

Assignment 15

(a) Distinguish between a contract for sale of goods, a contract for the sale and supply of goods and a contract of hire purchase.

(b) Explain the extent of the buyer's rights to reject goods which are not of satisfactory quality.

A suggested solution for this assignment can be found in the Lecturer's Guide.

CHAPTER 17

Sale of goods: transfer of ownership, performance and remedies for breach of contract

INTRODUCTION

It is important to distinguish between the concepts of *ownership* and *possession* in the study of sale of goods contracts. It is quite possible, during performance of the contract, for ownership ('*property in the goods*', or '*title*' as the Sale of Goods Act (SGA) 1979 calls it) to be vested in one party, while the other (usually the buyer) temporarily has possession only. Possession merely gives a party the right to physical control of the goods. Ownership empowers the owner permanently to dispose of the goods in any way he or she chooses: he or she may lawfully sell them, give them away, or even destroy them or abandon them; he or she will not be answerable in law to anybody for doing so. Similarly, if a person dies, or becomes bankrupt, only the property which that person owns forms part of his or her assets. Property like a hired car or library books cannot be disposed of in this way.

In a sale of goods contract, possession and ownership are not necessarily transferred at the same time. There are two reasons why it is crucial to know when ownership has been transferred:

1 *Risk*. Unless the contract specifies to the contrary, risk (liability for loss or damage to the goods) rests with the owner.

2 *Bankruptcy*. All goods owned by the bankrupt form the assets from which creditors may be paid. If a buyer has taken delivery of goods but not yet acquired ownership of them before being made bankrupt, an unpaid seller can recover them. Similarly, if a seller still has the goods in his or her possession but has transferred ownership to the buyer before going bankrupt, the goods will be treated as the property of the buyer, not of the seller's creditors.

This chapter explains the operation of the rules in the SGA 1979 which govern the *transfer of ownership*. It examines devices which a seller may use to protect its rights to payment after it has lost possession of the goods, and to avoid the burden of risk.

A sale of goods contract is *performed* when the seller delivers goods which form the subject matter of the contract and the buyer accepts and pays for them (s 27). The seller must ensure that the goods conform to the express and implied terms of the contract and are delivered in accordance with what the parties have previously agreed, in compliance with the SGA 1979, or the buyer may be relieved of the duty to accept and pay for the goods. This chapter examines the seller's and buyer's respective duties with regard to performance of the contract, and looks at the remedies which may be available for breach.

THE STATUTORY RULES GOVERNING TRANSFER OF OWNERSHIP FROM SELLER TO BUYER

The goods must be ascertained for property in the goods to pass: s 16

Ascertained goods, which may also be called 'specific goods', are defined in s 61 as 'goods identified and agreed on at the time a contract of sale is made'. A large number of consumer sales are for such goods; the concept is clearly illustrated by a self-service purchase.

Not all goods are ascertained when the contract is made: for example, where the buyer orders goods which have not yet been manufactured, or which, like grain or coal, will be allocated to the purchaser from bulk goods in the seller's possession. In such circumstances the parties have an agreement to sell. Ownership is transferred once the goods have been allocated to the contract, as explained below.

The parties' intention is crucial: s 17

The property in ascertained goods will be transferred at the particular time or in the particular circumstances which the parties intend. This may be specified in the contract itself, or be implied from the parties' conduct, custom of the particular trade or any other relevant circumstances. In *Lacis* v *Cashmarts* (1969), it was held that in self-service shops ownership is transferred when payment is made.

Where no intention is indicated: s 18

If no intention is indicated the following rules are applicable:

Rule 1: In an unconditional contract for the sale of specific goods in a deliverable state property passes when the contract is made. 'Unconditional' means that there is no term in the contract which postpones transfer of ownership until the buyer or seller performs some act. The phrase 'deliverable state' generally indicates that the goods are ready to be handed over to the buyer or put into the hands of a carrier.

> **Underwood v Burgh Castle Brick and Cement Syndicate** (1922)
> A contract was made to sell an engine which at that point was cemented to the seller's floor. It was held that it would not be in a deliverable state until it was dismantled and ready for transport.

Rule 2: In a contract for specific goods, where the seller is bound to do something to the goods to put them into a deliverable state, the property does not pass until it has been done and the buyer notified. For example, if you make a contract to buy a particular sports trophy and then leave it with the shop to have it inscribed, the property in the trophy will pass when the shop phones to tell you that it is ready for collection.

Rule 3: In a contract for sale of specific goods in a deliverable state where the seller is bound to weigh, measure or test the goods to fix the price, property passes when the seller does so and notifies the buyer. This is common in international contracts for the sale of bulk goods. Such processes take place on arrival at the port of destination and allow for final price adjustments.

Rule 4: Where goods are delivered to a buyer on approval (sale or return) property passes to the buyer when:

1 *'He signifies his approval to the seller' or otherwise indicates adoption of the transaction,* for example, treating the goods as if they were his own.

> **Kirkham v Attenborough** (1897)
> The buyer pledged the goods: this indicated adoption of the transaction, since it was inconsistent with the rights of the owner.

2 *Or the buyer retains the goods beyond the time fixed for their return, or, if no time was fixed, retains them for an unreasonable time.*

> **Poole v Smiths Car Sales (Balham) Ltd** (1962)
> Poole left his car with Smiths, who were dealers, so that they could find him a buyer. No time limit was fixed, but three months later the car had not been sold and Poole's many requests for the return of the car had been ignored. It was held that title had passed to Smiths under rule 4.

Transfer of property in unascertained goods

Under s 18, rule 5, ownership of unascertained goods is transferred when:

1 the goods are in a deliverable condition; and

2 either the seller or buyer with the consent of the other does something which *unconditionally appropriates* the goods to the contract.

Such appropriation can arise in many different ways dependent on other terms in the contract, but it must consist of behaviour which is clearly an irrevocable step in performance of the contract.

> ***Hendy Lennox v Graham Puttick*** (1984)
> In a contract to supply generators, appropriation took place once the sellers had assembled the goods and the buyers received invoices and delivery notes indicating the serial numbers.

> ***Federspiel v Twigg*** (1957)
> Bicycles were packed up and labelled, and shipping arrangements made by the seller, as stipulated by the contract. The buyer had paid for the goods, but prior to shipping them the seller went bankrupt. The buyer claimed that he had acquired title to the goods because of the seller's actions. It was held that at the point when the seller went bankrupt, the goods had not been appropriated. The seller might yet have changed his mind prior to handing the goods over to the shipper. He could have sent a different set of bicycles which still conformed to the order. The unfortunate buyer consequently had to join the queue with all the other creditors.

However, if the buyer is to arrange transport the goods are usually treated as appropriated once set aside and packed up and labelled or otherwise identified.

Reservation of title

Remember that the statutory rules for transfer of ownership, explained above, apply only if the parties indicate no contrary intention in the contract. The contract may include a reservation of title clause to protect the seller against loss in the event of non-payment. Where such a clause is effective, the buyer obtains possession and use of the goods, but will not obtain ownership unless or until he or she pays. This has important consequences:

1 the seller can recover the goods from the buyer if the buyer fails to make payment;

2 should the buyer die or become bankrupt before payment, any goods subject to a reservation clause can be recovered by the seller, since they do not form part of the buyer's assets.

Reservation clauses can be divided into two kinds:

1 *Simple reservation of title*. The seller simply stipulates that property in the goods will not pass until the buyer has paid for the goods.

    A reservation of title clause may protect all debts owed by the buyer to the seller, not just the debt for the goods to which it directly relates.

Armour and Carron Ltd v Thyssen (1990)
A reservation of title clause stating that the buyer would obtain title to goods supplied by the seller once money owing under this and other contracts with the seller had been paid, was held to be valid. Thus, the seller could recover steel supplied to the buyer from the receivers when the buyer company went into liquidation.

    A simple reservation of title clause is effective only if the relevant goods are in the buyer's possession, readily identifiable and likely to remain so. It gives no protection if the goods are sold on, or mixed with the buyer's other property so that the goods are no longer identifiable. It could, therefore, be useful to the seller of a large piece of machinery bought for use in the buyer's pie factory. It would not protect a seller of a consignment of flour which the buyer stored in a silo, mixed with supplies from other sources and which is used for making pastry in the pie factory.

Borden v Scottish Timber Products Ltd (1981, CA)
Resin supplied by the sellers was used by the buyers in the manufacture of chipboard. It was held that the reservation clause did not protect the seller once the goods had lost their identity by ceasing to be a separate commodity.

2 *Extended reservation of title clauses*. These are often called *Romalpa* clauses. It may be in the interests of the seller to allow a buyer to sell on, or to use the goods in its manufacturing processes, since this may promote the necessary cashflow to enable payment to be made. A suitably worded clause can require a buyer to store the seller's goods separately to prevent their getting mixed with similar goods. It may also permit the seller to trace the value of any of the money still owed to the seller to the proceeds of sale of goods in which the seller's goods became mixed in the manufacturing process.

Aluminium Industrie Vaasen v Romalpa Aluminium Ltd (1976)
The sellers supplied large quantities of aluminium to the buyers. The contract required that until the sellers were paid:

1 the consignment must be stored separately until used;

2 the sellers became owners of goods manufactured by the buyer and containing the sellers' aluminium; consequently the buyers must separately store these goods and account to the sellers for the proceeds of any sales;

3 proceeds of the sales were to be banked separately from the rest of the buyers' income and handed over on request.

The buyers went into receivership. It was held that the reservation of title provision entitled the sellers not only to recover the £50 000 worth of unused foil still in the buyers' store, but also to trace the remainder of the price still owed to the £35 000 proceeds of sale of the goods in which the sellers' goods had been combined. The buyers were bailees (holders of the goods on the owner's behalf) until payment was made. Under equitable rules, they effectively were in a position of trustee to the sellers and had to account for the proceeds resulting from the use of the goods in their possession.

The *Romalpa* decision was controversial insofar as it appeared to make it possible for sellers to enforce rights equivalent to a charge (mortgage) over manufactured products containing their goods, or over the proceeds of sale of such goods. Charges on the property of a limited company are enforceable against other creditors only if registered under ss 395–396 of the Companies Act 1985, at the Companies Registry. Registration is required to publicise the existence of a charge to protect the rights of other potential and existing creditors. It is also intended to prevent creditors with an unregistered charge from jumping the queue awaiting payment if funds run out.

The judge who first tried the *Romalpa* case, asserted that no registrable charge was created here. When the case reached the higher courts the issue was not discussed. The *Romalpa* decision has never been overruled, but in successive cases the courts have interpreted it very tightly. By nice distinction of fact they have generally avoided giving the seller the protection as regards rights to goods manufactured by the buyer which include the seller's goods, or the proceeds of sale of such goods. Consequently, unless a clause comes within the same terms as those approved in the *Romalpa* case, it will be treated as merely creating a charge which will not be enforceable unless registered.

Today a *Romalpa* clause will be likely to be upheld only if both the following conditions are satisfied:

1 it must specifically state that the buyer is to become the bailee of the goods: this puts the buyer in a similar position to a trustee and requires it to take care of the bailor's (seller's) property and account for the profits of sale;

2 the goods must be of a type that remain identifiable after the manufacturing process so that they may be recovered.

Re Peachdart (1983)
A sale of leather contract stated that the seller's title should vest in goods made from leather supplied by the seller, and that proceeds of sale of the handbags manufactured from it were traceable. It was held that the seller's title was not protected once the buyer used the seller's goods: this intention was not apparent from the language of the parties. Exclusive ownership rights were lost in relation to each piece of leather as soon as work began on it.

TRANSFER OF TITLE BY NON-OWNER

Sometimes a seller has no right to transfer ownership of the goods to the buyer. The goods may, for example, have been stolen, either by the seller or by somebody from whom the seller acquired them, innocently or otherwise.

The general rule is *nemo dat quod non habet*, which roughly translated means 'you cannot give what you have not got': a seller who does not own the goods, or who sells them without the owner's authority cannot transfer ownership to the buyer. Some exceptions have been developed to protect a third party in good faith without actual or constructive knowledge of the true owner's rights. A bona fide buyer may acquire good title in the following circumstances.

Estoppel

If the true owner allows the buyer to believe that the seller is the owner of the goods or has the true owner's permission to sell, the true owner cannot later deny that this is so (s 21).

Pickard v Sears (1837)
Machinery belonging to X was in Y's possession. It was consequently seized by Z, who was executing a court judgment. During the next three months X made no attempt to tell Z of his claims, although he had contact with him on other matters. It was held that X could not deny Z's apparent ownership of the goods.

Factors Act 1889: sale by a factor

A factor is a mercantile agent (see Chapter 15). A buyer from a factor acquires good title if the buyer can prove that:

1 the factor had possession of the goods with the owner's permission; and

2 the sale was within the factor's normal course of business as a mercantile agent; and

3 the buyer bought the goods in good faith unaware of the factor's lack of authority.

Sale under a voidable title

If the owner of the goods agreed to sell them as a result of a misrepresentation by a rogue buyer, a voidable title is transferred (s 23). This means that the rogue acquires ownership, but this may be lost if the owner takes steps to avoid the contract before the rogue passes the goods on. As it is usually impossible to find the rogue to tell him or her that the deal is off, notification to the police has been held to be sufficient (*Car & Universal Finance* v *Caldwell* (1964)). Unfortunately, even if the true owner succeeds in avoiding the contract in time, the party who bought the goods from the rogue buyer in good faith is likely to be saved by s 25 (see below).

Sale by seller in possession of the goods or title documents

A seller may not immediately relinquish possession of goods to the buyer once the contract has been made. An unscrupulous seller in such circumstances could then sell the goods again to a third party. Provided this buyer takes in good faith and without notice of the previous sale, he or she will gain good title to the goods (s 24).

Sale by buyer in possession of goods or title documents

This covers the resale of goods by a buyer who has obtained possession of the goods or evidence of ownership of them, but has not acquired ownership rights. Such a buyer is effectively placed in the same position as a factor. Provided that the second buyer acts in good faith, he or she will acquire ownership of the goods (s 25).

Newtons of Wembley Ltd v *Williams* (1964, CA)
The claimants agreed to sell a car to X, with ownership to pass when X's cheque cleared. X was given possession of the car but the cheque bounced. The claimants took steps to avoid the contract by notifying the police and thus destroyed X's voidable title. X then sold the car to Y, who in turn sold it on to the defendant who bought in good faith. It was held that although X no longer had any title to the goods when he sold them, s 25 enabled the defendant to acquire good title to the car.

This section does not operate unless the original buyer obtained possession of the goods because he or she agreed to buy them from the original owner.

Shaw v *Commissioner of Police* (1987)
A party who had acquired possession of a car by telling the owner that he had found a potential buyer for it was not a 'buyer' within the meaning of s 25. Therefore, he had not passed good title to the sub-buyer.

Purchase of a motor vehicle currently the subject of a hire-purchase contract

This is covered by the Hire Purchase Act 1964, s 27. It protects a private purchaser who acts in good faith, not car dealers.

It is very common for somebody who is purchasing a car on hire-purchase to sell it on before finishing paying for it. As the hirer has the registration documents it is very difficult for a private purchaser to know that the hirer/seller is acting illegally. Trade buyers have access to a register to check the car's provenance, so they are not protected by these provisions.

In *Hudson* v *Shogun Finance* (2002) (facts above at page 97) the Court of Appeal held that s 27 only protects the innocent buyer when the hirer is the debtor of the finance company. The rogue who had sold the car on to Hudson was not the debtor since he had misrepresented his identity to the company. The contract had been formed with the person he represented himself to be and whose signature he had forged on the contract. That person was not liable because it was not his agreement because of the forgery.

THE PASSAGE OF RISK

Until risk passes, the buyer may refuse to take delivery of goods which are damaged in transit. Once risk has passed to the buyer, the seller is relieved of liability for loss of or damage to the goods, unless caused by the seller's negligence.

Unless there is evidence of a contrary intention, risk passes when ownership is transferred. In practice, it is very common for the parties to agree that the buyer will acquire risk before ownership (s 20). In such circumstances it is essential that buyers acquire appropriate insurance, since their own policies will cover only the goods which they own. If the goods are damaged in transit by a third party, the buyer who is not covered properly stands to suffer considerable loss; even if the goods are lost or damaged beyond repair, the buyer still owes the seller the price, and would not be able to recover any losses by an action in negligence against a third party.

The Sale and Supply of Goods to Consumers Regulations 2002, s 4(2) amended s 20. Where the sale is to a *consumer* the goods remain at the seller's risk until delivery.

Even if risk and ownership pass at the same time, a buyer who has not yet taken delivery of the goods may need extra insurance; an existing policy may cover only goods which are actually on the buyer's premises, or at least in the buyer's possession.

PERFORMANCE OF THE CONTRACT

The duties of the seller

To deliver the goods

'Delivery' in its statutory meaning ('the voluntary transfer of possession from one person to another' (s 61)) does not necessarily involve actual physical transfer of the goods from seller to buyer; it includes 'constructive' delivery.

Actual delivery takes place in most consumer contracts, but in many commercial contracts *constructive* delivery occurs. Sometimes actual delivery is redundant as the buyer already has possession of the goods. For example, when a party with possession of goods under a hire-purchase contract exercises its option to purchase. On other occasions it may be sufficient to notify the buyer that goods are ready for collection, or to give the buyer the means to take control of the goods, for example by giving the buyer the key to the warehouse in which the goods are stored.

Goods in the possession of a third party are not delivered until the third party acknowledges that they are being held on the buyer's behalf (s 29(4)). This will require notice by the seller. The buyer may not ever take physical delivery of the goods, which will continue to be stored by the third party until sold to someone else, but the notice from the seller enables the buyer to dispose of the goods.

Delivery also takes place when the goods are handed over to a carrier, whether or not the carrier is the buyer's agent (s 32). This does not apply to a contract with a consumer buyer under s 4(3) of the Sale and Supply of Goods to Consumers Regulations 2002. The risk remains with the seller until delivery to the consumer takes place.

Once delivery has taken place, all risks pass to the buyer: the seller has no further contractual duties regarding the safety of the goods.

The arrangements for delivery may be found in the contract, but failing this the rules specified in s 29 apply:

1 *The place of delivery.* This is the seller's place of business, or the seller's home if he or she does not have business premises (s 29(2)). If the contract is for specific goods, which to the knowledge of the parties are at a different location, that will be the place of delivery.

2 *The time of delivery.* If no time is fixed and the contract requires the seller to send the goods to the buyer, this must be carried out within a reasonable time and at a reasonable hour (s 29(3)). What is reasonable is determined according to the circumstances of the contract. An unreasonable time would entitle the buyer to refuse to accept the goods. *Tender of delivery at a reasonable time is equivalent to actual delivery.* If the goods are delivered at a reasonable time and the buyer actively or passively fails to accept them, the buyer is in breach. The seller, by tendering performance, is freed from any legal obligation to make further attempts to deliver. Refusal by the buyer to accept the goods does not generally entitle the seller to repudiate the contract. In practice the issue is generally resolved by the parties agreeing a fresh delivery time.

Time of performance may be 'of the essence' of the contract. It is common for a contract to state a time for performance. Failure to deliver by that time is a breach of contract entitling a party to claim damages if they have suffered actionable loss. Late delivery does not necessarily entitle the buyer to reject the goods, however. This is possible only if the issue of time is a *condition* of the contract or, as it is sometimes described, 'of its essence'. Time will be of the essence of the contract if:

(a) its importance is expressly stressed under the terms of the contract; or

(b) its importance is impliedly indicated by the terms of the contract and/or circumstances surrounding it which are known to the seller (a contract requiring delivery of a wedding cake to where the reception is taking place would indicate pretty clearly that the time of delivery is crucial, without the buyer spelling out that it is required that day); or

(c) the contract originally required delivery within a reasonable time but the seller failed to fulfil this requirement so that a new delivery date was agreed. The new delivery date is 'of the essence'.

To supply goods which comply with the terms of the contract

The buyer may be entitled to reject delivery if the goods do not meet the specifications laid down in the contract, or fail to comply with the implied conditions under ss 12, 13, 14 and 15 (see the previous chapter).

The duties of the buyer

To accept delivery of the goods

Under s 27, the buyer has a duty to accept delivery of the goods. The buyer must do this at the specified time, if time is of the essence; otherwise it must be done within a reasonable time. Failure to accept delivery is a breach of contract which makes the buyer liable for any reasonable costs incurred by the seller as a result: for example, transport and storage expenses.

Under s 35, acceptance is deemed to occur when the buyer:

1 tells the seller that he or she accepts delivery; or

2 fails to notify rejection within a reasonable time; or

3 does something with the goods which is 'inconsistent with the rights of the seller'. This would include selling the goods to a third party.

The buyer is not generally legally obliged to accept anything less than complete performance of the contract. The rules are as follows:

1 *Variation in quantity of goods supplied (s 30).* If a specified amount is required by the contract and more or less delivered, the buyer is not generally bound to accept. If they choose to do so, the buyer must pay pro rata, i.e. proportionately. In a non-consumer sale the buyer is not allowed to reject the whole consignment if the

shortfall or excess 'is so slight that it would be unreasonable for him to do so' (s 30A). It is up to the seller to prove that rejection is unreasonable. Where only approximate amounts have been ordered ('about 20 tonnes'), variations within a reasonable margin must be accepted.

2   *Delivery by instalments.* The buyer need not accept delivery by instalments unless this has been agreed in the terms of the contract (s 31). If the buyer rejects an instalment or the seller makes a defective delivery of one, it is a question of fact in each case whether this gives the innocent party the right to repudiate the contract.

The innocent buyer need not return rejected goods. Where the buyer rejects the goods because of a breach by the seller, the buyer has no obligation to return the goods (s 36). The seller must make arrangements for collection.

To pay for the goods

The buyer's duty to pay for the goods is concurrent with the seller's duty to deliver. The buyer is not entitled to take possession of the goods until payment has been made, unless the parties have made alternative arrangements. Sometimes the parties may agree that payment is to precede delivery. It is also common for goods to be supplied on credit.

REMEDIES FOR BREACH OF THE SALE OF GOODS CONTRACT

The buyer's remedies

These differ according to the importance of the term(s) which have been breached by the seller.

The right to reject the goods and refuse payment

This is repudiation of the contract and is not possible unless the seller has breached a condition of the contract by, for example, failing to supply goods of satisfactory quality. If the seller sues the buyer for refusing to accept and pay for the goods, the buyer may raise the seller's breach as a defence and counterclaim for any losses.

If the buyer discovers that part of a consignment of goods delivered by the seller does not comply with the terms of the contract, the buyer has the right to accept those goods which meet the contract standards and to reject the rest (s 35A).

The right to reject goods is limited. It is lost as soon as the buyer is deemed to have accepted the goods (s 35). The courts have often held that acceptance has resulted from the buyer using the goods for anything more than a very short time and/or retaining and continuing to use the goods after having complained about them, or agreeing to them being repaired.

Bernstein v Pamson (1987)
After three weeks and with only 140 miles on the clock, the engine of the claimant's brand new Nissan seized up on the motorway, due to some sealant coagulating in the cooling system. It was held that the engine was clearly not of appropriate quality and the claimant was entitled to damages. However, he had lost his right to reject the car since a reasonable time had elapsed since taking delivery. The judge held that a reasonable time meant long enough to give the car a reasonable road test, not necessarily long enough to discover latent defects. It was held that it would be unfair to allow the buyer a protracted time to reject as this would unreasonably prevent the sellers from closing their books on the transaction.

Since all cases are judged on their particular facts, apparently conflicting decisions may occur:

Rogers v Parish (1987)
It was held that a top of the market Range Rover could be rejected after seven months, with a 5000 mileage. It had been a martyr to endless mechanical problems from the moment of delivery, and had spent much of its existence in the garage while many unsuccessful repairs were attempted.

The buyer must have a reasonable time to examine the goods. When deciding whether the buyer has accepted the goods, the court must consider whether the buyer had a reasonable opportunity to examine the goods after delivery (s 35(5)). This amendment was introduced in 1994, largely to protect the rights of consumers, but as the courts have always taken this into account it is uncertain whether it is likely to make much difference.

A buyer who is sold defective goods may agree to have them *repaired instead of rejecting* them. If this is treated as acceptance, the buyer loses the right to reject the goods and recover the price. The reality is that many consumers do not initially realise that they have the right to reject defective goods, so that they agree to the seller's apparently kind offer to repair the goods. At best this causes inconvenience to the buyer, who is temporarily deprived of the use of the goods: sometimes a whole saga of delay and incompetence starts to unfold. At this point the buyer may find out that he or she need not have agreed to the repair in the first place and seeks to reject the goods. To safeguard the buyer in such situations a 1994 amendment to the SGA 1979 states that a buyer is not to be assumed to have accepted the goods merely by agreeing to their being repaired (s 35(6)). This may increase the opportunities for a buyer to reject the goods.

Rights of rejection are less comprehensive in a non-consumer sale (s 15A). If there is a breach of condition under ss 13–15, a consumer buyer may reject the goods prior to acceptance, however trivial the damage. A buyer who is not a consumer (not buying for personal use) is not entitled to reject the goods if the breach is so trivial that it would be unreasonable to allow the buyer to reject.

The right to request specific performance

If the seller refuses to deliver the goods and this amounts to a breach of condition, specific performance (explained fully in Chapter 9) may exceptionally be available to the buyer if the goods are sufficiently unique.

The right to damages

A breach of condition entitles the buyer to claim damages, as well as exercising other rights. Damages are the only remedy for breach of warranty. How far damages are recoverable is partly governed by the rules relating to remoteness and quantum explained in Chapter 9, but the 1979 Act also regulates the process:

1 *Damages for non-delivery (s 51).* If there is a market for the goods, the buyer may recover the difference (if any) between the price agreed with the seller and the current market price; if the price has increased between formation of the contract and its breach, damages will be payable. The buyer is also able to recover any losses 'directly and naturally resulting in the ordinary course of events' from the failure to deliver.

2 *Damages when goods have been accepted (s 53).* If the seller has breached a condition, but the buyer has by acceptance of the goods lost the right to reject, the breach will be treated as one of warranty and damages will be recoverable for all actionable loss.

Lee v York Coach & Marine (1977)
The claimant bought a secondhand car from the defendants in March. She later discovered that the brakes were in such a dangerous condition that had she tried to stop in an emergency they would have failed. She had repairs done which cost £100. In September she gave notice to the sellers of her wish to reject the car. It was held that the car had been supplied to her in a state which was a breach of condition under s 14 of the SGA 1979. However, since she had failed to notify her wish to reject within a reasonable time, she was entitled only to damages for breach of warranty.

Note that because of recent amendment, the SGA 1979, s 35(6) says that agreeing to, or even asking for, repairs does not necessarily indicate acceptance. This might be helpful to a buyer in the same position as Ms Lee. However, an attempt to reject a secondhand car six months after sale would probably be regarded as being too late.

The Sale and Supply of Goods to Consumers Regulations 2002, s 4(5) amended the SGA s 48 and gave additional rights to the consumer buyer. The SGA s 48B gives the consumer buyer the right to demand repair or replacement of goods which do not conform to the contract at the time of delivery. Alternatively, the buyer (s 48C) has the right to ask for a reduction of the purchase price or rescission of the contract.

If the buyer requires repair or replacement the seller bears all the necessary costs and must fulfil his obligation within a reasonable time. However, the seller is not bound to repair or replace goods where this is impossible or disproportionate in comparison to a price reduction or rescission. The value of the goods had they conformed to the contract, the significance of the non-conformity and whether an alternative remedy would not significantly inconvenience the buyer are relevant to determining disproportionality. If the buyer's request is found to be disproportionate, price reduction or rescission should be granted (s 48B).

The seller's remedies

The seller has similar rights to the buyer and may thus repudiate the contract for breach of condition by the buyer. A seller is also entitled to damages if the buyer fails to pay for the goods (s 49), or refuses to take delivery of them (s 50).

If the seller has not been paid they have additional rights which may be exercised against the goods themselves. The seller is able to use the goods as security for the money owed from the buyer (s 39). The Act gives the seller the following rights:

1 a right of lien (to retain goods still in the seller's possession)

2 a right to stop the goods in transit to the buyer

3 a right of resale.

The right of lien

If the seller has retained possession of the goods, the seller may be able to hold on to them until the buyer pays the price in full, even if title has passed to the buyer (s 41). The right exists if:

1 the goods have not yet been paid for and there are no arrangements for credit; or

2 the goods were supplied on credit which has now expired; or

3 the buyer becomes insolvent, i.e. is unable to pay its debts in the ordinary course of business, or as they come due (s 61).

Under s 43, the right of lien is lost if:

1 the price is paid; or

2 the seller loses possession of the goods to a third party for delivery to the buyer and does not reserve the right to dispose of them; or

3 the seller waives the right, i.e. agrees not to exercise it.

The right to stop the goods in transit

This right under ss 44 and 45 can be exercised only if the buyer becomes insolvent. It may be exercised even though the buyer has title. Transit begins when the goods are in the hands of a carrier and ends when the buyer or their agent takes delivery. There is no right to stop the goods if the carrier is the agent of the buyer.

The right will be lost if the buyer or its agent intercepts the goods and obtains possession before the goods reach their destination.

The unpaid seller exercises the right by taking physical control of the goods, or by notice to the carrier or other custodian of the goods.

The right of resale

Under s 48, this right may be exercised if the buyer has failed to pay and:

1 the goods are perishable; or

2 the seller has notified the buyer of their intention to resell if payment is not made and the buyer fails to pay within a reasonable time.

On resale the new buyer acquires ownership of the goods.

If the seller makes a loss on resale he or she may sue the buyer for damages to cover this. If the seller makes a profit, he or she can keep it.

Quiz 17

1 When, under the SGA 1979, does title to the following goods pass?

   (a) A watch purchased by Boland, but retained by the shop for engraving.

   (b) An order to a coal merchant for 5 tonnes of smoke-free coal.

2 What is a *Romalpa* clause?

3 When may a third party, without title to goods, transfer a good title?

4 Burnham orders a consignment of 200 Easter eggs from Pemberton, a confectionery wholesaler. Pemberton delivers them to Carshalton Carriers, whose lorry is hijacked by Sherwood, and Burnham never receives them. What is the legal position?

5 What is the significance of making time of the essence of the contract?

6 When is a buyer deemed to accept goods under s 35 of the SGA 1979?

7 When does a buyer have the right to reject goods?

8 What rights may be exercised by Ashdown in the following circumstances?

 (a) Honor has failed to perform her contractual promise to pay for a consignment of strawberries which are still in Ashdown's possession.

 (b) Ashdown dispatched a cargo of carrots to Selly and then heard that Selly had gone bankrupt.

 ## Assignment 16

Is it true to say that the law gives more protection to the seller than to the buyer where transfer of risk and title are concerned?

A suggested solution for this assignment can be found in Appendix 2.

CHAPTER 18

Rights at work: the contract of employment and health and safety at work

INTRODUCTION

The employer and employee relationship is primarily based on the contract of employment. To some extent this is governed by the common law of contract described earlier in this book, but this has been considerably augmented by statutory regulation. This has restricted employers' traditional freedoms to select, hire and fire staff at will, and to contract on their own terms.

This chapter focuses on the formation and terms of the employment contract, as well as on employers' liability in tort and criminal law for the health and safety of their employees.

THE EMPLOYMENT CONTRACT: A CONTRACT OF SERVICE

Employees and independent contractors

A business may be served both by its own employees under a *contract of service* and by independent contractors under a *contract for services*. The distinction is important, since it determines the employer's liability in tort for harm caused to third parties (see Chapter 12). An employer has greater legal obligations to an employee than to an independent contractor. These include liability for paying National Insurance contributions and sick pay, and responsibility for deduction of income tax. An employee may also enjoy statutory protection against unfair dismissal and redundancy. References to 'employees' in this chapter are to staff with a contract of service with the relevant employer.

The form of the contract of service

The validity of a contract is not dependent on its form. It can arise quite informally by word of mouth; writing is not essential to the existence of the contract. However, s 1 of the Employment Rights Act 1996 (ERA) obliges an employer to provide an employee with a *written statement* of the key terms of the employee's contract within two months of starting work. This statement must include:

1 the parties' names;

2 the date when the employee started the job;

3 the date on which the employee's continuous employment began. This may not be the same as 2 above if, for example, the employee was already employed by the same employer but in a different post. The length of continuous employment is crucial to rights relating to unfair dismissal and redundancy, which are discussed below;

4 a note of any disciplinary and grievance procedures;

5 full particulars of:

    (a) pay entitlement;

    (b) hours of work;

    (c) any holiday entitlement and pay;

    (d) any sick leave and pay entitlement;

    (e) any pension rights (unless these are controlled by a statute which itself ensures notification);

    (f) length of notice required to be given to and by the employee;

    (g) the title of the employee's job and a brief description of what it involves;

    (h) if the job is not intended to continue indefinitely, the period for which it is expected to last, or the date it is intended to end if it is for a fixed term;

    (i) the place(s) where the employee will be required to work (employees required to work outside the UK for more than one month must be told how long this will be for, what currency they will be paid in, any entitlement to additional benefits and any terms relating to their return to the UK);

    (j) any collective agreement directly affecting the job.

Failure to provide this statement does not invalidate the contract. It is merely intended to provide employees with sufficient written evidence of some of the conditions under which they are employed to enable them to enforce their statutory rights. The statement does not represent all the terms of the contract, which are described below.

Sources of the terms of the employment contract

The terms of the contract will not generally be found in one written document since they may be both express and implied and may be traced to a number of sources.

Express terms are stated in any written contract of employment, but are also to be found in the written statutory information described above. They may also consist of promises made by word of mouth prior to acceptance.

The court may *imply* a term from any of the following sources:

- custom and practice;
- works and staff rules;
- collective agreements;
- statute;
- common law rights and duties of employers and employees.

Custom and practice

Relevant business practices acceptable nationally, locally or in the particular workplace may be implied as terms of the contract. To be enforceable they must be reasonable, certain and not contrary to law.

> ***Sagar v H. Ridehalgh & Son Ltd*** (1930, CA)
> In Lancashire, weaving factories employers customarily made deductions from pay for poor work. This was held to be a term of the contract.

This source of terms has diminished in importance with the increased formalisation of the employment contract. In the event of conflict with the written contractual terms, the written terms prevail.

Works and staff rules

While not necessarily terms of the contract, failure to obey works and staff rules is likely to be treated as evidence of failure to obey reasonable orders. If the rule does not have the status of a contractual term, this is advantageous to the employer; a rule may be introduced and varied at will without the consent which would be required from the employee to make a contractual term or variation binding. Policy considerations may influence judicial decisions on such issues.

> ***Dryden v Glasgow Health Board*** (1992)
> It was held that no smoking policies did not fall within the scope of contractual terms. The employer had a discretion to make appropriate rules for good workplace management.

Collective agreements

The terms of an agreement between union and employer may expressly or impliedly form part of a contract of employment. With the decrease of union recognition in recent years, only a small minority of workers' contracts are likely to be influenced by such agreements.

Statute

Legislation increasingly restricts the freedom of employers to impose the terms of their choice on employees. For example, the Working Time Regulations 1998 (implementing the Working Time Directive) impose limits on the hours which an employee can be asked to work and include requirements for minimum rest breaks and annual paid holidays.

Terms implied at common law

The common law implies certain terms into contracts of employment which impose duties on both employer and employee. For example, the common law requires employees:

1 to do their job with reasonable care and skill;

2 to obey all reasonable orders;

3 to act in good faith towards the employer.

Each of these duties is implied in the contract. They are discussed in detail below.

The common law duties of the employee

The duty to work with reasonable care and skill

Essentially this means that an employee must not be negligent. What is a reasonable standard depends on the status of the employee within the organisation and the level of qualification, skill and experience held by the employee. Grossly negligent performance may entitle an employer summarily to dismiss the employee.

The duty to obey reasonable orders

An order is usually treated as reasonable as long as it does not require the employee to do something outside the job description, since under the terms of the contract the employee has expressly or impliedly agreed to do anything necessarily incidental to performing the job.

> ***UK Atomic Energy Authority v Claydon*** (1974)
> Claydon's contract stated that he could be asked to work in any base in the UK. He was held to have failed to obey a reasonable order when he refused a transfer.

An order is not reasonable if its performance is likely to endanger the personal safety or liberty of the employee.

The employee must be able to show that *imminent* danger will result from carrying out the order. Compare the following two cases.

Ottoman Bank v Chakarian (1930)
The defendant was an Armenian refugee who had escaped from Turkey where he was under sentence of death. It was held that in the circumstances it was not reasonable to expect him to accept a posting in Turkey.

Walmesley v UDEC (1972)
Walmesley was ordered to accept a transfer to Ireland, which he refused because he was frightened of being harmed by the IRA. Since he was unable to prove any imminent and specific threat of harm, he was held to be acting in breach of his contract.

An employee cannot be ordered to break the law.

Morrish v Henlys (Folkestone) Ltd (1973)
An employee who had refused to falsify the company's accounts was held not to be acting in breach of contract.

In determining what is reasonable, current standards of good industrial relations practice are taken into account.

An employee cannot choose how far to perform an employer's reasonable orders. Some forms of industrial action, short of going on strike, may entitle the employer to dock pay for part performance. The employees must receive prior notification of the employer's refusal to accept part performance.

Wiluszynski v London Borough of Tower Hamlets (1988, CA)
Council employees who refused to answer councillors' enquiries could legally be deprived of all their earnings for the five weeks that this action continued, even though they were carrying out all other aspects of their work. The employees had received specific and prior notice of the consequences of their action.

The duty to act in good faith

Employees must act with complete honesty towards their employers when carrying out their contractual duties. The motivation of employees is irrelevant to their liability.

Dalton v Burtons Gold Medal Biscuit Company Ltd (1974)
An employee who falsified a clock card to benefit another employee had breached his duty of good faith. It was irrelevant that he obtained no personal benefit from the dishonest action.

The duty to act in good faith may be divided into three separate obligations:

1 *Not to act in conflict with the employer's interests.* Employees must not compete with the employer's business, even if they do so in their spare time. If the contract requires the employee to work for the employer exclusively, doing any paid work for another person is a breach of duty.

2 *Not to reveal confidential information.* The employee must not reveal confidential information about the employer's profits, customers, work systems, products or services. This duty remains enforceable, though to a more limited extent, even after an employee has left the employer's service. (There is detailed information about breach of confidence by employees in Chapter 27.)

3 *To account for all profits.* Taking bribes is obviously a gross breach of duty, but this duty may be breached by an employee who makes any unauthorised profit from the job. Employees are therefore not entitled to any secret commission. Tips may be retained in jobs where these are seen as part of payment, as in the restaurant trade.

The common law duties of the employer

It is implied in the contract of employment that the employer will:

1 pay the employee as agreed by the contract;

2 not undermine the trust and confidence of the employee;

3 provide the employee with safe working conditions.

The duty to pay the employee

Most employees (not just those with a contract of service) are entitled to a minimum wage, under the Minimum Wage Act 1999. The current rates, which were raised in October 2002 are £4.20 per hour for adults and £3.50 for young people between 18 and 21.

The employer has no right to make pay deductions unless, like income tax or National Insurance contributions, these are authorised by statute or agreed in writing with the employee. In practice, the contract of employment often provides for employer's deductions, and the employee thus waives the protection of the common law in this respect.

The obligation to pay the employee exists *whether or not the employer has provided work.* In general, there is no duty to provide work but if the nature of the work means that the employee is likely to obtain a benefit other than payment from doing the work, the employer may be under a duty to provide work. For example, actors and other performers require the publicity that performance brings. Similarly, apprentices are entitled to the opportunity to practise the skills they have contracted to learn.

Not to undermine the trust and confidence of the employee

This is aimed at preventing the employer from indulging in unreasonable and abusive conduct towards the employee; it is reciprocal to the employee's duty to act in good faith. A wide variety of behaviour can give rise to a breach of this duty: for example, failing to provide extra support to staff at busy times (*White* v *London Transport Executive* (1982)), criticising a supervisor in front of employees who worked under him (*Associated Tyre Specialists* v *Waterhouse* (1976)), failure to protect an employee against harassment (*Bracebridge Engineering Ltd* v *Darby* (1990)).

> ### *Isle of Wight Tourist Board* v *Coombes* (1976)
> A manager, within earshot of his personal secretary, said to another employee: 'She is always an intolerable bitch on Monday mornings.' He did not attempt to apologise and it was held that his behaviour shattered a close and confidential working relationship.

Breach of this duty may be grounds for a claim that the employee has been *constructively* dismissed. If the employer's conduct is sufficiently serious, the employee is entitled to leave without notice.

To provide safe working conditions

Employers must take all reasonable care to provide safe working conditions for their employees. Liability for breach of this duty is also imposed through the law of tort, both at common law and statute. In practice, actions for personal injury to employees are brought by an action in tort rather than for breach of contract. In the following section this is explained in that context.

THE LAW OF TORT: EMPLOYERS' CIVIL LIABILITY FOR INDUSTRIAL INJURIES

Two possible rights of action in tort may be open to an employee injured at work:

1 an action for breach of the employer's common law duty of care;

2 an action for breach of statutory duty.

Employers' common law liability

This is a *non-delegable duty*. This means that an employer cannot avoid liability merely by showing that a hazard has been created by a third party. The responsibility to maintain safety remains with the employer. Therefore, if independent contractors cause a spillage on which a member of the employer's staff slips and breaks a leg, the employer may be liable. The employee will have to prove that in the given circumstances, in a properly managed workplace, the employer would have seen that the spillage was cleared up. Liability is, therefore, not strict, but requires an employer to take reasonable care, as in a negligence action.

The common law duty comprises three interlinked obligations:

1 to provide competent staff;

2 to provide safe premises, plant and equipment;

3 to provide a safe system of work.

Competent staff

The employer must take reasonable care to ensure that staff are competent to do their work so that they are not a danger to their fellow employees. Reasonable care must be taken in the selection, training, supervision and discipline of the workforce. The duty includes preventing hazards arising from activities that are not necessarily incidental to the job in hand.

> **Hudson v Ridge Manufacturing Co. Ltd** (1957)
> An employee, who had previously been reprimanded more than once for skylarking, injured a fellow employee when playing a practical joke. It was held that the employer was liable since it had been alerted to the fact that the employee was a potential danger and should have taken adequate steps to control him.

Safe premises, plant and equipment

This includes providing appropriate tools, machinery and materials maintained to an adequate standard. The premises must also be reasonably safe.

> **Pagano v HGS** (1976)
> An employer which failed to maintain its vehicles in a safe condition, despite having been alerted to the problem by complaints from its workforce, was held liable for breach of duty.

Under the Employers' Liability (Defective Equipment) Act 1969, if equipment is defective due to the fault of a third party such as a manufacturer or repairer, the employer may be held liable even though they are not personally to blame and could not have known of the defect. Equipment may include the materials that employees are required to handle while carrying out their duties.

Knowles v Liverpool CC (1993)
The council was held liable for injuries caused to an employee by a defective paving stone which unexpectedly shattered while he was laying it.

A safe system of work

This encompasses a huge variety of activities. It includes providing protective clothing with instructions about its use, setting up safe working procedures, ensuring sufficient washing and first aid facilities, and appropriate use of warning signs.

An employer's liability may arise from a mixture of breaches of these three interdependent duties. For example, a computer operator claiming repetitive strain injury might be able to prove (i) lack of proper equipment (the seating and desk not being at an appropriate height), and (ii) failure to maintain a safe system of work (if employees are required to use keyboards for lengthy periods without a proper break).

Historically, claims against employers have been for physical injuries, but recently cases have come before the courts in which employers have been found liable for stress-induced mental illness.

Walker v Northumberland County Council (1995)
The employers, who knew that Mr Walker had already suffered psychiatric illness due to stress at work, increased his workload. This caused the illness to recur so badly that he had to take early retirement. The judge, who awarded substantial damages, said that there was no difference in principle between mental and physical injury in the context of the employer's duty to provide reasonably safe working conditions.

Increasing numbers of claims for stress-related illness have come before the courts since the decision in *Walker*.

In *Hatton* v *Sutherland* (2002) the Court of Appeal laid down guidelines which stressed the need to avoid imposing too great a burden on employers:

- No occupation should be regarded as intrinsically dangerous to mental health.
- The employer should be alerted to the risk to an employee when a reasonable employer would foresee that risk.
- Injury to health must be reasonably foreseeable, not just emotional stress.
- It is reasonable for the employer to assume that the employee could cope with the level of stress normally associated with the job. Often it will be up to the employee to bring the issue to the employer's attention rather than suffering in silence.

- A breach of duty must be judged by the normal criteria: the magnitude of the risk, the gravity of harm and the practicability of taking precautions.

- If the only way to resolve the risk is to dismiss the employee, the employer will not be in breach if the employee is allowed to continue working.

- The duty can often be performed by the offer of counselling or other treatment.

- The issue of causation is often problematic for employees given that stress-related illness can come from a number of sources, not just the working environment.

Civil liability for breach of statutory duty

Any criminal or administrative legislation which does not expressly give rights to take action in tort for damages may be treated by the courts as being capable of doing so. This means that an employee who is the victim of an industrial accident or illness may be able to sue the employer for breach of a duty imposed on the employer by legislation designed primarily to impose public rather than civil law duties on an employer. The claimant will have to prove the following:

1 *The legislation gives the right to sue for damages*. The legislation may make this explicit one way or the other. Section 47 of the Health and Safety at Work Act 1974 clearly rules out an action for damages for breach of the employer's *general duty*; no action is possible here. However, it also states that action is possible for breach of any regulations made under the authority of the Act unless expressly excluded. If no explicit reference is made, the court will have to decide whether such a remedy was intended by the legislation. The courts have been generous in their approach to claims by employees, and many successful actions have resulted from breach of the Factories Act 1961 and related legislation.

2 *The employee is part of the class of persons protected by the legislation*. Sometimes legislation is very limited in its application. For example, breach of a regulation to protect a machine operator might not protect a different type of employee.

Knapp v The Railway Executive (1949)
A train driver injured in an accident caused by failure to close level-crossing gates was held not to be protected by legislation intended to protect members of the public.

3 *The defendant is in breach of the duty*. The extent of the duty is specified by the statute. It may be advantageous to sue under statute if the standard of care it imposes is higher than the reasonable care required at common law, or if the burden of proof is placed on the employer to show that he or she discharged the duty. If strict liability is imposed, the claimant does not have to prove that the defendant was lacking in care and that the harm suffered resulted from it. The

duty may operate only in very strictly defined situations, however, and this may defeat the action.

Chipchase v British Titan Products (1956)
Building safety regulations required the provision of platforms of at least 34 inches wide when work was being conducted six and a half feet above ground level. The claimant, who was working at a height of six feet, was injured when he fell from a platform which was only nine inches wide. It was held that he had no right to claim for breach of the regulations since he had been working six inches below the regulated height when the accident happened.

CRIMINAL LAW REGULATION OF SAFETY IN

THE WORKPLACE

Since the Factories Act 1802, the welfare of employees has increasingly been regulated by statute as well as by the common law. In recent years the UK's membership of the EC has led to an increase in development of the law in this area.

The Health and Safety at Work Act 1974 was intended to implement a general policy of integrated statutory control of health and safety in the workplace. Powers are delegated under the Act to enable the Department of Employment (now the Department of Work and Pensions) to make regulations covering specific areas of workplace safety. The Act was an important development in three respects:

1 it imposed general duties on both employers and employees to maintain health and safety;

2 it created the Health and Safety Executive, with powers to enforce the legislation;

3 it gave wide powers to the Department of Employment to make detailed legally binding regulations to cover particular hazards.

The employer's and employee's statutory duties

The employer's general duty to employees: s 2

Employers have a duty 'to ensure as far as is reasonably practicable the health, safety and welfare of all their employees'. (This means only those under a contract of service to an employer.) Employers are not made strictly liable by the 1974 Act. They are responsible only if they have failed to take *reasonably practicable* precautions. This has been criticised for its vagueness. It is very similar to the common law duty of reasonable care, but the reference to practicability indicates that the resources of employers may be relevant in judging how much can be expected of them.

The scope of the duty is spelt out in s 2 and encompasses particular areas of employer responsibility which closely mirror the employers' common law duty in tort.

The employee's duty: s 7

Employees are also placed under a two-part duty:

1 to take reasonable care for their own health and safety and for that of others likely to be affected by their acts and omissions at work;

2 to co-operate with the employer as far as is necessary to enable it to carry out legal responsibilities.

The employer's duty to persons other than employees: s 3

Section 3 places the employer under a duty to conduct its business as far as practicable in a way that does not endanger persons other than employees who might be affected by it. This includes independent contractors, as well as visitors to the premises. Section 3 imposes a similar duty on self-employed persons. The s 3 duty is a negative requirement not to expose them to risks, compared with the positive duty in s 2 'to ensure as far as practicable'.

Health and safety policies: s 2

The 1974 Act seeks to ensure that employees are involved in and kept informed about health and safety provision in their workplace. An employer with a workforce of five or more must have a written health and safety policy and ensure that this is kept up to date and brought to the attention of the employees. A workplace safety committee must assist in the process. The employer must consult health and safety representatives from trade unions if required by Department of Trade and Industry regulations.

The powers of the Health and Safety Executive (HSE)

HSE inspectors are given wide powers to enter and investigate workplaces and to enforce sanctions under the 1974 Act. These include the following powers.

Prosecution of any offence specified in the Act

Offences may arise not only from breach of duty, but also from obstruction of the inspectors.

Improvement notices: s 21

If in an inspector's view the statute is being breached and this state of affairs is likely to continue, the inspector may issue a notice requiring the contravention to be corrected within specified time limits. Compliance may be enforced by prosecution if necessary.

Prohibition notices: s 23

If the inspector believes that the way the business is being conducted is likely to result in serious personal injury, a prohibition notice may be issued. This prohibits continuance of the relevant activity until the situation is resolved. These notices have to set out clearly the nature of the problem and may include advice about how it can be remedied. Section 24 gives rights to appeal against an order to an employment tribunal.

Ministerial regulations

The 1974 Act empowers the Department of Employment to make specific regulations to ensure performance of duties under the Act. Progress was initially slow in this area, but the need to comply with EC Directives issued between 1989 and 1991 forced the Department to issue the Management of Health and Safety at Work Regulations 1992. These came into force progressively between 1993 and 1997 and replace most of the provisions of statutes like the Factories Acts and the Offices, Shops and Railway Premises Act 1963. These regulations expand the scope of obligations imposed on employers by the Health and Safety at Work Act, since they incorporate aspects of EC law not envisaged by the 1974 Act.

Quiz 18

1 What are the main differences in the legal obligations of an employer to an employee and to an independent contractor?

2 Angelica is employed by Juniper plc as personal assistant to the managing director. What contractual duties may Angelica have breached in the following circumstances?

  (a) She takes an evening job with Coltsfoot Ltd.

  (b) When serving refreshments at a meeting at Juniper plc, she drops a full coffee pot into the lap of Lupin, the chairman of the board.

  (c) After the meeting, Hawksbeard, a visiting consultant, who had enjoyed Lupin's discomfiture, gives Angelica a £10 tip.

3 Heather, who is employed by Rush, was run over on work premises by a forklift truck driven by Bogbean. Her injuries were aggravated by difficulties in locating the first aid kit. What are Rush's liabilities?

4 What powers are available to HSE inspectors who discover that a health and safety offence has been committed?

Assignment 17

Evaluate the ways in which the law regulates employers with regard to the health and safety of their employees.

A suggested solution for this assignment can be found in the Lecturer's Guide.

CHAPTER 19

Rights at work: protection against discrimination

INTRODUCTION

Since the 1960s some statutory measures have been introduced to attempt to control sex, race and disability discrimination. The main current domestic legislation is the Equal Pay Act 1970 (EPA), the Sex Discrimination Act 1975 (as amended by the Sex Discrimination Act 1986) (SDA), and the Race Relations Act 1976 (RRA). The Disability Discrimination Act 1995 (DDA) gives a person who suffers adverse discrimination because of his or her disability similar rights to those of victims of sex and race discrimination. The implementation in 2000 of the Human Rights Act 1998 has widened the scope of anti-discrimination law.

EU law has also already assisted development of English law through Article 119 (now 141) of the Treaty of Rome and the Equal Treatment and Equal Pay Directives. The early years of the twenty-first century will see the scope of the law widening through implementation of Framework Directive (2000/87/EC). This will increase the scope of sex, race and disability discrimination and introduce direct protection against discrimination on the grounds of sexual orientation, age and religious belief.

THE EQUAL PAY ACT 1970

The EPA 1970 was amended in 1983 under the Equal Pay (Amendment) Regulations to comply with the EC Equal Pay Directive regarding equal payment for work of equal value. Historically, women's work has been undervalued, with low rates of pay in those areas of employment most often filled by women, like cleaning, nursing, catering, and shop work. Where men have been employed alongside women, they have often been paid at a higher rate than women doing similar, or even identical, work. The main provisions of the Act are discussed below.

The equality clause: s 1

It is an implied term in every woman's contract of employment that she has the right to be paid at the same rate as any man in her workplace who is doing:

1 the same or similar work; or

2 work which is rated as equivalent work by a job evaluation scheme; or

3 work of equal value.

A claim may be brought for breach of this implied term.

The same or similar work

A number of successful claims have been brought by women who were able to show that they were being paid less than a man who was effectively doing the same or broadly similar work, although the man's job was sometimes dignified by a superior title.

> **Capper Pass v Lawton** (1977)
> A woman employed to cook meals for the directors' dining room was held to be doing essentially similar work to the assistant chefs in the canteen. The only differences were that the canteen chefs cooked more meals for greater numbers, were supervised and worked for four hours more every week than she did.

To justify unequal treatment the job done by the man must be more onerous in terms of its responsibility, anti-social hours or physical functions.

> **Noble v David Gold & Sons (Holdings) Ltd** (1980)
> Male warehouse workers were paid more than women working alongside them. This was held to be justified by the fact that the men loaded and unloaded goods while the women's work was lighter and involved sorting, labelling and packaging goods.

Notional responsibilities which are not actually performed will not be treated as a material difference.

> **Shields v Coomes (Holdings) Ltd** (1978)
> It was claimed that a male counter assistant at a betting shop was paid more than a female counter assistant because he was there for security purposes. The employer was unable to prove that the male assistant had received any special training for this, or that he had ever had to deal with troublemakers. There was, therefore, no material difference between his function and the woman's, so she won her claim.

Work rated as equivalent by a job evaluation scheme

A woman is entitled to claim breach of the equality clause if her employer has a valid job evaluation scheme in operation, under which the woman's job is graded at the same level as a man's but he is paid more, or if the woman's job would have been graded at a higher level under the scheme if the evaluation had not been made according to different values for men and women. This claim is given additional force by the 1975 Equal Pay Directive, which requires that the same criteria be applied to both men and women and the scheme drawn up in such a way as to avoid sex discrimination.

The Act does not compel an employer to carry out such schemes and, due to the relatively small number in operation, claims in this area of the statute are uncommon.

Work of equal value

Before 1983, many women were unable to claim successfully under the 1970 Act as they were unable to prove that the work they did was sufficiently similar to that being done by men. The comparative value of the work was irrelevant unless a job evaluation scheme was in operation. The Act was amended in 1983 to take account of the Equal Pay Directive 1975. To determine the value of the work, the demands of the relevant jobs must be assessed and compared by the tribunal. It must take into account the skill, knowledge, trade or professional qualification, physical and mental effort, and levels of responsibility and decision-making.

Hayward v _Cammell Laird Shipbuilders_ (1988)
The House of Lords held that the work of a cook in the works canteen was of equal value to that of other skilled workers such as joiners, painters and insulation engineers, and she was entitled to the same basic pay as they were. It was irrelevant that her entitlement to sickness benefits, holiday leave and meals entitlement were superior to other skilled workers.

Murphy v _Bord Telecom Eireann_ (1988)
The European Court of Justice closed a loophole in the 1970 Act. If the Act is given its literal meaning, a woman would have no claim if she was paid less for doing work of greater value than a man who is doing work of less value for higher pay. Such an interpretation was held to be a breach of Article 141 of the Treaty of Rome which requires that men and women 'receive equal pay for equal work'. The claimant was entitled to be paid at least at the rate of the male comparator.

In assessing whether work is of equal value, it is important to determine _the area of comparison and the choice of comparator_. The comparator must be or have been employed at the claimant's workplace or at another workplace where the same conditions of service apply. In *McCarthys* v *Smith* (1981, CA) it was held that the comparator need not be employed contemporaneously with the claimant. This prevents an employer from replacing a man with a woman and paying her less.

> **Pickstone v Freemans plc** (1988, HL)
> The claimant worked in a warehouse alongside men doing similar work and who were paid the same as her. She chose as her comparator a male checker in the warehouse, claiming that her work was of equal value to his. The House of Lords held that she was entitled to choose whom she wanted to be compared with.

This prevents an employer from slipping a 'token male' into the same line of work as the woman, paying him at the same rate.

The procedure in equal value claims is lengthy and complicated:

1 the applicant applies to the employment tribunal;

2 the case is referred to ACAS and settlement attempted;

3 if no settlement is reached, the employment tribunal decides whether on the face of it there is a reasonable likelihood that the woman's work is of equal value. The burden of proof is on the applicant. The employer is automatically discharged from liability if it can show that under a job evaluation scheme the woman's job has been graded lower than the male comparator's;

4 if the applicant makes out a reasonable case the tribunal refers the matter to an independent expert, who carries out a study and reports back to the tribunal (which is not bound by the report).

Defence to a claim under the EPA 1970

Under s 1(3), if the employer can prove that the reason for a pay differential between men and women is 'genuinely due to a material factor which is not the difference of sex', it will not be liable. Effectively, the employer is saying that the difference in pay between men and women is coincidental and that it can be shown to be linked to material differences between the two parties other than their sex. Such differences have been held to include levels of qualification, length of service, place of work and anti-social hours of work. Organisational and economic factors may also justify a pay differential, but it is a question of fact for the court to decide in each case.

> **North Yorks County Council v Ratcliffe** (1995, HL)
> Paying dinner ladies less than men judged to be doing work of equal value could not be justified on the ground that it was done to enable the employers to make the winning bid in compulsory competitive tender negotiations. It was 'the very kind of discrimination which the Act sought to remove'.

THE SEX DISCRIMINATION ACT 1975

This statute makes it illegal to discriminate directly or indirectly *against* persons on the grounds of their sex or marital status. Treating men and women differently does not amount to illegal discrimination unless it results in members of one sex being treated less favourably than the other.

Discrimination against women: s 1

Direct discrimination

This is overt discrimination and occurs if a woman is treated less favourably than a man. Reserving a job for male candidates only is an obvious example. See *Batisha* v *Say* (1977), where a woman who applied for a job as a cave guide was turned down on the ground that it was 'a man's job'. Such glaring discrimination is easy to spot, but the Act also recognises more subtle forms.

Indirect discrimination

This is covert discrimination. It occurs when a person imposes requirements or conditions (for instance, a minimum height requirement) which are likely to be able to be satisfied by a much smaller number of women than men and are likely to prove detrimental to women. Such a condition is illegal unless it can be shown to be justifiable in the circumstances.

> **The Home Office v Holmes** (1984)
> A requirement that employees worked full-time not part-time was indirectly discriminatory against women. Their opportunities to go out to work full-time were more likely to be limited by child care responsibilities than men's. The nature of the job did not justify the full-time requirement.

> **Price v Civil Service Commission** (1978)
> A requirement that candidates for the executive officer grade should be under the age of 28 was indirectly discriminatory against women. Fewer women than men could comply with it since many women in their twenties would have taken career breaks to have children.

Discrimination against men: s 2

The provisions of the 1975 Act must be read as applying equally to men. Although this statute was enacted primarily to combat sexual discrimination against women, men are given equal rights under its terms. In some years men have brought more successful cases than women.

Sexual harassment

Although this is not specifically identified as discrimination in the SDA, a complainant can succeed on proof that a person of the opposite sex would not have been subject to the same treatment.

> ### *Porcelli v Strathclyde Regional Council* (1986)
> Ms Porcelli worked as a technician in a laboratory with two male colleagues who mounted a campaign of sexual insults and physical intimidation to try to make her leave. It was held that she was the victim of discrimination since the behaviour of her colleagues was 'a particular kind of weapon which ... would not have been used against an equally disliked man'.

The Framework Equal Treatment Directive of 2000 states that harassment is to be treated as direct discrimination and the SDA must be amended to include a definition by 2003.

Sexual orientation and gender reassignment

The SDA and EC law offer no direct protection against discrimination on grounds of sexual orientation. In *R v Ministry of Defence, ex parte Smith* (1995) it was held that a complainant would have to show that he or she was being discriminated against on the basis of his or her sex compared with a homosexual person of the opposite sex. The European Court of Justice held in *Grant v South West Trains* (1998) that neither Article 119 (now 141) of the Treaty of Rome nor the Equal Treatment Directive protects against this type of discrimination.

Human Rights legislation has provided some redress. The European Convention on Human Rights (Article 8, Article 13 and Article 14 which prohibits discrimination) does not refer expressly to sexual orientation but can be interpreted purposively. The ECHR in *Smith and Grady v UK* (1998) held that the ban on lesbians and gay men in the armed forces violated their rights under Article 8 (the right to privacy and family life) and Article 13 (the right to an effective domestic remedy). This led to a radical change in policy by the Ministry of Defence which lifted the ban. The implementation of the Convention in the English courts by the Human Rights Act 1998 enables further developments of English law in this area.

The scope and effectiveness of EC law in this area will increase with the implementation of the Treaty of Amsterdam (see page 30 above). An Equal Treatment Directive adopted in November 2002 requires member states to introduce legislation to outlaw discrimination on grounds of sexual orientation by 2003. A consultation process has been set up by the Department of Trade and Industry to decide on the content of the new legislation.

Transsexuals have the protection of the SDA (*Chessington World of Adventures* v *Reed*, 1997) and the Equal Treatment Directive. In *P* v *S and Cornwall County Council* (1986) it was held that such complainants should be compared with a person of the opposite sex who is *not* undergoing gender reassignment. The rights of transsexuals were further extended by the decision of the ECHR in *Goodwin* v *UK* (2002), which held that transsexuals might amend their birth certificates to reflect their new gender. This enables transsexuals to marry, thus potentially impacting on employment law in relation to spouses' pension rights.

Discrimination on the grounds of marital status: s 3

In the field of employment, it is illegal to discriminate against persons on the ground of their marital status. Direct and indirect discrimination are covered in the same way as by s 1.

Discrimination on grounds of victimisation: s 4(1)

It is illegal to discriminate against persons who have asserted their rights under the EPA 1970 or under the SDA 1975, or who have been involved in any legal proceedings relating to those statutes.

The scope of employment: s 6

The legislation acknowledges that there are many situations where discrimination may come into play in relation to employment, and it covers most aspects of the employment process. For example:

- advertising jobs;
- interview and selection procedures;
- the terms of the employment contract;
- training;
- promotion;
- other facilities available to employees (like a canteen, social club or medical service);
- membership of trade unions and professional bodies.

Note that rates of pay and pension provisions are expressly excluded from the operation of the 1975 Act. As pensions are not covered by the EPA 1970, inequalities between the sexes are still largely without statutory redress under UK law. However, cases brought both in the European Court and in the domestic courts for breach of Article 141 of the Treaty of Rome and the Equal Treatment Directive have provided some helpful results.

> ### Barber v Guardian Royal Insurance (1993, ECJ)
> The European Court held that it was contrary to Article 141 for a man who had been made compulsorily redundant to be entitled only to a deferred pension if a woman of the same age and in the same position would be entitled to claim her pension immediately.

The genuine occupational qualification (GOQ): s 7

Qualities like physical strength and stamina are not treated as sex specific. A woman cannot automatically be excluded from consideration for a job because it involves heavy lifting. However, it is acknowledged that in a minority of jobs the sex of the employee may be an essential qualification for the job. The burden of proving that there is a genuine occupational qualification for a particular job lies with the employer. This may be possible in the following situations.

The essential nature of the job

For example, when it is in the interests of the authenticity of a dramatic performance. It is, therefore, legitimate to appoint a man to play a male role. A job may be reserved for a man or a woman specifically if this is essential for physiological reasons, such as life models for art classes and striptease artists.

Issues of privacy and decency

This includes lavatory and locker-room attendants, and jobs in private homes.

> ### Etam plc v Rowan (1996, EAT)
> Being female was not a GOQ for a shop assistant selling women's clothes. A male applicant could fulfil the bulk of the job, and the task of supervising changing rooms could be carried out by a female staff member without any inconvenience to the employer.

Lack of facilities

This may be relevant, for example, if the job requires staff to live on the premises where appropriate separate sleeping or sanitary facilities cannot reasonably be provided.

Single-sex hospitals and prisons

Employing persons of one sex only may be justifiable provided that the hospital or prison, or the relevant section of them, provides care to persons of one sex only.

Vicarious liability: s 41

The employer is vicariously liable for anything done by employees in the course of their employment, whether or not it is done with the employer's knowledge and approval. This has been interpreted purposively in the context of the SDA and RRA to cover harassment (*Jones* v *Tower Boot Co.*, 1997). See below at page 285. The current trend is to interpret course of employment generously. In *Chief Constable of Lincolnshire* v *Stubbs* (1999), inappropriate sexual advances made by a male police officer to a woman during a leaving party for a colleague at a pub were treated as coming within the scope of employment. (More information about vicarious liability can be found above at page 285)

Enforcing the Act: s 63

A complainant may apply to take the matter before an employment tribunal. An application must be made within three months of the alleged discriminatory behaviour. Initially, conciliation procedures may be implemented, but if these fail the case will be heard by the tribunal.

There is no longer any statutory limitation on the amount of damages which may be awarded. The employer may also be ordered to take practical steps to correct the situation.

Protection against less favourable treatment due to pregnancy and parental responsibilities

The Equal Treatment Directive and the Pregnant Worker's Directive 92/85/EC (PWD) have led to changes in UK employment law and its interpretation by the courts, which give women a fair degree of protection at work while they are pregnant and for some months afterwards. The ERA 1996 includes rights to time off for ante-natal care, maternity leave, pay during such absences and the right to return to work after the birth. The Employment Relations Act 1999 amended and clarified these rights, in response to the PWD. It also enabled implementation of the Parental Leave Directive 97/75/EC (PLD) entitling employees to time off to deal with domestic emergencies involving the care of their dependants. The Employment Rights Act 2002 enables further implementation of the PLD including the introduction of paternity leave and adoption leave with pay. The SDA also protects against discrimination on the grounds of pregnancy and covers all employees, including agency workers and the self-employed.

Webb v EMO Cargo (1994, HL)

Mrs Webb was recruited to cover for an employee on maternity leave and was dismissed when it was discovered that she herself was pregnant. The House of Lords initially decided that her action under the SDA must fail, since a man absent for sickness for the same period of time would have been fairly dismissed. The case was referred to the European Court of Justice which held that this comparative approach was inappropriate: pregnancy and sickness were not the same. Under the Equal Treatment Directive she had been directly discriminated against. When the case returned to the HL (*Webb v EMO Cargo (No 2)* (1995)), it was held that she had been discriminated against directly under the SDA, though it was suggested that this would not have been the case if the contract had been for a fixed term.

The Equal Opportunities Commission

This body enjoys a variety of powers derived from the Sex Discrimination Act, which are aimed at ensuring effective implementation of the legislation. It has issued a code of practice as a guide to employers regarding implementation of the Act. The Commission is also able to:

1 take proceedings in the county court to obtain an injunction to restrain an employer from illegal behaviour;

2 assist victims of alleged discrimination with information, legal advice and representation, and attempted conciliation;

3 carry out research and educational projects;

4 conduct formal investigations of workplaces;

5 issue and enforce non-discriminatory notices.

THE RACE RELATIONS ACT 1976 (RRA)

In structure this Act, which was amended by the Race Relations (Amendment) Act 2000, is very similar to the SDA 1975. It embraces similar concepts of direct and indirect discrimination on racial grounds (s 1) and there is a defence of genuine occupational qualification. Like the SDA 1975, the RRA 1976 makes discrimination illegal in the provision of education and services, as well as in employment.

The changes arising from the Race Relations (Amendment) Act 2000 (RRAA) removed immunities previously enjoyed by public authorities under the RRA. (See page 285 below.) The RRAA also places a duty on specified public authorities to strive to eliminate unlawful discrimination and to promote equal opportunity and good relationships between people in different ethnic groups.

Meaning of 'racial grounds'

Under s 3, 'racial grounds' are defined as meaning any of the following: colour, race, nationality, or ethnic or national origins. Note that under this section nationality includes citizenship. Ethnicity is interpreted more widely than race.

Mandla v Dowell Lee (1983, HL)
School rules forbidding turbans and requiring hair to be cut to a specified length were held to discriminate indirectly against Sikhs, who constituted a distinct ethnic group under the Act. The House of Lords held than an ethnic group existed for the purposes of the Act if the group was regarded by its members and by outsiders as a clearly distinguishable community with its own cultural traditions and a long-shared history. Other relevant factors were said to include a common geographical origin, or language, religion, or literature.

The Commission for Racial Equality v Dutton (1989, CA)
Applying the principles of the above decision, the Court of Appeal held that gypsies constituted an ethnic group which had not merged wholly with the general population, although it was no longer derived from a common racial stock.

Crown Suppliers (PSA) v Dawkins (1991, EAT)
The Act does not give protection against discrimination on purely religious grounds. The complainant, a Rastafarian, therefore failed in his claim that he had suffered unlawful discrimination when he was dismissed for refusing to obey his employer's order to cut his hair and beard. It was held that Rastafarians were a religious sect which could not be regarded as a separate ethnic group. Their shared history of only 60 years was not long enough, and there was insufficient difference between them and other members of the Afro-Caribbean community, to bring them within the *Mandla v Dowell Lee* criteria.

Direct discrimination: s 1(1)(a)

Persons discriminate against somebody on racial grounds if they treat him or her less favourably than they would or do treat others because of his or her colour, race, etc. Less favourable treatment to one person may arise as a result of discrimination against a third party.

Showboat Entertainment Centre Ltd v Owens (1984, EAT)
The complainant was held to have been unfairly dismissed for disobeying a management instruction to exclude young black men from the amusement centre where he was employed.

Indirect discrimination: s 1(1)(b)

This occurs when a condition is imposed on members of a racial group which is applied equally to people who are not members of that group, but which considerably fewer members of the racial group are able to satisfy. The fact that they cannot comply with it must be to their detriment. If the condition can be shown to be justifiable on other grounds, e.g. health and safety, this is a defence available to the employer.

Panesaar v Nestlé (1980)
A rule forbidding long beards and hair in the defendant's factory indirectly discriminated against Sikhs, but was held to be lawful on hygiene grounds.

Racial harassment

The RRA does not define harassment but has been interpreted to cover it. A complaint will be successful provided that the complainant can prove that a person of a different race would not have been similarly treated.

Burton v De Vere Hotels (1996, EAT)
Two black women claimed that they had been racially harassed when racist comments were made by a comedian and customers at a dinner where they were working as waitresses. The Employment Appeal Tribunal held that the employer had subjected them to a 'detriment' under s 4(2)(c) of the Act since the employer could have taken steps to prevent the occurrence.

The Framework Equal Treatment in Employment Directive of 2000 states that harassment is to be treated as direct discrimination. The RRA will be amended to include a definition reflecting the wording of the Directive by 2003.

Discrimination by victimisation: s 2

It is illegal to discriminate against persons who have asserted their rights under the RRA 1976, or who have given evidence in any proceedings under the Act.

Discrimination in employment: s 4

The content of this section is very similar to the corresponding provisions of the SDA 1975 and makes it illegal for an employer to subject an employee to racial discrimination with regard to most aspects of employment except for pensions.

The genuine occupational qualification: s 5

Choosing to employ a member of a particular racial group may be justified in the following circumstances.

Authenticity in the provision of entertainment, modelling or catering services

It is justifiable to advertise for a black actor to play Othello, or for somebody Chinese to work in a Chinese restaurant.

Special welfare services

This defence may also be applicable to jobs involving the provision of services to a specific racial group, where applicants may be required to be members of that group themselves.

Vicarious liability: s 32

This operates similarly to s 41 of the SDA (see above).

Jones v Tower Boot (1997, CA)
The complainant was subjected to verbal and physical racial abuse in his workplace from other employees, for which his employer was held to be vicariously liable. The Court of Appeal stated that to give proper effect to the Act it was necessary to interpret 'course of employment' purposively. Otherwise, the more appalling the behaviour of the employee, the less likely it would be that the employer would be liable.

Until the implementation of the RRAA in April 2001 a chief constable was not vicariously liable for the acts of other members of the force (*Chief Constable of Bedfordshire Police* v *Liversidge*, 2002). However, a chief constable is now vicariously liable in the same way as any other employer.

Enforcement of claims under the 1976 Act: ss 54–55

Cases concerning employment must be referred to an employment tribunal within three months of the alleged incident, though this time limit may be extended on the grounds of justice and equity (s 54).

Conciliation may be attempted (s 55), but if this fails the case proceeds to a tribunal hearing. If the claim is successful, damages awarded may include compensation for humiliation or hurt feelings. The employer may be ordered to take action to resolve the situation; the employer may be required to pay increased damages if the order is not obeyed.

The Commission for Racial Equality: s 43

This body, which consists of 8–15 members appointed by the Secretary of State, has a statutory duty to work towards the elimination of racial discrimination and to promote equality of opportunity between the members of different racial groups. The Commission has a wide variety of powers, such as the issue of relevant codes of practice. The Commission also has advisory, monitoring, inspection and enforcement powers similar to those exercised by the Equal Opportunities Commission.

THE DISABILITY DISCRIMINATION ACT 1995

There are more than 60 000 disabled people of working age in the UK, but only 30 000 of them are in employment. On average they are paid 20 per cent less than able-bodied people. This Act seeks to prevent less favourable treatment at work of people with disabilities and outlaws discriminatory practices in recruitment, terms of employment, transfer and training, employment benefits and dismissal and other detrimental treatment. Interpretation of the Act is aided by the code of practice, issued by the Secretary of State in 1996.

What is a disability?

Section 1 defines disability as a physical or mental impairment which has a substantial and adverse long-term effect on a person's ability to cope with everyday activities. The impairment must be medically recognised and relate for example to mobility, manual dexterity, eyesight, hearing, memory, concentration or comprehension. Progressive conditions are also included (for instance, multiple sclerosis, HIV/AIDS). Severe disfigurement may be a disability (birthmarks, scars, skin diseases), though not if self-inflicted (tattoos). Certain conditions, such as addiction to alcohol, nicotine and other substances are specifically excluded by the Act, as are certain personality disorders such as pyromania and voyeurism.

Since the Act, a variety of illnesses and conditions have been held to be disabilities under the Act: *Cox* v *Post Office* (1997), asthma; *O'Neil* v *Symm & Co.* (1998), ME: Chronic Fatigue Syndrome; *Clark* v *Novacold* (1998), soft tissue injuries; *Howden* v *Capital Copiers* (1998), acute abdominal pain.

To be 'substantial' the condition must affect a person's ability beyond the differences to be found between able-bodied people. The conditions must have lasted or be going to last for at least 12 months.

When does discrimination occur?

Section 5 states that an employer discriminates against a person if:

(a) for a reason related to their disability, he or she treats them less favourably than he or she would treat others without such a disability; and

(b) he or she cannot show that the discrimination was justified.

Comparison may be made with any person to whom the reason for less favourable treatment does not apply, whether disabled or able-bodied.

This definition does not cover indirect discrimination and an employer must know of the disability in order to be liable for discrimination. Those protected by the Act include the self-employed, as well as those with a contract of service. However, workplaces employing fewer than 20 people are not affected by the Act. Certain employees (such as firefighters and members of the police or armed forces) do not enjoy the protection of the Act.

The Act, while protecting the disabled against less favourable treatment because of their disability, does not prevent positive discrimination in their favour.

Justification

The employer will not be liable if he or she can prove material and substantial reasons. The code of practice states that the reasons must be related directly to the particular circumstances of the case and not just based on general assumptions about the nature of the disability. An employer, therefore, may be justified in refusing to employ as a model for cosmetics someone who suffers from a disfiguring skin complaint in the relevant body area. However, there are no real and substantial reasons for refusing to shortlist a blind person for a job involving computers, in the belief that due to being blind he or she will be automatically incapable of using one. Similarly, it is not justifiable to dismiss a person with learning difficulties on the basis that he or she is slower than the average worker if the difference in productivity is insignificant.

Reasonable adjustments

Section 6 requires an employer to make reasonable adjustments to arrangements on the basis of which employment is offered, including 'to any physical feature of the premises which place disabled people at a substantial disadvantage with people who are not disabled'.

Adjustments may include structural or physical changes to the workplace, flexible hours, or transferring an employed person whose capabilities have deteriorated to an appropriate vacancy.

Whether it is reasonable to expect the employer to make the adjustment will be decided on the basis of proportionality. Thus, the effectiveness and practicability of the measure are relevant, as well as the size of the employer's business, the cost of alterations, the financial and other resources of the employer and the value of the employee to the business.

> **_Tarling v Wisdom Toothbrushes_** (1997)
> Ms Tarling had a club foot which made it difficult for her to stand for long periods. This impaired her work performance, which led to her dismissal. Her employer knew that a special chair was available, on four weeks' free trial at a subsidised cost which reduced the price to £200. No steps were taken by the employer to obtain one. It was held that her dismissal was discriminatory and due to the failure of the employer to make reasonable adjustments.

The Disability Rights Commission

This was created by the Disability Rights Commission Act 1998 with similar powers to the Equal Opportunities Commission and the Commission for Racial Equality. It replaced the National Disability Council, which had advisory powers only.

Future impact of EU law

The Act will require amendment once the EU Framework Directive of 2000 is implemented. For example, harassment will need to be defined by the Act and treated as a form of direct discrimination.

HOW WELL DOES THE LEGISLATION WORK?

The four statutes described above have come in for a fair amount of criticism, both from the members of the relevant interest groups, who say that they are ineffective, and from those who say that such measures are unnecessary, undesirable or in themselves likely to promote discrimination. It is claimed that the legislation places unreasonable restrictions on employers and actually restricts access to employment for the relevant groups. Successive governments have shown resistance to full implementation of EU equality requirements, though EU law has led to development of anti-discrimination law and its impact continues to be felt.

Hard evidence suggests that the legislation does not prompt huge numbers of claims. For example, during 2001 ACAS received 52 000 complaints of unfair dismissal, compared with 3825 complaints of race discrimination.

There are various opinions about why this is so. Those critical of the effectiveness of the legislation say that:

- employees lack knowledge of their rights;
- employees fear repercussions from management and fellow employees if they assert their rights;
- employees lack the necessary support to overcome the difficulties mentioned above;

- the attitude of employment tribunal panels (often predominantly white and male) may demonstrate a lack of understanding of the relevant equality issues.

Those critical of the existence of the legislation claim that it is under-used because:

- there is no/very little sex or race discrimination at work;
- many unsuccessful actions are taken by troublemakers or those with 'a chip on their shoulder', which makes them interpret any slight as an insult to their race or sex.

Anecdotes and urban myths abound, as do generalisations in this emotive area. It can, however, be asserted with some degree of certainty that:

1 the use of the legislation has helped to raise people's perceptions of issues to which they had given little thought previously. Since most prejudice rests on ignorance and thoughtlessness, such stimulus can only be healthy;

2 some valuable modifications in employment practice have been introduced by some employers since the legislation was enacted;

3 the possibility of legal action inhibits some undesirable behaviour, like blatantly advertising jobs in a sexually or racially discriminatory way, which would have gone unchecked in the past.

FURTHER DEVELOPMENT OF ANTI-DISCRIMINATION LEGISLATION

Age

There is currently no direct legislative prohibition of age discrimination under English law. In fact, the Employment Rights Act 1996 effectively sanctions discrimination by denying protection from unfair dismissal and the right to redundancy pay, to people past retirement age. (See below at page 292.) The Employment Appeal Tribunal in *Simpson* v *British Temken* (1998) held that this appeared to be incompatible with EC law since it was discriminatory on grounds of gender. Statistics show that a much higher proportion of men over 65 continue in work compared with women. The case was referred to the European Court of Justice, but at the time of writing no decision has been handed down. A government initiative to promote voluntary action by employers occurred in 1999 with the publication of a Code of Practice on Age Diversity. This stated an intention to promote good practice to reduce discrimination and promote a more age diverse workforce. An EU Equal Treatment Framework Directive of 2000 requires legislation by member states to outlaw age discrimination in employment by 2006.

Religion or belief

Implementation of the 2000 Framework Directive by 2003 will make it unlawful for employers to discriminate directly or indirectly on matters such as rules regarding uniform or dress or leave for the purpose of religious observance. Genuine occupational requirements will protect from liability those organizations whose ethos is based on religion or belief such as churches and religious schools.

Quiz 19

1 (a) Ms Antelope, who is employed as a cleaner by Cheetah plc, is paid less than the packers.

(b) Mr Buck was refused a job at the Warren Family Planning Clinic because of his sex.

What legal rights may they have?

2 What is the difference between direct and indirect discrimination?

3 When may it be legal to advertise a job as being open only to members of a particular ethnic group?

4 What aspects of employment discrimination come within the scope of the Sex Discrimination Act 1975 and the Race Relations Act 1976?

Assignment 18

Mary applied for a job in a men's clothing shop, which was a branch of a large high street retailer. There were four male employees employed in that particular branch. Although Mary had significant retail experience she was unsuccessful in her application, the successful applicant being a man. When Mary enquired of the human resources manager as to why she had been unsuccessful she was told that whilst she was a very good candidate reluctantly they had to appoint a man in the light of possible embarrassing situations where personal measurements had to be taken for made-to-measure clothing.

Mary feels particularly aggrieved and feels that she has a legitimate claim for sex discrimination.

Explain to Mary the main purpose of the sex discrimination laws, any possible defences the shop may have to an action and, if there is discrimination, identify in detail the distinction between what constitutes direct or indirect discrimination.

(20 marks)

(ICSA English Business Law: May 2002)

CHAPTER 20

Rights at work: protection against dismissal and redundancy

INTRODUCTION

This chapter focuses on the legal consequences which result when the employment contract is brought to an end by the employer. Three legal concepts are crucial to this area:

1 *Wrongful dismissal*. At common law an employee dismissed without appropriate notice may sue in the civil courts for breach of contract at common law.

2 *Unfair dismissal*. Provided that the required notice is given, dismissal is lawful at common law, but may nonetheless be unfair as an employee is potentially vulnerable to dismissal at the whim of the employer. Since 1971, statutory rights have existed which protect employees found to have been dismissed unfairly. An employee may be entitled to bring a claim before an employment tribunal, whether dismissed with notice or not. Unless the employer can prove that it was fair to dismiss the employee (because of incompetence, for example), he or she may have to pay compensation to the employee who might, in exceptional cases, be reinstated.

3 *Redundancy*. An employer may need to reduce the size of the workforce, but an employee consequently made redundant may have a statutory entitlement to compensation.

These concepts are explained in detail below.

WRONGFUL DISMISSAL

This is a breach of contract action which may be brought by either party if the contract of employment is terminated without the appropriate notice, or, in the case of a fixed-term contract, if termination is enforced before the contract's completion date.

Summary dismissal (without notice) may be justified only if the employer can prove that the employee was guilty of gross misconduct. This usually involves theft, fraud, violence or drunkenness, reckless behaviour or wilful refusal to obey a reasonable order.

Minimum notice periods

Under the Employment Rights Act (ERA) 1996 the following notice periods apply unless a longer period is specified in the contract (s 86):

- up to one month in employment: no notice;
- one month to two years' employment: one week's notice;
- two to ten years' employment: one week's notice for every completed year;
- over ten years' employment: 12 weeks' notice.

Remedies for wrongful dismissal

An employee is entitled to sue for breach of contract in the county court or High Court to recover any lost earnings payable during the notice period, as well as any commissions and gratuities which the employee would normally have acquired. An apprentice is entitled to be compensated for loss of prospects. An employee may also obtain compensation for benefits lost where the wrongful dismissal prevented the employee from completing the necessary period of continuous employment to entitle the employee to pursue a claim for unfair dismissal (see below).

UNFAIR DISMISSAL

This area of the law, which has been subject to constant change, is currently largely governed by the ERA 1996 (as amended by the Employment Relations Act 1999).

Any employee entitled to sue for wrongful dismissal may also be entitled to bring a claim for unfair dismissal to an employment tribunal. However, an employee who has not been dismissed wrongfully may qualify to claim for unfair dismissal. Employers, therefore, are no longer necessarily free to dispense with an employee's services unless they can satisfy the tribunal that they acted fairly and with reasonable cause within the legislative criteria.

Certain types of employee are not eligible to claim unfair dismissal. These include:

1 employees over retirement age (see above at page 289 regarding the issue of age discrimination);

2 employees whose contracts of employment require them to work primarily outside Great Britain;

3 employees on short-term contracts who have waived their rights to claim.

Eligibility to claim

Claims must be brought within *three months* of the termination of the contract. The following criteria must be satisfied:

1 continuous employment;

2 the employee must prove the fact of the dismissal;

3 the employer must prove the dismissal was not unfair.

The employee must have been continuously employed for at least one year

A previous requirement that part-time workers must have been continuously employed for five years has been abandoned. It was held by the House of Lords (*R v Secretary of State for Employment, ex parte The Equal Opportunities Commission* (1994)) to breach Article 119 (now Article 141) of the Treaty of Rome. It was discriminatory to women, who are more likely than men to work part-time. The number of hours worked per week is now also irrelevant in computing continuous employment.

Employment remains continuous despite certain interruptions:

- sickness;
- pregnancy and maternity leave;
- temporary lay-offs;
- holidays;
- change of job with the employer or its associate;
- takeover by a new employer.

Until 1999 the continuous employment qualification period was two years (ERA 1996, s 108(1)) but the legality of this provision was challenged in *R v Secretary of State for Employment, ex parte Seymour-Smith and Perez* (1997) and the Court of Appeal held that it was discriminatory to women, since they are more likely to take career breaks than men. The House of Lords referred the case to the European Court of Justice to determine whether the requirement was in breach of the Equal Treatment Directive. In June 1999, the government introduced a one-year qualification under the Unfair Dismissal and Statement of Reasons for Dismissal (Qualifying Period) Order 1999.

Employees must prove that they have been dismissed

Dismissal may be actual, constructive or deemed.

1 *Actual dismissal*. The employer clearly indicates an intention to dispense with the employee's services.

2 *Constructive dismissal*. The employee resigns claiming that the employer's behaviour made it impossible for the employee to stay. Breach of the employer's duty not to undermine the trust and confidence of the employee is often the ground for such a claim. A number of such cases have arisen from an employer's failure to prevent sexual harassment and bullying.

3 *Deemed dismissal.* An employee who has been on maternity leave but has given appropriate notice that she wishes to return to work, is deemed to be dismissed if the employer refuses to let her resume her job.

In the following circumstances dismissal does *not* occur:

1 *The employee fails to return to work after leave of absence has expired.* This may deprive an employee of the right to return but it is not a dismissal.

2 *Completion of purpose of employment.* Employees will not be able to claim that they were dismissed if they were appointed to complete a specific project. Once this is done, their employment ceases. This is common in seafaring and fishing contracts.

3 *Resignation.* The employee must neither have resigned voluntarily, nor have been forced into doing so (see constructive dismissal above).

The burden of disproving unfairness lies with the employer

The employer must prove:

(a) grounds for the dismissal;

(b) that in the circumstances it is fair.

Section 98 of the ERA 1996 lays down five grounds, any of which may justify dismissal:

- lack of appropriate qualifications/capability to do the job;
- the employee's conduct;
- the employee was redundant: the job had ceased to exist;
- continuance of employment would result in illegality;
- any other substantial reason.

There are numerous cases to illustrate the application of these criteria, including the following examples. Each case is judged on its particular facts.

1 *Lack of qualification or capability.* The missing qualification must be essential to the proper performance of the current job.

> ### Litster v Thom & Sons Ltd (1975)
> Litster was given a job on condition that he obtained an HGV licence. However, he failed the test and was transferred to a fitter's post. Later he was given notice. It was held that he had been unfairly dismissed. The lack of a licence had not prevented him from serving his employer. (Presumably if he had been sacked immediately on failing the driving test that might have been justifiable.)

Negligence may justify dismissal. One isolated act of negligence is unlikely to be sufficient grounds for dismissal unless it is gross negligence and/or endangers the life and limb of third parties.

Taylor v Alidair (1978)
An airline pilot who landed a plane in such a careless manner as seriously to disturb his passengers and crew was held to have been fairly dismissed.

Dismissal is not deemed fair if the employee's lack of capability can be attributed to the fault of the employer.

Davison v Kent Meters (1975)
A production line worker was held to have been unfairly dismissed for wrongly assembling several hundred components since she had been neither properly trained nor supervised.

Long-term sickness may make dismissal fair if it places an unreasonable burden on the employer. The employer must prove that they made proper enquiries, including where appropriate with the employer's medical adviser.

2 *Misconduct.* This covers a multitude of obvious evils, including lying, fighting, theft, and dangerous and careless behaviour, but a wider range of behaviour may constitute grounds for fair dismissal. Employees who are guilty of rudeness to superiors, drinking on duty, or who refuse to co-operate with management instructions may also be fairly dismissed. The crucial factor is that the misconduct must be incidental to the job that the employee was employed to do.

Thomson v Alloa Motor Co. (1983)
A petrol pump attendant was dismissed after she managed to demolish one of the pumps by carelessly driving her car into it. This was held to be unfair. Her dubious driving skill was not relevant to how she did her job.

Conduct which occurs in the employee's spare time may be incidental to employment if it reflects adversely on the employee's suitability for the job or reasonably reduces the employer's confidence in the employee.

Moore v C & A Modes (1981)
It was held that it was fair to dismiss a shop assistant who was arrested for theft in another shop. This clearly reflected adversely on her honesty; it was reasonable for the employer to suspect that she might help herself to the firm's property.

It is generally a mistake to sleep with the wife of an employer.

Whitlow v Alkanet Construction (1987)
Whitlow was asked by a senior executive to do some work at his house, where he departed from management instructions by starting an affair with the executive's wife. He was held to have been fairly dismissed since he was in breach of his duty of good faith.

Dismissal was held to be fair in all the following cases: *Atkin* v *Enfield Hospital Management Committee* (1975), failure to wear appropriate clothing; *Boychuk* v *Symons Holdings* (1977), wearing provocative badges in breach of instructions and several warnings; *Newman* v *Alarm Co.* (1976), conducting a sexual relationship in the company's time; *Parsons* v *McLoughlin* (1981), fighting; *Minter* v *Wellingborough Foundries* (1981), refusing to attend a training course.

3 *Redundancy*. This topic is dealt with in depth later in this chapter.

4 *Statutory restriction*. The employer claims that the employee can no longer be legally employed, or can no longer legally perform the job. Disqualification from driving is an obvious example, provided driving is central to the job description. Dismissal is not automatically fair in such circumstances. The nature of the job, the length of disqualification, the type of criminal offence from which it arose and the possibility of redeployment must all be considered.

Mathieson v Noble (1972)
A travelling salesman who lost his driving licence arranged to pay for a driver out of his own pocket, but his employer dismissed him. It was held that he should not have been dismissed unless and until it was evident that this arrangement was unworkable.

5 *Some other substantial reason*. A variety of circumstances which do not fit into any of the above categories may make dismissal reasonable.

Farr v Hoveringham Gravels Ltd (1972)
A term in Farr's contract required him to live within reasonable travelling distance of his workplace, as he was sometimes needed to cope with emergencies outside working hours. His employer was held to have fairly dismissed him after he had moved house to an address 44 miles away.

Gorfin v Distressed Gentlefolks' Aid Association (1973)
It was held that dismissal of an employee to resolve a personality clash may be reasonable to restore harmony to the workplace where all other reasonable steps to resolve the situation have failed.

Economic reasons may also be treated as 'substantial', provided that the employer can show that these are based on good business practice. Employment tribunals seem readily convinced by such arguments. Employees who leave in protest at attempts to impose detrimental changes to their contracts may well fail in a claim that they have been constructively and unfairly dismissed. If, for instance, the employer can show that the new terms will result in cost saving, necessary to the continuance of the business and maintenance of most of the existing workforce, these are likely to be treated as substantial reasons.

St John of God (Care Services) Ltd v Brooks (1992, EAT)
A hospital, after large cuts in government funding, offered its staff new contracts which reduced pay and overtime and removed paid holiday entitlement. The EAT held that the employer had proved substantial reasons for its decision, which must be examined with reference to all the relevant circumstances and not just to its impact on the employees.

Fairness of dismissal

Section 90(4) states that fairness is judged by deciding whether in all the circumstances of the case the employer acted reasonably. This 'shall be determined according to equity and the merits of the case'. It is not enough for the employer to prove that the employee received contractual notice and that one of the relevant criteria is satisfied. Good industrial practice demands that dismissal (except for gross misconduct, justifying summary dismissal) must not come out of the blue. The employee must be given adequate warnings that his or her job is under threat or the dismissal may still be unfair.

To justify the dismissal, the employer must prove that he or she dealt with the problem in a reasonable way in the particular circumstances. The employer will have to prove that dismissal was the last resort and that the employee had been given every opportunity to change the situation, by spoken and written warnings and, where appropriate, by providing training, support and supervision. In some cases redeployment is an option which the employer should explore. If the employee was dismissed after disciplinary proceedings, the employment tribunal should take into account whether the employer has complied with the ACAS Code of Practice on Disciplinary Practice and Procedures in Employment.

Dismissal is automatically unfair in certain specified circumstances

Certain classes of employees, who are vulnerable to victimisation, are automatically treated as unfairly dismissed in certain circumstances. The following employees are entitled to take their case to the tribunal without having to satisfy the continuous employment requirement.

- Section 99, ERA 1996 (as amended by the Employment Relations Act 1999): women dismissed in connection with the exercise of maternity rights: when the amendment is implemented, this right will be extended to cover *any person* exercising rights to parental leave to time off for domestic incidents;
- Section 100, ERA 1996: health and safety representatives;
- Sections 102 and 105, ERA 1996: trustees of occupational pension schemes;
- Section 103, ERA 1996: employees representing the workforce in redundancy consultations;
- Sections 103A and 105A, ERA 1996 (as amended by the Public Interest Disclosure Act 1998) protects employees dismissed for 'whistle blowing';
- Section 104, ERA 1996: employees who have taken legal action against their employer to enforce statutory rights;
- Section 105, ERA 1996: employees who have been made redundant;
- Section 152, Trades Union and Labour Relations (Consolidation) Act 1992 (TULRCA): trade union membership or activity. This protection is extended by s 14 and Sch 5 of the Employment Relations Act 1999 (adding s 238A to TULRCA) to include protection for employees participating in official industrial action;
- Section 12, Employment Relations Act 1999: employees accompanying workers to a disciplinary hearing.

Remedies for unfair dismissal

Reinstatement: ERA 1996, s 116

This may be ordered at the request of the employee if it is a practicable option. If granted, the employee resumes the job under the same pay and conditions as before.

Re-engagement order

The employer may be ordered to find a job for the employee which is reasonably comparable to the post from which the employee was dismissed. The new job may be with an associated employer (s 114, ERA 1996).

Compensation

An employer may be liable to compensate an employee who is unfairly dismissed.

The basic award (s 119, ERA 1996) is intended to protect the employee against the losses caused by a break in continuous employment and is, therefore, calculated in the same way as the statutory redundancy award with reference to the employee's age, current gross weekly pay and years of service:

● an employee aged 18–21 is entitled to half a week's pay per year of service;

● an employee aged 22–40 is entitled to one week's pay per every year of service;

● an employee aged 41–65 is entitled to one-and-a-half week's pay per year of service.

The compensatory award is intended to redress losses arising from the dismissal so far as these may be seen as the fault of the employer (s 123, ERA 1996). The ceiling was raised by s 29(4), ERA 1999 from £11 500 to £50 000. The conduct of the employee is relevant to the size of the compensatory award and may be reduced if the behaviour of the employee contributed to the dismissal. The Secretary of State may vary the minimum of the basic award and the upper limit of the compensatory award with reference to the Retail Price Index (s 29, Employment Relations Act 1999).

The additional award may be payable (s 117, ERA 1996, as amended by the Employment Relations Act 1999) where an employer fails to comply with an order to re-engage or reinstate an employee. It consists of 26–52 weeks' pay.

REDUNDANCY

A redundant employee may have the right to make one or both of the following claims:

1 *Redundancy payment*. While it is legitimate to reduce the size of a workforce, thus rendering some employees surplus to requirements, those employees may have statutory entitlement to compensation for losing their jobs.

2 *Unfair dismissal*. Employees who can prove that the method by which they were selected for redundancy did not meet the standards of good industrial practice, may additionally have a claim for unfair dismissal which might result in a compensatory award or an order for their reinstatement.

Redundancy payment

Eligibility

In order to be able to claim compensation the claimant must be able to prove the following:

1 *One year's continuous service with the relevant employer*.

2 *Relevant employee status*. Certain categories of employees excluded from claiming unfair dismissal are also excluded from statutory redundancy protection. See above at page 292.

3 *Dismissal.* To be able to claim, employees must be able to prove that they have been actively or constructively dismissed within the meaning of s 136, ERA 1996. Dismissal includes the expiration of a short-term contract where renewal is not offered. An employee is also dismissed if the employer dies, or if the employer is a partnership or company which is dissolved or wound up. An employee who leaves voluntarily having been warned of the threat of redundancy is not dismissed.

4 *Redundancy has caused the dismissal.* Under s 139, ERA 1996 redundancy may occur where:

(a) the employer ceases to carry on business or ceases to carry on business at the location where the employee worked; or

(b) the employer restructures the business or changes production methods so that fewer employees are needed.

(An employee may also be redundant if dismissed by the employer who intends to take any of the above actions.)

Change of workplace location

Where the employee's contract contains a term that the employee may be required to work at any place of business the employer directs, the employee is not made redundant by being moved. If no term exists, it is a question of fact whether or not redundancy has occurred. Distance is often a material fact in deciding this. Where compliance with the employer's order would force the employee to move house or undertake a much longer journey to work than before, the employee will be able to claim to have been constructively dismissed in circumstances which make the employee redundant. Compare the following two cases.

O'Brien v Associated Fire Alarms (1969)
Reduction in the amount of business available in Liverpool resulted in the employer offering O'Brien a transfer to its Barrow-in-Furness branch. Taking it up would have increased his journey to work very considerably. When he turned the offer down he was dismissed. It was held that he had been made redundant.

Managers (Holborn) Ltd v Hohne (1977)
An employee dismissed when he refused a transfer from an office in Holborn to one in Regent Street (a short tube ride) had not been made redundant.

Offers of suitable alternative employment

Employees offered suitable redeployment cannot, if dismissed, claim that they have been made redundant (s 138(1), ERA 1996). What is suitable is a question of fact to be determined by the tribunal in each case. Factors like travelling distances, domestic problems and lack of appropriate educational facilities for the employee's children may all have to be taken into account. An employer must show reasonable sensitivity and regard for the individual employee, but there are limits to this.

> **Fuller v Stephanie Bowman Ltd** (1977)
> A secretary working at her employer's Mayfair branch did not act reasonably when she refused to transfer to the Soho office because it was situated over a sex shop.

Under s 138(2), ERA 1996, an employee who takes up an alternative post has at least four weeks to decide if it is workable. If the employee gives up within the time limit, any rights to redundancy pay are not prejudiced.

Time limitation on redundancy claims

Employees must start their claims within six months of the date when a short-term contract expired or when their notice period expired. Late claims may be admitted by the tribunal if this is judged to be just and equitable.

Financial entitlement

This is calculated with reference to the age of the employee and the length of service up to a maximum of 20 years:

- 18–21: half a week's pay per year of service
- 22–40: one week's pay per year of service
- 41–64: one-and-a-half weeks' pay per year of service.

A week's pay is currently subject to an upper limit of £220, so the maximum statutory redundancy payment is £330. There is, of course, nothing to stop an employer from voluntarily exceeding this. The Secretary of State is empowered to vary this sum (s 227) and under the Employment Relations Act 1999 may do so with reference to the Retail Price Index.

Unfair dismissal arising from redundancy

An employee who has been made redundant may have an additional claim for unfair dismissal (s 98). To avoid liability, the employer must show that he or she acted reasonably in selecting the employee for redundancy. Criteria determining selection should include safeguards against bias. The employee must have been given proper warning, adequate consultation must have taken place, and proper consideration must have been given to the provision of alternative employment. (The relevant awards of compensation are described above at page 299.)

What is reasonable is judged with reference to the size and resources of the employer's business. A successful claimant is entitled to the same levels of compensation as any other unfairly dismissed employee.

TRANSFER OF UNDERTAKINGS

In the event of a new employer taking over an existing business entity, current employees enjoy protection of their job security and existing conditions of service under the Transfer of Undertakings (Protection of Employment) Regulations 1981 (amended by the Trade Union and Employment Rights Act 1993). The legislation was prompted by the Acquired Rights Directive 1977. The interpretation of the regulations by the English courts has, therefore, had to conform to a purposive interpretation in accordance with the Directive and relevant decisions in the European Court of Justice.

The meaning of 'transfer' and 'undertaking'

Regulation 3 states that a transfer may be 'by sale, or some other disposition' like a gift, or by operation of law (for example, if the original employer goes into liquidation). Certain types of transfer are, however, specifically excluded, such as transfer by share takeover, where the employer (the company) remains unchanged despite a change of shareholders.

An 'undertaking' is defined in the regulations as 'any trade or business', which has been interpreted widely by the courts. It includes, for instance, contracting out of public services by competitive tendering, and schools contracting out from local authority control. Thus, the undertaking need not have a commercial purpose. It may represent a small part of the transferor's enterprise as long as it retains its 'identity' as an economic entity. No one factor is crucial to this definition and the ECJ has warned against the application of technical rules in this context. The bottom line is whether there is evidence that the unit transferred retains a minimum level of independence, enabling it to enjoy a separate existence either on its own, or as a discrete part of a larger undertaking.

Rask & Christensen v ISS Kantineservice (1993, ECJ)
The European Court of Justice held that this issue could be resolved by looking at whether staff or tangible assets (such as premises) were being transferred and how far, if it all, the activities of the undertaking would be changed by the transfer.

Isles of Scilly v Brintel Helicopters and Ellis (1995)
A separate identity may in the service industry just comprise the transfer of staff and functions.

Who is protected?

Any employee in the business or the part of the business being transferred who was employed immediately before the transfer took place is protected. Employees who can prove they were dismissed earlier for reasons connected with the transfer can also sue. Employees include (Regulation 2) not just those with a contract of service but also apprentices and workers supplied by an agency.

The rights of the employees

Both collective and individual rights are created by the regulations.

Information and consultation

Both old and new employers must inform the relevant trade union or elected employee representatives of the transfer, when it will take place and why it is happening. Information as to the legal, economic and social implications of the transfer is also required, including any measures which either employer may need to take in relation to them. Consultation with union or elected representatives is required regarding such measures as, for example, a reduction in manpower.

Job security

This enjoys only limited protection.

Regulation 8 states that the employer is not legally entitled to dismiss an employee for reasons connected with the transfer unless there is 'an economic, technical or organisational reason [ETO] entailing changes in the work force'. Thus, where redundancy occurs, it may be treated as fair under the ERA 1996. Regulation 8 states that in this context an ETO represents substantial grounds for dismissal.

Continuation of existing terms and conditions of employment

Regulation 5 states that the transfer does not terminate the employee's contract of employment: almost all the existing rights, duties and liabilities of the old employer are transferred to the new one. With the exception of pension rights (Regulation 7), the terms of the existing contract remain in force. Reasonably similar pension rights have to be granted and existing pension rights are protected.

An employee may object to continuing in employment with the new employer, but if the employee leaves, this is not to be treated as (constructive) dismissal.

The new employer is able to make changes in the terms and conditions only if they remain comparable to the old ones. Failure to comply with this may entitle the employee to claim constructive and unfair dismissal if the change is shown to be in relation to the transfer (Regulation 8, above).

Quiz 20

1 Distinguish between wrongful and unfair dismissal.

2 On what grounds may Tiger Enterprises claim that they fairly dismissed the following employees?

   (a) Zebra, who was given a job as a trainee lorry driver three years ago and has just failed the HGV test for the sixth time.

   (b) Camel, who sexually harassed Ms Wart-Hog at the works' Christmas party.

   (c) Possum, a van driver who has crashed his vehicle three times.

   (d) Rhino, who was recently convicted of being drunk and disorderly one Saturday night.

3 Have the following employees been made redundant by Lynx plc?

   (a) Aardvark, who heard rumours of redundancy and resigned.

   (b) Porcupine, a senior computer programmer, whose current workplace is being closed down. He is told that he is being transferred to another branch 80 miles away.

4 What procedures should be observed by an employer before making employees redundant?

Assignment 19

Explain briefly the circumstances in which a worker is entitled to a redundancy payment on the termination of his or her employment.

(ICSA English Business Law: December 1994)

A suggested solution for this assignment can be found in the Lecturer's Guide.

CHAPTER 21

Business organisation

INTRODUCTION

This chapter provides an outline description of the commonest forms of business organisation (the sole trader, the partnership and the registered company) and the legal consequences which flow from setting up a business in each of these ways. First, though, it is necessary to gain understanding of three concepts which are recurring themes in the law relating to business organisation – legal personality, incorporation and limited liability.

LEGAL PERSONALITY, INCORPORATION

AND LIMITED LIABILITY

Legal personality

Under English law all human beings are endowed with a legal personality from birth until death. A person's legal personality is made up of that person's legal rights and duties. These are subject to change throughout the lifetime of the subject. A child has only very limited rights and few duties. The average adult has a complex bundle of rights and duties determined by the adult's current status: for example, as a married or single person, employer, employee, taxpayer, receiver of welfare benefit, debtor or creditor.

Incorporation

It is not just human beings who have legal rights and duties: the law permits the creation of artificial or legal persons (corporations) which have a legal personality, separate from the members.

A corporation is brought into being (incorporated) by operation of law. Some form of legal process must be completed before it comes into existence. This chapter is primarily concerned with corporations created exclusively for commercial purposes by registration in compliance with the Companies Acts. You should also be aware that other types of corporation exist for a number of different purposes, like education (the universities) or management of a profession (The Chartered Institute of Surveyors). The BBC is another example. These corporations were all created by the Crown by royal charter. Parliament may grant corporate status to an organisation by passing a special Act; the nationalised industries were all created in this way.

All types of corporations have certain characteristics in common:

1 *Creation by operation of law*. The necessary legal process (charter, Act or registration) must take place to bring the corporation into existence. Once created the corporation will continue to exist unless or until the appropriate legal procedure takes place (the winding up of a registered company, withdrawal of royal charter or repeal of statute). Any change in membership does not affect the existence of the company. Even if all the members of a corporation were to die simultaneously, the company would continue to exist.

2 *One or many members*. Incorporation may create an office held by one person (a corporation sole), like a bishop or the Public Trustee, but most corporate bodies have at least two members (a corporation aggregate).

3 *Its own legal personality*. The corporation's rights and duties are conferred by the charter or law under which it was created. The company's legal personality is distinct from that of the company's members, who are merely the means of operating the organisation. They may be the cause of breaches of a contract, tort or crimes in the execution of their policies, but it is the company which is legally liable for the wrongdoing. For example, a registered company which pollutes a river may be prosecuted and fined. Payment of the fine will come from the company's bank account, not the pocket of the managing director whose order caused the pollution.

Limited liability

Because a corporation's legal liabilities are its own and not its members', the members are not generally liable for the company's debts. The members of a registered company do not enjoy complete immunity, but their liability is generally limited to the sum which they have agreed to invest, even if the company runs out of money and cannot satisfy its creditors.

THE SOLE TRADER

Any person may set up in business and trade under his or her own name or a business name. Such a sole trader has independent control of the business and all the profits are theirs. He or she also has total responsibility for the legal liabilities and financial risks of the business. The sole trader provides all the start-up capital; often this will involve a bank loan secured by a mortgage on the sole trader's home. Since he or she is personally liable for all business debts, the sole trader may be bankrupted by the creditors of the business.

THE PARTNERSHIP

This is a type of unincorporated association, which simply means that it is an organisation without any legal personality distinct from its members. There any many different kinds of unincorporated associations which exist for social, educational, political and business purposes. You may belong to one: they include sports clubs, pressure groups, local chambers of commerce, trade unions and political parties, not to speak of the Scouts, Guides and Woodcraft Folk. What distinguishes a partnership from these organisations is the motivation of the partners: they have joined together intending to carry on a business with a view to making and sharing profits.

The partnership is the favoured method of business organisation for many professionals like doctors, solicitors and accountants. They can share facilities which a sole practitioner would be unable to afford. It is also very common for small businesses to operate from this base, as it enables start-up capital and expertise to be drawn from a number of people. Partners, like sole traders, often raise their contributions through a bank loan and are also personally liable for business debts. The Partnership Act 1890 governs the creation and regulation of partnerships.

Forming a partnership

It is usual to formalise the existence of the partnership by written agreement; this is sometimes described as the partnership deed. Writing is not essential though. The partnership relationship may be implied from the conduct of two or more persons carrying on a business in common (as joint proprietors) with the intention of making and sharing the profits arising from their enterprise. The partnership relationship, with all its ensuing rights and duties, exists from the time when the business is up and running. Planning to run a business does not in itself create the partnership.

For clarity and for evidential purposes it is wise to have a written partnership agreement, which indicates the nature and purpose of the business, its name and address, the amount of capital invested by each partner, and how profits are to be shared and paid. If there are *sleeping partners*, whose only involvement is providing capital and taking a share of the profits, the agreement should specify which partners are actually responsible for the management.

The partnership agreement, whether written or unwritten, is a contract governed by the rules which you have studied earlier in this book.

The partnership may trade under the names of the partners (Glossit, Over and Dodge (Estate Agents), Bloggs Bros, Smith & Daughters), or under a business name (Speedy Cleaners).

Numbers of partners

There must be at least two partners. Until 2001 section 716 of the Companies Act 1985 imposed a maximum of 20 on commercial partnerships. It was believed that a business of such size should more appropriately be run as a registered company.

However, the Partnership (Unrestricted Size) No. 17 Regulation 2001 (2001/2422) has removed this restriction completely. No such limits have ever applied to professional partnerships such as accountants and surveyors, since the rules of their professional organisations do not permit incorporation.

The partnership relationship is a fiduciary one

This means that the partners are placed in a position of trust with each other and have the following duties:

- to make full disclosure to each other of all issues relevant to the business;
- to declare any personal financial benefit received by a partner in carrying out the firm's business;
- not to compete with the firm without the consent of the other partners.

Each partner acts as the agent of the others

When transacting business on behalf of the firm, a partner is treated as its agent. Partners can act only within their legal authority and must carry out their duties with reasonable care and skill. The Partnership Act 1890 states that partners have apparent authority to carry out any transaction relating to the business, therefore, any resulting contract is binding on the other partners whether or not they actually authorised it. Failure to perform the contract could result in an action for breach against any or all of the partners. For example, if a partner ordered headed writing paper for the firm, the other partners will be jointly liable for its cost, even though it had previously been decided by majority at a partners' meeting that new supplies were not needed. Similarly, if a partner committed a tort while carrying out the firm's business, the other partners would be vicariously liable for it. A negligently performed job could give rise to this sort of liability.

The partners are jointly and severally liable for all partnership obligations

As the partnership has no legal existence distinct from its members, all the partners are personally liable for its debts and other legal obligations. If the firm does not have sufficient funds, the partners have to make good the shortfall out of their own pockets.

Legal action can be taken against a partnership in its own name, but the partners remain jointly or severally liable for what is owed. This means that if a judgment debt is not paid, it can be enforced against all or any of the partners. This may result in one partner having to pay the entire debt, though that partner may seek a contribution from the others.

Like a sole trader, a partner may be personally bankrupted if the assets of the business are not sufficient to cover its debts.

Limited liability partnerships

The Limited Partnerships Act 1907 enabled the creation of a partnership with *limited liability* for some of the partners. At least one partner must retain unlimited liability for the partnership debts. The liability of the others, provided that they play no part in running the business, is restricted to the amount specified in the partnership agreement. In practice, such partnerships are extremely rare, as any body seeking limited liability is more likely to seek registration as a company. The Department of Trade and Industry started a consultation procedure in 1997 to discover the views of interested parties on the introduction of fully limited liability partnerships in the UK.

As a result, the Limited Liability Partnerships Act 2000 was passed and came into effect in April 2001. By April 2002 over 200 such partnerships had come into existence. To set up a limited liability partnership (LLP) it must be registered with the approval of the Companies Registrar. An incorporation document is required. Once registered the LLP takes on a legal identity of its own, with each partner's liability limited to the amount of their investment in the firm. It enjoys all the advantages of incorporation and relatively few of the disadvantages. An LLP can hold property and sue and be sued in its own name. The *ultra vires* rule, which binds companies to their stated objects (see below page 324) does not affect the LLP, so that it is free to pursue any business venture with the agreement of a majority of the partners. It is not subject to the same rules as companies concerning its internal governance and may regulate its relationships with its members and make its own management rules.

Despite incorporation, the LLP is still treated as a partnership for the purposes of tax. This is a key advantage and puts partners in a better financial position than if they were company shareholders. However, certain legal responsibilities follow incorporation. The LLP must present its annual audited accounts to the Companies Registrar and the accounts are then available for public scrutiny. Insolvency procedures governing companies also apply to an LLP.

Dissolving the partnership

A partnership may come to an end for a number of different reasons.

1 *Lapse of time*. Most partnerships are formed in the belief that they will be continued indefinitely, but a specified lifetime may be stated in the partnership agreement. For example, two people might decide to run catering facilities for the duration of an exhibition or a trade fair.

2 *The sole purpose of the partnership is achieved*. The example in 1 above is also relevant here.

3 *Death or bankruptcy of a partner*. Usually the partnership makes provision for such occurrences, but failure to do so could result in dissolution.

4 *Illegality*. If the purposes of the partnership subsequently become illegal, the partnership contract is frustrated (see Chapter 8). A partnership created for the

import of certain goods would be dissolved if the import of those goods was subsequently banned by Department of Trade and Industry regulations.

5 *Notice from a partner*. Unless the agreement provides otherwise, the partnership will terminate if one party decides to leave. Usually provision is made for this.

6 *Court order*. A partner may ask the court to order dissolution on the grounds of mental or physical incapacity of a partner, or because of misconduct by a partner prejudicial to the business or which amounts to wilful and persistent breach of the partnership agreement. The court may also dissolve the partnership if it is just and equitable to do so. Dissolution will be ordered if the business cannot be carried on without making a loss.

Public scrutiny of partnerships

Unless the partnership is an LLP, its affairs, unlike those of a registered company, are not subject to any more public scrutiny than those of an individual trader: relevant tax returns must be made and the planning requirements of the local authority concerning business use of the premises must be met. The public have no right to inspect the accounts of the partnership and there is no legal duty to audit them.

If a business name is used, the Business Names Act 1985 requires that the names of the proprietors be displayed at the place of business and on any letterheads of business stationery.

THE REGISTERED COMPANY

This is a corporation created in compliance with the registration procedures in the Companies Act 1985 and monitored by the Companies Registry.

The purposes of the registration process

This serves:

- to check that, before it starts trading, a business is financially viable, has a reasonable chance of success, and is likely to be reputably managed for legal purposes;
- to provide a public record of all such businesses, which may be inspected by interested parties before trading with or investing in them;
- to guard against fraud;
- to enable continuing supervision of the company by the Companies Registrar.

A registered company is generally required to provide a regular update of the information required on registration.

Types of registered company

The public company

A public company is so called because its shares may be transferred freely to members of the public. If the company is *listed* the shares may be traded on the Stock Exchange. This enables capital to be raised easily. An applicant for listing must satisfy the requirements of the Financial Services Act 1986. In practice only large public companies will be eligible. Most of the members of a public company will aim to share in its profits without taking any part in its management.

In order to be registered as a public company the following four criteria must be satisfied:

1 the memorandum of association of the company must state expressly that the company is to be a public company;

2 the name of the company must indicate its public status. The suffix 'plc' (or its Welsh equivalent) must follow the company name;

3 the company's authorised capital must not be less than the statutory minimum: currently £50 000. At least 25 per cent of this must already be paid up. This means that at least £12 500 must have been paid for shares;

4 it must have limited liability.

The private company

Any registered company which does not fulfil the four criteria stated above is a private company. This is the type of company usually formed by a sole trader or a partnership seeking the advantages (like limited liability) which incorporation may bring. Since the implementation of the Single Member Private Limited Companies Regulations 1992, a private company may be formed with only one member, though a company secretary must also be appointed.

Shareholding in a private company is usually limited to participants in the business (and sometimes their families). Most, if not all, of the shareholders may be engaged in managing the business. Such companies are sometimes described as 'quasi-partnerships'. The transfer of the shares will be controlled by the company rules. If a member leaves he or she may have to sell back his or her shares to existing members of the company, or obtain the company's permission before selling them to a third party.

A private company may apply to register as a public company if it becomes able to fulfil the necessary criteria.

The Companies Act 1985 was amended by the Companies Act 1989 to assist deregulation of private companies. The legislation aims to remove unnecessary bureaucracy and to lessen the administrative burdens of small businesses. The process of registration has not changed, but a private company may choose by a unanimous vote of its members to opt out of certain obligations under the 1985

Act, like holding an annual general meeting or appointing auditors. This is clearly a sensible choice for a company incorporating a previous partnership of three or four people.

Holding and subsidiary companies

During the latter half of the twentieth century it became increasingly common for public companies to operate in groups. One (the holding company) controls the others (subsidiary companies). Such a relationship exists where the holding company has the capability to control the voting majority within the subsidiaries. Under the Companies Act 1985 there is a duty to disclose this relationship to ensure that the public are not misled in their dealings with any of the members. The holding company is also obliged to present group accounts as well as its own (s 277).

The consequences of incorporation

Once registered the business is said to be incorporated. This has an effect on the financial and general legal liabilities of the company, its directors, its shareholders and any outsiders who have dealings with the company or are affected by its actions.

The company is a separate entity distinct from its members

Once registration has been successfully completed a new legal person is created: its legal liabilities are entirely separate from those of its members. What the courts have described as a *veil of incorporation* prevents the members being held responsible for the company's liabilities, however close their connections with it. This is clearly illustrated in the following case.

> **Salomon v Salomon & Co. Ltd** (1897, HL)
> Mr Salomon had a boot factory. He set up a company and sold the business to it for £39 000. He was paid £9000 in cash and £20 000 in shares, the remaining six shares being held by members of his family acting as his nominees. Mr Salomon lent the company the remaining £10 000 of the purchase price, and this debt was secured by a charge on the company's property. In due course the company got into financial difficulties and had to be wound up leaving unpaid debts. As a secured creditor, Mr Salomon recovered what he was owed in full, but there were insufficient assets left to satisfy the other creditors. They argued that the company was a sham used by Mr Salomon as a front for his own business activities, and that he should have to pay off the creditors personally. The House of Lords disagreed, holding that the company had been created properly in accordance with the Companies Act and was a separate entity on whose behalf Mr Salomon acted as agent. It was irrelevant that after incorporation ownership and management stayed in the same hands as they had before. The company had borrowed the money and was legally liable to pay it back to its secured creditor who took preference over the other creditors.

Generally the *Salomon* v *Salomon* approach has been strictly adhered to, though to a very limited extent the courts have created exceptions to prevent fraud. There was no evidence of fraud from the evidence in *Salomon* v *Salomon*. Although Mr Salomon may seem to outward appearances to have been sailing rather close to the wind, he did not deceive anybody. His fellow shareholders knew what was going on. The charge on the company's assets was appropriately registered; the creditors could have found out about it before dealing with the company had they chosen to do so. In law they had notice of it. The court may be prepared to question whether a company owner is personally liable for its debts if it appears that the alleged company is a mere façade for the fraudulent activities of the owner. This is known as *'lifting the veil of incorporation'*.

Jones v Lipman (1962)
Mr Lipman contracted to sell land to Mr Jones and then changed his mind. He set up a company and conveyed the land to it to defeat Mr Jones's attempt to get a decree of specific performance. It was held that since Mr Lipman had absolute control and ownership of the company and had set it up specifically to defraud Mr Jones, he could not escape performance.

The veil may be lifted to make a director personally liable for negligent advice given on behalf of the company provided that a 'special relationship' exists under the principle in *Hedley Byrne* v *Heller* (1963). (See pages 155–8 for a full explanation of the *Hedley Byrne* principle.)

Williams and Another v Natural Life Health Foods Ltd and Mistlin (1998, HL)
Natural Life was a very small company consisting of Mr Mistlin, the director who owned all the shares except his wife's nominal holding. Apart from Mr Mistlin, there were only two company employees. Mr Williams and his partner bought a franchise to run a healthfood shop from Natural Life. They were given a brochure which described the company and Mr Mistlin's knowledge and expertise in glowing terms. They also received some financial projections of the potential of their franchise. All this information was compiled by Mr Mistlin, but he had no personal dealings at all with Mr Williams, who negotiated the sale with one of Mr Mistlin's employees. The turnover of Mr Williams's shop always fell substantially short of the projected levels and he went out of business within 18 months of opening. Mr Williams claimed that he had been negligently advised by Mr Mistlin.

The House of Lords held that Mr Mistlin was not personally liable. The veil of incorporation could only be lifted in very exceptional circumstances, particularly where one-person companies were concerned, otherwise their owners would unreasonably be deprived of the protection of incorporation. Negligent advice by a director to an outsider dealing with the company could only give rise to personal liability of the director if the necessary special relationship under *Hedley Byrne* principles existed. This required a voluntary assumption of responsibility by the director and reasonable reliance by the recipient upon it.

A voluntary assumption of responsibility by Mr Mistlin could not be presumed merely because he compiled the relevant literature: in any one-person company the owner was likely to be the individual with most of the skill and knowledge relevant to the running of the company. Mr Mistlin had no personal dealings with Mr Williams and there was no evidence that he or anybody on his behalf conveyed 'directly or indirectly to the prospective franchisee that the director assumed personal responsibility towards the prospective franchisee' (per Lord Steyn).

Objective assessment of the evidence indicated no grounds for reasonable belief by Mr Williams that Mr Mistlin was assuming personal responsibility, given the lack of direct dealings or undertakings to this effect.

There are a number of statutory exceptions to the separate entity rule, mainly relating to tax and insolvency law. For example, under s 213 of the Insolvency Act 1986, if during the liquidation of a company it becomes evident that the directors were trading fraudulently, they may be required personally to contribute to the payment of the company's creditors. (Fraudulent trading in this context includes continuing to trade when the directors are or should be aware that the company is unable to meet its current debts.)

Company members may enjoy limited liability for the company's debts

The company has unlimited liability to its creditors, but the liability of its members may be limited.

Company law does not permit a company's members to be completely free of financial liability, as this would promote irresponsible trading. Members' liability for company debts may, on registration of the company, be limited to the value of the capital which they have agreed to invest. Limitation of liability is seen to be in the public interest since it encourages investment in business enterprise and, therefore, promotes the economy.

Liability may be limited by shares or by guarantee.

1 *By shares.* The majority of companies raise their capital this way. If the company is unable to meet its debts, the maximum amount that any shareholders can be asked to contribute is the amount, if any, which they have still to pay for their shares. Their loss is therefore limited to the value of their shares when they joined the company.

2 *By guarantee.* A minority of companies limit their liability in this way. These companies generally exist for educational or charitable purposes, like private schools or museums. Since they are not formed for the purpose of making a profit, it is not appropriate for them to have a share capital. The liability of such a company's members is limited to the amount which they have agreed to contribute if the company is wound up. The guaranteed sum is usually minimal.

Exceptionally, a company may be registered with *unlimited liability*. Its members agree to subsidise the company to an unlimited extent in the event of liquidation. This liability is, therefore, owed by the members to the company rather than to the company creditors.

The company may be legally liable

1 *Criminal offences*. There are certain crimes, like rape and bigamy, which a company *cannot* by its physical nature commit. Apart from these obvious exceptions, a company may be prosecuted for any crime which is committed in the course of carrying out the company's business. For example, prosecutions are common for using false trade descriptions, and for breach of health and safety regulations and anti-pollution controls. After the Zeebrugge ferry disaster it was established that a company could be charged with manslaughter.

2 *Tort*. The company is vicariously liable for the torts of its employees and agents committed in the course of their employment. Where the law imposes a non-delegable duty (for employee safety, for example) on the company, it remains personally liable even though the damage was caused by a third party.

3 *Breaches of contract*. Generally a company is liable on its contracts in the same way as any other person. (This is dealt with in detail in the next chapter.)

Ownership and management

The company is owned by its members and managed by its directors. In a very small company, membership and management may be synonymous, but generally company membership does not give rights to dictate how the company is run on a day-to-day basis; it may not even entitle a member to vote at company meetings, since the rights of holders of some classes of shares may be limited under the internal rules of the company.

Public accountability

Once the company has been registered certain information about it is open to public scrutiny through the Companies Registry. This information must generally be updated yearly through the *annual return*, though unlimited companies are exempt from this. Other company records may be inspected by the public at the company's registered office. The Department of Trade and Industry (DTI) has wide statutory powers to investigate companies where malpractice is suspected. It is legally entitled to obtain a warrant to search premises. A DTI inspector may require company officials to produce and explain any company document. A report of the investigation is usually made public.

Continuous succession

Once registered a company continues to exist until the legal process of liquidation brings its life to an end. 'Liquidation' means the realisation of the company's capital and other assets. These are distributed to creditors and shareholders according to strict rules of priority. The shareholders often lose much, if not all, of their investment. There are two kinds of liquidation: compulsory and voluntary.

1 *Compulsory liquidation* by court order under the Insolvency Act 1986. This most commonly occurs where the company is unable to pay its creditors who then petition the court. The Official Receiver is appointed as liquidator.

2 *Voluntary liquidation*. Here the process depends on whether the company is still solvent. If so, the members control the liquidation process. If the company has become insolvent the creditors appoint a liquidator to distribute the company's assets.

The advantages of incorporation as a registered company

Turning a business into a registered company may be a sound move for its proprietors.

Limited liability of investors

Investors in a limited liability company are able to restrict their financial responsibility to the company. They cannot be personally bankrupted to pay business debts.

Transferability of shares

When a member ceases to belong to the company, this does not affect the existence of the business, although it might destroy a partnership. The member's interest in the business can be transferred by sale or other means to a new member. In a public company such rights of transfer are unfettered and a sale of shares may take place under the auspices of the Stock Exchange. A private company's rules may impose considerable restrictions in order to protect the close personal relationship of the small number of members all actively engaged in running the business.

Tax

Incorporation and the subsequent separation of the financial interests of the business from the personal financial interests of the members may prove advantageous for tax purposes.

Separate property rights

The assets of a business become its own property on incorporation. This is advantageous in a number of ways. For example, a member who leaves cannot disrupt the business by claiming any particular asset as his or her own; he or she is entitled to recover only his or her financial stake at its current value. Similarly, if the company goes into liquidation members cannot be personally bankrupted when the company's assets are exhausted before all its debts are satisfied. All they will lose is their financial stake in the business.

Raising capital

Unincorporated businesses are very restricted as regards obtaining new capital. The only options are to increase the number of members or obtain a bank loan. Recruiting new members while increasing capital, results in business profits being spread more widely and perhaps more thinly. Bank loans involve large interest payments and usually are unobtainable without the security of a mortgage on the members' own homes. A company may be able to borrow money secured by a charge on its own assets. A public company may advertise publicly to attract loans through an issue of debentures.

This advantage is likely to be enjoyed only by a company with large enough assets to secure the loan. The members of very small private companies (quasi-partnerships) are usually required personally to secure the debt by mortgages on their homes.

Continuity

Once registered the company's existence continues regardless of any changes in membership. Only winding-up proceedings can bring the company to an end.

THE IMPACT OF THE HUMAN RIGHTS ACT 1998 (HRA)

ON BUSINESS ORGANISATIONS

Businesses directly bound by ECHR duties are those designated under the HRA as 'public authorities' (like Thames Water below). However, any business may have rights which can be protected by action under the HRA against state or other public authority interference. Additionally, the court, as a public authority itself, has a duty not to infringe any Convention rights of any party. This informs how decisions are reached and remedies awarded.

Property rights

A business may be able to protect its property by reference to Protocol 1 Article 1. This states that every human and *legal* person has a right to the peaceful enjoyment of property. This right is not absolute and interference may be justified in the public interest or where necessary to the collection of debts owed to the state. The right is breached if the interference prevents a fair balance being maintained between the rights of the claimant and the public interest. For example, a compulsory purchase order of business premises without adequate compensation would probably be judged to be in breach of the right. The business also may be liable for breach of this Article. In *Marcic v Thames Water Utilities (No. 2)* (2001, CA) it was held that Thames Water had breached Mr Marcic's right of peaceful enjoyment of his house due to constant flooding caused by failure to maintain an appropriate sewage system.

Privacy

As an employer an organisation may be subject to Convention duties regarding employees, such as Article 8, which protects respect for privacy and family life. A business may need to adjust working practices to accommodate requests by employees for more flexible working hours. Article 8 may also restrict employer access to employees' emails and phone conversations. Article 8 also protects business privacy, since the court must take care that it is not breaching this Article when granting search orders to premises in civil proceedings (see pages 21–2 above). The court must consider carefully whether the terms of the order are fairly balanced between the competing interests of the parties and that it is a proportionate response.

Fair trial

A business and its members enjoy the right to a fair trial under Article 6. This includes right of access to the courts and an impartial hearing. However, this right may be waived in civil proceedings where an arbitrator is used and in most cases where the parties settle out of court (see above at page 23). Article 6 also includes the right to avoid self-incrimination. In *Saunders* v *UK* (1997) the ECHR held that by subjecting Saunders to coercive questioning (refusal to answer was itself a criminal offence) DTI fraud investigators had breached his rights under Article 6.

Freedom of speech

Advertising, publishing, film, journalism and other media businesses may be affected by Article 10 (freedom of expression). The court when granting an injunction to prevent publication must ensure that it is not itself in breach of its Convention duties. Any restriction should be no more than is necessary in a democratic society to protect national security, public safety, health and morals, reputation or rights of others, or against breach of confidence. In *Venables* v *News Group Newspapers* (2001) the High Court issued a gagging order to prevent the press publishing information about the murderers of James Bulger. This was held to be justifiable, to prevent them being identifiable and thus in danger once they left prison. It can be seen from the examples above that, directly and indirectly, business organisations are just as likely to be affected by human rights law as any individual.

IN CONCLUSION

By now you should be aware of the different legal consequences of operating a business in the three forms described in this chapter. Before you move on to study in more detail the formation and operation of a registered company, it might be wise to go back and check that you understand the concepts of legal personality, incorporation and limited liability, as these underpin much of the content of the next three chapters. To assist you a comparison of partnerships and registered companies follows.

The differences between a partnership and a registered company

The partnership

Creation

A written partnership agreement is usual but not essential. The parties' conduct (jointly doing business with a view to profit) will create a partnership.

Numbers

Minimum: at least two.

Maximum: 20.

Legal personality

The partnership has no separate legal personality of its own: partners are vicariously liable for any breaches of civil law caused by a fellow partner in the course of the business.

Any partner may be personally liable for crimes relating to the business.

Limited liability

Partners have unlimited liability for the debts of the business, unless registered as a limited liability partnership

Supervision and publicity

The running of a partnership is not supervised by any outside authority.

Partnership accounts and other documentation are confidential to the partners unless the partnership is an LLP.

Termination

Completion of object, lapse of time, partner leaves, bankruptcy, mental disability or death of partner.

The company

The company does not exist until the registration procedures of the Companies Acts have been complied with.

A one-person private company is possible.

No maximum is prescribed.

Once registered a company has its own legal personality separate from that of its members. Members cannot be made liable for its illegal activities.

The company's liability is unlimited.

Members may have limited liability for company debts.

A limited liability company is monitored by the Companies Registrar through its annual return. Particulars and accounts are open to public inspection.

The DTI has wide investigative powers.

Once created a company has continual succession.

It will not cease to exist unless or until the legal processes involved in winding up are complete.

Quiz 21

1 How may incorporation take place?

2 In relation to incorporation, what is meant by:

 (a) limited liability?

 (b) continuous succession?

 (c) a corporation aggregate?

3 What is the main difference between a partnership and other incorporated associations?

4 Thames, Dover and Wight are members of a partnership called Outdoor Adventures. What is the legal position if:

 (a) Thames, without consulting the others, bought two new four-wheel drive vehicles from Humber; and

 (b) as a result of Thames's purchase, the partnership now has insufficient sums to pay its creditors?

5 What are the main differences between a public and a private company?

Assignment 20

Sharp and Cool are in business together selling computers to industry. The business is continuing to expand and Sharp and Cool recognise a need to seek outside finance to assist cashflow. They have received conflicting advice from business associates on the question of whether they should trade through a limited company or continue to trade through a partnership. They ask you what factors should help them to decide.

(ICSA Introduction to English and EC Law: June 1994)

A suggested solution for this assignment can be found in the Lecturer's Guide.

CHAPTER 22

Forming a registered company

INTRODUCTION

This chapter is concerned with the statutory procedures which must be complied with when a company is set up. Company law is largely statutory. Its developments have been greatly influenced by the impact of EC law; radical reforms took place in the 1980s to assist harmonisation with the legal systems of other EC members. It is primarily enacted by the Companies Act 1985, as amended by the Companies Act 1989. You can generally spot an amended section by the capital letter A appended to it. All statutory references in this and succeeding chapters will be to the Companies Act 1985 unless otherwise specified. Radical reforms are in the pipeline subsequent to the 2002 Government White Paper (Modernising Company Law). These are unlikely to be implemented before 2004. Where relevant, the proposals are flagged up in this and subsequent chapters.

PROMOTERS

The role of the promoters

The promoters of the company are those who set it up. However, this does not include a solicitor, accountant or other professional providing services to assist the process.

The promoters' role varies, but it always involves the formalities of registration. It may also involve finding directors and obtaining premises, plant and equipment. However, these latter functions may not be required of promoters, since large numbers of companies do not start from scratch on being registered. They have their origins in an established small business for which incorporation is the next logical step. The promoters of such a company will usually move from being partners to directors.

The promoters' liability for pre-incorporation contracts

Section 36C makes promoters personally liable for all contracts entered into before the company has completed the registration process, even if made in the name of the future company. This is entirely logical since the company does not exist as an independent being until its registration is complete. While it may be essential for the promoters to make contracts on behalf of the business before incorporation, they cannot be treated as the agents of the company since it has no independent existence as yet. It, therefore, cannot legally authorise the making of a contract. Even when it is incorporated it cannot ratify the contracts because they were made before incorporation brought the company into being. Therefore, it is fair to give the other party to the contract the right to sue the promoters if the contract is not performed. The promoters may sue or be sued on such contracts regardless of whether the other party knew that the company did not yet exist.

> **Phonogram v Lane** (1982, CA)
> The claimant contracted to supply finance to the defendant for the purposes of a company to manage a pop group called 'Cheap Mean and Nasty'. The claimant knew that the company was still at pre-registration stage, but this did not prevent him from suing the defendant for breach of contract.

Section 36C allows a promoter to avoid personal liability by *express agreement* with the other party to the contract. Such agreements fall into two kinds:

1 the contract may stipulate that the liability of the promoter will cease once the company has been registered and has entered into a contract on the same terms;

2 a gentleman's agreement: the promoter may enjoy complete immunity if the other party agrees to enter into a gentleman's agreement from which the intention to form a legally binding relationship is excluded. This means that in reality the pre-incorporation contract does not have the status of a contract at all.

THE REGISTRATION PROCESS

The following information must be delivered to the Companies Registry with the appropriate fee:

1 *the memorandum of association;*

2 *the articles of association* – these must both be signed by at least two subscribers (one in the case of single member private companies) who have agreed to buy at least one share each. Details of the contents of the articles are given below;

3 *a statutory declaration* signed by the company's solicitor/secretary/director that the legal requirements have been complied with.

The Registrar will issue the *certificate of incorporation* provided that the legal formalities have been complied with and the company appears to be formed to pursue a legal object.

A private company may start trading at once, but a public company cannot do so until the Registrar grants it a trading certificate. This will be done only if 25 per cent of the share capital has been paid up.

The memorandum of association

This is the company's constitution and governs the relationship of the company to the outside world. It contains the following information:

1 the company's name;

2 the registered office;

3 the liability of the members;

4 the authorised capital;

5 the objects of the company.

The company's name

The chosen name must not be the same as or too similar to the name of another registered company. Where a company has limited liability this must be made evident by placing 'plc' after the name of a public company and 'Ltd' or the Welsh equivalent after the name of a private company (s 25).

Some names can be used only with permission from the Department of Trade and Industry; these include any which suggest a connection with a government department or local authority. The Registrar must refuse to register a name if its use would be a criminal offence or it is deemed offensive (s 26).

R v Registrar of Companies, ex parte Attorney-General (1991)
Lindi St Clair attempted to register a company in the name of *Hookers Ltd.* This was rejected by the Registrar as offensive, but Ms St Clair was allowed to register it as *Personal Services Ltd.* (Later, objections to the legality of the company's objects were successfully raised. These were held to be objectionable because they encouraged prostitution. The court ordered the Registrar to strike the company off the register.)

The company's name must be displayed outside the business premises, on all business stationery and on the company's seal. Under s 349, it is an offence to fail to do so, which may result in the company and/or the officer responsible being fined. The officer responsible for the default may also be personally liable on any transaction not honoured by the company, because it was not clearly identified as being a party to it.

To protect use of a company name on the Internet, it is also necessary to register its website's 'domain' with its Internet service provider. Registrations are accepted on a 'first come first served' basis. Failure to act quickly could prevent a company from using its company name for Internet purposes. Worse still, another company could use the name, and the only possible protection would be an action under the Trade Marks Act 1994 (see below Chapter 26) or a passing-off action (see Chapter 27).

The registered office

The full address is not required (this is notified separately to the Registrar), but its domicile (England or Wales) must be given.

The registered office represents the official contact point for the company. It is here that official notices may be sent, or claim forms served. Information which may be inspected by members of the public is kept here. This includes the registers of members, directors and debenture holders.

The address of the registered office must appear on the company's letterheads and any changes notified to the Companies Registrar.

Members' liability

This indicates whether members' liability is limited or unlimited.

Authorised capital

This indicates the amount of capital which the company proposes to hold and how it is divided up into shares. For example: 'The capital of the company is £100 000 divided into 100 000 shares at £1 each.'

The objects clause

The company must state the purposes (objects) of its business. This may include a statement of the powers relevant to the fulfilment of the objects and specify related transactions which the company may enter into. Even if an activity is not specifically authorised, it may be legitimate if it is necessarily incidental to the furtherance of the company's business.

A company is registered to trade only within the limits of its objects clause: any other activity is unauthorised because it is *ultra vires* (in excess of the company's powers). Therefore, any contract not within the powers stated in the objects clause is potentially void (and until the European Communities Act 1972 was void and could not be enforced by or against the company). Before 1972, therefore, the drafting of objects clauses was crucial to companies' capacity to contract.

Ashbury Railway Carriage Co. v Riche (1875, HL)
The objects of the railway company were limited to the manufacture, sale and hire of railway rolling stock. It made a contract to construct a railway. The House of Lords held that the contract was void because it exceeded the company's specified objects, which were concerned with rolling stock not the railway on which such stock might be used. It was irrelevant that a majority of shareholders supported the project.

Promoters often resorted to very lengthy, vague or complicated objects clauses to avoid restriction on later business developments. Provided that the clause did not permit the company a completely free rein but indicated that any new enterprise was capable of being linked to the main objects, the courts were generally prepared to sanction such an extension of activity.

> **Bell Houses Ltd v City Wall Properties Ltd** (1966, CA)
> The objects clause of a land development and building company stated that it had the power 'to carry on any other trade or business whatsoever, which can in the opinion of the directors be advantageously carried on in connection with or ancillary to any of the above businesses and the general business of the company'. It was held that this entitled the directors to make a consultancy contract under which they had introduced a financier to the defendant developer. It was sufficiently ancillary to their business.

The Companies Act 1985 was amended in 1989, and s 3A now provides that an objects clause may state that 'the object of the company is to carry on business as a general commercial company'. This enables it to carry on any trade or business which it chooses and gives it the power to do anything incidental or conducive to this end. Such a wide clause gives directors almost unlimited powers, which might not be acceptable to shareholders. It also makes it harder for members of the public to ascertain the nature of the company's business.

Before the UK's entry into the EC, a company might choose to hide behind its objects clause and the *ultra vires* doctrine to avoid liability on a contract. The other party could not plead ignorance of the limitations on the company's objects since it was deemed to have *constructive notice* of the memorandum of association because it is a public document which the other party could have inspected.

> **Re Jon Beauforte (London) Ltd** (1953)
> The company's objects were stated as dressmaking, but it had abandoned this and taken up manufacturing veneered panels. The company became insolvent, but those who had been supplying it with goods were unable to claim money owed. Orders had been placed on writing paper describing Beauforte as veneer panel manufacturers. Suppliers were thereby given *actual* knowledge that the company had departed from its authorised objects. They had *constructive* knowledge of the true objects since the memorandum of association was open to their inspection.

When the UK entered Europe, reform was necessary to conform with the First Company Law Directive. This largely abolished the *ultra vires* and constructive notice principles as regards dealings between a company and third parties. Section 35 of the Companies Act 1985 (as amended by the Companies Act 1989) represents the current law and has produced the following results:

1 the company is treated as having the capacity to make any contract even if it is in excess of its objects clause. The good faith of the other party is not relevant;

2 if the directors of a company exceed their powers as laid down in the articles of association, any resulting act or transaction involving a third party is binding unless there is evidence that the third party did not act in good faith (s 35A). Good faith is presumed. The third party has no duty to enquire whether any restriction exists (s 35B). Under s 711A, the third party is not deemed to have notice of the company's memorandum or articles. Proof of bad faith would probably require evidence of wilful neglect to make enquiries in the light of reasonable suspicion that the directors are exceeding their authority;

3 the company can sue for breach if the third party fails to perform the contract, as well as being liable for breach itself if it failed to perform;

4 the *ultra vires* rule still operates *within* the company. Section 35 does not prevent the operation of the *ultra vires* rule in the relationship of the company to its members. Where the directors have planned to exceed their authority but have not yet done so, a company member who finds out in time may seek an injunction to stop them;

5 the shareholders may ratify (confirm) the *ultra vires* activity by a special resolution, but this does not absolve the directors from liability to the company for any damage arising from their breach of duty in failing to observe the terms of the memorandum. A separate special resolution is required to relieve the directors from such liability.

Despite the good faith requirement in s 35A, there is still a danger that the directors in their personal capacity may enter into potentially fraudulent transactions with the company. To guard against this, s 322A provides that if the purported transaction by the company is made with:

1 a director of the company or its holding company, or

2 any person connected with the director or any company with which the director is associated,

the transaction is *voidable* by the company.

This gives the company a choice not to go through with the transaction. Whether or not the company avoids the transaction, the director can be required to account for any profits arising and must indemnify the company for any damage caused to it.

Changing the memorandum

Most of the contents of the memorandum can be changed, but this generally requires the proposal of a special resolution and a vote carried by a specified majority. The country of domicile of the registered office cannot be changed. With a special resolution, which requires at least a 75 per cent majority, the following can be changed:

- name;
- objects;
- a public company to a private one: re-registration will be required;
- unlimited liability to limited liability.

Usually an ordinary resolution carried by a simple majority is required to increase authorised share capital, unless the articles require otherwise. If the company wishes to change from limited to unlimited liability, *all* members must agree. *The Registrar must be notified of all changes within 15 days.* A copy of the relevant resolution is required, as well as an altered copy of the memorandum.

The articles of association

The articles regulate the *internal* management of the company and the relationships between it and its members.

The Companies Act 1985, s 8 lays down a set of draft articles (Table A) which are adopted automatically by any company limited by shares if the promoters do not choose to register specially composed articles. Public companies almost always draft their own articles in order to include provisions in compliance with Stock Exchange rules for listed companies.

Contents

The articles state all the rules necessary to the internal conduct of the company's business. For example:

- the number of directors;
- the method of their appointment;
- powers of directors;
- the procedures for calling and conduct of meetings;
- voting rights of members;
- keeping of accounts;
- the payment of dividends.

The company may, therefore, empower itself within the confines of the law. The Companies Act prohibits some activities and permits others subject to compliance with certain procedures. For example, shares cannot be issued at a discount (s 100).

Alterations to the articles

Changes to the articles require a special resolution carried by a 75 per cent majority, but this may be dispensed with if the members unanimously agree. Subject to the observation of this formality, changes can be made provided that:

1 there is no resulting conflict with the memorandum, or any statutory requirement or current court order;

2 the alteration is made in good faith for the benefit of the company as a whole.

The fact that personal hardship is caused to one shareholder is irrelevant if overall the change is beneficial to the bulk of shareholders. This rule protects the interests of shareholders as members of the company and not in any other capacity.

Sidebottom v _Kershaw Leese & Co._ (1920)
Mr Sidebottom held shares in a company and also carried on a business in competition with it. The company changed its articles to contain a requirement that any shareholders who competed with the company must transfer their shares at a fair value to a person nominated by the directors. Clearly the share transfer provision was beneficial to the company and necessary to prevent unfair competition. The fact that the claimant suffered hardship in the conduct of his other business was irrelevant.

The courts try to ensure that this power is not used oppressively to discriminate against a minority of shareholders. As long as the court is satisfied that the shareholders reached the decision in the honest belief that it would potentially benefit every shareholder, the good faith criterion will be satisfied.

It is not possible to prevent alteration by requiring a majority greater than 75 per cent, or by a declaration in the articles that they cannot be altered. There are, however, some means by which proposed alterations may be blocked (for example, if the articles give a member additional voting strength to oppose change). Such blocking mechanisms may be challenged by members on the grounds of unfair prejudice. (This issue is covered in greater detail in Chapter 25.)

The memorandum and articles represent contractual terms

Under s 14, a contract exists on the terms set out in the memorandum and articles, between:

1 the company and each of its members; and

2 the members of the company.

The company and each of its members

Failure by one of the parties to carry out its obligations under the memorandum or articles is actionable as a breach of contract. The parties are bound by these terms, though the company is in the stronger position since it makes the rules and has the power to initiate their alteration.

Hickman v Romney Marsh Sheep Breeders Association (1915)
The articles of the association stated that in the event of a dispute between a member and the association, the matter must be referred to arbitration. Mr Hickman was expelled from the association and sued it claiming breach of contract. It was held that he could not take court action until the arbitration process had taken place as required by the terms of his membership contract with the association.

The members of the company

A personal action by one member against another is possible.

Rayfield v Hands (1960)
The articles required the directors to buy a retiring member's shares at a fair price. Refusal to do so entitled a retiring member to obtain a decree of specific performance against the directors.

Members' capacity to sue on the terms imposed by the articles and memorandum is limited to enforcing their rights as members. The fact that a breach of the articles results in damage to them in their personal capacity does not allow them to sue for that breach.

Eley v Positive Life Assurance Co. (1876)
The articles stated that Eley would be the company's solicitor for life. When the company dismissed him, he unsuccessfully attempted to sue for breach of the articles. It was held that the interest which he was attempting to protect was a personal employment right, not one related to his status as a company member.

The articles may, however, provide evidence of terms to be implied in a separate contract giving rise to personal rights. For example, this enables directors to sue for remuneration owed to them under the terms of the articles. They must sue on the contract which appoints them, but its terms may be clarified by reference to the articles if necessary.

Soden v British Commonwealth Holdings plc (1997)
The rights and obligations imposed by the Companies Acts may also be implied terms within the contract arising under s 14.

Proposed reform

The White Paper 2002 proposes that the memorandum and articles of association shall be replaced with a single document setting out the constitution of the company. This could be amended by special resolution by the members.

BUYING A COMPANY 'OFF THE SHELF'

Instead of going through the registration process, the promoters of a company may buy a ready-made company from a business specialising in providing such a service. The seller registers companies and then renders them dormant, relieving them of a duty to appoint auditors or prepare annual accounts. When the company is sold, the shares are transferred to the buyers, who then register themselves as the new directors and secretary. The name and objects of the company may have to be changed to fit the needs of the buyers' business, unless originally registered as a 'general commercial company'.

Apart from saving the promoters time and effort, buying a company off the shelf is generally cheaper than completing the registration process.

Quiz 22

1 What documentation must be received by the Companies Registry before a company can be registered?

2 What difference has EC law made to the contractual capacity of a company?

3 Dogger and Portland are the directors of Maritime Pursuits Ltd. They want to change their company to one with public status. What will they have to do?

4 What is the significance of the Table A draft articles for company promoters?

5 How may changes be made to a company's articles?

Assignment 21

(a) What is the purpose of the objects clause in the company's memorandum and to what extent may the wording restrict the trading activities of a company?

(10 marks)

(b) How far does the objects clause affect the ability of a third party to enforce a contract against the company?

(10 marks)

CHAPTER 23

Running the company: raising and maintaining capital

INTRODUCTION

In general terms, the company's capital includes all its business assets, including premises, equipment, stock in trade and goodwill. This chapter is concerned with capital in more specialised terms: that which can be raised through the issue of shares or through loans made to the company.

The Companies Acts lay down detailed rules concerning the raising of share capital. A company will not be registered unless the Registrar is satisfied that the proposed share capital is sufficient to buffer potential claims from company creditors. The Acts also aim to ensure that once share capital has been raised, it is maintained at safe levels.

A company may need to borrow money and may do so under the relevant powers in its objects clause. Security to lenders may be obtained from registered charges on the company's property which require registration under the Companies Acts.

Capital may be raised in two ways:

1 by selling shares (share capital): the buyers become company members;

2 by obtaining loans (loan capital): the lenders do not become members by virtue of their loan. They are creditors of the company.

SHARE CAPITAL

The memorandum of association states the authorised or nominal capital of the company; this represents the maximum share capital which the company has the authority to raise. It can be increased by an ordinary resolution passed by a simple majority of members. It is not indicative of the number of shares that have been issued or the money raised by sales.

There are different categories of share capital:

1 *Issued capital*. This refers to the number of shares issued to members and represents some guarantee of progress for the company's creditors.

2 *Called-up capital.* The amount of capital raised by a call on shares. A shareholder, on being allotted shares, may not have to pay for them at once but may be called on to do so at a later date.

3 *The paid-up capital.* This should be the same as the called-up capital unless a shareholder has failed to pay what is due. The amount of paid-up capital is a good indicator of the company's financial health.

4 *Uncalled capital.* The difference between the called-up capital and the nominal value of the shares.

5 *Reserve capital.* This is created by the company passing a special resolution which removes issued capital from the directors' control in order to provide a fund out of which creditors may be paid in the event of a winding up. This is not a common practice.

Classes of shares

The articles prescribe the rights derived from the shares issued. For example, Table A states that the company may issue shares with whatever rights or restrictions may be determined by the passing of an ordinary resolution. Different classes of shares may give rise to different rights. A shareholder's rights are also to some extent governed by the size of its shareholding: this will govern the amount of dividend payable and the strength of the shareholder's voting power.

There are different classes of shares which a company might choose to issue.

Ordinary (equity) shares

A company may choose to issue only this type of share. They commonly carry most of the voting rights.

Preference shares

If the company chooses to declare a dividend, the preference shareholders are entitled to payment at a fixed rate promised to them when the shares were allotted to them. It will represent a percentage of the value of their shares. How great an advantage they enjoy is dictated by the fortunes of the company. They may be the only shareholders to receive a dividend, or may be paid at a higher rate than the ordinary shareholders. If the company is doing well, the ordinary shareholders may do better than the preference shareholders, since the latter, having received their dividend at the prescribed rate, are not entitled to share with the ordinary shareholders in the distribution of any surplus profits. The articles may entitle them to other benefits: they may take priority over ordinary shareholders with regard to recovery of capital during a winding up.

Redeemable shares

Section 159 permits the issue of any class of shares on a short-term basis. The holder takes them for a specified period of time, after which the company buys them back. This can be a useful means of raising capital for a new small business. These shares may have preference or non-preference status.

Deferred/founders' shares

These may be held by the promoters of the company. They carry increased voting rights but rank below ordinary shares for payment of dividends and the return of capital.

The issue of shares

The first issue of shares takes place when the company is floated. Subsequent issues may be made provided that there is compliance with any procedures in the company's articles. These may include a *rights issue*, which is a sort of special offer, restricted initially at a favourable price, to existing shareholders.

Any company which intends to issue shares may issue a *prospectus* to describe the venture. A public company may advertise its shares for sale to the public, but that does not mean that it has an automatic right to sell through the Stock Exchange. The right to sell on the Stock Exchange is governed by rules formulated by the Stock Exchange under the Financial Services Act 1986 which implements EC directives.

A large public company may have the financial stature required to qualify its securities for admission to the Official List of the Stock Exchange. The information given by the company in its listing application then becomes public knowledge.

The Companies Act places a number of restrictions on share issue. These exist to prevent the company reducing its capital to the prejudice of its creditors, for whom the company's share capital assets represent some security. The principal restrictions relate to the price of shares and a company's acquisition of its own shares.

Price

Under s 99, the company can transfer shares only in return for *money or money's worth*. Shares can be given in return for services rendered to a private company. A public company is prohibited from doing this.

Under s 100, on first issue the shares cannot be sold at *less than their face value* as stated in the memorandum, unless (under s 97) the sale is to underwriters when a discount of up to 10 per cent is permissible.

Shares can be issued at a *premium*, i.e. at more than their face value. Any money so raised is counted as part of the company's capital, not profits, and it must be treated as such. Funds from the premium issue must be kept in a separate account and may be used for certain purposes only (s 130):

1 paying up unissued shares for issue as bonus shares to members;

2 writing off the preliminary expenses of the company.

A company's acquisition of its own shares

In the interests of capital maintenance, the general rule is that a company cannot acquire its own shares since a likely (and undesirable) result is that Peter is robbed to pay Paul: the shareholder would be paid from the company's assets, but since the shares would be cancelled after purchase, the company's share capital would be reduced.

Section 143 states that, subject to certain specified exceptions, the company may *not* acquire its own shares by sale, subscription or any other means. The company *may* acquire its own shares in the following circumstances:

1 no valuable consideration is paid for the shares;

2 the purchase is to effect a formal reduction of capital which has been approved by the court;

3 the court orders the purchase of shares to protect the interests of a minority of shareholders. Such orders may be made in certain situations specified by the Act. For example, under s 5 when an unsuccessful application is made to challenge a change in the articles;

4 where shares are forfeited or surrendered as required by the articles, by the shareholder who has failed to pay.

Becoming a shareholder

Acquiring shares from the company

When the shares are first issued by the company, an interested party may apply to buy some. This is an offer which the company may accept by a letter of allotment. At this point a contract for sale of the shares comes into existence. However, the shareholder does not become a member of the company until his or her name is placed on the company's register of shareholders. The company must issue a certificate of registration which is evidence of the shareholder's title to the shares. Under s 185, the company has a duty to do this within two months of the issue of the letter of allotment.

Acquiring shares from an existing shareholder

A shareholder in a public company may freely transfer his or her shares; restrictions may be imposed by private companies. Section 183 requires the transfer to be formally notified to the company. The company must register the change of shareholder and issue a new certificate of registration within two months of receiving the instrument of transfer (s 185).

Once registered, the buyer of shares acquires all the rights attaching to that class of shares as dictated by the articles. In a limited company the buyer's liability for the company's debts is limited to the value of its shares. The shareholding makes the shareholder part owner of the company. Unless the company is wound up a shareholder cannot withdraw his or her capital investment from the company, but may transfer his or her shares to somebody else.

The rights of shareholders

To be paid any dividend declared by the company

A dividend is a bonus payment which can only be paid out of profits (s 263). Dividends are declared at the company's discretion, so the shareholders have no automatic right to a dividend unless the company chooses to issue one.

To vote at company meetings

Shareholders may vote at company meetings provided that their shares attract voting rights. This is determined by the articles. Voting rights may be used for the personal benefit of the shareholder and do not have to be exercised in the best interests of the company.

To recover the capital value of their shares if the company goes into liquidation

This right can be exercised only subject to the superior rights of the company's creditors. The shareholders do not necessarily have equal rights in relation to each other. Those with superior status have a right to be repaid before others. The articles determine the status of shareholders in this respect.

To transfer their shares

Shareholders may transfer their shares subject to any restrictions laid down in the articles. Restrictions are usual in the articles of a private company. Disputes regarding interpretation of such restrictions may be brought to court. The court will interpret any ambiguity in favour of the shareholder. To be legitimate the restriction must be used in the best interests of the company; evidence of bad faith by the directors would invalidate it.

LOAN CAPITAL

Section 3A gives a company the powers to borrow money to further the business; these are usually made explicit in the memorandum of association, which indicates how far the company's assets may be used as loan security. When it obtains loans in this way the company creates a mortgage of its property. This is described as issuing debentures.

Debentures

A debenture is the written evidence of a secured loan to the company. There are three forms of debentures.

The single debenture

Any company may obtain a loan from any person or organisation prepared to lend it the money. In practice such loans most often come from a bank.

Series debentures

The company may look to its own members for loans and issue a series of debentures to participants who have equal rights to repayment. They are generally protected by a trust in the same way as holders of debenture stock.

Debenture stock

Public companies are entitled to issue debenture stock, which may be offered to the public through the Stock Exchange in the same way as shares.

In order to protect the debenture holders, the company creates a trust with control over the company's assets, with the power to appoint a receiver. The trustee, which is often an insurance company, has the status of a company creditor, with the legal duty to act on behalf of the debenture holders. The terms of the trust deed may require the company to take certain precautions to protect the lenders' interests, including insurance of company assets and limiting its borrowing powers.

The debenture holder agrees to lend a specific sum of money repayable with interest after a certain length of time. Extra perks may also be offered as an inducement to buy debenture stock. When the facilities for the Wimbledon tennis championship were being expanded, the company responsible raised the capital through an issue of debentures. Investment entitled the debenture holders to special facilities at the ground and priority booking rights.

A debenture is a transferable security and may therefore be disposed of in the same way as shares. The company is required to keep a list of debenture holders and issue registration certificates which are evidence of ownership for the registered holder.

Charges: the security behind the loan

If the company does not have the funds to repay debenture holders at the appointed time, the company's assets securing the loan will have to be realised to honour the debt.

The chargeable assets of the company include its premises, plant, machinery and goods (including stock in trade). As well as this tangible property, intellectual property like patents and copyright are also chargeable assets, as are book debts and business goodwill.

Registration of charges

All charges issued to secure debentures must be registered with the Companies' Registrar within 21 days of being created. Failure to register within this timescale renders the charge void. This does not relieve the company from liability to pay the debt, but it prevents the debenture holder from having any enforceable security for its loan.

Types of charges

Two kinds of charges are possible: fixed and floating.

1 *Fixed charges*. Specific assets to the value of the loan link with it as soon as the charge is created. Such a charge prevents any disposal of the assets over which the charge exists, and therefore only a limited variety of assets are suitable to being charged in this way. Land and large items of plant and machinery are the assets which are most appropriate for a fixed charge.

2 *Floating charges*. Here the charge relates to the company's assets at large. At the point the loan is created the security enjoyed by the debenture holder does not attach to any specified assets, but the debenture holder will be entitled to repayment of its loan from any of the assets held by the company at the time of repayment. A floating charge may, therefore, relate to any of the company's more fluid assets which are subject to constant change, like stock in trade. This facility, which is available only to registered companies, is helpful to companies with few fixed assets.

Any of the following circumstances will cause the floating charge to *crystallise* and attach to particular assets:

● the company ceases trading;
● winding up is commenced;
● the company fails to repay the debenture holder at the due date;
● the occurrence of any other event specified in the charge deed as triggering crystallisation.

A debenture holder is better protected by a fixed charge rather than by a floating charge. The value of a floating charge is likely to fluctuate. In the event of a winding up, the fixed-charge holders or statutorily protected creditors (employees, for example) take preference over the floating-charge holder.

Summary of the differences between shares and debentures

Shares	Debentures
The shareholder is a part owner of the company and may have voting rights.	The debenture holder is a company creditor; he or she does not have voting rights.

Shares	Debentures
Dividends are not payable out of capital. Since dividends are issued from profits at the company's discretion, a shareholder does not know if he or she will get any dividend, or what it will amount to.	The debenture holder must be paid interest on the loan, and this is payable out of capital. Debenture holders know how much interest they will get.
Risk: the entire value of the shareholding may be lost.	Since the loan is secured by a fixed or floating charge, the debenture holder has some security.
The company cannot usually buy its own shares.	The company can buy its own debentures.
Shares cannot be issued at a discount.	Debentures may be issued at a discount.

Quiz 23

1 What is the difference between issued and called-up capital?

2 Why might a company issue redeemable shares?

3 In what circumstances may a company acquire its own shares?

4 Silver, Gold and Copper all own shares in Metals plc and seek your advice on the following problems:

   (a) Silver complains that he has never received a dividend.

   (b) Gold, a preference shareholder, has just discovered that he has no right to vote at a company meeting.

   (c) Copper, a preference shareholder, has heard rumours that Metals may soon be wound up and is worried about his investment.

   (d) Brass, a debenture holder, is also worrying about whether he will recover his investment.

Assignment 22

Rashida has won £1000 in a raffle and wants to invest it in a company. She seeks your advice on whether she should buy shares or debentures. Explain the differences between the two investment methods to her, indicating the advantages and disadvantages of each.

CHAPTER 24

Daily management of the company: functions of directors, secretary and auditors

INTRODUCTION

Although the company is an independent legal entity, it needs human beings to manage it. The key management figures are the directors. The company secretary has important administrative functions, while financial accountability is monitored by the auditors. This chapter examines the work of these officials and takes a brief look at insider dealing.

THE DIRECTORS

The directors act as the agents of the company; they are primarily responsible for the daily management of the company and development of company policy. Decisions on such issues are made by the directors at board meetings.

A large company may have a correspondingly large board of directors. A number of these may be lay (non-executive) directors, who provide their services on a voluntary basis and whose primary function is attendance at board meetings. They do not play any direct role in the day-to-day management of the company; this is in the hands of its executive director(s). The value of independent directors is controversial: it is argued that their presence is important to ensure independent decision-making and an objective view of company policy. The Stock Exchange's Combined Code: Principles of Good Governance and Code of Good Practice 1998 requires that the majority of the board of a listed public company be made up of lay directors. A more cynical view is that their lack of relevant knowledge and experience may render their contribution largely useless. It is also said that they are likely to be too readily influenced by executive directors.

Appointing the directors

The first directors are named in the memorandum of association. Subsequent directors are appointed by ordinary resolution passed by a simple majority at a company general meeting. The articles of association state the procedure for replacement of a director who leaves or dies before a general meeting is due to be called. For example, Table A says that the remaining directors make the appointment.

Directors need not be shareholders of the company, but the articles may require them to hold qualifying shares.

Executive (managing) directors

Since they are responsible for the day-to-day management of the company, executive directors work for the company full-time and have expertise and experience relevant to the company's business. They may be engaged by the company under a contract of service; provided the articles do not state otherwise, a person may be both an employee and a director of a company, subject to some restrictions:

1 a contract of employment for more than five years cannot be offered to any person who is already a director without the approval of the shareholders in a general meeting (s 319);

2 company articles generally prohibit directors from voting on their terms of employment at a directors' meeting;

3 directors' service agreements are open to public inspection at the company's registered office.

In a small private company (quasi-partnership) all the directors will be full-time managers but will decide informally how much the company can afford to pay them.

To prevent a conflict of interest for executive directors and to discourage malpractice in listed companies, the Combined Code requires companies to put in place open and transparent procedures for appointing executive directors and their remuneration. A company's annual report should state the relevant policies for the information of shareholders. The code also requires that a committee of non-executive directors should decide, within agreed terms of reference, a company's policy for paying its executive directors. This committee is also responsible for determining the specific remuneration rights for each executive director, including pension entitlement and compensation payment.

Alternate directors

If the articles permit, a director may appoint someone else to represent him or her at a board meeting if unable to attend. In practice, this function is usually exercised by another director.

Shadow directors

There is a danger that company members whose voting powers enable them to manipulate the directors' decision-making may choose to exercise their powers while avoiding the legal responsibilities which appointment as a director brings.

Section 741 provides a safeguard: 'a person in accordance with whose instructions the directors of a company are accustomed to act' is subject to the same liability and controls as any other director.

The powers of the directors

These are indicated by the articles. Table A states that 'the business of the company shall be managed by the directors'. Examples of directors' powers include issuing shares and borrowing money on the security of the company's assets.

Limitation on the exercise of powers

The directors' powers must be exercised subject to the company's objects clause; they are the agents of the company and their powers are limited to those of the company.

The Companies Acts impose restrictions on the way directors may use their authority, and this may also be limited by the articles. The powers must be exercised in the best interests of the company to fulfil the purposes for which they were given.

Protecting third parties against abuse of directors' powers

If the directors exceed their power the company may be bound by a resulting transaction. The third party may enforce the transaction as long as it acted in good faith under s 35, which was previously examined in detail in Chapter 22. The common law also provides some limited protection:

1 *Directors with apparent authority*. This is governed by the law of agency (see Chapter 15). If the board of directors know that a maverick director is exceeding his or her authority but do not disown that behaviour, the company will be bound by any resulting contract with a third party. In law the directors are estopped from denying that the contract was authorised.

> **Freeman & Lockyer v Buckhurst Park Properties Mangal Ltd** (1964)
> The articles of the defendant company permitted the appointment of a managing director. None was appointed, but one of the directors was known by the others to be conducting business with outsiders as if he had these powers. The company was held liable on contracts resulting from this abuse of authority. The board had been fully aware of the director's behaviour and could not deny his apparent authority after the event.

2 *The indoor management rule (the rule in* Turquand's *case)*. Where a director enters into a contract in breach of the company's internal management rules in the articles, the other party may enforce the contract as long as it did not know that the rule had been broken.

Royal British Bank v Turquand (1856, HL)
The articles of a company required that the directors could borrow money for the company only if the loan was specifically authorised by the shareholders passing an ordinary resolution in a general meeting. It was held that the company was bound by an unauthorised loan agreement as the lender could reasonably assume that the shareholders had authorised it.

The rule in *Turquand's* case has largely been eclipsed by s 35 as regards the exercise of directors' powers (see Chapter 22). It may be relevant to unauthorised transactions by a company employee.

The duties of directors

The directors have a number of duties arising from the exercise of their powers:

1 *To the company's employees: s 309.* Directors are required to have regard to the interests of the company's employees. Since the Act gives the workforce no means of enforcing this duty, its importance is doubtful.

2 *To the company's creditors: Insolvency Act 1986, s 214.* If the directors should be aware that the company cannot reasonably avoid going into liquidation, they should take steps to minimise losses to creditors. Breach of this duty may result in the directors becoming personally liable for the creditors' losses.

3 *To the company.* The 'company' in this context means its membership – the body of shareholders. Duties are imposed at common law and by statute.

Directors' common law duties

Directors owe two common law duties to the company; a duty of care and a fiduciary duty. Provided that directors have not acted *ultra vires* or fraudulently, the fact that damage has been caused by their behaviour is not in itself evidence of lack of reasonable care and skill.

Re City Equitable & Fire Insurance Co. Ltd (1925)
Due to fraud by a managing director, the company suffered major losses resulting in its liquidation. The other directors were held not to be negligent in failing to notice the managing director's misconduct. The court laid down criteria for judgement of what is a reasonable standard of care:

1 the director must act honestly for the benefit of the business;

2 what is reasonable care must be judged with reference to the experience, knowledge and skill of the relevant director. Directors cannot be expected

to exercise greater care than these qualities equip them for. Less would be demanded of a lay director than of a managing director;

3 a director is not generally expected to give continuous attention to the company's affairs, since directors' duties are essentially intermittent in their nature (today it is unlikely that any court would excuse a managing director who failed to exercise continuous attention);

4 delegation of duty by a director to an appropriate company official is not evidence of a breach of duty provided it is in accordance with business practice and does not infringe the company's articles.

Where it appears that a director has breached the duty of care an action in negligence may be started, after members at a general meeting have voted in favour of such action. A director who is found to have been negligent must personally indemnify the company for its losses.

It is possible for the directors to be informally excused (without passage of a resolution) their negligent conduct by unanimous agreement of members with voting rights. This may be done even if the negligent directors themselves control the voting.

Directors' second common law duty is to act with the *utmost good faith* in dealing with the company. This duty is derived from the directors' position as fiduciaries to the company. This has three consequences.

1 *Directors must avoid any conflict between their own financial interests and those of the company.* If they breach this duty, they must account to the company for any resulting profit.

IDC v Cooley (1972)
Cooley was an architect employed as managing director of IDC. He was put in charge of negotiations with a gas board, which had approached IDC concerning the design of a gas holder. During the negotiations it became clear that the gas board was unwilling to place the contract with IDC. At this point Cooley resigned, falsely pleading ill health. Then he took on the design contract with the gas board. It was held that Cooley must pay the profits from the contract to IDC, since he had abused his position as agent of the company to obtain the contract. It was irrelevant that IDC had not necessarily lost the contract because of his behaviour.

2 *Directors must make full disclosure of any personal interest which they have in company business.* Generally the articles provide that as long as directors fully declare their interests they may retain them, but they must not vote at a board meeting on any issue relating to those interests.

3 *Directors must exercise their powers in good faith and for their proper purposes.*

Hogg v Cramphorn (1967)

The directors, who honestly believed that a threatened takeover was not in the company's best interests, issued 5000 additional shares to be held on trust for the company's employees. It was held that this was a misuse of the directors' powers.

If a contract is made in breach of the directors' fiduciary duty the contract is voidable, and therefore the company is able to choose whether to go through with it or not. Provided that the directors have not acted fraudulently or in breach of the law, the shareholders may vote to ratify their actions. For example, in *Hogg* v *Cramphorn* (above) it was held that provided that the employees were excluded from the vote, the remaining shareholders could vote to ratify the directors' action.

Directors' statutory duty to declare contractual interests: s 317

As has already been explained, as fiduciaries of the company, directors have a common law duty to reveal anything about their financial position which might be material to the company's business. The Companies Act imposes a specific duty to declare any direct or indirect interest which they have in a contract or proposed contract with the company. Directors must also disclose an interest where the company is contemplating making a contract with anybody 'connected with the director'. This includes:

1 a director's spouse;

2 any company in which the director has at least a 20 per cent of voting capacity;

3 the trustees of any trust whose beneficiaries include the director;

4 a partner of the director;

5 the partner of any person connected with the director.

Failure to make proper disclosure makes the transaction voidable and is a criminal offence punishable with a fine.

The disclosure must be made at the meeting where the contract is first discussed. The directors' duty to volunteer information is limited to giving the board of directors a general indication of the interest. If the members ask any detailed questions, these must be answered honestly.

Guinness plc v Saunders (1990)

During a takeover bid a payment of over £5 million was made to a director who disclosed his interest to a committee of the board consisting of only two other members and himself. It was held that this was not sufficient to discharge the duty under s 317. The disclosure must be made to the whole board.

Information and control for shareholders of directors' dealings with the company

Some transactions between a director and the company require the shareholders' approval.

1 *Disclosure in the company accounts: s 232*. The accounts must give details of a director's *material interest* in contracts of a specified minimum value. (Contracts not exceeding £1000 or, if greater, not more than 1 per cent of the company's assets up to a maximum of £5000 are exempt.) The directors determine what is a material interest.

2 *Shareholders' approval of substantial and material property transactions: s 320*. The shareholders may avoid any transaction involving the sale or acquisition of property by the company to or from a director or a director of a holding company where the value of the property exceeds £10 000 or, if less, exceeds 10 per cent of the company's net assets. The director or any connected person is liable to the company for profits arising from the contract; any directors who gave their approval may also be liable.

The Combined Code: Stock Exchange regulation and monitoring of directors' duties

All listed companies are required to comply with the Combined Code.

This code, which came into operation in 1998, largely encompasses the requirements of two previous codes which had their origins in the Cadbury Report (1992) and the Greenbury Report (1995). It also implements recommendations of the 1998 Hempel Report.

The Combined Code has a considerable impact on directors' duties since it emphasises the need for:

(a) effective and transparent management to maximise profits for shareholders by enhancement of the company's prosperity; and

(b) a balance of power and authority at the head of the company, to prevent one individual from having 'unfettered powers' of decision-making.

Listed companies are expected to provide specified evidence of compliance with the code in their annual accounts and report. This should also ensure that shareholders are fully informed. Although the code is not legally binding, a company which does not comply may be deprived of its Stock Exchange listing, unless it is able to provide written proof of why compliance did not occur.

Reforms of this area of the law are also proposed by the Law Commission, which in 1998 issued a Consultation Paper: *Company Directors: Regulating Conflicts of Interest and Formulating a Statement of Duties* (Law Commission, No. 253). The aim was to obtain a wide range of views of ways in which the complex and vital rules laid down in the Companies Acts need to be rationalised and modernised in keeping with the current business environment. The paper stresses that the law concerning the duties of directors needs to be more accessible. It recommends a comprehensive statutory statement of directors' duties, which possibly might include a new duty of care. The Company Law Review 1999 reiterated the need for statutory restatement.

The Government White Paper 2002 (Modernising Company Law) affirms these proposals in principle. It states that directors' common law duties should be codified. General duties (apart from the duty to creditors) should be similarly treated. To ensure that directors are fully aware of what is required of them it is proposed that all new directors should receive guidance in simple language. This would clearly summarise the main legal requirements of insolvency and company law. It would also indicate the essential points of fraudulent trading law.

The rights of directors

Fees and expenses

Executive directors' remuneration is determined by the terms of their service contracts. Lay directors' entitlement is specified in the articles, but they are entitled to expenses.

Loans to directors

Section 330 generally forbids such loans, but exceptions are made under other provisions of the statute. Under s 334, a loan may be made to a director of the company or of its holding company provided the loan does not exceed £5000. Subject to the approval of the shareholders at a general meeting, directors may obtain a loan to enable them to carry out their duties.

The removal and retirement of directors

Removal by ordinary resolution with special notice: s 303

A director may be removed from office before the expiry of its term. This is done by an ordinary resolution of the company, for which special notice is given. The director must be given a copy of the special notice prior to its distribution to the shareholders so that the director can attach a written statement to it. Under s 304 the director is entitled to address the meeting.

Directors are entitled to use weighted voting rights even if these have been created specifically to prevent removal.

Bushell v Faith (1970, HL)
The company's articles stated that in the event of a resolution to remove the directors, their shares would carry three votes per share instead of one. Mr Faith, who held 100 shares, was able to use this measure to defeat his sisters who held 100 shares each.

Although executive directors may be removed in the same way as any other director, the company may have to pay damages if the removal is in breach of an executive director's contract of employment.

Retirement

Directors may retire from office for one of two reasons: age or resignation.

1 *Age*. Directors of a public company must retire once they reach the age of 70 (s 293).

2 *Resignation*. These rules are specified in the articles: directors retire in rotation. Table A requires a third of the directors to resign at each AGM on the basis of their length of service. Retiring directors may offer themselves for re-election.

The disqualification of directors

There are no special qualifications for holding office as a director. However, some people are disqualified from being appointed to or continuing to hold the office of director for any of the reasons set out below.

1 *Bankruptcy*.

2 *Unsound mind*.

3 *Absence from board meetings*. Failure to attend for over six months without permission.

4 *Failure to fulfil any shareholding requirements imposed by the articles*. A director does not have to be a shareholder but the articles may make this obligatory.

5 *By court order under the Company Directors Disqualification Act 1986*. Any person (not just an existing director) may be disqualified by the court from being a director, liquidator, administrator, receiver or manager of a company's property or from being in any way directly or indirectly concerned in running a company. Such an order may be made in the following circumstances:

   (a) *Conviction for an indictable offence in the Crown Court*. The offence will be connected with setting up or managing a company. The maximum disqualification period is 15 years.

   (b) *Persistent failure to make the annual return*. Persistent means three times over a five-year period. The maximum disqualification period is five years.

   (c) *Fraudulent trading*. The maximum disqualification period is 15 years.

   (d) *Unfit conduct by a director of an insolvent company*. Unfit behaviour includes:
   - breach of directors' duties;
   - misapplication or wrongful retention of company property;
   - failure to comply with Companies Act requirements concerning accounts and annual returns.

● failure to co-operate with the liquidator in accordance with the requirements of the Insolvency Act 1986.

The maximum period for disqualification is 15 years.

6 *On application by the Secretary of State.* The disqualification must be in the public interest.

THE COMPANY SECRETARY

This is a key post since the company secretary is the company's principal administrative officer. The company secretary has a wide range of duties with responsibility for ensuring that the company fulfils its obligations under the Companies Acts. The secretary is not involved in managing the company or in carrying on its business, but has responsibility for running the registered office. In a large company the company secretary's job may involve hiring staff, buying office equipment and administering a pension scheme, as well as carrying out any functions designated by the articles or statute.

Qualifications for office

In *private companies* no specific qualifications are needed. In *public companies* the directors must be satisfied that their appointee has appropriate skills and experience to do the job (s 286). In addition, the appointee must satisfy one of the following requirements:

1 already be acting as the company secretary; or

2 for three of the last five years have been the secretary of a public company; or

3 hold a UK qualification in law; or

4 be a member of an approved organisation, for example ICA, ACCA, ICSA, ICMA, CIPFA; or

5 appear to be capable of acting as a company secretary because of experience gained as the holder of another office or membership of an appropriate body.

The directors are responsible for appointing the company secretary. Every company must have one and the company secretary must not be the sole director (s 283).

The functions of the company secretary

Ensuring compliance with the Companies Acts

The secretary must make sure that all the documentation open to public inspection is kept in order and up to date. This includes the registers of share and debenture holders. The secretary is also responsible for supervising the completion of the *annual return*.

The annual return updates the information about the company which was required for registration, so that most of the information which may be obtained by looking at the register can be found in the return. Sections 364 and 364A require the following information to be included:

1 the names and addresses of the current directors and secretary;

2 particulars of other directorships held by board members;

3 the address of the registered office;

4 particulars of the company's share capital.

The return should be delivered to the Companies Registry every year on the anniversary of the company's incorporation or delivery of its last annual return. Under s 363 failure to deliver it is a criminal offence by the company and its directors and secretary.

Since the implementation of the Cadbury Report in 1993, the secretary's duty in formulating the return has become more onerous. The secretary of a listed company must indicate in the annual return how far the company has complied with the code of best practice. The report stressed the secretary's responsibility for monitoring the directors' progress in fulfilling the requirements of the code. Failure to declare progress in conforming with the code may result in the company having its listed status removed by the Stock Exchange.

The secretary has authority to act as the company's agent

Company secretaries have authority to make a wide variety of contracts incidental to their functions. These include engaging office staff, buying or hiring office equipment, and purchasing such other goods and services as are necessary to running the company office. As long as the other party acts in good faith in the reasonable belief that the company has authorised the contracts, they will be enforceable against the company whether or not the secretary had actual authority or not.

Panorama Developments v Fidelis Furnishing Fabrics Ltd (1971, CA)
The company secretary of Fidelis Furnishings hired cars, claiming that they were to be used to transport customers to the company premises. In fact he was putting them to his own use. It was held that the company was liable on these contracts, which came within the scope of the secretary's apparent authority. The Court of Appeal stressed that the status of the company secretary had become greatly enhanced in the twentieth century and carried much greater responsibility than the largely clerical role of the nineteenth-century company secretary.

Some activities, however, do not come within the secretary's authority. These include borrowing money and making a trading contract, as these actions are not incidental to the administration of the company.

THE AUDITORS OF THE COMPANY

The duty to appoint an auditor

Every company has a duty to appoint an auditor (s 384). A private company may choose not to make an annual appointment (s 379A). Where it does so choose, the original auditors are deemed to be re-elected every year until a resolution is passed to the contrary. The appointment is made initially by the directors and the appointee remains in post until the end of the first general meeting before which the accounts are laid (s 385). Subsequent auditors are appointed by the shareholders.

Recent deregulation measures have made it possible for small private companies to avoid many of the audit requirements imposed by the Companies Act. Since 1994, very small private companies with a turnover of less than £90 000 are completely exempt from the requirement to have an annual audit. Private companies with a turnover of at least £350 000 may obtain a compilation report prepared by an independent accountant.

Under s 389, the auditor must be suitably qualified. This means that the auditor must be a member of a recognised accountancy body. This includes the Institute of Chartered Accountants and the Chartered Association of Certified Accountants.

The functions of the auditors

The functions of the company's auditors are to check that the company's accounts genuinely reflect its actual financial position and to issue a report on the accounts to the shareholders. To perform these functions efficiently the auditors will have to do more than just check the in-house accountant's arithmetic; the company's stock in trade and money-handling procedures will have to be inspected and the company advised of any undesirable practices taking place in the management of the business.

The powers of the auditors

The Companies Act gives the auditors considerable powers to help them acquire the necessary information to perform their functions. Section 389A gives them access to all the company's books and records and allows them to question company officials. It is a criminal offence knowingly or recklessly to make a misleading or materially false statement to an auditor.

The liability of the auditors

Contract

The auditors' contract with the company must be performed with reasonable care and skill. Failure to do so can make the auditors liable for breach of contract. Only the company has the right to sue, as there is no privity of contract between the auditors and individual shareholders.

Tort

Negligence liability will arise if the auditors do not act with reasonable care and skill, but this duty is owed only to the company, not to existing or potential shareholders. (See the House of Lords' decision in *Caparo* v *Dickman* (1990) in Chapter 11.)

INSIDER DEALING

Anybody with inside information about the present or future value of the company's securities, who uses that information for their own profit and without disclosing it to any other relevant parties, may be guilty of insider dealing; this is a criminal offence. Insiders include the company's directors, shareholders and employees, and any other people who have access to relevant information about the company because of their office or professional status. Therefore, an auditor who bought shares in the knowledge that a takeover was imminent which would increase their value, would be guilty of insider dealing if that information was not public knowledge.

Such dealing has been an infringement of the Companies Acts since 1980. The current law is to be found in the Criminal Justice Act 1993, Part IV, which was prompted by the need for the UK to comply with EC Directive 89/92 on insider dealing. It is an offence to deal in securities while in possession, as an insider, of inside information and if the price of securities is affected by this information. Defendants may avoid liability if they can prove that when they entered into the transaction they did not do so with the intention of making a profit or avoiding a loss.

The Act does not create civil liability for insider dealing, therefore the company or individual shareholders do not have any right to recover damages for the losses which they have suffered. Where the insider is a director, the profits from the deal are technically recoverable by the company, as by dealing in this way the director will have acted in breach of fiduciary duty. There are no reported decisions where such action has been taken.

Quiz 24

1 Bombazine was approached by Linen, a director of Textiles plc, and asked to supply catering services for Textiles' hundredth anniversary party. She incurred costs in preparing for the event, but has now been told that Linen had acted without the authority of the board of directors who had vetoed his proposal. What are her rights?

2 Textiles plc is having severe financial problems. What duties does it owe to:

   (a) its creditors?

   (b) its employees?

3 Textiles' board has voted to employ Threads Ltd to carry out an efficiency study. The principal shareholder and managing director of Threads is Taffeta; she is married to Cotton, a director of Textiles plc. Cotton has not mentioned the connection. What is the legal situation?

4 What is the legal position of the following Textiles' directors?

   (a) Tweed, who has gone bankrupt.

   (b) Denim, who has not attended a board meeting all year.

   (c) Twist, who was so consumed with worry over Textiles' affairs that he had a nervous breakdown.

Assignment 23

Explain the statutory and other means by which directors may be controlled in the exercise of their duties and discuss how far they might be reformed.

CHAPTER 25

Company meetings and shareholder participation

INTRODUCTION

The day-to-day management of the company is in the hands of the directors, and usually there is little that the shareholders can do to influence this. They are, however, statutorily entitled to a certain amount of information from the directors. For example, shareholders are entitled to a copy of the annual company accounts under s 238. They also have the right to attend general meetings of the company. A general meeting is one which all members of a company are entitled to attend. This must be distinguished from a board meeting which is for directors only. A class meeting is one which is restricted to holders of particular classes of share.

Under the Companies Act, some kinds of business can be transacted only at a general meeting. The directors are statutorily required to call one in certain circumstances and this duty may be enforced by the shareholders. Some radical changes which the directors may wish to implement require a majority vote from the shareholders at a general meeting of the company. For example, a majority of shareholders must support a motion to do any of the following:

- a change of company name;
- a change of company objects;
- a change to the company's articles;
- a voluntary winding up.

GENERAL MEETINGS

The annual general meeting (AGM)

In general, every company must hold an annual general meeting (s 366), though members of a private company may choose not to hold one (s 366A). The first AGM must be held within 15 months of when the company was registered. After that each AGM must be held no later than 15 months after the last one.

Under s 369, 21 days' notice of the AGM must be given in writing to the shareholders. The purpose of the AGM is to allow the shareholders to question the directors about the annual report, to vote on any motions put before the meeting and to elect new directors.

Proposed reforms

The government White Paper 2002 (Modernising Company Law) proposes that in future there will be no requirement for a private company to hold an AGM, but an opt-in procedure will exist for any company which does wish to do so. A public company will still require an AGM unless there is a unanimous agreement of all members not to hold one. Very small public companies could benefit from this flexibility.

Extraordinary general meetings (EGMs)

It may be necessary to call an EGM if something occurs which needs to be dealt with so urgently that it cannot wait until the next annual general meeting. The directors' powers to call the meeting are stated in the articles, but a duty is imposed by law in certain situations:

Serious reduction of capital: s 142

A director of a public company must call a meeting within 28 days of discovering that the company has suffered a serious loss of capital. A serious loss occurs where the company's net assets amount to half or less of its share capital. The meeting must be held within 56 days of notice being given.

The shareholders requisition a meeting: s 368

The directors must call an EGM if required to do so by a requisition of the shareholders who hold at least one-tenth of the paid-up share capital. Notice of the requisition, explaining why the meeting is needed, must be delivered to the company's registered office. It must be signed by the relevant shareholders. Within 21 days of the delivery, the directors must issue notice of the meeting. This must take place no later than 28 days after the date of issue of the notice.

Meeting by order of the court: s 371

A director or shareholder may ask the court to order that a meeting be convened with a specified agenda and a quorum of one. This is intended to resolve deadlock in a two-person company.

Requisition by retiring auditors: s 392A

An auditor who has retired because of concerns about the financial management of the company may requisition a meeting to allow the members to consider the reasons for the auditor's resignation.

Rules concerning meetings

Notice of meetings

The length of required notice varies according to the type of meeting and the nature of the business to be transacted. It may be reduced by agreement of the shareholders. An AGM generally requires 21 days' notice, while an EGM generally requires only 14 days.

Under s 369, all members must agree about reduction of notice for an AGM. For notice of an EGM to be reduced, the majority of members holding 95 per cent of shares must agree. This may be relaxed in relation to private companies.

The notice must contain the following information:

- the date, time and place of the meeting;
- the status of the meeting: whether it is an AGM or an EGM;
- the agenda;
- an indication of a member's right to appoint a proxy (a proxy need not be a company member). A shareholder may appoint a proxy to *vote* at a general meeting of a public or private company (s 372). A member of a private company may appoint a proxy to *speak* on the member's behalf.

Quorum

The quorum is the minimum number of people who must be present to enable the business of a meeting to be legitimately transacted. This is usually specified in the articles; if not, two people are sufficient (s 370). The meeting cannot take place if it is not quorate within 30 minutes of its starting time. If during the course of the meeting numbers drop below the required minimum, the meeting must be adjourned.

Resolutions

These are the proposals put before the meeting on which members may vote. A requisition of shareholders representing at least one-tenth of the total voting rights, *or* at least 100 shareholders who have each paid up at least £100 on their shares, may require the company to circulate details of any resolution in advance. This enables shareholders to propose a resolution at the meeting. Resolutions may be amended at the meeting provided that this does not take them out of the scope of the notified business.

There are three categories of resolution:

1 *Ordinary resolution*. This requires only a simple majority of members who vote to support it. This type of resolution is required to increase share capital (s 121), or to remove a director (s 303).

2 *Special resolution*. A 75 per cent majority of members present and voting is necessary for a special resolution to be successful. This is required to change the objects clause of the memorandum (s 4), or to make any change to the articles (s 9) or to re-register a private company as a public one. Twenty-one days' notice is usually required.

3 *Extraordinary resolution.* Fourteen days' notice must be given and a 75 per cent majority is required. Under the Insolvency Act 1986 (s 84) a company may be wound up by passing an extraordinary resolution stating that its liabilities prevent it continuing in business.

Proposed reform

The government White Paper 2002 (Modernising Company Law) proposes abolition of the extraordinary resolution and its replacement with a special resolution with 14 days' minimum notice.

Resolutions requiring special notice

The following resolutions cannot be put before the meeting unless the company received special notice of them at least 21 days before the date of the meeting:

1 a resolution for the removal of an auditor or to appoint a new one (ss 391 and 391A);

2 a resolution to remove a director (s 303);

3 a resolution to reappoint a director who has reached retirement age.

When the company receives the special notice it must take the necessary steps to inform the members. Usually this accompanies notice of the meeting. Where a director or an auditor is threatened with removal, he or she must be sent a copy of the special notice and is entitled to defend himself or herself by circulating a written statement to members and to address the meeting.

Avoid confusion: A special notice is *notice* which must be given to the company, not to the members. A special notice has nothing to do with a special *resolution*. 'Special' in that context refers to the size of majority required for the resolution's success (75 per cent).

Chairing the meeting

The articles usually specify who is to take the chair. If they do not, or if that person is not present, any nominated member may be chair. Usually this will be a director. The duty of the person in the chair is to run the meeting, but the permission of members must be sought before adjourning the meeting unless it becomes disorderly.

Voting at meetings

This may be by show of hands or by poll. A show of hands does not take into account the possible variation in voting strength of members specified in the articles. Proxies cannot vote on a show of hands. The articles may exclude the use of a poll to select the chair or adjourn a meeting. Otherwise, voting must be conducted by poll on the request of:

1 a minimum of five persons (proxies included); or

2 a member or members holding at least one-tenth of the voting rights;

3 a member or members holding shares to the value of at least one-tenth of the paid-up capital.

PROTECTING THE RIGHTS OF MINORITY SHAREHOLDERS

The decisions of the directors may successfully be challenged by a majority of shareholders who disagree with their proposals. Problems may arise if the directors are also the majority shareholders, since this permits them to make decisions with which the minority disagree.

The common law approach: the rule in *Foss* v *Harbottle*

The courts have generally been reluctant to assist a minority of shareholders even where damage to the company's interests is alleged. The justification for this approach is that the damaged party alone can sue and that the individual shareholder has no right to sue on the company's behalf. This is known as 'the rule in *Foss* v *Harbottle*' since it has its origins in this case.

Foss v *Harbottle* (1843)
Mr Foss, a shareholder in a company set up to open a public park, tried to sue the directors who he claimed had made an unfair profit from the sale of the land to the company. It was held that he had no right to take action. The directors' conduct had been sanctioned by the majority vote. Any damage caused by the directors' behaviour was to the company, which made the company the appropriate party to sue the directors.

A number of exceptions exist and an individual shareholder may intervene in the following circumstances.

1 *To challenge an illegal or* ultra vires *decision*. A shareholder may obtain an injunction to restrain the company from such behaviour. If such behaviour has already occurred the shareholder may be powerless.

2 *If the directors have acted fraudulently*. Proof of fraud is difficult since it is necessary to show that the directors actually intended to deceive or were reckless, and as a result misappropriated the company's property. Proof of gross negligence is not sufficient. Where the board consists of a number of directors, they may not all be

implicated and it will be necessary to prove that the board was effectively controlled by the fraudulent directors.

3 *Disregard of the procedures laid down in the articles*. The court will have to be satisfied that more than a technical procedural breach has occurred.

Edwards v Halliwell (1950)
(This is a trade union case, but the same principles apply in this instance.)
  An increased subscription was levied without the voting majority specified in the articles. It was held that this entitled an individual member to challenge the resolution.

However, in *MacDougall* v *Gardiner* (1875) it was held that a resolution passed on a show of hands could not be challenged on the grounds that the articles required a poll to be used at the request of at least five members.

The procedures by which shareholders may take action

Any shareholder can take action, whether or not that shareholder has voting rights. The following actions are available.

1 *A derivative action*. The claim is taken on behalf of the company, the purpose being to enforce its rights rather than the rights of the shareholder.

2 *A personal action*. The claim is to permit the shareholder to be compensated for losses arising from the damage caused to the company.

3 *A representative action*. One shareholder takes action on behalf of the other shareholders.

Remedies

The court may issue an injunction to prevent continuance of the improper behaviour. Damages may also be payable.

Statutory protection of minority rights

The Companies Act 1985 and other statutes provide some protection in a number of specific circumstances. These include the following:

1 a dissenting minority may ask the court to cancel an alteration to the memorandum provided that they hold at least 15 per cent of the nominal value of the issued share capital (s 5);

2 a minority of 50 shareholders, or those members holding at least 5 per cent of issued shares, may ask the court to cancel a change in the company's status from public to private company (s 54);

3   section 122 of the Insolvency Act 1986 permits any member to petition the court for the company to be wound up on the just and equitable ground. (This may be used to resolve deadlock between directors of a small quasi-partnership.)

However, the protection given under s 459 (below) is capable of application in a wide variety of situations.

The statutory right to petition the court on the grounds of unfair prejudice: s 459

The rights to sue given by the exceptions to the rule in *Foss* v *Harbottle* have often proved more illusory than real. The statutory right to petition has considerably undermined the effect of the rule in *Foss* v *Harbottle* and has extended the rights of a minority of shareholders. The concept of unfair prejudice is more flexible; it may exist even where the directors did not act intentionally or in bad faith.

In order to take action under s 459:

1   the petitioner must be a member of the company;

2   the petitioner must have evidence that the company's affairs have previously been or are currently being carried on in a way that is unfairly prejudicial to the interests of members;

3   it is enough to show that only the interests of the petitioner are being unfairly prejudiced as long as this affects the petitioner in his or her capacity as a company member, not in his or her personal capacity.

Whether or not unfairly prejudicial behaviour has actually occurred is a matter for the court to decide on the particular facts of each individual case.

Petitioners may succeed even though not entirely without spot or sin themselves; but the morality of their behaviour is relevant to judging whether they have been unfairly treated.

Petitions have most commonly been sought on the following grounds:

- exclusion of the petitioner from the management of a small private company where the members are also directors and it is easy to vote someone off the board;
- failure to lay accounts before members;
- reduction in voting power;
- insufficient information and advice about a proposed takeover bid.

Where a petitioner is successful, under s 461 the court may make any appropriate order. These include:

1   regulation of, or restrictions on, those eligible to manage the company;

2   an order requiring the company to purchase shares from a minority shareholder;

3   the amendment of the company's memorandum or articles, which can then be changed only with permission from the court.

Section 459 has been used successfully by minority shareholders of small private companies. It is less likely to be helpful to shareholders in large public companies who in practice are likely to remain largely powerless.

In 1998 the Law Commission issued a report entitled 'Shareholder Remedies' (Law Commission, No. 246) which recommends reform of the law to make proceedings under s 459 more accessible and affordable:

(a) proceedings should be simplified and the cost reduced by intensive case management. Alternative dispute resolution should be employed wherever possible (see Chapter 2 above);

(b) there should be a presumption of unfair prejudice against a private company limited by shares where the petitioner either has been removed from a directorship or substantially prevented from carrying out a director's duties. If the company is unable to rebut the presumption, the court should have the power to order a buy-out of the petitioner's shares on a pro-rata basis;

(c) petitioners should have the right to request that the company be wound up.

Shareholders' powers to initiate Department of Trade and Industry intervention

Where serious abuse of corporate powers is suspected, the shareholders may be able to instigate an inquiry by Department of Trade and Industry inspectors, and this may result in the company being wound up. The relevant statutory provisions are as follows:

1 under s 431, a minority of at least 200 shareholders, or those holding at least one-tenth of the issued shares, may apply to the Secretary of State for an investigation to be carried out;

2 under s 432, the Secretary of State may initiate an investigation in any circumstances suggesting that the company's members have not been kept appropriately informed (this section also empowers the Secretary of State to investigate where there is evidence of fraud, unlawful behaviour by the company or misfeasance or misconduct towards members);

3 under s 124A (Insolvency Act 1986), the Secretary of State may, if justified by the results of an investigation, petition for the company to be wound up on the grounds that it is just and equitable for this to happen.

Current minority rights are limited

You will now be aware of the great limitations on the rights of minority shareholders. If they are unhappy with the way the company is being run, the common law, despite exceptions to the rule in *Foss* v *Harbottle*, is unlikely to prove helpful. The statutory rules provide greater protection, but often only in extreme circumstances.

Dissatisfied shareholders in a public company will probably be best advised to sell their shares, unless the level of malpractice is such that the Secretary of State is prepared to intervene. Shareholders in private companies cannot generally freely dispose of their shares so this option is not open to them. They, however, are more likely to find that petitioning under s 459 on the grounds of unfair prejudice will provide a helpful outcome.

Proposed reform

In its White Paper 2002 (Modernising Company Law) the government proposes a consultation process to identify alternative dispute resolution procedures in order to avoid litigation between shareholders and companies. A cost-benefit study of arbitration schemes will be carried out.

CONCLUSION: THE FUTURE OF COMPANY LAW

In 1998 a Company Law Review was set up by the Department of Trade and Industry to investigate the means by which company law could be effectively and coherently reformed. It published its final proposals in 2001. The government White Paper of 2002 (Modernising Company Law) represents the 'first part' of the government's response to this review. The first volume contains a statement of government policy for the future of company law, accepting many of the review proposals. The second volume contains 225 draft clauses, forming only part of the final draft of the Companies Bill. The White Paper seeks comments from interested parties on many of the proposed reforms. Those directly relevant to the content of this book are referred to in the relevant chapters above.

The legislation resulting from this White Paper will give the Secretary of State powers to develop the law and update it in future by regulation, promoting comprehensive and coherent legislation, unlike the piecemeal and reactive reforms of the past. When in place it should also free UK company law from the overly elaborate regulation which has dominated it for over 150 years and which has been disproportionately restrictive and burdensome to private companies. Parliament is unlikely to start to process the new legislation before 2004, but when it is finally implemented the shape and content of company law should change radically.

Quiz 25

1 What is a general company meeting?

2 What are the principal differences between an annual general meeting and an extraordinary general meeting?

3 Titan is a director of Atlantis plc who has just celebrated his seventieth birthday. What procedures must be fulfilled if he is to continue to serve on the board?

4 Consider the rights of the following shareholders in Vulcan Ltd:

    (a) Brunhilde, who is unhappy about the company's decision to become a public company.

    (b) Siegfried, who has been voted off the board.

5 What is the difference between a derivative and a representative action by a shareholder?

Assignment 24

Explain the statutory and other means by which minority shareholders may be protected and discuss whether they are sufficient.

A suggested solution for this assignment can be found in the Lecturer's Guide.

CHAPTER 26

Statutory intellectual property protection: copyright, designs, patents and trade marks

INTRODUCTION

The law gives rights not only in relation to tangible property, i.e. goods capable of physical control like a car, but also in relation to the ownership of the intangible fruits of your labours arising from the use of mental as opposed to physical energy. This is called *intellectual property*.

Mental effort is obvious in the creation of a book, film, piece of music or a design of a 100 per cent efficient mousetrap. It is just as important in developing a successful business through original marketing strategy, or a novel way of packaging or labelling your goods. For your business to be successful you will have built up healthy goodwill and a good business reputation by your imagination and creativity. The law acknowledges ownership of such things and provides remedies for infringement of your ownership rights. Some infringements are criminal as well as civil offences.

Intellectual property, like any other property, may be disposed of by its owner through sale, will or gift. Licences may be granted to enable use of the property by someone other than the owner. The law of intellectual property seeks to ensure a balance between the owner's wish to control his or her business interests and the public interest in preventing monopolies and other non-competitive practices.

Intellectual property rights are protected by both statutory and common law rules. This chapter explains statutory intellectual property rights, including copyright, patents and registered trade marks. Owners are entitled to take legal action against infringement of their rights by third parties. Intellectual property rights are heavily influenced by EC law and international treaties.

STATUTORY REGULATION OF INTELLECTUAL PROPERTY

Copyright

Copyright is regulated by the Copyright, Designs and Patents Act 1988 (CDPA). The scope of copyright is very wide and includes (s 1):

- original literary, dramatic, musical and artistic works;
- sound recordings, films, TV and radio broadcasts and cable programmes;
- typographical arrangements of published works.

These terms have been defined in the Act or by the courts.

1 *Original: s 2.* This means 'not copied' rather than 'unique'. The issue of originality concerns the way an idea is expressed rather than the idea itself. It is also measured by the amount of independent work and effort which it required. A famous person may be the subject of a number of biographies. Information conveyed in the first biography does not become the exclusive property of the author and may well appear in subsequent works by different authors. The original author has rights to the 'copy' (the form of words or other form of expression used), not to the information which was conveyed. Commonly available knowledge may be 'original' because of its form of presentation. For example, in *McMillan & Co.* v *Cooper* (1923) a street directory was held to be original for copyright purposes.

2 *Literary: s 3.* This is not nearly as grand as it sounds and includes anything written, spoken or sung (other than a dramatic or musical work) if recorded in some tangible form. It covers tables, compilations, and computer programs and their preparatory designs. Writing of any sort, including letters, lists of customers,

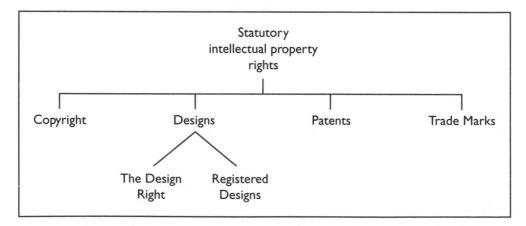

Figure 26.1 Classification of different types of intellectual property

reports and business plans may, therefore, attract copyright. To a limited extent copyright therefore protects privacy.

3 *Artistic: s 4*. Again the scope is wide. As well as covering works of 'artistic crafts-manship', like sculpture and paintings, textile patterns and clothing designs, it includes more prosaic items. Charts, maps, plans, graphs and diagrams are all protected. It also covers buildings and models for buildings.

To attract copyright the item must be more than a scheme or idea existing in the mind of the creator; it must be in a *tangible form* like a book, film, audio tape or a piece of writing, or a musical notation. If you tell somebody your scheme for a business plan or sing them your jingle before it is written down, they may possibly be liable for breach of confidence (see Chapter 27) if they steal your idea, but not for infringement of copyright.

Performers enjoy similar rights to copyright owners, in relation to their work under Part II of the Act. A bootleg recording at a pop concert would involve breach of copyright in the songs and breach of the performance rights of the members of the band.

Acquisition of copyright: ss 154–158

No formal process exists. Copyright is automatically acquired provided that the qualification criteria laid down in the CDPA 1988 are fulfilled.

A work will attract copyright if there is sufficient connection between it and the UK. It is sufficient that the author has British citizenship, or is domiciled or resident in the UK, or if the work is first published in the UK. Copyright also applies to works created or published in other countries to which the Act applies. This covers foreign states with whom Britain has reciprocal copyright links.

The duration of copyright: ss 12–15

How long the copyright period lasts depends on the type of work. Literary, dramatic, musical or artistic works enjoy copyright for 70 years from the end of the calendar year in which the author dies. Films are protected for 70 years from the end of the calendar year in which the last of the following die – director, writer, musical composer. Broadcasts and cable programmes enjoy copyright for 50 years from the first broadcast. Copyright in sound recordings lasts 50 years from the end of the calendar year in which they were released.

Crown copyright: s 163

The copyright in works created by civil servants and other Crown employees belongs to the Crown and lasts for up to 125 years.

The ownership of copyright: ss 9–11

The author (creator) of the relevant work is also generally the owner of the copyright. However, the copyright in any work created by an employee in the course of employment belongs to the employer. Course of employment is construed widely, and even relevant works created by employees in their spare time and without an express or implied order from the employer are likely to be treated as the employer's property, if relevant to the employee's job.

Copyright may be transferred in the same way as any other item of property. The owner may dispose of it by sale, gift or will. It may also be transferred by operation of law: if the owner becomes bankrupt, it will form part of the assets which may be sold towards satisfaction of the owner's creditors.

The rights of commissioners of photographs and films: s 85

This is relevant to anybody running a photography or video-making business. The photographer or film maker is owner of the copyright in the photograph or film, but the party who *commissioned* it has the right to prevent its publication without that party's consent. This only protects commissions for domestic use.

> **Williams v Settle** (1960)
> Wedding photographs commissioned by the claimant included pictures of her father. He was subsequently murdered and the defendant photographer sold copies of the photographs to the press. This was held to be a breach of the claimant's moral rights.

A person who is the subject of an unsolicited photograph (for example, by a street photographer) has no moral rights under the Act since the work was not commissioned.

The rights of the copyright owner

Copyright owners have exclusive rights to copy, adapt or present the work publicly.

Infringement of copyright

Any exercise of the owner's exclusive rights by a third party without lawful authority is a *direct infringement* (ss 17–21). It is irrelevant that it is being done for private use and that no profit is being made. Not surprisingly, thousands of such infringements take place every day as many people tape CDs or 'pirate' their friends' computer software. It is highly unlikely that any action will be taken against them. However, where copyright materials are being used in public places greater caution is required. For example, where a business uses background music to soothe (or irritate) its customers.

Secondary infringement (ss 22–26) occurs if the copyright is exploited commercially, and includes importation or sale of infringing items.

The CDPA 1988 provides some limited *defences* (ss 29–40). Where these apply, use of copyright material will not amount to an infringement. For example, making a copy for research or private study, limited use of quotations for the purpose of critical review or inclusion in a current affairs programme. Libraries and educational institutions also enjoy some limited protection.

Licensing

The copyright owner, or a collecting organisation like the Performing Rights Society, may grant permission to do something which would otherwise be an infringement. The licensee may be required to pay royalties for this privilege. A business wishing to use background music on disc or tape should apply to the Performing Rights Society for a licence.

If owners of copyright unreasonably refuse licences, they may be ordered compulsorily to grant them by the Secretary of State: for example, on the recommendation of the Monopolies and Mergers Commission (s 144) where the public interest is prejudiced.

Sanctions

Breach of copyright entitles the owner to take civil action (s 96). Some forms of secondary infringement (including those mentioned above) also give rise to criminal liability (s 107) provided the defendant should reasonably have known that copyright existed.

Rights in performances and recordings

A composer of a piece of music is protected by copyright as explained above. Part II of the CDPA and the Copyright and Related Rights Regulations 1996 similarly protect the rights of performers and recording companies. Bootleg audio or video recordings at, for example, a rock concert will therefore breach the performers' rights as well as those of a company legitimately recording the event. Breaches also arise from the illicit copying of existing recordings.

Copyright and Internet users

Everybody who accesses the Internet should be aware of the copyright implications. If you download or print off materials you find on a website, you may be infringing the copyright of the author, or the performance or recording rights of other people. If you are the proprietor of a website, you will have copyright in the design of the website and materials on it, provided that these are your own original work, but you may be infringing the rights of others if you reproduce their materials on your site without a licence. Internet service providers may also be infringing copyright if they are unable to show that they took reasonable steps to monitor the contents of the websites which they facilitate.

A European Community Directive (2001/29/EC) is due to be implemented in the UK by 31st March 2003. Its purpose is to harmonise the basic rights of authors of materials transmitted through e-commerce and the information society. Minor amendments to the CDPA and related legislation are being undertaken to fall in line with the Directive. The details of these legislative changes are outside the compass of this text.

Protection for design owners: the design right and registered designs

The design right (governed by Part III of the CDPA 1988) attaches *automatically* to any sufficiently *original* design, giving similar protection to copyright. An *aesthetically pleasing* and *inventive* design may also be registered under the Registered Designs Act 1949. The registered owner obtains a monopoly on the design similar to a patent.

The design right

The author of a design acquires copyright of that design, but that gives protection only against infringements of the copy (wrongful copying and publication). Ownership of the design right enables the owner to control the use of the design for manufacturing purposes. Nobody else may make items to that design without the owner's consent.

Designs for a huge variety of items are protected by this right. Some of these would also qualify for registration under the Registered Designs Act 1949 (see below) because of their attractive appearance and unique innovatory features. Others might qualify for copyright protection as works of artistic craftsmanship. Where these other rights exist the design owner will rely upon them rather than on the more limited design right. The majority of designers will be protected only by the design right.

The implicit intention of the Act is to ensure a limited protection for owners of sufficiently original designs for items capable of mass production. Such items are often functional, not necessarily visually attractive and include a multitude of items in everyday use. The limits to design right protection are intended to prevent undesirable restraint on industrial development. Some areas of industrial design are very fast moving, but would be frozen in a time warp if adaptations were an infringement of an existing design right. Also it is unfair to restrict other designers unreasonably in the exercise of their creative skill.

Section 213(2) of the CDPA 1988 defines 'design' as 'The design of any aspect of the shape or configuration (whether internal or external) of the whole or part of an article'. Only designs for *three-dimensional articles* are covered. Designs for surface decoration are not protected. The design *must be original*. Original is described as 'not commonplace' in the relevant design field at the time of creation (s 213(4)). This is interpreted much more stringently than the originality test for copyright, but the design need not be unique.

The right does not exist unless and until it has been recorded in a design document, or an article has been made to the design (s 213(6)). Like the law of copyright, it does not protect ideas. The design may be computer generated.

The person who creates the design is first owner provided that the design was not created in the course of employment or in carrying out a commission (s 215). If it was, the employer or commissioner will be first owner.

The right lasts for a maximum of 15 years from the end of the year when the design was created in tangible form. If goods made to the design are marketed within five years of the year of creation, however, the design right will last for only ten years from the marketing date (s 216).

The design right is acquired in the same way as copyright (ss 217–220). It is part of the owner's personal property and may be sold, given away, or disposed of by will or by operation of law (s 222). The owner has exclusive rights to exploit the design for commercial purposes, either by reproducing the design document or by making articles to the design (s 226).

The provisions of ss 226–227 concerning infringements mirror those explained above in relation to copyright. Infringement gives rise to civil liability only (s 229) and the remedies are the same as those of a copyright owner.

Licences may be granted by the owner to third parties enabling them to exercise any of the exclusive rights to exploit the design (s 222). During the last five years of the right, anybody is entitled to a licence (s 237). Licences may be compulsorily ordered if it is in the public interest to prevent unreasonable restriction of competition (s 238). The Crown may, without a licence, use the design to supply articles for the use of the defence and health services. Compensation for loss of profit may be paid (ss 240, 243).

Registered designs

Some designs may qualify to be registered under the Registered Designs Act 1949 (RDA) as amended by the Registered Designs Regulations 2001, Registered Designs (Amendment) Rules 2001 and the Registered Designs (Fees) Amendment Rules 2001. This amending legislation was necessary to implement the Designs Directive (98/71/EC) which aims to harmonise registration requirements across the EC, in order to eradicate differences which may adversely affect trade. This legislation, implemented in December 2001, has extended the scope of the right and made the process more flexible.

The rights arising from a registered design relate to the appearance of the product, its shape and any patterns or design on it. It is not concerned with its function, unlike a patent which is concerned with how a product works. In order to be registered the 'design' must relate to a 'product', which is 'new' and has 'individual character' as defined by the RDA, s1.

1 *Design*. This is the appearance of the whole or part of a product resulting from 'the lines, contours, colours, shape, texture or materials of the product or its ornamentation'. To be registered the design must therefore be visible to the user when the product is being used.

2 *Product*. This includes 'any industrial or handicraft item' except a computer program. It covers three-dimensional designs such as lamps, door furniture, water-filter jugs or one-dimensional designs such as patterns for wallpaper, floor covering, or clothing fabrics.

3 *New*. The design must differ materially from any existing 'publicly available' design. This is more generous to the designer than the old law, which required

'substantial' difference. 'Publicly available' means products being currently marketed as apposed to museum exhibits.

4 *Individual character*. The overall impression of the design on the user of the product must be different from that of any similar publicly available design. Under the old law 'eye appeal' was required which meant that the design had to be aesthetically pleasing. While this may be relevant to determining the existence of individual character it is no longer essential.

Designs for components of other products may be registered as long as they fulfil the above criteria.

Protection for spare parts remains very limited. The Directive proved very contentious on this issue and member states were unable to agree on its operation. This part of the Directive is suspended from operation currently, so the UK's existing law is retained. The design for a spare part must be for a product which is capable of standing alone. The product must not rely in its shape or configuration on another item. This is aimed at preventing unreasonable hindrance of development in the design field; it also prevents a designer of spare parts from acquiring a monopoly (*Ford Motor Co. Ltd and Iveco Fiat SpA's Design Application* (1993)). In that case, designs for car doors, bonnets, boot lids and windscreens were held to be excluded.

The person who created the design is generally the owner, unless acting in the course of employment or carrying out a commission when ownership lies with the employer or commissioner respectively (s 2). Only the owner can apply for registration. UK citizenship or resident status is not necessary. Applications are filed with the Designs Registry, a branch of the Patents Office. The procedure is complex so the owner of the design may use the services of a design agent to prepare the application.

The registrar will register the design if searches indicate that the design is new and the other statutory criteria are satisfied. Modifications may be required. Registration generally takes about six months. It must be completed within a maximum of 15 months from the time of application. A fee, currently £60, is payable for registration.

A design will initially be registered for five years, which runs from the date of registration. This may be renewed for up to five further five-year periods on application to the registrar with payment of further fees (s 8). Most designs become outdated within about six to ten years as fashions and technology change, making it unlikely that renewal applications will be made more than once.

The owner of a registered design has the *exclusive rights* of commercial exploitation of the design (s 7): this entitles the owner to manufacture, import, sell or hire items made to the design. Items made to the design should be appropriately marked with the number under which it is registered. This is a clear indication of registration. Failure to do so may provide an infringing party with the defence that they acted innocently without knowledge that the design was registered. These rights are infringed by anybody who exercises them without a licence granted by the owner. Civil proceedings may be taken by the owner.

The owner may issue *licences* to use the registered design. To protect unreasonable restrictions on the development and exploitation of designs, the registrar has powers to grant *compulsory licences* (s 10) if, having registered the design, the owner fails to exploit it. The registrar may also be ordered to issue licences on the recommendation of the Monopolies and Mergers Commission, where the owner is unduly restricting the issue of licences (s 11A).

The Crown is given rights to use the registered design under Sch 1 of the Act. These are similar to those concerning the design right (see pages 368–9 above).

It is a *criminal offence* to falsify the register (s 34) to register a design. Under s 35, it is also an offence to claim falsely that a design has been registered.

Patents

Patents are regulated by the Patents Act 1977. The registration of a patent enables an inventor to obtain a monopoly over its exploitation. The invention may be a *device* (for example, a mouse trap, an electric can opener, or a solar-powered heating system) or a *process* (for example, making glass or waterproofing fabrics). The possibilities are manifold.

The criteria for registration of a patent are stringently interpreted (ss 1–4):

1 *The invention must be new*. It must not currently form part of the state of the art in the UK or elsewhere (s 2). This means in effect that only the inventor and close associates must know of it and the information must clearly be confidential. Publication of information in, for example, a trade or academic journal anywhere in the world may put the invention into the public domain. Similarly, if the invention is already in use industrially its novelty is lost. Once an unpatented invention becomes part of the state of the art it enables other people to develop it; the public interest would not be well served by the grant of a patent, as this would put a stranglehold on technological development already initiated by others.

2 *It must be an inventive step*. This is defined as something which would be not 'obvious to a person skilled in the art'. It must involve originality of thought and represent a new development in the relevant industry. It may be something deceptively simple, but which solves a problem which has existed for some time. It might cause even a lay person to say 'Why didn't I think of that?'

> *Parks-Cramer Co. v Thornton Ltd* (1966, CA)
> An invention of an overhead vacuum cleaner with long vertical tubes reaching almost to the floor for cleaning narrow spaces between rows of fixed machinery, was held to be original. It solved a problem which had vexed the textile industry for many years.

3 *It must be capable of industrial application*. The invention or process must be capable of being produced or used under industrial conditions, which includes agriculture. Plant and animal varieties cannot be patented nor can biological

371

processes which could be used to produce plants or animals. Micro-biological processes and the products of these processes may be patented. This includes genetic engineering processes.

Some inventions will not be registered, for example those encouraging 'offensive, immoral or anti-social behaviour'. Current taste dictates what is appropriate here, but presumably ingenious instruments of torture or sex toys might be excluded.

Certain things are not 'inventions' for the purposes of the 1977 Act. These include some things like computer programs and literary works which are protected by copyright. Scientific discoveries and theories also do not qualify; they are not directly capable of industrial application.

The right to register a patent

The inventor is usually entitled to apply to patent the invention. This right is transferred to the employer, however, if the invention was created by an employee in the course of the employee's normal, or specially assigned, duties (s 39). Employers may try to protect themselves by putting a term in employment contracts claiming ownership of employees' inventions. This will not be applicable if an employee's duties do not involve potentially inventive activity.

Electrolux v Hudson (1977)
In their spare time at home, Mr and Mrs Hudson invented an adaptor which allowed any brand of vacuum cleaner using disposable bags to be used with any brand of vacuum bags. Mr Hudson worked as a storekeeper for Electrolux, but it was held that the invention belonged to him and to Mrs Hudson. The nature of his job did not cover such creative activity.

The inventor is entitled to be named in a patent application being made in some other person's name (usually an employer) (s 13).

If the invention is of 'outstanding benefit' to the employer, the employee is entitled to be compensated by them (s 40). The Comptroller of Patents or the court may order compensation if the employer does not voluntarily provide it.

The registration process: ss 14–19

This is a lengthy and highly complex business. A patent agent is usually employed. The different stages of the process have to be completed within certain time limits. Unless these are adhered to and the necessary fees paid, the application will be rejected. Here is an overview of the process, which concentrates on key features:

1 *The application.* An application for a patent must be made to the Patent Office in the required form and must include a full description of the invention. This must convey sufficient information to enable a reasonably skilled person in the rele-

vant field to make the item or to carry out the process. It will involve lengthy written instructions and any necessary drawings. The inventor must indicate the specific purposes which the invention is intended to fulfil. The claim must not be too wide or it will be rejected, or at least require amendment. Some devices and processes have a very wide field of potential application, but the patent when granted may not necessarily cover them all. Some uses may not even exist yet as a twinkle in a technologist's eye, and it is not in the public interest to allow an inventor to monopolise their development.

2 *Search and publication.* Once the application has been received, initial checks and searches are carried out and the Patent Office publishes the application in its journal. This has two consequences:

(a) the published invention is now part of the state of the art; subsequent applications for a similar patent may fail the novelty test. If the application fails it cannot be re-submitted;

(b) on registration the applicant will be entitled to take action for any infringements occurring after the publication date.

3 *Substantial examination and registration.* Full examination of the specification and claim now takes place. Final checks are made against searches and any other information received since the publication date. Further amendments may be required. Provided the invention still meets the registration criteria, the patent will be granted. Notice of this appears in the *Patents Journal*.

Duration of patents

Patent rights exist for up to 20 years. Renewal fees are payable.

Ownership rights

A patent is the personal property of the owner and can be disposed of by operation of law or in any way the owner chooses, for example sale or will. It can also be security for a mortgage (s 30).

Infringement

Protection under the 1977 Act is very wide: a large number of activities carried on without the consent of the patent owner are actionable. Infringements include the manufacture of patented products and the use of patented processes; they also arise from import into the UK of such products manufactured in breach of a patent (s 60). The owner of the patent may take civil action against infringement.

Defences to infringement include non-commercial use of products or processes and scientific investigations for the purpose of testing them.

Licensing

The owners of patents can grant licences to whoever they choose. The owner may request that the Patent Office indicates in the register that licences are available as of right (s 46), which could be a useful move if the owner has not been successful in marketing licences privately.

After three years the Patent Office may grant licences either if the patent is not being worked, or if demands for relevant products are not being met (s 48). Wide Crown exploitation of certain patents by government departments is permitted (s 55), in connection with defence, health and nuclear energy policies.

Criminal liability

Under ss 109–113, offences include falsification of the register and false claims that a patent exists or has been applied for.

Trade marks

The purpose of trade marks

Trade marks are used as a marketing strategy to enable providers of goods or services to ensure that their products are immediately clearly recognisable by their potential customers. A competitor who markets a similar product in a similar way may be breaking the law. If the distinguishing feature has been registered as a trade mark under the Trade Marks Act 1994, the competitor may be sued for infringement. Registration creates rights of ownership in the mark which can then be disposed of as any other personal property.

Not all distinguishing characteristics are registrable, but the tort of passing off may provide a remedy for the misuse of unregistered marks and other distinguishing features. Passing off is covered in the next chapter.

The law relating to trade marks has recently been updated and expanded by the Trade Marks Act 1994, which replaces the 1938 Act. The 1994 Act implements an EC Directive aimed at harmonisation of trade mark law throughout the European Union.

The marks capable of registration

Section 1 of the Act defines a trade mark as any sign capable of being represented graphically which is capable of distinguishing the goods or services of one undertaking from another. 'Represented graphically' means capable of being represented in the form of pictures, words or numbers. This has greatly extended the scope of trade mark law. As well as designs, letters and numerals (which were all covered previously) it will now be possible to register shapes of goods or their packaging (like the Coca-Cola bottle). Moving images clearly come within this definition, as do musical jingles (like Direct Line Insurance), and even perfumes since these can be graphically represented by their notation or chemical formulae, respectively.

A mark must be distinctive. It may be verbal or non-verbal in form. *Verbal* marks include the following:

1 *Names of people.* Names can be trademarked but will have to be represented in some way that makes them distinctive and immediately recognisable as that of one trader alone. This can be achieved by a signature (Walt Disney), or by a very

distinctive style of lettering (McDonald's, Marks & Spencer). A business may prefer to trade under a made-up name (Kwikfit) to ensure a distinctive character.

2 *Names of products*. To prevent other businesses from being unreasonably restricted in the advertisement of their products, names will not be treated as distinctive if they relate to the character, quality, geographical origin, intended use or any other characteristics of the product. 'Wholemeal Flour' or 'Best Butter' could not be registered, but 'Floss Mill' and 'March Hare' would not offend. Invented words may well be distinctive for registration purposes: in themselves they convey no clear and ordinary meaning to the average person. Snickers and Hovis, for example, without their associations with chocolate bars and bread, are completely meaningless. In this way monopolisation of the use of ordinary words is avoided.

Non-verbal marks include emblems, symbols and other pictorial representations, as well as combinations of letters or numbers. This enables eau de cologne to be marketed under the 4711 trade mark. Advertising jingles come within the definition, which also embraces distinctively shaped goods or packaging, for example Jif lemons, Coca-Cola bottles.

A mark will not be registered if it is insufficiently distinctive, against the public interest or public morality, or identical or too similar to an earlier trade mark.

1 *Insufficiently distinctive*. As determined by the above rules:

Phillips Electronics NV v Remington Consumer Products (1998)
A drawing of one of the heads of a three-headed electric razor was held not to be sufficiently distinctive. It did not sufficiently identify the manufacturer but merely referred to the function of the goods.

A trade mark must, therefore, be sufficiently distinctive to enable the public clearly to identify the origin of product and not confuse it with others.

Interlego AG's Trademark Application (1998)
The applicant wanted to use a Lego brick shape as the trade mark for Lego toys. The application failed on the ground that members of the public identified Lego toys by the name of the manufacturer rather than by the shape of a constituent part of the toys.

2 *Against the public interest or morally offensive (s 3)*. These criteria are interpreted in the light of current taste and attitudes. 'Hookers' or 'Hustlers' condoms might prove problematic. Would Robinson's golliwog be registered today?

3 *Identical or too similar (s 5)*. Marks which are identical or very similar to an earlier trade mark and applied to the same or similar goods or services:

Berlei (UK) Ltd v Bali Brassiere Co. (1969)
Both parties manufactured brassieres and corsets. Berlei successfully claimed that
the use of the name Bali would lead to confusion with their product.

Some emblems enjoy special protection. These can be used as a trade mark only
with permission from the registrar (s 4). They include royal coats of arms, pictorial
representations of members of the royal family, and any of the flags of the UK. The
use of any device or words suggesting that the product has been patronised or
authorised by royalty is similarly protected.

The registration process

The applicant for registration must own the mark. There is no nationality or resi-
dence qualification. Application is made to the Trade Mark Registry. It must include
a representation of the mark and state the product to which it may apply. A fee is
payable (s 32). The registrar decides whether the mark is sufficiently distinctive and
carries out any necessary searches (s 37). If the application is acceptable, the registrar must publish notice of the application to enable interested parties to raise
objections (s 38). Provided no objections are sustained, the registrar will on payment
of a fee register the trade mark (s 40), for use in relation to a particular class of goods
or services.

Duration of protection

Registration lasts ten years and renewal is possible every ten years.

Infringements: s 10

These may be committed only in the course of trade. They may arise from the
wrongful application of an identical or similar mark in connection with identical or
similar goods for which use of the mark is registered.

'Application' of the mark includes not only putting it on the product or its packing, but also offering products for sale under the sign, or using it on business papers
or in advertising. Therefore, many people in the marketing process other than the
manufacturer of goods or the provider of a service may commit an infringement.

Using the mark merely to identify the relevant goods in accordance with honest
commercial or industrial practice is not an infringement. Provided that your business is selling or servicing a particular product, it is perfectly legal to use the name
on your own advertising materials. Thus, Comet Warehouses legally advertise that
they stock Hotpoint and Hoover washing machines.

Licensing the use of trade marks

Only the owner may grant licences for use of the mark by others (s 29). The licence
may impose restrictions on the range of products to which the mark may be applied,
or the manner of its use, or the locality within which the licence may be exercised.

Assigning the right to use a trade mark

Like all other intellectual property, a trade mark is part of the proprietor's personal property. It is transferable by assignment (in writing), by will or by operation of law.

Remedies for infringement of statutory intellectual property rights

These are largely similar whichever type of intellectual property is involved.

Injunction

An injunction may be granted to prevent the commission or continuance of the infringement.

Damages

Damages may be awarded to compensate for consequential losses to the proprietor.

Account of profits

Any profit on the sale of relevant goods may be forfeit. This prevents the defendant from retaining any financial gain resulting from the illegal behaviour.

Seizure, delivery up or destruction orders

These remedies are relevant to infringement where goods have been manufactured or marked in breach of patent or trade mark rights.

THE IMPACT OF EC LAW AND INTERNATIONAL TREATIES ON INTELLECTUAL PROPERTY RIGHTS

Intellectual property rights have considerable implications in relation to international trade. Consequently, their operation and development have been considerably influenced by EC law. A number of internationally-binding treaties to which the UK is signatory are also important.

The EU context: conflict with English law

EC law takes precedence over English law in the event of conflicting rights (see Chapter 3). The Treaty of Rome imposes obligations to promote free trade within the Community. Thus, free movement of goods must be encouraged, restrictive trade practices are prohibited and a dominant trading position must not be abused. Discrimination against nationals of other member states is also prohibited. It is easy to see that the exercise of some rights like licensing could be a breach of the treaty; the European Court of Justice has had to decide on issues like this in a number of cases.

	Copyright	Design right	Registered design	Patents	Trade marks
Statute	Copyright, Designs and Patents Act 1988, Parts I & II	Copyright, Designs and Patents Act 1988, Part III	Registered Designs Act 1949 (as amended 2001)	Patents Act 1977	Trade Marks Act 1994
Scope	Original, literary, dramatic and artistic works	Original design for 3D functional items	New design for any industrial or handicraft item, includes shape, pattern and ornamentation	New thing/process, inventive step, industrial application	Distinctive identifying symbol for goods or services
Acquisition	By owner on creation, no formalities	By owner on creation, no formalities	Registration: Design Registry	Registration: Patents Office	Registration: Trade Mark Registry
Duration	Max: 70 years from author's death	Max: 15 years (5-year renewal)	Max: 25 years (5-year renewal)	Max: 20 years	Renewable indefinitely (10-year renewal)
Property rights	Personal property: transferable by assignment, will, intestacy, operation of law				
Licensing	Voluntary, compulsory, Crown	Voluntary, compulsory, Crown	Voluntary, compulsory Crown	Voluntary, compulsory, Crown	Voluntary only

Figure 26.2 Types of intellectual property and protection

In addition to the UK's treaty obligations, any relevant Directives must be complied with. For example, the Trade Marks Act 1994 implements a Directive aimed at harmonising this area of law throughout the Community; it has greatly widened the scope of trade mark protection in this country.

A number of recent changes to copyright law have been the result of EC Directives. The length of copyright was extended to its current limits in 1995 in compliance with EC law. Additional rights to protect copyright in databases were also added in response to EU requirements by the Copyright and Rights in Databases Regulations 1997.

Currently under the European Patent Convention the proprietor may register a patent with effect in any member state specified in the application. The EU also proposes to develop a Community patent. A consultation process began in 1997. A unitary system is planned which would grant to successful applicants a patent effective in all member states.

The wider international context

The UK is signatory to a number of treaties with a large number of other countries, both in and outside the EU. These treaties give reciprocal rights to protection of intellectual property in signatory states. For example, through the Berne Convention and the Universal Copyright Convention, UK citizens and residents enjoy copyright protection of their work in any of the signatory states. Almost all countries are signatory to one or other of these. The Patent Co-operation Treaty enables patent holders from the UK to apply for registration in any signatory country.

The European Patent Convention enables UK residents with clearance from the UK Patent Office to apply to register their patents in any of the signatory states named in their application. An application may be filed directly with the European Patent Office or through the Patent Office in London.

International registration of trade marks was possible from 1995 for members of states which are signatories to the Madrid Protocol.

Quiz 26

1 Advise Pipit whether she has copyright in the following work:

(a) a piece of music which she has composed;

(b) an idea for a short story which she and Bunting discussed in the pub and which Bunting has now written;

(c) a flow chart which she produced at work and which is now being used by her employers in publicity leaflets;

(d) a booklet of mathematical tables.

2 Heron has designed a series of figurines representing different types of fish. He would like to know his legal rights over this design.

3 Puffin, who works for Fulmar Fish Foods, has designed a new fish-smoking process.

    (a) What criteria will the process have to satisfy if it is to be patented?

    (b) Who will own the patent?

4 (a) Nuthatch Products advertise a peanut spread with a musical jingle.

    (b) Bullfinch plc market fruit pies which they call 'Yummies'. Jackdaw plc has registered its trade mark 'Yum-Yums' under which it markets lollipops.

    (c) Merlin Ltd want to market a game pie called 'Queens Favourite'. The wrapper bears a picture of Windsor Castle.

Will these parties be allowed to register their trade marks?

Assignment 25

Explain briefly what types of works are entitled to copyright protection under the Copyright, Designs and Patents Act 1988. In what ways may copyright be infringed and what rights are accorded to copyright holders?

(ICSA English Business Law: June 1994)

A suggested solution for this assignment can be found in the Lecturer's Guide.

CHAPTER 27

Common law protection of intellectual property: passing off, malicious falsehood and breach of confidence

INTRODUCTION

Intellectual property rights at common law arise informally; they relate to interests more diffuse than those covered by statute, like confidentiality, business reputation and goodwill. Where such rights are infringed, action under one or more of three distinct torts may be possible. These are:

1 passing off;

2 malicious falsehood;

3 breach of confidence.

PASSING OFF

This tort protects the goodwill and reputation of a business. It is committed where the defendant falsely attributes to their product some distinctive feature (for example, packaging, logo, definitive or distinctively presented name) which is likely to persuade members of the public that it is associated with the claimant's business.

The tort may be committed in a number of different ways:

1 *The defendant presents its goods or services in a similar, distinctive get-up to that used by the claimant for a similar product.*

White Hudson & Co. Ltd v Asian Organisation Ltd (1964, PC)
The claimants had for five years marketed their cough sweets in distinctive red cellophane wrapping labelled 'Hacks', and people buying them often asked for 'red paper cough sweets'. The defendants were held liable for passing off their cough sweets as the claimants' when selling their product in similar wrapping paper labelled 'Pecto'.

2 *The defendant uses a false description imputing a definitive characteristic of the claimant's product to its own.*

Erven Warnink BV v Townend & Sons (Hull) Ltd (1979)
The defendants marketed a drink made of eggs and sherry under the name of 'Keelings Old English Advocaat'; this competed very favourably with the more expensive 'Warninks Advocaat' which carried a heavier excise tax as it was made of brandy and eggs. It was held that the defendants were liable for passing off what should properly have been described as egg flip as advocaat. Advocaat proper was recognised by the public as an entirely distinct drink because of its spirit base.

3 *The defendant claims the claimant's work as its own.*

Bristol Conservatories Ltd v Conservatories Custom Built Ltd (1989)
The defendants were held to have acted illegally when they showed prospective customers photographs of conservatories constructed by the claimants, as evidence of their own work.

4 *The defendant falsely suggests that the claimant vouches for the defendant's work.*

Associated Newspaper Holdings v Insert Media Ltd (1991)
It was held that the insertion of an advertising leaflet between the pages of a newspaper would be likely to make readers believe that the newspaper approved of the products advertised.

To succeed in an action the claimant must prove the following:

1 *The defendant made a false statement*. The statement must be untrue, but the defendant need not have known this. The motive of the defendant is irrelevant. The statement may be express or implied.

2 *The statement was made in the course of trade*. 'Trade' has been defined widely by the courts and includes non profit-making organisations.

3 *The statement must be published to the claimant's customers*. The law of passing off exists to protect the goodwill of the claimant. The claimant must, therefore, currently be engaged in running an established business with the same catchment area as the defendant. Where a business organisation enjoys only very local goodwill, the use of a similar marketing technique 200 miles away will not be seen as illegal. However, the court may take into account likely geographical expansion.

4 *Damage to the claimant's business must be reasonably foreseeable.* The claimant does not have to prove that the defendant intended to cause damage. Where the public is not reasonably likely to connect the claimant's business with the defendant's activity, no liability exists.

Granada Group Ltd v Ford Motor Co. Ltd (1973)
Ford Motors could not legally be restrained from marketing a car under the name 'Granada'. The claimant and defendant were not engaged in a similar field of business activity; therefore it was unlikely that the public would be confused about the origin of the car and associate it with the TV company.

Compare:

NAD Electronics v NAD Computer Systems (1997)
The public might well be confused by the use of the name NAD by these two companies. The claimant manufactured high quality hi-fi equipment while the defendants were computer manufacturers. There were, therefore, similarities in their respective products since many computer systems include CD players and loudspeakers. Their products were also likely to be sold alongside each other in the same retail outlets.

5 *Damage or sufficient probability of damage must result.* Any of the following may evidence actionable damage:

(a) loss of sales to the defendant because customers believe the product to be manufactured by the claimant;

(b) loss of business reputation: the defendant's goods are inferior and people are likely to associate them with the claimant;

(c) the unique character of the claimant's product is being eroded or its status diminished by the defendant's conduct.

Taittinger SA v Allbev Ltd (1993, CA)
The Court of Appeal held that EC law's limitation of the name 'Champagne' to wines produced in the Champagne area of France gave the name a distinctive character. The defendant, by selling a soft drink described as 'Elderflower Champagne', was marketing its product in a way which would inevitably lead to an erosion of the distinctiveness of the name 'Champagne'.

Note the relationship of registered trade mark protection to passing-off actions.

If a product is marketed under a registered trade mark, the proprietor who alleges infringement merely has to prove that:

1 the mark is registered in relation to a relevant product; and

2 the conduct of the defendant amounts to an infringement within the definition of the Trade Marks Act 1994.

The mark is protected immediately on registration, even if as yet the product has not been marketed. It may therefore be easier to assert your rights under a registered trade mark than to commence a passing-off action. However, an action in passing off may be brought where the relevant product does not have the protection of a registered trade mark. Not all products are sufficiently distinctively marketed to qualify for registration. A passing-off action may arise from conduct which does not amount to an infringement of a trade mark.

Passing off on the Internet

If you have a website you may obtain exclusive use of this *domain* by registering its address (for example: lawtutorsonline.co.uk) through your Internet service provider. However, if it bears a close resemblance to the name of another business, which has not sought registration and which the public might confuse with yours, you may be liable in passing off.

Marks & Spencer plc v One in a Million Ltd (1998)
The defendant registered the domain name, marks&spencer.co.uk, and then offered to sell it to the claimant. This was held to be a threat to pass off by the defendants. The claimant obtained an injunction which required the defendant to transfer the domain name to the claimant.

MALICIOUS FALSEHOOD

Like passing off, this tort protects a claimant against false statements damaging to the goodwill and reputation of its business. The claimant must prove the following:

1 *A false statement published by the defendant relating to the claimant's business.* The statement must be untrue and likely to cause damage to the claimant's business. It may consist of an express attack on the claimant's business reputation, but an untrue statement of an apparently innocent kind may give rise to liability.

Ratcliffe v Evans (1892)
The defendant untruthfully stated in a local newspaper that the claimant had ceased to trade from a particular address. He knew this was untrue, but wished to get the claimant to abandon his business premises. Liability existed here since the statement was likely to deprive the claimant of customers.

Conduct may amount to a statement.

Wilts United Dairies Ltd v Thomas Robinson & Sons Ltd (1958)
Condensed milk manufactured by the claimant was bought and stockpiled by the government during the war. Long past its sell-by date (and in an inferior condition) it was sold to the defendant on the condition that it was to be used only as animal feed. The defendant sold it for human consumption. It was held that the inferior quality of the milk sold suggested that this was the normal standard of the claimant's product and, therefore, the defendant was liable in malicious falsehood.

2 *Damage must be reasonably foreseeable.* It must be reasonably likely that potential customers will be influenced. Comparative advertising, where the defendant merely puffs its goods by claiming that they are superior to those of the claimant, is unlikely to give rise to liability.

White v Mellin (1895)
It was held that no liability existed where the defendant attached labels to the claimant's product claiming that his own was superior.

The defendant will be liable if it has infringed normal business practice.

De Beers Products Ltd v International General Electrics (1975)
Apparently weighty statements about the accuracy of the claimant's instruments, backed up with reference to plausible, but actually specious scientific data, amounted to malicious falsehood.

3 *The statement must be made maliciously.* The defendant must have made the statement either knowing it to be false or not caring whether it was true or false, or believing it to be true but publishing it because motivated by the intention to cause the claimant damage. An untrue statement made in good faith will not give rise to liability.

4 *The claimant must suffer damage as a result.* Proof of a general drop in custom will be sufficient.

Note the relationship of malicious falsehood and passing off:

1 *Dual liability may exist.* Where passing off involves the sale of inferior goods, this is also an implicit assertion that the claimant produces goods of poor quality; this may also be malicious falsehood.

2 *Both parties to a passing-off action must be in competition*. A passing-off action is limited to situations where both parties are engaged in competing businesses. Malicious falsehood can be pursued against any defendant who attacks another party's business reputation.

If the claimant has a choice it is easier to succeed in a passing-off action. It is hard to prove the malice and falsity crucial to success in malicious falsehood.

BREACH OF CONFIDENCE

This area of the law gives limited protection to privacy in private and business life. If one party confides information to another, a legal duty may be created not to reveal that information to anyone else. Liability for breach of confidence will exist where the following criteria are satisfied:

1 the claimant expressly or implicitly reveals confidential information to another person;

2 a relationship of trust already exists between the parties or is created as a result. It will be apparent from the circumstances that this information is private and that the confidant is being relied upon to keep it confidential;

3 the confidant makes use of the information or passes it on to a third party;

4 as a result the claimant suffers damage.

What information is confidential?

It is very difficult to define what information will be treated as confidential: it is a question of fact in every case and is judged objectively by the courts. Personal information may enjoy protection.

> **Stephens v Averay** (1988)
> The claimant, Mrs S, confided in the defendant, Mrs A, details of her previous sexual relationship with Mrs T. This information was newsworthy because Mrs T had recently been murdered by her husband; Mrs A leaked the story to a newspaper. It was held that she was liable in breach of confidence.

In the context of business, confidential information includes trade secrets which do not enjoy statutory protection; for example, plans for an invention or industrial processes peculiar to the claimant's business. It may cover ideas and information not yet protected by copyright. It could also include information forming the subject of a competitive tender prior to its submission; leakage of such information could cause the claimant to lose the contract. For example, in *PSM International* v *Whitehouse &*

Willenhall Ltd (1992), drawings, price quotations, and business plans were treated as confidential; but not all information which the claimant might wish to keep private is necessarily treated by the courts as confidential.

> **Faccenda Chicken v Fowler** (1986)
> Lists of the claimant's customers' names and details of van rounds used by the defendant (an ex-employee of the claimant) to assist him to set up a competing business were not held to be confidential information.

Equitable principles are very influential here; the moral justification for secrecy or revelation and the issue of public interest will be relevant. However, even information which would have been treated as confidential ceases to be so once it enters the public domain.

> **Attorney-General v Guardian Newspapers (No. 2)** (1990)
> (The *Spy Catcher* case.) Memoirs of an ex-secret service officer were published in breach of a confidence clause in his contract of employment. The information would have been regarded in law as confidential because of its national security implications. *The Guardian*, by publishing details from the book, were not liable for breach as the book had been widely published and commented on in the media abroad and, therefore, a duty of confidentiality no longer existed.

When does a duty of confidence arise?

This will be determined by reference to the nature of any relationship or legal obligation already existing between the parties. Such a relationship is capable of arising as a result of an informal request, or by operation of law or a contract term.

Informally

An informal duty of confidence exists between friends, family members or business colleagues, employer and ex-employee. The confidant may be told of the need for discretion, or this will be obvious given the nature of the information and any other attendant circumstances.

Operation of law

Usually for a duty of confidence to arise by operation of law the relationship of the parties will be one where the law treats the relationship as a fiduciary one between the parties, for example solicitor and client and doctor and patient. In such relationships there is an automatic duty of confidence. The fiduciary relationship exists regardless of whether or not the parties are joined by a contract. A National Health Service doctor or a solicitor acting under the Legal Aid scheme is in a fiduciary relationship with the patient or client.

However, the courts have recently indicated that a fiduciary relationship is not essential. This has widened the scope of the tort of breach of confidence, giving greater rights of privacy to claimants who in the past would not have been able to sue. In *A-G v Guardian Newspapers* (1990, HL), Lord Keith held that 'breach of confidence involves no more than an invasion of privacy ... the right of privacy is one which the law should in this field seek to protect'. Potentially this enables claims by any person whose private life is exposed by a third party who passes on information about them without their consent.

Douglas and OK Magazine v Hello Magazine Ltd (2001, CA)
Michael Douglas and Catherine Zeta-Jones sold the exclusive rights to publish pictures of their wedding to *OK* magazine. *Hello* gate-crashed the wedding and obtained photographs. The Court of Appeal held that breach of confidence had occurred and awarded limited compensation. However, it refused to issue an injunction to prevent *Hello* from using the photographs, as it held that by selling the rights to *OK* the happy couple had shown that they were prepared to give up the full degree of privacy usual to a private event.

Every case ultimately turns on its facts and not every breach of confidential information is actionable, however embarrassing the revelations may be for the claimant.

A v B sub nom Garry Flitcroft v Mirror Group Newspapers Ltd (2002, CA)
A professional footballer who had had a one-night stand tried to obtain an injuction to prevent a report from the woman concerned being published in the press. His application was refused.

The CA stated that a transient sexual relationship may not be treated as confidential by the courts, if it involves an element of public interest and a party to such a relationship other than the claimant does not want it to remain confidential.

The court stressed that a technical approach to the law was not required in such cases. 'A balancing of all the interests involved and the particular facts' was needed.

Contract

In a business context it is very common for a confidence clause to be an express term of any consultancy contract, and in some other contracts for the provision of services where access to confidential information is involved. Such a term might also be implied in a contract of service as part of the duties of good faith and trust and confidence (see Chapter 18). This obliges both employer and employee not to reveal confidential information about each other to outsiders. A specific confidentiality clause is effective only if it does not unreasonably restrain trade (see Chapter 8).

What sort of damage is actionable?

A claimant will have to prove that the breach of confidence operated to the claimant's detriment. Economic loss may have been suffered, but the courts also acknowledge loss of privacy and attendant distress.

The public interest defence

If a defendant can show that there was a duty to reveal the confidential information because this was in the public interest, liability will be avoided.

W v *Edgell* (1990)
A doctor informed the Mental Health Review Tribunal about his patient's psychopathic tendencies. He was held not liable for breaching doctor–patient confidentiality: his action was in the interest of public safety.

The impact of the Human Rights Act 1998

Article 8 of the ECHR gives the right to respect for privacy and family life, so an action under the HRA may be taken to enforce this right, providing an alternative to a breach of confidence action, if the defendant is a public authority. ECHR rights are not absolute. Article 8 states that interference by a public authority with the privacy of the individual may be justified so far as necessary 'in a democratic society to ensure national security, public safety or the economic well-being of the country, for the prevention of crime, the protection of health and morals or for the protection of the rights and freedom of others'. The court must therefore balance the rights of the claimant against the right to freedom of expression of the defendant and the public interest in receiving the information.

The court as a public authority is bound by the ECHR. This means that in every case, not just those brought under the Human Rights Act, it has a duty to ensure a fair trial under Article 8 and have regard to the ECHR where relevant to the issues raised by the facts of the case. This is always likely to impact on cases involving breach of confidence (see *A* v *B sub nom Garry Flitcroft* v *Mirror Group Newspapers Ltd* (2002) above).

REMEDIES FOR PASSING OFF, MALICIOUS FALSEHOOD

AND BREACH OF CONFIDENCE

The following remedies are available for each of the three torts:

1 *Injunction.* To prevent publication and/or require the defendant to hand over relevant goods or documentation.

2 *Damages.* To compensate the claimant for loss and damage.

3 *Account of profits.* The defendant may be required to hand over the fruits of his or her wrongdoing.

The court may award any of the above remedies. The health club proprietor who passed on to the press pictures which he had illicitly obtained of the Princess of Wales using club facilities was alleged to have acted in breach of confidence. He and the relevant newspaper settled out of court; they had to hand over the photographs and negatives, as well as paying a very substantial sum in damages.

Quiz 27

I What torts may have been committed in the following situations?

 (a) Rockall told Dogger, a fellow inventor, of his plans to develop a voice-activated tin opener. Dogger has now patented the item.

 (b) Wight, a professional photographer, discovers that Lundy has been using samples of Wight's work to help him obtain photographic commissions.

 (c) Fairisle, an opera singer, discovers that Plymouth, a professional rival, told Bight that Fairisle was temperamental, unreliable and given to cancelling engagements at the last minute.

2 What must a claimant prove in a claim for breach of confidence?

3 What remedies are available to a victim of malicious falsehood?

4 Why may a party seek to register a trade mark rather than rely on the common law protection of a passing-off claim?

Assignment 26

Throughout the 1990s your company, Natural Juice plc, has been manufacturing and marketing pure fruit juice in distinctively shaped containers which closely resemble the relevant fruits, for example oranges and grapefruit. At a recent meeting the advertising director has expressed concern that rival companies may start to package and market their drinks in a similar way. He fears that this may confuse the public and affect sales. He wishes to know whether the law provides the means of protection against this potential threat to company sales.

Advise the advertising director.

(ICSA English Business Law: December 1993)

CHAPTER 28

Study skills, and revision and examination hints

INTRODUCTION

This chapter, which aims to help you to acquire the skills essential to successful study, is divided into three sections:

1 beginning to study;

2 writing law assignments;

3 revision and examination technique.

BEGINNING TO STUDY

Time management

It is important that you set aside a realistic amount of time each week for your private study, as this is an essential supplement to the tuition which you receive. Attending a lecture is the first step towards understanding a topic, but you must personally reinforce this initial learning in you own time.

Make yourself a study timetable with realistic goals. Short bursts spread across the week may be more appropriate than aiming to study in lengthy blocks, particularly in the early stages of your course.

Note-taking

Your notes are an essential lifeline. It is probably best not to take lecture notes 'in rough'. Your good intentions to write them up later may not be fulfilled. Use a loose-leaf folder and write on one side of the paper only. That enables you to add notes later on when you read the textbook.

When taking notes, summarise what you hear or read in your own words and use plenty of side headings. Do not take unnecessary notes. If your tutor provides lecture outlines you may not need to write many lecture notes.

Reading

It is very important that you always read the relevant section of the textbook, as well as any other materials provided by your tutor, as soon as possible after each lecture. At first you may find this heavy going, but if you persevere it does get easier. Do not worry about understanding every word. If you get bogged down at the beginning of the course do not struggle endlessly with the early topics. Keep up with the reading relevant to your lectures and light will dawn.

While you need to read your chosen textbook thoroughly, it is always useful to consult other texts (see Appendix 1). Make good use of the index or contents section of an additional text to find the bits you need. Do not be afraid to skim.

WRITING LAW ASSIGNMENTS

Assignments may take two forms:

1 *Problem or 'situation based' assignments.* These involve a scenario to which you are expected to apply principles of law and draw reasoned conclusions.

2 *Discursive assignments*: essays and reports.

Very different types of answers are demanded by these two methods of testing your knowledge and abilities.

Answering problem questions

A good answer to such a question will require the following:

1 a clear explanation of the relevant points of law;

2 an analysis of the given facts in the light of the relevant law, indicating the likely outcome.

Sometimes the facts will be deliberately vague to encourage you to indicate that a decision could go either way. It is crucial that you give reasons to support your conclusion. It is not good enough to write at length about the legal principles, which are generally raised by the problem, and follow that with an assertion that X or Y will win. Giving clearly analysed reasons why you are making such an assertion is what earns you marks. Here are some tips to help you.

1 *Read the problem thoroughly and think about what is involved.* This is crucial to spotting the relevant legal areas and to your grasp of the relationship of the parties and their names. Underline the 'triggers', the points of fact in the story which indicate the points of law to be explained. Refer to your books and notes to make sure that you understand these points of law.

2 *Briefly jot down the relevant points of law that relate to the behaviour of the parties.* If the facts of the problem are complicated, representing the relationship of the parties in diagram form may assist.

3 *Now write your answer in full*. It is a good idea to have a brief opening paragraph giving an overview of the problem faced by the parties and indicating how the law affects this. Next, proceed to the first 'trigger': stick to the point of law which it raises. Do not write about the law at large. If the examiner expressly tells you the legal situation on a particular point, this does not need to be debated. For example, if a contract question specifically states that a price has been stipulated, you do not need to discuss the existence of consideration. Link each point of law to the relevant trigger and explain its implications. There is no need to worry about the evidence which would have to be proved in real life. For instance, if postal contractual acceptance is involved, do not worry about whether the offeree can actually prove that the letter was posted. Explain the outcome if the postal rules are applied. Then proceed to the next trigger point and repeat the process.

4 *When stating a point of law try to indicate its source*. Name relevant cases or statute sections, or otherwise indicate that you know you are quoting a legal rule by saying, for example, 'in law ...'. There is no need to explain the facts of the case, though a brief reference may be useful to stress its relevance.

5 *Conclude with a brief summary*. This gives polish to your answer and should always form part of a coursework assignment. In an exam, if you are short of time, it is not important as it should not include any new argument. Remember that there is not necessarily a right or a wrong answer. You are being tested on your reasoning. The facts of the problem may be capable of more than one interpretation, each indicating a potentially different result.

Check your answer carefully, rewriting and polishing if necessary.

This approach is demonstrated in the analysis of the following problem (Assignment 3 in Chapter 4). The italicised words are the 'triggers'.

Iris made an offer to sell her piano to Diana for £500 on Monday. Diana replied 'I will buy it *if I can raise the money*'. Iris *promised that she would not sell to anyone else before Saturday*, and added that Diana could collect it that day at *any time before noon*. On Wednesday Diana phoned and left a message with Iris's daughter Athene, saying that *she had got the money* and *would come to collect the piano on Saturday morning. Athene forgot to pass on the message*. On Thursday Iris was visited by Juno who said that she would pay £600 for the piano. *Iris accepted this offer*. Later that day Iris *posted a letter to Diana telling her that she could not have the piano*. Mercury, the postman, delivered it to the wrong address and Diana, *who never received it*, appeared with a *hired van* to collect the piano at ten o'clock on Saturday morning.

Advise Iris of her legal position.

The issues of law raised by the problem

1 Binding acceptance is essential to contract formation.

2 Promises are not contractually binding without consideration.

3 Acceptance must be communicated.

4 Revocation can take place up to the moment of acceptance.

5 Notice of revocation is necessary to make it effective.

Note that you are told that an offer was made by Iris, so you do not need to discuss whether or not an offer exists.

The points of law pinpointed by the 'triggers'

1 *If*: conditional acceptance is not binding, therefore no contract formed yet.

2 *Promise*: Iris is not bound to keep offer open until Saturday, unless Diana pays to keep the offer open (*Routledge* v *Grant*).

3 *She had got the money, and would come to collect the piano*: intention to accept?

4 *Athene forgot to pass on the message*: has acceptance been communicated? (*Entores* v *Miles Far East Corporation*, *Brinkibon*)

5 *Posted a letter ... never received it*: revocation possible up to time of acceptance (*Payne* v *Cave*). Notice essential (*Dickinson* v *Dodds*). Postal revocation is not effective until received (*Byrne* v *Van Tienhoven*).

6 *Hired van*: acceptance by conduct (*Brogden* v *Metropolitan Railway*), or does she verbally accept before she is told of the revocation? If effective acceptance a contract results. Iris is liable for breach and must compensate Diana for resulting losses.

You will find a suggested solution based on this analysis in Appendix 2 (page 403).

Writing discursive assignments

Students often incorrectly assume that writing essays and reports is easier than answering problems, but careful analysis is necessary to ensure that you discover exactly what you are being asked and how you are required to present the relevant information. A question rarely tells you to write everything you know about a topic. Drifting from the point or failing to present the required analysis will lose you marks. The important points to remember are as follows:

1 *Make sure you understand the question*. Analyse it carefully looking for the *key words*. These tell you what information is required and *how* to present your answer. 'How' words include: 'compare', 'discuss', 'distinguish between', 'critically assess', 'what are the advantages/disadvantages of', 'explain'. Sometimes you may be required to present information in the form of a memorandum or

report. Head this appropriately with the relevant title and present it under relevant side headings, using numbered points if appropriate.

2 *Carry out your researches*. Apart from checking your existing knowledge of the topic, you may need to refer to additional sources and make notes of relevant points.

3 *Plan your answer in writing*. You need to jot down the points to be made, paragraph by paragraph.

4 *Write your first draft*. Take care to use your own words; do not copy chunks from books or notes. If quoting, indicate this. Proof-read and amend and correct where necessary.

5 *Copy out the corrected draft*. Check it thoroughly.

Some suggested solutions for essay-style questions can be found in Appendix 2.

REVISION AND EXAMINATION TECHNIQUE

Revision

Effective preparation is essential to success: lack of it undermines your confidence and thus doubly impairs your examination performance. You may find the following tips helpful.

Time planning

1 *Make yourself a realistic revision timetable*. This must take into account all your other commitments and your likely concentration span. Short periods (30–45 minutes) are usually the most effective. Hours spent unremittingly at a desk are likely to produce little more than a sense of virtue and a headache.

2 *Prioritise your study time*. Where you have a choice, study at the times of day when you find it easiest to concentrate. While you may be sacrificing time that you would probably rather spend elsewhere, it is important that you view this short-term loss as producing long-term gains. If you have family commitments, be aware of the need to take time for yourself at this important point in your life. What is good for you will be good for your family, too. If you go out to work, check your entitlement to study leave.

3 *Stick to your timetable*. It is very important to ensure that you revise across the syllabus and do not get bogged down in the areas that you are least confident about. Keep to your schedule as tightly as possible, but be prepared to adapt and rationalise if necessary. Once you have given the allotted time to a particular topic, do not tweak it, polish it or check whether you remember it. Press on to the next goal.

Revision technique

1 *Thorough reading is essential.* Your primary aim is to consolidate your existing knowledge. Ensure that you have the basics of each topic at your fingertips. These act as recall points: magnets and foundations to which more peripheral knowledge will stick. If you have fully covered your revision you may choose to read something new, to avoid getting stale. Possibly, if you are this well prepared, you should consider taking some time off to give yourself space for assimilation and refreshment. It is possible to over-prepare, though this is likely to be a problem for only a minority of students. If you are struggling against time constraints or the intricacies of subject matter, it may be best to stick to one clear source of information like lecture notes or handouts.

2 *Note-taking while you read.* This generally helps concentration and can provide useful reference points for last-minute revision. List the main points of each topic. Reduce cases to a couple of sentences, briefly conveying the essence of the facts and decision *in your own words*. If you can do this it proves your understanding of the essential points. Consequently, you will be much more likely to remember them. It is also good practice for the examination, when your own words are what will count.

3 *Testing your knowledge.* When you have covered a topic, identify relevant questions from past papers. Draft answer plans, or try writing a timed answer. Use textbook quizzes. Suggested solutions may be helpful as a guide to question-answering technique. Get someone to ask you questions: while a fellow student is best, any long-suffering friend or family member will do.

4 *Working out your battle plan.* Most of us find taking exams hard. This is largely because it is an alien experience, not something which we often do. It is possible, however, to make some plans for effective use of time in the examination and to forearm yourself by studying past papers. What you face on the day is likely to resemble papers of previous years, in terms of both form and content. Observe how questions are formulated. Decide which questions in each paper you would answer, avoiding any where the examiner does not make it clear what is required. Identify the advantages and disadvantages of different types of question. Remember that although it is often easier to pick up a good mark with a question that covers a number of different topics, this will require a reasonably lengthy exposition. If a question focuses on one small area this can be useful when you are running short of time, since you may be able to convey the main points quickly. While it is too much to hope that these skills will become second nature, there is no doubt that studying the form and content of papers, practising effective analysis routines and considering the best use of time, will help you to make the correct choices on the day.

5 *Maintaining your morale.* The exam season is a depressing and stressful time for many students. While this is to some extent inevitable, there are many ways of reducing the problem. Take good physical care of yourself: your brain will work

more efficiently if you have enough sleep, exercise and the right sort of food. Give yourself rewards: try to do something you find pleasant in some of your breaks between study sessions. If you can, network with your fellow students to avoid feeling isolated. It helps to know that you are not the only one who is finding things difficult. Remember that feeling stressed can be beneficial: most people work better under a degree of pressure. Feeling too relaxed can inhibit effective revision. Do not be afraid to ask for help from teachers or personal tutors who will have had much experience of helping students prepare for exams. A trained counselling service is usually available to any college or university student.

The examination

However thoroughly you have revised, you will not reap your just rewards unless you acquit yourself well in the exam room. There are certain survival tactics that will help to keep you calm and promote efficiency. Some are very obvious, but are worth thinking about in advance so that they do not get overlooked in the heat of the moment.

1 *Do make sure that you know the location of the exam and how to get there.*

2 *Do arrive in plenty of time with all appropriate equipment.*

3 *Do not be in too much of a hurry to start writing.* Read the exam paper thoroughly before you start. Check the instructions and mark the questions you like the look of.

4 *Do start with the question that you like best.* But check that it really is as good as you first thought; under stress it is easy to misread.

5 *Do plan your answers.* It may be advisable to spend between 20–25 per cent of your time on planning, particularly if you are dealing with a complex problem. Always re-read a question and briefly list the points you wish to make before you begin to write your answer. Make sure that you are answering the question that the examiners asked, not the one you wish they had asked. Examiners constantly remark that failure to grasp the point of a question is the biggest cause of lost marks. Embrace the full scope of the question: check that you have spotted all the 'triggers' in a problem. In essay questions, make sure that you have correctly analysed the 'key words' indicating the topics involved and the method of presentation required (see above).

6 *Do keep an eye on the time.* Set a time limit for each question and stick to it. Remember that most people pick up the majority of marks in the first 50 per cent of the writing time per question. If you do find yourself running out of time, answer any remaining questions in note form. Remember that if you fail to answer the required number of questions, you are potentially throwing away a vital percentage of marks (probably 20–25 per cent).

7 *Do not leave before the end of the exam.* Use any spare time to check your paper: correct clerical errors, ensure that each question is numbered properly. If you have finished with more than a very few minutes in hand the chances are that something is wrong, so use the time to try to put it right. Check what you have written and see if anything needs amending. If you have left out any questions, make a stab at some answers: you might gain the crucial few marks that separate a pass from a failure (or a distinction from a pass). Even if it is the exam paper from hell, do not run away from it. Having entered the exam (often at considerable expense) you have nothing to lose from having a go. If you write nothing, nothing is what you will get. You are in with a chance: exploit it. If you placed a bet on a horse, would you shoot it before the race?

8 *Do present your work as clearly as possible.* Never copy the question from the exam paper; this only wastes valuable time. You can answer questions in any order you like, but do make sure that each question is numbered correctly. Present each question on a fresh page, leaving space to insert any forgotten points at the end of the exam. It is best to use dark ink. Take care with your handwriting, and if you have time, underline the cases and statutes that you have quoted. This all helps to keep the examiners on your side: remember that they may be marking hundreds of scripts and will be grateful for a clearly presented paper.

GOOD LUCK!

Appendix 1: Additional resources

Your studies will be more rewarding if you look beyond what is in this book. Coursework assignments may require some research from specialist textbooks. Here are some suggestions.

Background information

Apart from quality newspapers, TV and radio programmes are a useful source of information about current legal topics. Regular useful slots include *Watchdog* on BBC1, a lively consumer affairs programme. *You and Yours* and *The Money Programme*, and *The Law Programme* on Radio 4 all deal interestingly with a variety of topical legal issues. *Which?* magazine is published monthly by the Consumers Association, 2 Marylebone Road, London NW1, and provides a lot of very accessible information on consumer rights.

Specialist texts

The English legal system

The English Legal System: Slapper and Kelly, Cavendish Press, 3rd edn 2002.

The law of contract

Davies On Contract: Upex (ed.), Sweet & Maxwell Concise College Texts, 7th edn 1995.
Casebook on Contract: Poole, Blackstone Press, 5th edn 2001.
For reference: *The Law of Contract*: Cheshire and Fifoot, Butterworth, 14th edn 2001.

Sale of goods

For reference: *Sale of Goods*: Atiyah, Longman, 10th edn 2001.

Consumer law

Consumer Law: Text, Cases & Materials: Oughton, Blackstone Press, 2nd edn 2000.

The law of tort

Textbook on Torts: Michael Jones, Blackstone Press, 7th edn 2002.
Casebook on Torts: Kidner, Blackstone Press, 6th edn 2000.
For reference: *Street on Tort*: Brazier (ed.), Butterworth 1999.

Employment law

Employment Law: Sargeant, Longman 2001.
Cases and Materials on Employment Law: Pitt, Longman, 3rd edn 2003.

Company law

Company Law: Smith and Keenan, Longman, 17th edn 2002.
For reference: *Principles of Modern Company Law*: Gower, Sweet & Maxwell 1997.

Intellectual property

Intellectual Property: Bainbridge, Longman, 5th edn 2002.
Cases and Materials in Intellectual Property: Bainbridge, Longman, 2nd edn 1999.

Interested in taking your law studies further?

If you are looking for a distance-learning package, Law Tutors Online can provide you with tuition via the Internet, including virtual tutorials and individual email support. Tuition is available for students following London University's External Programme LLB and LLM courses, also ILEX Part II. Study support for individual subject areas may be arranged. Visit the website at http://www.lawtutorsonline.co.uk or email lto@lawtutorsonline.co.uk for more information.

Information points

The following organisations provide a range of resources which may be useful to you in your researches. If you have access to the Internet (your college library should be able to assist here) you will be able to find out easily which is available to you. Subject to any specified copyright restraints, you may download and print off documents for your personal study use. Websites also often have useful links to other relevant sites.

Name	Nature of resources	Contact
ACAS (Advisory, Conciliation and Arbitration Service)	Good employment law resource, helpful phone enquiry service	Clifton House, 83–117 Euston Road, London, NW1 2RB Tel. 0207 396 5100 http://www.acas.org.uk
CCTA (Government Information Service)	Access to government departments and lots of links	http://www.ukonline.gov.uk
CRE (Commission for Racial Equality)	Race relations law, reports, reform proposals	Eliot House, Allington Street, London, SW1 5EH Tel. 0207 939 0000 http://www.gov.uk/index.html
DTI (Department of Trade and Industry)	Consumer and employment law resource	DTI HQ, 1 Victoria Street, London, SW1 0EH Tel. 0207 215 5000 http://www.dti.gov.uk/
EOC (Equal Opportunities Commission)	Sex discrimination law, reports, reform proposals	Overseas House, Quay Street, Manchester, M3 3HN http://www.eco.org.uk/index.html
Europa	EU website: legislation, cases and useful links	http://www.europa.eu.int./index-en.htm
LCD (Lord Chancellor's Department)	Information about Parliament, current legislation, the courts, House of Lords' judgments, legal system reform proposals	30 Great Peter Street, London, SW1P 2BU Tel. 0207 210 8500 http://www.open.gov.uk/lcd.home.htm
OFT (Office of Fair Trading)	Consumer law information	15–25 Breams Buildings, London, EC4A 1PR Tel. 0345 224499 http://www.oft.gov.uk/
Smith Bernal	Court of Appeal judgments available on-line	http://www.smithbernal.com.index2.htm
Copyright Licensing Agency Limited	Copyright information	90 Tottenham Court Road, London, W1P 0LP Tel. 0207 436 5931 http://www.cla.co.uk
Patent Office	Patents and trade marks information	Central Enquiry Unit, Cardiff Road, Newport, Gwent, NO9 1RH Tel. 01645 500505 http://www.patent.gov.uk
The Stationery Office (formerly HMSO)	Parliamentary legislation, Green and White Papers	http://www.hmso.gov.uk see also http://www.tso-online.co.uk

Appendix 2:
Suggested solutions and quiz answers

SUGGESTED SOLUTIONS

Assignment 1

To answer this question it is necessary to explain what is meant by alternative dispute resolution (ADR) and describe the forms it may take. An analysis of how such strategies help to obtain a workable settlement of claims out of court is also required. Finally, comment must be made on the influence of the Woolf reforms in furthering the use of ADR.

Many commercial disputes are regularly settled by arbitration and it is common for provision for arbitration to be agreed in advance in a contract between the parties. A professional arbitrator with relevant expertise hears evidence from both parties and imposes a solution. The process is governed by the Arbitration Act 1996, which seeks to ensure autonomy for the parties. It largely excludes the jurisdiction of the court except in relation to determination of points of law. These may be taken to the court subject to any prior agreement between the parties. This process is ideal for settling cases where technical issues of fact are involved and the parties are on an equal footing. It is likely to result in a more amicable outcome than litigation. It is quicker and usually cheaper than litigation. It is not generally appropriate for consumer disputes and cannot be imposed on a consumer (Consumer Arbitration Act 1988).

Arbitration facilities are offered to consumers by some trade associations like ABTA. A breach of the trade association's code of practice may trigger a right to use the service, which may give greater protection to the consumer than the law. The procedure is conducted in writing and a fee is payable. This is refunded to the consumer if the claim is successful. It is useful for settling claims which are simple in law and on the facts, where the complainant has documentary evidence and is articulate on paper.

Conciliation is sometimes used. The conciliator's function is to help the parties reach a solution to their conflict and to suggest a solution, though there is no power to impose this. Conciliation is commonly used in employment cases. Any party to a dispute before the employment tribunal is offered the services of ACAS in an attempt to avoid the need for a full hearing.

Mediation is increasingly used. The mediator assists parties to communicate and thus find a solution to their dispute. This may involve the mediator initially meeting with each party separately and acting as a channel of communication, before a face-to-face meeting or series of meetings can be arranged. It is a particularly valuable tool in relationship breakdown cases and is one of the services provided by the Community Legal Service. Health trusts are also using the process in cases of medical accidents. It can be very valuable where liability and quantum of damages are not in dispute and the trust is prepared to explain how the accident occurred and, if appropriate, offer compensation. It is well documented that often this is all a party requires and it can do much to relieve distress.

In the great majority of cases settlement out of court is a much better way to resolve a claim than a resort to litigation. The latter is costly, time-consuming and often stressful for all involved. It may involve financial risk for a party with a less than strong case who may find themselves with no remedy as well as shouldering the bill for the other party's costs. It does have certain drawbacks, however, where there is an imbalance of power between the parties. The party who is in the financially weaker position may be manipulated by the stronger one into accepting a settlement for much less than is fair. However, it may be argued that in some cases it is better that they should receive something rather than nothing, particularly if there is any uncertainty as to the strength of their case.

The Civil Procedure Rules contain strategies like pre-action protocols requiring early disclosure of all relevant evidence to try to ensure that parties do not litigate where the strength of the case does not justify this. Judges are empowered to encourage the parties to settle the case independently and to impose sanctions on a party who persists unnecessarily to litigate. As a result there has been a considerable drop in the number of claims being initiated.

ADR strategies are clearly key to the settlement of increasing numbers of cases. In general it may be fairly argued that this is generally a desirable outcome, since through such means much unnecessary litigation is avoided.

Assignment 3

Diana's rights in contract will depend on whether she is able to prove that she made a binding acceptance of Iris's offer before it was revoked. Diana's initial response to Iris's offer is not a legally binding acceptance, as she is only conditionally agreeing to buy. The law requires an acceptance to be unconditional. Diana does not legally bind herself at this point, since in effect she is saying that if she cannot get the money she will not buy the piano.

Iris's promise to hold the offer open until Saturday is not legally binding as it is gratuitous. Diana has provided no consideration in return. In *Routledge* v *Grant*, a promise to keep an offer open for the sale of a house was held not to be binding because the potential buyer had given no consideration to the seller for keeping the offer open. Iris is doing Diana a favour by restricting her own freedom to sell the piano, as there is no guarantee that Diana will buy the goods. Diana has promised nothing in return, so no contract to keep the offer open until Saturday can result. Iris is, therefore, free to revoke the offer at any time. If she does not do so effectively, the offer will continue to exist until midday on Saturday, as we are told that Iris said that the piano could be collected any time before noon.

An acceptance, to be binding, must also be communicated. This generally means that the offeror must know that the acceptance has been made (*Entores* v *Miles Far East Corporation*). Diana's phone statement may well indicate a commitment to enter a contract, but no communication to Iris has taken place as Diana did not speak to Iris directly and Athene failed to pass the message on. In a business context it may be sufficient for acceptance to be received (*Brinkibon*) at business premises, but Athene is not Diana's employee or agent.

By selling the piano to Juno, Iris revokes her offer to Diana. Offerors may revoke their offers any time up to the moment of acceptance (*Payne* v *Cave*). However, revocation is not effective unless or until the offeree has notice of it. The offeror may give such notice directly but it is also possible for the offeree to discover the revocation indirectly through a third party (*Dickinson* v *Dodds*). Here Iris attempts postal revocation, but it is not communicated as Diana does not receive the letter. In *Byrne* v *Van Tienhoven* it was held that postal revocation is ineffective unless received by the offeree. Therefore, Iris's offer, which is not due to lapse until noon on Saturday, remains open to Diana.

Diana will claim that turning up with a van before the deadline is sufficient communication of her acceptance. Conduct may be an adequate form of communication. In *Brogden* v *Metropolitan Railway*, Brogden's counter-offer was never formally accepted by the company, but the fact that it was prepared to order or take delivery of coal was held to be effective acceptance.

The facts of the problem are not clear about exactly what happens at this point. If Iris did not see the van, and on opening her front door immediately told Diana that she had changed her mind, revocation will at last be communicated and no contract will result. If she does not see the van acceptance has still not been effectively communicated, so revocation is still possible. If, however, Diana acted quickly and reinforced her conduct with appropriate words a contract will be concluded between the parties. If a contract has resulted, Iris, who cannot deliver the piano, is in breach. Diana is entitled to be compensated for consequential financial losses like the cost of hiring the van.

While Diana did not communicate her acceptance effectively by phone, Iris's offer remained open until Saturday morning, as her postal revocation was never communicated. At this point a contract may still result if effective acceptance results from Diana's conduct, or possibly by word of mouth.

Assignment 9

Since we are told that Handyman has taken all reasonable care, no liability in negligence can arise as regards any user of its product who suffers skin cancer, or to Peter, Max and Paul. For negligence liability to exist, a claimant must prove that the defendant breached a duty of care which was owed to the claimant and caused damage to the claimant through failure to take reasonable care.

(a) Liability under the Consumer Protection Act 1987 (CPA) for defective products is strict (s 2), which means that a claimant does not have to prove any failure to take care on the part of the defendant, only that the goods are defective. The wood preserving fluid is clearly defective under the Act, which states that a product is defective if dangerous (s 3). However, the Act also provides a special defence, called the developments risk defence, which will protect Handyman. Section 4 provides that the defendant will not be liable if at the point when it put the product onto the market, it complied with all current safety standards. It must also have been developed in accordance with current research and technological processes in the relevant field. As the problem tells us that in the light of current scientific knowledge the skin cancer is an unpredictable side-effect, Handyman is not liable.

(b) Handyman may be liable under the CPA 1987 as *importer* or *marker* of the goods, but may be able to claim that the accident was caused by Peter or that he was at least partially to blame (contributory negligence). Under s 2 of the CPA 1987, the party who first imports the defective goods into the EC is a potential defendant. Therefore, if Handyman was actually responsible for the initial importation of the ladders, it may be sued. Even if it was not the initial importer, by putting its name on the goods it may be identifying itself as the marker of them (s 2) and this also makes Handyman potentially liable. The collapse of the ladder suggests that it is dangerous and, therefore, defective under the Act. However, Peter will not win his case if he failed to use the ladder in accordance with any instructions (s 3), or if, when using it, he failed to take reasonable care for his own safety. The ladder may not be defective at all if adequate safety instructions were supplied and Peter suffered injury only because he ignored them. Even if the ladder was clearly defective or was supplied without relevant instructions, damages against Handyman may be reduced on the grounds of contributory negligence if Peter failed to take reasonable care for his own safety.

(c) Handyman is not liable to Max under the CPA 1987 for the cost of the repairs to the washing machine. It may be liable to Paul under the Act for the damage to his property, excluding the damage to his computer. Under the CPA 1987, liability for damage to property may be claimed subject to certain limitations. Max will be unable to recover the costs of repairing the defective washing machine since this is pure economic loss. The Act seeks to make defendants liable for damage caused by their products to *other property* belonging to the claimant. It does not make them liable to compensate the claimant for the defective quality of the product itself (s 5). Even if Max's claim was not one for pure economic loss, it would still not be recoverable as under s 5 claims for damage to other property cannot be entertained unless at least £275 is being claimed.

Paul has rights to sue under the Act, as it protects not just the user of the product, but other persons affected by its use. Section 2 states that the defendant is liable for damage wholly or partly attributable to the defect. Paul can claim any sums in excess of £275 for all the damage caused to his flat's decor. He cannot claim for the damage to his computer because it is used for the purpose of his business. Section 5 states that only damage to private property is recoverable.

While Handyman has no liability to any party in negligence, it may be liable under the CPA 1987. As a marker or importer of the ladder, Handyman may be liable to Peter for his personal injuries unless it can show it was not at fault. Handyman is similarly liable to Paul for the damage to his personal property. It is not liable to Max, since his claim is for pure economic loss.

Assignment 14

(a) If an agent enters into a transaction on behalf of its principal, it will not be binding on the principal unless the agent acted with legal authority. To protect the interests of third parties who have acted in good faith, a principal may be bound by a transaction which it did not actually authorise. In such circumstances it will have been reasonable for the third party to believe that authority existed and the principal is legally prevented (estopped) from denying that this is so. In such circumstances the agent is said to act with *apparent* or *ostensible* authority.

Apparent authority may arise in three situations. First, an agency relationship once existed but has now been terminated. If the principal failed to give appropriate notice it will be bound by any transaction, made in the principal's name by the ex-agent, with a party who reasonably believes that the agent still has authority. A wife has implied authority to pledge her husband's credit. If a couple cease to cohabit, the husband will continue to be liable for debts run up in his name unless he takes reasonable steps to inform potential creditors that his wife no longer has his authority.

Secondly, if the principal allows a third party to believe that someone is the principal's agent even if no such relationship exists, the putative agent has apparent authority and the principal cannot deny it. In *Barrett* v *Deere*, a debtor went to a counting house belonging to his creditor. He paid the money to someone who appeared to be an employee with authority to receive payment. This rogue then made off with the money. It was held that the debtor was discharged as the creditor was estopped from denying the apparent authority of the rogue. An employer is obviously expected to take responsibility for the conduct of their workplace; denial of knowledge of the presence of a trespassing rogue would not be sympathetically received by the courts.

Thirdly, if an agent enters a transaction in excess of its actual authority, the other party may assume that the agent has authority as long as the principal has not taken appropriate steps to notify the party of the limits to it, and there is nothing to alert that party to the irregularity. In *Todd* v *Robinson*, an agent was authorised to purchase goods at not more than a specified price. The principal was held liable on a contract with a third party to purchase the relevant goods more expensively. There was held to have been no evidence which should have alerted the creditor to the absence of authority.

(b) Max will be liable on the contract to purchase the photocopier only if Nick is deemed to have acted with apparent authority, or if Max is treated as an undisclosed principal. Here Nick has actual authority from Max, but it is generally limited to showing clients round houses. Max's instruction before his departure 'to keep things ticking over' may have marginally extended that authority to include making minor purchases of stationery and stamps, but clearly was not intended to encompass major financial outlay. Therefore, when Nick purchases the photocopier, he has clearly exceeded his actual authority. However, we are told that Nick did not represent himself as Max's agent but as the business owner. It can, therefore, be argued that the photocopying firm cannot claim that their representative had reasonable belief that Nick was acting with Max's apparent authority if he claimed to have been transacting on his own behalf.

The photocopying firm might try to claim that as Nick is Max's agent, Max was an undisclosed principal and consequently bound by the contract. However, this argument is defeated on three grounds. First, the existence of a principal was apparently expressly ruled out by Nick's misrepresentation. Secondly, an undisclosed principal is not bound by transactions falling outside the actual authority of his agent. Thirdly, if Nick, when signing the contract made it look as if he were sole business owner, with sole rights under the contract, this would also preclude any obligations for Max under the contract (*Humble* v *Hunter*).

The most likely outcome here is that Max will not be liable for the cost of the photocopier as Nick is unlikely to be treated as his agent but as a person trading on his own behalf.

Assignment 16

To answer this question it is necessary to define what is meant by 'risk' and 'title' in the context of the Sale of Goods Act 1979 (SGA). The statutory rules concerning transfer must be explained and evaluated to determine the protection given to both seller and buyer. The approach of the courts must also be noted.

'Risk' means the liability for loss of the goods or damage to them. 'Title' (described in the SGA as the 'property in the goods') means ownership: the ultimate right to dispose of the goods. Title must not be confused with possession (physical control of the goods), the terms of which may be limited by the owner. It is crucial for a buyer to know when risk passes to them as at this point they will become responsible for insurance. Risk and title may be acquired before possession is obtained. The SGA states that risk and title pass simultaneously unless the parties agree to the contrary (s 20). However, as explained below, it is possible for a buyer to acquire the risk attached to the goods without immediately getting title to them, if this is retained by the seller under the terms of the contract, pending payment.

The SGA s 17 gives the parties the freedom to determine when title will pass. It states that this will occur when the parties intend, provided that (s 16) the goods have been 'ascertained'. Unascertained goods include goods which have been ordered, but which the seller will have to manufacture, buy in or separate from bulk supplies. Section 18, rule 5 states that such goods become ascertained once the seller takes an irrevocable step to allocate them to the buyer and the buyer has notice of this.

Section 18 lays down rules determining passage of title in ascertained goods. These rules are relevant only where the parties do not indicate their intentions in the contract. Rule 1 states that title passes once the goods are in a deliverable condition, in an unconditional contract. Thus once the goods are absolutely ready to be handed over to the buyer or carrier, title will pass. If something needs to be done to the goods (for example, putting an inscription on a watch) prior to delivery, title under rule 2 passes once this is done and notice given to the buyer. If the contract requires price to be ascertained by the seller by measurement of the goods or some other activity, title passes under rule 3 once this has been done, provided the buyer is notified. Rule 4 covers supply on a sale and return basis. Title passes when the buyer expressly or implicitly indicates acceptance. Evidence of such indication includes retaining the goods after a fixed date for return has passed.

Since the SGA permits the parties to determine when title passes, the seller may be able to impose a term retaining title until the buyer pays them, with risk passing to the buyer once the goods are deliverable or handed over to a carrier. Such a clause may enable the seller to recover the goods if the buyer refuses payment, or dies, or goes bankrupt.

A simple reservation of title under which title will not pass until the buyer pays for the goods, may be phrased to include all the debts owed by the buyer to the seller (*Armour & Carron Ltd* v *Thyssen*). However, a simple reservation is only useful if the goods remain in the possession of the buyer and are kept separate from the buyer's other goods. It is no help, for instance, where bulk goods are purchased and/or the buyer manufactures products which include the seller's goods.

An extended reservation clause (*Romalpa* clause) may be useful in such circumstances. In *Aluminium Industrie Vaasen* v *Romalpa Aluminium Ltd* it was held that such a clause may require a buyer to store such goods separately and permit the seller to trace the debt to the buyer's proceeds of sale of goods which include the seller's components. However, in subsequent cases the courts have interpreted such clauses very strictly, to prevent circumvention of the requirement to register charges on company property under ss 395–396 of the Companies Act 1985. Unless the clause strictly mirrors the wording of the clause in *Romalpa*, it will not be effective. This effectively made the buyers the trustees of the seller's share of the proceeds of sale of the buyer's products.

The law does not actively prioritise the rights of either party as regards transfer of title and risk. The SGA, s 17 gives the parties the opportunity to determine these matters themselves. The terms of the contract may thus reflect the wishes of the more powerful party unless commercial custom dictates different practice. How far the court gives support to a retention of title clause is also crucial.

QUIZ ANSWERS

Quiz 1

1 Source: the state; scope: geographical limitations; sanctions: imposed by or with the authority of the state.
2 Retribution and protection for society through containment, deterrence, rehabilitation.
3 Compensation for damage caused by defendant; possibly an equitable remedy to make the defendant alter behaviour.

4 Sparrow may be prosecuted for drunken and careless driving. He may also be liable in negligence to Finch and breach of contract to Wren.

Quiz 2

1 (a) Crown Court. (b) Court of Appeal Criminal Division. (c) Crown Court/Divisional Court of QBD. (d) County court. (e) High Court: QBD. (f) Employment tribunal. (g) County court.
2 Tribunals have specialist lay members. They are less formal, cheaper (but generally no legal aid), quicker and not necessarily bound by precedent. They have wide discretion.
3 A freezing order prevents the defendant from transferring his or her assets abroad or otherwise concealing them.
4 Arbitration: arbitrator's decision binding. Conciliation: conciliator may suggest a solution. Mediation: parties reach their own decision.

Quiz 3

1 European law, parliamentary legislation, case law.
2 Regulations have immediate effect and aim at uniformity. Directives require state legislation and aim at harmonisation.
3 First and second reading; committee and report stages; third reading; transfer to the other House; procedures repeated; royal assent.
4 Two of the following: Orders in Council, statutory instruments, regulations, bye-laws.
5 Literal rule: face-value meaning of the statute's words. Mischief rule: purposive approach.
6 General words take their meaning from any preceding specific words.
7 A precedent may be binding if it was decided by a court whose decisions bind the current court and the facts are sufficiently relevant to the current case.
8 *Ratio decidendi* may be binding. An *obiter dictum* is always persuasive.
9 They provide an accurate, accessible and reasonably contemporaneous record of judicial decisions.
10 Its decisions are merely persuasive, though its membership consists of Law Lords.

Quiz 4

1 (a) No: invitation to treat. (b) No: invitation to treat. (c) Yes: unilateral. (d) No: lacks communication. (e) Counter-offer by Esther. (f) No: offer revoked, if P knew of sale.
2 (a) No: conditional. (b) No: Failure to communicate. (c) Yes: if the postal rules apply. (d) No: failure to communicate.

Quiz 5

1 (a) Gratuitous: past consideration. (b) Binding: adequacy irrelevant. (c) Gratuitous: existing contractual duty. (d) Binding: exception to *Pinnel's* case. (e) Provides a defence under *High Trees* if Pink tried to repudiate.
2 The Contracts (Rights of Third Parties) Act 1999 may assist Grey since the contract is made for his benefit.

Quiz 6

1 Conditions: major terms, innocent party may repudiate and claim damages. Warranties: minor terms, damages only.
2 Capable of being breached in a number of ways, some serious enough to justify repudiation.
3 (a) Yes, if it should be visible to customers before they enter the contract. (b) Yes, regardless of whether the signer read or understood it. (c) No: contract concluded at reception. (d) No: too late, contract already concluded.
4 Liability for negligently caused damage to property may be excluded if reasonable.
5 Liability for breach of the conditions implied by statutes concerning the sale or supply of goods cannot be excluded at all. Liability for breach of contract may be excluded if reasonable.
6 UCTA 1977 protects non-consumers, but relates only to exclusion of liability in contracts or non-contractual notices. The regulations only protect consumers, who must be party to a contract. Any term of the contract, if deemed unfair, is not binding on the consumer.

Quiz 7

1 (a) Voidable. (b) Void. (c) Voidable. (d) Voidable. (e) Void.
2 (a) Misrepresentation. (b) Mistake: subject matter. (c) Misrepresentation, mistake: identity. (d) Undue influence.

Quiz 8

1 A contract for an illegal purpose (breaking the law) is completely void. Property is not generally recoverable. Severance is impossible. Under a contract perceived as merely undesirable to the public interest, property is recoverable and severance possible. Any void portion may be severed.
2 (a) To commit a crime. (b) Sexually immoral. (c) Dangerous to international relations.
3 (a) Necessary goods: reasonable price payable. (b) Non-necessaries: not enforceable. (c) Yes, if for his benefit. (d) No: contract of debt.

Quiz 9

1 (a) (i) Yes: divisible contract. (ii) Yes: acceptance of part performance. (b) Yes: full performance prevented.
2 Chambray committed an anticipatory breach. This would have entitled Linen to repudiate the contract, but as he did not exercise this right, it was lost when the contract was frustrated by destruction of the car. If the car was destroyed before the contract was made, the contract is void for mistake if neither party was aware that the goods no longer existed.
3 Remoteness: limits the amount of actionable *damage*. Quantum: concerns the amount of damages payable by the defendant to compensate for the actionable damage.
4 Specific performance will not be granted to enforce an employment contract, or one requiring continuing supervision. Discretionary: will not be granted to enforce any contract unless this is deemed fair to both parties.

Quiz 10

1 Duty, breach, consequent damage.
2 Reasonable foreseeability, proximity, justice and reason.
3 Lapse of time, third-party interference.
4 Basil has rights in contract against Tarragon. Basil and Rosemary also have rights in negligence and under the Consumer Protection Act against Marjoram.
5 Liability: Fault: Negligence, Strict: CPA. Defendant: Negligence: Manufacturer. CPA: Producer/marker/importer/supplier. Property damage: limited to claims over £275 under CPA, no limitations in negligence.

Quiz 11

1 (a) Yes: negligent statement (*Hedley Byrne* v *Heller*). (b) No: pure economic loss (*Muirhead* v *Industrial Tank Specialities*). (c) Yes: nervous shock (*Alcock* v *Wright*). (d) No: damage caused by the third party (*Smith* v *Littlewoods Organisation*).
2 Reasonable care.
3 An exception to the remoteness of damage rule, which makes a defendant liable in a personal injuries case for all the injuries flowing from the negligent act if they are due to some illness or condition suffered by the claimant, even if not reasonably foreseeable.

Quiz 12

1 (a) Public nuisance affecting the highway: non-delegable duty. (b) Under the Occupiers' Liability Act 1957, no liability if notice sufficient to discharge duty. (c) Lymeswold is a trespasser (Occupiers' Liability Act 1984). Red likely to be liable, as he could easily have prevented a child from obtaining access to his storeroom and should have foreseen Lymeswold's likely presence if children regularly visit his shop. (d) Private nuisance.

2 Contributory negligence if Wensleydale suffered head injuries.
3 Employers are vicariously liable for torts committed by an employee if incidental to the job. Generally there is no liability for independent contractors unless the employer's personal duty is non-delegable.

Quiz 13

1 (a) Applying a misleading description. (b) Supplying goods carrying a misleading description. (c) False description of services. (d) Misleading price.
2 Applying: active, personal. Supplying: passive: passing on someone else's description.
3 Section 1: strict liability (goods); s 14: fault (services).
4 If goods which are not reasonably safe are supplied or offered for sale, or if an agreement is made to sell or such goods are exposed for sale or in seller's possession with intention that they shall be supplied.

Quiz 14

1 Enables an individual to obtain personal credit up to a maximum of £15 000.
2 The point at which title passes. HP contract: if hirer exercises option to purchase. Conditional sale: if all instalments paid. Credit sale: on delivery.
3 (a) A DCS agreement providing running-account credit for restricted use. (b) A DC agreement providing fixed-term credit for unrestricted use. (c) A DCS agreement providing fixed-term credit for restricted use.
4 (a) Section 67 gives her the right to cancel within five days from receiving notice of cancellation rights. (b) If she has paid more than a third of the value of the goods, they are 'protected' under s 90 and cannot be taken from her without her consent unless the creditor gets a court order.

Quiz 15

1 (a) Actual express authority. (b) Actual implied authority.
2 Yes: Starboard failed to notify Compass about Port's dismissal and is estopped from denying Port's apparent authority.
3 If the third party wished to contract with the agent personally.
4 When the principal agrees/trade practice/routine tasks not requiring special skill.
5 When an irrevocable/enduring power of attorney exists.

Quiz 16

1 Contract: ascertained goods, title passes immediately. Agreement: non-ascertained goods, title passes once goods ascertained.
2 Title to goods does not pass until all instalments paid and hirer exercises purchase option.
3 They may all claim breach of the relevant implied conditions of the SGA 1979 and reject the goods, as well as claim damages for any other related loss: (a) goods do

not meet their description (s 13); (b) not of satisfactory quality (s 14(2)) or suitable for its purpose (s 14(3)); (c) carpet does not correspond with sample (s 15); (d) goods not suitable for their purpose (s 14(3)).

Quiz 17

1 (a) Section 18, rule 2: when engraving complete and Boland told that watch ready for collection. (b) Rule 5: coal must be made ascertainable, i.e. bagged up and irrevocably earmarked for Boland.
2 Specialised form of retention of title clause. If suitably worded it may require the seller's goods to be separately stored by the buyer; it may also enable the seller to obtain proceeds from sale of goods manufactured by the buyer, which includes the seller's goods if these remain identifiable.
3 Estoppel, factor, voidable title, sale by buyer/seller in possession, private buyer of car subject to hire-purchase.
4 If risk passed to Burnham, he is liable in the event of loss or damage to goods, therefore, Pemberton is entitled to payment. Under s 20, risk passes with title, but the parties may agree to the contrary. Handing goods to carrier: unconditional appropriation which will transfer title to Burnham.
5 Performance time: a condition of the contract, buyer may repudiate if not precisely performed.
6 When the buyer tells seller/fails to notify rejection in time/treats goods inconsistently with seller's rights.
7 If the seller in breach of the implied conditions (ss 12–15)/performance not complete (ss 30, 31, but note s 30A). Right lost on 'acceptance'. Must have reasonable time to examine goods first (s 35(5)).
8 (a) Resale. (b) Stoppage in transit.

Quiz 18

1 Employer is responsible for paying employees' NI contributions and sick pay and deduction of income tax. No such responsibilities for contractors, who also have no rights to claim for unfair dismissal or redundancy. Lesser duty to contractors under the HSAWA 1974 than that owed to employee.
2 (a) Good faith: conflict with Juniper's interests. (b) Lack of reasonable care and skill. (c) Good faith: failure to account for profits.
3 Common law duties: competent staff, safe work systems. Criminal liability under the HSAWA 1974.
4 Prosecution, improvement/prohibition notices.

Quiz 19

1 (a) Work may be of equal value under EPA 1970. (b) May be sex discrimination under the SDA 1975 unless genuine occupational qualification applicable.
2 Direct: overt restriction of employment opportunity to members of one sex or racial group. Indirect: conditions imposed which are more likely to be fulfilled by members of one sex or racial group rather than another.

3 If race or sex is deemed a genuine occupational qualification.
4 Appointment, terms of employment contract, promotion, training, facilities. But not pay and pensions.

Quiz 20

1 Wrongful dismissal: breach of contract; no qualifying period of employment; common law action in the courts; remedy – damages determined by the court. Unfair dismissal: employer has not necessarily breached the contract. One year's continuous employment; statutory rights, hearing: employment tribunal, compensation regulated by statute, reinstatement/redeployment possible.
2 (a) Lack of qualification. (b) Misconduct. (c) Negligence/incapability. (d) Conduct, but only if it reflects on Rhino's suitability for the job.
3 (a) No: he was not dismissed. (b) If a contract term requires acceptance of relocation, not redundant; otherwise distance is likely to be too great to be reasonable.
4 Fair selection procedures, warnings, consultation procedures, redeployment offers.

Quiz 21

1 Royal charter, Act of Parliament, registration.
2 (a) Financial liability of corporation members may be limited to their investment. (b) Once incorporated, corporation continues to exist until extinguished by relevant legal process. (c) At least two members.
3 A partnership is formed to make profits.
4 (a) Partners jointly bound if T had apparent authority. (b) All partners personally liable for partnership debts.
5 A company is public if: specified in the memorandum, limited liability, plc suffix, and it has at least £50 000 authorised capital, 25 per cent of which is paid up. Any other company is private.

Quiz 22

1 Memorandum and articles, details of directors and secretary, domicile of registered office, statutory declaration.
2 Company may be bound by a contract which exceeds its objects clause.
3 This resolution must go to a meeting of the company: 75 per cent majority. Re-registration required.
4 May be adopted, wholly or partially, as the company's articles.
5 By a vote at a company meeting passed by a 75 per cent majority.

Quiz 23

1 Issued capital: potential profit raised so far by the shares issued. Called-up capital: money actually raised by calls on issued shares.
2 As a short-term measure to raise capital.
3 No valuable consideration/court-approved reduction of capital/court order/shares forfeited.

4 (a) Company has no obligation to issue dividends. (b) Company's articles define voting rights: not all shareholders necessarily entitled. Preference shareholders enjoy no privileges in this respect: their preferential rights may compensate for lack of voting rights. (c) Any shareholder may lose all/some of investment on winding up: rank below the company's creditors. Preference shareholders may be paid before the equity shareholders if the articles so require. (d) Brass has made a loan to the company which is secured against its assets and should recover his investment.

Quiz 24

1 Bombazine has rights in agency law, rule in *Turquand's* case, s 35 of the Companies Act 1985.
2 (a) Section 214, Insolvency Act 1986. (b) Section 309, Companies Act 1985.
3 Cotton: in breach of his duty of good faith at common law and under s 317 of the Companies Act 1985: contract voidable.
4 Tweed and Twist are disqualified. Denim is disqualified unless he has permission.

Quiz 25

1 General meeting: all members.
2 AGM: compulsory, except for private companies exempt under s 366A. EGM: urgent business/statutory duty. Notice: AGM 21 days, EGM 14 days, but may be reduced with members' consent.
3 Retirement age: can continue to serve if the company votes in favour. Resolution requires special notice to the company 21 days prior to meeting. Company must ensure members notified before meeting.
4 (a) Section 54: petition to court if at least 50 shareholders/those who hold 5 per cent of shares agree. (b) Section 459: if he can prove unfair prejudice.
5 Derivative: shareholder acts in the company's interests. Representative: by one shareholder on others' behalf.

Quiz 26

1 (a) Yes: if written. (b) No: not a tangible form. (c) Employer owns the copyright. (d) If format sufficiently original. If created incidentally to her work, employer owns it.
2 Copyright: design drawings and figures (if works of art). Design right under CDPA 1988. Possibly design registrable: Registered Designs Act 1949.
3 (a) New, inventive step, capable of industrial application. (b) Owned by Fulmar. Puffin may get compensation.
4 (a) If sufficiently distinctive it is registrable: capable of graphical representation. (b) Not if too similar. (c) Not if it unjustifiably suggests royal family endorsement.

Quiz 27

1 (a) Breach of confidence. (b) Passing off. (c) Malicious falsehood.
2 (i) Confidential revelation. (ii) Relationship of trust between the parties. (iii) Information used by confidant/third party. (iv) Resulting damage.
3 Damages, injunction, surrender of profits.
4 Greater protection: goodwill need not yet exist. Simpler to prove.

Appendix 3:
Civil litigation terms:
the Woolf reforms

You will be aware from study of Chapter 3 that the language of civil litigation radically changed in April 1999 because of the Woolf reforms. Earlier textbooks use pre-Woolf language so here are some of the commonest terms in both forms in case you come across them in your further reading.

Before 26 April 1999	After 26 April 1999
Anton Piller order	Search order
Arbitration	Small claims track
Discovery	Disclosure
Ex-parte hearing	Hearing without notice
Further and better particulars	Further information
Guardian *ad litem*	Litigation friend (person taking proceedings on behalf of child/mental patient)
Inter partes hearing	Hearing with notice
Letter before action	Letter before claim
Mareva injunction	Freezing injunction
Plaintiff	Claimant
Witness statement	Statement of truth
Writ, summons	Claim form

Index